AF669170

ERICH FRAUWALLNER

The Philosophy of Buddhism

ERICH FRAUWALLNER

The Philosophy of Buddhism

(Die Philosophie des Buddhismus)

Translated by
GELONG LODRÖ SANGPO
with the assistance of
JIGME SHELDRÖN

under the supervision of
Professor ERNST STEINKELLNER

MOTILAL BANARSIDASS PUBLISHERS
PRIVATE LIMITED • DELHI

First Edition : Delhi, 2010
Translated from Die Philosophie des Buddhismus
fourth edition 1994, Berlin, Akademie-Verlag,
revised third edition 1969, first published, 1956

ISBN : 978-81-208-3481-1

MOTILAL BANARSIDASS
41 U.A. Bungalow Road, Jawahar Nagar, Delhi 110 007
8 Mahalaxmi Chamber, 22 Bhulabhai Desai Road, Mumbai 400 026
203 Royapettah High Road, Mylapore, Chennai 600 004
236, 9th Main III Block, Jayanagar, Bangalore 560 011
Sanas Plaza, 1302 Baji Rao Road, Pune 411 002
8 Camac Street, Kolkata 700 017
Ashok Rajpath, Patna 800 004
Chowk, Varanasi 221 001

Printed in India

By Jainendra Prakash Jain at Shri Jainendra Press,
A-45, Naraina, Phase-I, New Delhi 110 028
and Published by Narendra Prakash Jain for
Motilal Banarsidass Publishers Private Limited,
Bungalow Road, Delhi 110 007

DEDICATED

TO MY ESTEEMED FRIEND

ÉTIENNE LAMOTTE

CONTENTS

(brief)

PREFACE

THE PRESENT ENGLISH TRANSLATION of *Die Philosophie des Buddhismus* by Erich Frauwallner opens up a classic introduction to Buddhist thought to a broader English language readership. First published in 1956, the main body of the book has remained unchanged. Frauwallner added supplementary remarks to the third edition, published in 1969. The edition translated here is the fourth, published in 1994.

Frauwallner's original idea was to publish a series of anthologies with selected translations and introductory explanations to accompany his *Geschichte der indischen Philosophie (History of Indian Philosophy)*, of which the first two volumes were published in 1953 and 1956.[1] Of this planned translation series only the anthology of Buddhist philosophical texts translated here and a small selection of Śivaitic texts[2] were published in his life-time. An anthology of translations of Brahminical philosophical texts was published posthumously.[3]

Because of the exemplary selection of source texts translated in *Die Philosophie des Buddhismus* and particularly because of the clear and substantial introductions to these texts, this

---

[1] New edition by Andreas Pohlus: Shaker Verlag, Aachen 2003. English translation by V. M. Bedekar: *History of Indian Philosophy*, Motilal Banarsidass, Delhi 1973.

[2] *Aus der Philosophie der śivaitischen Systeme*, Berlin 1962.

[3] *Erich Frauwallner: Nachgelassene Werke II. Philosophische Texte des Hinduismus.* Gerhard Oberhammer / Chlodwig H. Werba (eds), Verlag der Österreichischen Akademie der Wissenschaften, Wien 1992. These translations from the *Upaniṣads* and the *Mahābhārata* to texts from the Sāṃkhya-, Vaiśeṣika-, and Nyāya-systems, as well as Mādhava's *Sarvadarśanasaṃgraha* are all that remained of the original plan.

anthology is an excellent and profound narrative of the unfolding of Buddhist thought, and it is still the only one of its kind. At the same time, to be sure, this book is not totally comprehensive. It covers the period of early canonical literature, with examples of its philosophically relevant ideas, followed by the principal philosophical concepts of mature Śrāvakayāna-Buddhism and, in the main part of the book, presents the first survey of the development of the philosophical systems of Mahāyāna-Buddhism. It does not, however, include such developments as the important post-systematic tradition of Buddhist epistemology and logic. Although as early as the 1930s Frauwallner was breaking new ground with articles, first critical editions, and translations of texts on concept formation and theory of language, as well as the proof of momentariness, at the time of his writing *Die Philosophie des Buddhismus,* research in general had not progressed sufficiently to allow a clear and comprehensive presentation of the main issues at stake in the epistemological tradition founded by Dignāga. It is for this reason, I think, that Frauwallner decided not to include a selection of major texts by either Dignāga or Dharmakīrti. As is evident from his overall plan for the continuation of the *Geschichte der indischen Philosophie,*[1] the Buddhist epistemological tradition was, of course, intended to be included, along with many other and much later traditions.

His articles on the sequence of Dharmakīrti's works (1954), on Vasubandhu's *Vādavidhi* (1957), or on the development of Dignāga's thought (1959) indicate that during these years Frauwallner had begun to clarify the philological and historical

---

[1] *Cf. Erich Frauwallner: Nachgelassene Werke I. Aufsätze, Beiträge, Skizzen.* Ernst Steinkellner (ed.), Verlag der Österreichischen Akademie der Wissenschaften, Wien 1984, Anhang C and D (= *Erich Frauwallner's Posthumous Essays.* Translated from the German by Jayendra Soni. Aditya Prakashan, New Delhi 1994, Appendix C and D).

basis for the next volumes of his *Geschichte*. In 1956, however, the year both the second volume of the *Geschichte* and the present anthology were first published, he does not seem to have been ready to include this philosophically creative development. He thus decided to conclude this presentation of Buddhist philosophy, which must have been written in close temporal relation to the first volume of the *Geschichte*, by introducing and providing translations from the last great ontological and soteriological system, the Yogācāra-Vijñānavāda. A comparable case is the lack of a more detailed account of the beginnings of Buddhist scholastic philosophy (Abhidharma), on the subject of which he began to publish a long series of *Abhidharma-Studien* only in 1963. Frauwallner was well aware of these limitations in his presentation of only the Buddhist philosophy of the "classical," i.e., the systematic period, as well as of the fact that from a vast literature he could take into consideration no more than a small sampling.[1] The remaining volumes of his *Geschichte* were evidently on his mind throughout these later years of his life. Nevertheless, he always adapted his own research and writing interests to the changing needs of his students, thus moving from Buddhist epistemology to Mīmāṃsā, and on to Abhidharma and Navya Nyāya. It was only after retirement, during his last years, that he could again concentrate on the earliest Abhidharma, publishing the last articles of the above-mentioned series.[2] Unfortunately, however, he did not have sufficient time left to realize his great plan for a comprehensive history of Indian philosophy from its beginnings to modern times.

---

[1] *Cf.* the last paragraph of his introduction to the present book.

[2] The whole series of articles was translated by Sophie Francis Kidd and published by SUNY Press: Erich Frauwallner, *Studies in Abhidharma Literature and the Origins of Buddhist Philosophical Systems*. Albany 1995.

Before saying a few words about Frauwallner's concept of Buddhist philosophy and the present English translation of his *Die Philosophie des Buddhismus,* it seems appropriate here to briefly address Frauwallner's life. Frauwallner's life has been portrayed and his scholarly progress delineated in a number of more or less detailed contributions,[1] but in brief:

Born December 28, 1898, he was drafted from the Academic High School into the Austrian Imperial Army in May 1916. As a combatant in the First World War, he took part in the Rumanian offensive and the "Battle of Isonzo". At the war's end he enrolled at Vienna University in the winter term of 1918/1919. Frauwallner studied Classical Philology and took courses in Indology and Iranian Studies. His doctoral thesis, *De synonymorum quibus animi motus significantur, uso tragico,*[2] was approved in 1921. In 1922 he took the state examination and started to teach Classical Greek and Latin at a secondary school in Vienna. Although a Sanskrit grammar had been in his possession since 1915, he had no academic mentor in Indology and Indian philosophy. Instead he used his methodological

---

[1] Gerhard Oberhammer: "Erich Frauwallner – 60 Jahre," *Religion, Wissenschaft, Kultur* 10. Jg., 1959. IV, pp. 397–99; *id.*: "Erich Frauwallner (28.12.1898 5.7.1974)," *WZKS* 20, 1976, pp. 5–36; *id.*: "Nachgetragene Gedanken zu E. Frauwallners 'Geschichte der Indischen Philosophie'," in *Erich Frauwallner, Nachgelassene Werke II. Philosophische Texte des Hinduismus.* Verlag der Österreichischen Akademie der Wissenschaften. Wien 1992, pp. 225–34; Robert Göbl: "Erich Frauwallner," *Österreichische Akademie der Wissenschaften, Almanach für das Jahr 1974,* 124. Jg., Wien 1975, pp. 476–81). The most detailed account of his life and work is contained in the "Preface" by Karin Preisendanz and Eli Franco in *Die Philosophie des Buddhismus* to be soon reprinted by the Akademie Verlag, Berlin. I gratefully acknowledge having received an almost completed manuscript of this preface at the end of 2006 and I am indebted to them for a number of facts and statements in my summary below.

[2] "On the synonyms by which the modes of the soul are signified, in tragic usage."

competence as a Classicist to guide himself.[1] In 1925 he published his first indological paper,[2] and in 1928 he received the *venia legendi*[3] for Indology on the basis of his first studies of Dignāga and Dharmakīrti. In addition to teaching at the secondary school he taught until 1938 as a sessional instructor at Vienna University. During these years he also turned to Classical Tibetan, which—just as he later did with Buddhist Chinese and Modern Japanese—he taught himself, and was able to interpret, for example, Dharmakīrti's theory of concepts and language from its Tibetan translation with such a degree of clarity and accuracy that to this day, it remains a wonder of philology.

After Austria's annexation by Nazi Germany, Frauwallner was appointed professor extraordinarius[4] of Indology and Iranian Studies in August 1939. Drafted once again in April 1943, he served in anti-aircraft units around Vienna until the end of the second world war. On June 6, 1945, he was dismissed from the University due to his political affiliations, and his *venia legendi* was revoked. At the end of 1948 he was sent into early retirement with a small secondary school teacher's pension. The difficult post-war years as private scholar with a wife, three children, and almost no income, were devoted to the first volume of his *Geschichte der indischen Philosophie*. This was the beginning of an exposition of Indian thought that in its methodology and presentation can be considered to be the basis of all further research in this field. His account of the history of Indian thought as a history of ideas, based directly on the original sources, is still unequalled. In analyzing the acceptance

---

[1] Karl Reinhardt's *Poseidonios* (Munich 1921) is probably the most recognizable model for Frauwallner's attitude in research.

[2] "Untersuchungen zum Mokṣadharma. Die nichtsāṃkhyistischen Texte," *Journal of the American Oriental Society* 45, pp. 51–67.

[3] Latin for "permission to lecture" after habilitation.

[4] I.e., a professor without chair.

and rejection of concepts and theorems that constitute the core of philosophical positions, he renders the content of new thoughts and new theories intelligible and thus is able to explain them as attempts to solve specific difficulties arising within older views.

In 1952, Frauwallner once again received his *venia legendi* at Vienna University and in 1955 he was again appointed professor extraordinarius. In 1956 he established a committee for the compilation of a "Handbuch der indischen Philosophie" at the Austrian Academy of Sciences, of which he became a full member in 1955, and in 1957 he founded the influential *Wiener Zeitschrift für die Kunde Süd- und Ostasiens.*[1] Appointed full professor at the newly founded Institute of Indology that opened March 21, 1960, he retired in 1963. Greatly respected throughout the international scholarly community, also known as a fascinating and motivating teacher, Frauwallner drew a number of gifted students to Vienna during his last years at Vienna University. He was honored in 1972 with an honorary membership in the Deutsche Morgenländische Gesellschaft and 1973 he became a corresponding member of the Academy of Sciences at Göttingen. Erich Frauwallner died on July 5, 1974.

Long left uninvestigated has been Frauwallner's relationship to the National Socialist Party (NSDAP) and the extent to which its racist ideology influenced his conception of the character and development of Indian philosophies. It is only quite recently that these aspects of Frauwallner's life and work have been focused upon more seriously.

While coming to terms with the National Socialist past ("Vergangenheitsbewältigung") was a process widely propagated in Germany after the war, and subsequently also in Austria, in less prominent fields of European scholarship, such

---

[1] Renamed *Wiener Zeitschrift für die Kunde Südasiens* in 1970, which celebrated its 50th volume in 2006.

as Indology, comparable necessary efforts concerning individual scholars is still just beginning. The recent recovery of Frauwallner's entire correspondence up to 1966 and the accessibility of various archives in Vienna, Berlin, and Munich, made it possible to conceive the research project "Erich Frauwallner und der Nationalsozialismus" that is presently being carried out by Jakob Stuchlik with funding provided by the Presidency of the Austrian Academy of Sciences.[1]

Jakob Stuchlik presented his PhD dissertation at the Department of Philosophy of Vienna University in 2005. Its second section contains[2] an analysis of Frauwallner's "Aryan approach" ("arischer Ansatz"), which is also the principal subject matter of the ongoing project. At the same time, although

---

[1] In 1997, the Academy published a comprehensive survey of its own fate and activities during the years of Austria's annexation (Anschluß) to the Third Reich: Herbert Matis, *Zwischen Anpassung und Widerstand. Die Akademie der Wissenschaften in den Jahren 1938 – 1945.* Verlag der Österreichischen Akademie der Wissenschaften, Wien. As for Frauwallner—who had become a "corresponding member" of the Academy in 1940—in 1946 he was acquitted of his political past by a denazification panel, which judged him to have been "less incriminated" ("minderbelastet"). However, a more substantial examination of the involvement of Austrian scholars with their political and ideological reality was not undertaken at that time, and the matter was closed. It seems that a closer investigation had to wait for a more distant generation of scholars. H. Matis dryly summarizes this aspect of the Academy's reorganization after 1945: "As the problem of 'denazification' was treated in a purely judicial manner, a thorough discussion of the period of National Socialism with lasting effects did not even come close to taking place." ("Indem das Problem der 'Entnazifizierung' rein juristisch abgehandelt wurde, kam eine nachhaltige und innerliche Auseinandersetzung mit der Ära des Nationalsozialismus gar nicht erst zustande." *Ibid.*, p. 67).

[2] Jakob Stuchlik: *Erkenntnispraxis mit offenen Augen. Überlegungen am Rande eines altindischen Übungsweges.* Dissertation, Universität Wien, 2005, pp. 72–149. The results of the above mentioned project will be published by the Austrian Academy of Sciences Press.

independently of Stuchlik's dissertation, Karin Preisendanz, University of Vienna, and Eli Franco, University of Leipzig, also wrote a lengthy preface, which addresses this issue, for the present book's new, fifth German edition by the Akademie Verlag, Berlin.

Frauwallner evidently had strong political convictions, as did many of those intellectuals who, after the catastrophes of the First World War and the fall of the Hapsburg Empire, made up a social stratum of German nationalists in Austria. Frauwallner had already joined the National Socialist Party (NSDAP) in 1932, when it was still illegal. He clearly shared such ideas as "the Aryan race", "blood", and other inherited propensities, which had long been used in Europe to account for the perceived differences in peoples and cultures. It was these ideas that formed a part of the theoretical basis of Frauwallner's understanding of historical differences in Indian philosophical thought, and he applied them to a periodization of Indian philosophical history. But these same ideas were then also incorporated into the NSDAP's ideology for their increasingly aggressive core slogans, which then in the end helped to pave the way for the holocaust.

In 1939, Frauwallner published the article "Der arische Anteil an der indischen Philosophie" ("The Aryan Share in Indian Philosophy"), which highlights in particular, as characteristic of the ancient systems of Indian philosophy, the aspects of atheism and of a purely scientific derivation of their teachings, attributing these features to the "blood" common to Aryan peoples. His promotion of these ideas seemed to have served two purposes. On the one hand, Frauwallner was clearly convinced that it was appropriate to use such ideas when interpreting his subject matter. On the other hand, by using them, he also sought to increase the academic value of his specific subject, the study of Indian thought, in the eyes of those holding power at the time. This shows that Frauwallner, in what was actually his first attempt to define typological features of a fundamental and pervading nature that would be convenient for distinguishing the early period from later periods of Indian philosophy, cannot be seen as merely a victim of Nazi ideology in the sense that he "fell victim to the spirit of the times."[1] He was fully confident of the meaningfulness of his historical hypothesis. Moreover, Stuchlik's dissertation also points out that the traditional notions of the Aryan race, blood, and other inherited propensities, which Frauwallner had presented in his article of 1939, were still on his mind in 1953, as seen in his attempts to define categories that differentiated the periods in the history of Indian thought in the first volume of his *Geschichte der indischen Philosophie.*[2]

Besides the personal difficulty of understanding, on a human level, Frauwallner's relationship with the NSDAP and its ideology, we are also faced with the difficulty of understanding why a scholar of Frauwallner's stature and range—whose interpretations and methods of presenting the Indian sources are impeccable models of philological and critical scholarship—used such archaic categories, as "blood", at all, and why, furthermore, the influence of these categories is not to be sensed in *Die Philosophie des Buddhismus.* The answer, to my mind, is simple enough. While in the distinct individual results of his philological and interpretational work Frauwallner produced untainted presentations of the sources, it was when he ventured into the wide-ranging comprehensive historical summary of the cultural phenomenon of Indian philosophical thought and its development that he fell back on such meta-conceptions from his socio-political environment and his own convictions.

---

1 "Verfallenheit an den Zeitgeist," G. Oberhammer in 1992 quoted in note 6 above, p. 225, note 1.

2 And also even later, as seen for example in the article "Indische Philosophie," in: *Die Philosophie des XX. Jahrhunderts.* Stuttgart 1959, (pp. 49–66) p. 50.

Leaving the human level aside and considering only the scholarly perspective, it is in this area that we can say today that he failed. On the one hand, he incorporated the notions of Aryan race, blood, and body ("Volkskörper") into his work based on his own convictions; on the other hand, he selected certain features that he identified in his subject, e.g., "rationality," "scientific approach without presuppositions,"[1] or the presence or absence of the idea of God, and took such features to be representative of typical characteristics of the Aryan race. While no longer accepting such concepts because they are either unfounded or unethically biased, scholars today are still grappling with the problem of how—without relying on racist theories—to otherwise explain the features highlighted by Frauwallner or dismiss them as being inadequately chosen or defined.[2] In short: when we read his *Geschichte*, it is reasonable and legitimate to accept those of Frauwallner's

---

[1] For a discussion of these characteristics as appropriate or useful in understanding the development of Indian philosophical traditions, in particular of the Sāṃkhya, *cf.* Jan. E. M. Houben, "Why did rationality thrive, but hardly survive in Kapila's 'system'? On the *pramāṇas*, rationality and irrationality in Sāṃkhya (part I)," *Asiatische Studien* 53, 1999, pp. 491–512, and " 'Verschriftlichung' and the relation between the *pramāṇas* in the history of Sāṃkhya," *Études de lettres* 2001.3: La rationalité en Asie / Rationality in Asia (ed. J. Bronkhorst, Lausanne), pp. 165–94, as well as Johannes Bronkhorst, "Mysticism et rationalité en Inde: le cas du Vaiśesika," *Asiatische Studien* 47, 1993, pp. 559–69.

[2] For a recent attempt at identifying other characteristics through which to demarcate periods in Indian philosophy and an explanation of these periods as being also based on changing intellectual or sociopolitical conditions, *cf.* Johannes Bronkhorst, "La grammaire et les débuts de la philosophie indienne," *Asiatische Studien* 58, 2004, 791–865, and "Systematic Philosophy between the Empires. Some Determining Features," in: (Patrick Olivelle ed.), *Between the Empires. Society in India 300 BCE to 400 CE*, Oxford University Press: Oxford 2006, pp. 287–313, as well as *Aux origines de la philosophie Indienne.* Collection Le Maître et le disciple. Infolio éditions: Gollion 2008.

interpretations and insights that remain valid even from our historically more informed perspective, while at the same time we can discard all those of his ideas that originated in a specific and discernible set of social and cultural conditions that, hopefully at least in the majority, are no longer ours.

The book translated here, *Die Philosophie des Buddhismus,* is, however, not tainted by any of these racist ideas, although it was written at the same time as the *Geschichte*. So we must ask: why? My answer may appear inexcusably flippant, but I can see no better. For Frauwallner, from its beginnings up to the development of its philosophical systems, Buddhism belonged to the early period of cultural phenomena that he had determined in his *Geschichte* as dominated by the Aryan component of Indian societies. Like Oldenberg[1] and de La Vallée Poussin,[2] both held in high esteem by Frauwallner,[3] he had no awareness, as we have today, of the multicultural melting pot in the eastern Ganges Valley, with its minor kingdoms and small stratum of immigrant Aryan tribal peoples.[4] Since in this anthology of Buddhist philosophy, Frauwallner focused exclusively on Buddhist philosophy, there was no reason to

---

[1] E.g., Hermann Oldenberg, *Buddha, sein Leben, seine Lehre, seine Gemeinde.* Stuttgart-Berlin 1881.

[2] Louis de La Vallée Poussin, *Indo-européens et Indo-iraniens.* (Histoire du monde III). Paris, [2]1936.

[3] *Cf.* his *Geschichte* I, pp. 464–66.

[4] *Cf.* Michael Witzel, *Das alte Indien.* Verlag C. H. Beck, München 2003, pp. 50ff. Frauwallner considered the Buddha to be a member of this group of immigrant Aryan tribes, which was a ruling class. However, today even this has become highly uncertain (*cf.*, e.g., Richard Gombrich, *Theravāda Buddhism. A Social History from Ancient Benares to Modern Colombo.* London–New York 1988, pp. 49f. – Greg Bailey and Ian Mabbett, *The Sociology of Early Buddhism.* Cambridge University Press 2003. – Johannes Bronkhorst, *Greater Magadha. Studies in the Culture of Early India.* Leiden-Boston: Brill 2007, pp. 1–72.)

explain the appearance of this historical phenomenon as such, or its relationship to other cultural phenomena of India. Here he acted as an interpreter of a strictly defined phenomenon, the development of systematic philosophy in Buddhism. It is for this reason that the book is what it is: an impeccable scholarly account of early and systematic Buddhist thought, reliable in its translations and precise in its introductory explanations. In this, being a product untainted by racist conceptions, it provides corroboration for my hypothesis above, namely that only when writing comprehensive history, which had to include a determination of periods and an identification of their characteristic aspects, did Frauwallner refer to his personal ideological convictions. Although there probably will always remain a certain blemish to Frauwallner's reputation, based on his political past and some of his personal views, since this book is free from any ideas related to those and since it is still the best of its kind, there should be sufficient benefit to warrant the publication of this English translation.

At this point it seems worthwhile to remark on Frauwallner's concept of "Buddhist philosophy," which he used as the title of his book. "The Buddha himself ... proclaimed exclusively a doctrine of liberation," Frauwallner says, and he avoided "the philosophical questions of his time," which had no relevance for this doctrine. The development of philosophy within Buddhism occurred when "in the course of the last centuries before the Common Era the general development of Indian philosophy had led to the formation of complete philosophical systems."[1] To my knowledge, however, Frauwallner does not expressly state anywhere what actually constitutes "philosophy"

[1] *Cf.* the *Introduction* in this book, p. 1, as well as *Geschichte der indischen Philosophie* I, 1953, pp. 17ff. and 156–60 (= *History of Indian Philosophy* I, 1973, pp. 8ff. and 124–27).

and in particular "Buddhist philosophy,"[1] or why he considered his selections from the Buddhist literature as "philosophically valuable." Apparently the book itself is intended to provide an answer to these questions. And here, in fact, we find philosophy represented mainly in the form of metaphysics or ontology, as well as soteriology: limitations of which, as stated above, Frauwallner was well aware.

As a whole, within the religion[2] of Buddhism in its various forms, "Buddhist philosophy" can be roughly defined as encompassing all the theoretical traditions that developed over time in the analysis, elaboration, and argumentative establishment and defense of the so-called Four Noble Truths[3] *(catvāry āryasatyāni)*, which serve all followers of the Buddha as a succinct summary of the Buddha's teaching and are thus the theoretical framework of philosophy for Buddhists everywhere. Of these Truths, the first, the Truth of Suffering, is the basis of Buddhist ontology; the second, the Truth of the Origin of Suffering, the basis of a Buddhist psychology or in other words, of an ontology of the mental; the third, the Truth of the Cessation of Suffering, is the basis of Buddhism as a religion, since it teaches a goal to be pursued; and the fourth, the Truth of the Way leading to the Cessation of Suffering, is the basis of Buddhism as a moral and meditational practice. Following the formation of the various philosophical systems, from the

---

[1] For a recent straightforward, lucid and succinct lecture elucidating the concepts of "philosophy" as well as of "Buddhism as religion" and "as philosophy" *cf.* chapter 1 in Mark Siderits, *Buddhism as philosophy. An Introduction*, Aldershot UK 2007.

[2] "Religion" in the broader sense of a belief that liberation from a frustrating and painful existence or from eternally repeated existence is possible and can be achieved through appropriate mental and moral practices.

[3] Or "the Four Truths of the Noble One, i.e., the Buddha," *cf.* K. R. Norman, "Why Are the Four Noble Truths Called 'Noble'?," in: *Ānanda: Essays in Honour of Ananda W. P. Guruge*, Colombo 1990, pp. 1–13.

fourth century c.e. on, discussions concerning epistemology and logic began to develop in an effort to examine the sources of correct and valuable knowledge that shapes every-day and spiritual practice and is oriented towards liberation, as well as the methods of acquiring such knowledge. The theories and argumentations elaborated in the Buddhist tradition of epistemological thought are primarily related to the first two Noble Truths and were ultimately created in order to strengthen the authority of the Buddha, who had been the first to recognize and proclaim them. While in many aspects, to be sure, many theories and ideas of this philosophical tradition appear deceptively emancipated from their religious origins, nevertheless they cannot be separated from their Buddhist presuppositions and purposes, just as medieval European logic cannot be separated from Christianity.

Although the above mentioned four principal truths of the Buddha remain as the core of Buddhism and all of its later manifestations, it would be more appropriate to speak of "Buddhist philosophies" in the place of the book title's singular philosophy. For—beyond the Buddha's few and basic theoretical concepts, all intended as direct explanations of facts of experience, none responding to metaphysical questions—there is nothing resembling one comprehensive or unified "Buddhist philosophy." In fact, the present book describes a considerable variety of theories and systems of Buddhist thought, all of which are related to the same fundamental heritage, but which were often developed in vivid inner-Buddhist polemics and result in quite contradictory ultimate views.

As for Frauwallner's approach to translation, it was straightforward: to remain as close as possible to the original text while presenting it in a clear and readable way in order to mediate an accurate impression of its meaning. For technical terms, he maintained a single translation even when various meanings were suggested. For clarity regarding such variations of meaning he relied on the strengths of context and explanation. This method had the added advantage of revealing the fact that these literary documents were firmly embedded in strong terminological traditions.[1]

The same approach has also been taken by the translator of the present book, Gelong Lodrö Sangpo. Born in Stuttgart, Germany, Jürgen Balzer studied Educational Science and became a teacher at an elementary school. In 1984 he underwent his first ordination in the Karma Kagyü Sangha, in France, and he then moved to Gampo Abbey, located in Canada. In 1987 he received the Bhikshu ordination in the USA and afterwards he completed the traditional three year retreat and a four year study retreat. He became one of the co-founders, in 1996, of the Nitartha Institute for the transmission of Buddhist learning and practice, and is a senior teacher at the Vidyadhara Institute, the monastic college *(shedra)* of Gampo Abbey. Over the years he has specialized in the systematic traditions of Buddhist Abhidharma, and has prepared an annotated English translation of Louis de La Vallée Poussin's French translation of the *Abhidharmakośabhāṣya* that is now edited in preparation for its upcoming publication. Since Lodrö Sangpo's mother tongue is not English, he was assisted in the initial stages of the present translation by a Canadian, Bhikshuni Migme Chödrön, and in its later stages particularly by the expertise of Jigme Sheldrön (aka Donna Ross), a Canadian, who is also very familiar with the intricacies of the German language.

My own task in this enterprise was limited to ensuring that Frauwallner's sometimes idiomatic Austrian German was correctly represented; discussing ambiguous linguistic points and terminological questions; and providing parts of the

---

[1] *Cf. Geschichte der indischen Philosophie I,* pp. 5f. and the Introduction to the present volume, pp. 4–5.

bibliographical supplement with literature related to the book published since 1969. I take this occasion to express my sincere gratitude, not only for the enormous amount of work invested by Lodrö Sangpo and his colleagues, all members of the Chökyi Gyatso Translation Committee, but also for their thorough and dedicated approach to this task, as well as for their patience, over the years, with the intervening periods of silence on my part due to time constraints. From start to finish, this cooperation was a most pleasant experience and of great benefit to me as well. In addition, I would like to gratefully acknowledge the help received from Hisataka Ishida in checking the URLs—newly added to the book—for most of the now freely and easily available original Sanskrit, Tibetan, Pali, and Chinese source-materials used by Frauwallner, and in compiling the bibliographical supplement. For easy access to these URLs, go to the webpage of the Chökyi Gyatso Translation Committee:

http://www.gampoabbey.org/translations2/index.html

My thanks go further to Stephanie Johnston, Lodrö Yarda, and Lars Keffer for their tips and help with the layout and artwork in the book.

While this translation attempts to be literally faithful to the 1994 edition of *Die Philosophie des Buddhismus,* in the process of translating we thought it helpful, for the benefit of the reader, to insert additional headings into the text and to enlarge the index. All other additions by the translator are enclosed within square brackets. Besides this we have created an Appendix, which includes one of Frauwallner's more important articles, namely, "Amalavijñāna and Ālayavijñāna. A Contribution to the Epistemology of Buddhism" (1951), since it nicely complements the long Yogācāra section of the book; a bibliography of Frauwallner's work; and the selective bibliography of related publications since 1969.

It is my hope that, in spite of the author's personal commitments, this English translation of an anthology of pivotal documents from the rich world of Indian Buddhist philosophy together with introductory essays that are still unsurpassed gems of intellectual history writing will be duly appreciated by a new readership.

Vienna, December 2008 Ernst Steinkellner

CONTENTS
(detailed)

INTRODUCTION[1]

In Indian philosophy the systems of the Buddhists occupy a leading position. The Buddha himself, it is true, proclaimed exclusively a doctrine of liberation and scarcely ever expressed his view on the philosophical questions of his time, but when, in the course of the last centuries before the Common Era, the general development of Indian philosophy had led to the formation of complete philosophical systems, the Buddhists also began to develop their old doctrine into a system. At that time they had already developed specific noteworthy views, such as the doctrine of the momentariness of all entities or the denial of the existence of a soul. Most importantly, however, the schools of the Mahāyāna raised the fundamental question of the reality of the phenomenal world, tried to accurately prove its unreality, and created a carefully thought-out epistemological idealism in order to establish their view. At the same time, they contributed decisively to the elaboration of the epistemology and logic that reached their full flowering at the end of the classical period of Indian philosophy and that belong to the most significant contributions of Indian philosophy in general. In addition, the philosophy of the Buddhists exerted a strong influence on the following period, with above all the Vedānta having derived a lasting stimulus therefrom.

In spite of its great importance, however, Buddhist philosophy is still little <2> known in wider circles. A satisfactory presentation is lacking and the sources themselves are scarcely

---

[1] Angle brackets (< >) throughout the translation indicate the original page numbers of Frauwallner's *Die Philosophie des Buddhismus* (fourth German edition). Square brackets ([ ]) indicate additions by the translator.

Frauwallner's own cross references—as well as newly added cross references—to German page numbers are indicated by: S. (= Seite = page).

accessible to those unfamiliar with the original languages. Some sources have in fact been translated, but as they make up only a small part of an extensive literature, one could only with great difficulty gain from them a general overview. In addition, the study of these translations is so laborious that they are seldom heard of beyond specialized circles. An opportunity for a wider circle of readers to familiarize themselves with the world of ideas of the Buddhist philosophers without great hardship still does not exist.[1]

The present work is intended to provide this opportunity. Through the use of selected texts, the intention is to provide an initial introduction, which should subsequently facilitate further more detailed study. There are, however, great difficulties associated with such an undertaking. In the Indian philosophy of the older period, with which we are dealing exclusively, there are very few texts that were intended to set forth the doctrines of the different systems for outsiders. Doing so was a matter of oral instruction, as, overall, the spoken word always predominated in the philosophical and religious life of India. What we are left with from this period, insofar as it was meant for the intramural use of the schools, consists essentially of originally orally transmitted mnemonic sayings and verses, and, insofar as it was used in <3> discussions with other schools, of polemic works. Neither are the kind of presentations we might wish for.

---

[1] Two works that contain a selection of Buddhist texts in translation have recently [i.e., in the 50's] appeared: *Buddhist Texts through the Ages,* edited by E. Conze, in collaboration with I. B. Horner, D. Snellgrove, A. Waley, Philosophical Library, New York 1954, and *Buddhistische Geisteswelt, vom historischen Buddha zum Lamaismus,* Texte, ausgewählt und eingeleitet von G. Mensching, Darmstadt 1955. Both provide well-selected samples from all layers of Buddhist literature. The purely philosophical texts in both works, however, take up only a modest space and the development of philosophical thoughts is not pursued further.

The mnemonic texts provide key words for the memory in the most concise form, which were meant to be handed down together with oral explanations and which therefore are almost incomprehensible without such explanations. They were, as well, not so much intended to record the fundamental doctrines but rather the systems in their totality, and in particular the details and formulations of disputed points peculiar to each school, which so easily vanish from memory.

The polemic texts, on the other hand, usually continue old debates already in progress for generations, with which the reader must be familiar if he wants to properly understand the particular discussions. In this case the fundamental issues, the broad strokes, become less important than the details to which the dispute has turned its focus.

What is most important for us must, in both cases, first be extracted from the texts through hard work and must all too often be inferred from isolated comments and indications. In addition, it must be said of Buddhist works that large parts of them are philosophically without interest. In such cases we are faced primarily with discussions of the practice-oriented path of liberation in which technical details are presented and elaborated upon in wearisome depth, in the midst of which that which is philosophically valuable is almost completely squashed. Finally, the study of all of these works is also made more difficult for the reader because of the hitherto unavailability of a sufficient presentation of the Buddhist philosophy—one which could supply the prerequisites necessary to put these texts into proper perspective and to comprehend them. Instead, the reader must first gain most of the necessary prerequisites through his own efforts. <4>

I have chosen to counter all these difficulties in the following way. I will not render large sections of text in their entirety, but have selected philosophically valuable sections and arranged them according to pertinent viewpoints so that the reader may easily follow the development of the individual thoughts. I have, however, placed particular emphasis on the explanation of the texts. First, the reader is oriented by a brief synopsis about the author and his teachings. The texts and their detailed elucidation then follow.[1] As for how exactly this is carried out, I would like to note that I differentiate strictly between *translation* and *explanation*. A translation must pass on the contents of the original as accurately as possible to the reader who is not familiar with its language. If the original is solemn and long-winded, then the translation can only be solemn and longwinded. If the original is difficult and obscure, then the translation should not feign smoothness and clarity. Otherwise it is not a translation but a reworking. The translator must reproduce unaltered even logical mistakes made by the author. To point them out and to explain them is a matter for the elucidation. The elucidations themselves are rather extensive, especially those related to the concise mnemonic texts. In such cases, I have preferred to give a single uninterrupted explanation instead of disconnected separate comments, and I have placed this explanation at the beginning of the text. These elucidations are not intended to be a thorough scholarly commentary, but it is my hope that they contain everything necessary for an initial understanding of the texts.

As to the difficult issue of *rendering the philosophical terminology*, I have proceeded in the following way. As we are concerned here with a language that is, in contrast to that of classical philosophy, familiar to only a very few readers, the retention of the original terms was not a possibility. I have therefore translated everything, as a matter of principle. Indian terms are, however, included in parentheses in order to avoid

---

[1] Translating Indian commentaries instead of presenting one's own explanations has the disadvantage that these commentaries themselves often require an explanation and quite frequently read foreign thoughts into these texts.

errors and ambiguities. In doing so, I have made an effort to adhere to the same translation of a given term throughout this book. Further, I have distinguished here as well between *translation* and *explanation*. Indeed, even the Indian who familiarizes himself with a philosophical system must first get to know the terminological meaning of the different terms. As far as possible, therefore, I have chosen translations that express roughly the same as what the word in question means at first glance for the Indian. The exact philosophical meaning will become apparent from the comments. Above all, I have avoided the use of terms from the European philosophical terminology because, however convincing they often appear on first sight, as a rule they mislead and arouse false ideas. First and foremost, I have made an effort to adhere throughout to the Indian characterization of the thoughts and to reproduce it as accurately as possible, for only in this way is a correct understanding of this foreign world of ideas possible. To give just one example, the term *fundamental cognition (ālayavijñāna)* of the Yogācāra school tempts one immediately to translate it as *subconsciousness* [Unterbewußtsein], but Buddhist philosophy is also cognizant of the term *consciousness* [Bewußtsein]. Historically, to be exact, it designates it earlier as *saṃjñā* [Bewusstsein (ideation); *see* for example S. 21], and later as *saṃvit* [Bewußtsein (awareness), as in *svasaṃvitti*, i.e., Selbstbewußtsein (self-awareness); S. 391]. If it now designates the fundamental cognition as *cognition (vijñāna)* and not as *consciousness*, then it defines it deliberately as a mental phenomenon to which very definite qualities belong and which is essentially different from consciousness. In my opinion, the translator must capture this distinction and should not blur it.

Additionally, in a field as little examined as that of Buddhist philosophy, much remains a matter of personal view. I, of course, express my own views. My *Geschichte der indischen*

Philosophie[1] *[History of Indian Philosophy]* and separately published scholarly treatises detail the reasoning underlying these views. In a work such as the present one, there is no place for a discussion of differing views. I would, however, like to briefly deal with two points.

Up to now, the great Madhyamaka teacher Nāgārjuna has been considered to be a southern-Indian. É. Lamotte, by contrast, basing himself on the *Mahāprajñāpāramitopadeśa*,[2] recently advocated the view that Nāgārjuna was active in the north-west of India. This is correct insofar as this work must actually have originated in the north-west. I do not, however, consider it to be a work of the great Nāgārjuna, and hence I continue to adhere to the old view.

A second point concerns the distinction between Asaṅga and his teacher Maitreyanātha. P. Demiéville has, in this regard, recently demonstrated in great detail that, according to Indian tradition, the works attributed by some scholars to a teacher of Asaṅga's named Maitreyanātha were revealed to Asaṅga by the Bodhisattva Maitreya; that <7> the belief in such revelations was quite common in Buddhist circles at that time; and that nothing entitles us to deduce from this tradition a historical teacher of Asaṅga's named Maitreyanātha.[3] I, however, do not take the legend as my starting-point in this case. I find rather, that the most important scriptures handed down under the name of Asaṅga fall into two groups that differ sharply[4] from each other

---

[1] E. Frauwallner, *Geschichte der indischen Philosophie.* Salzburg, Otto Müller Verlag, I. Band 1953, II. Band 1956.

[2] *Cf.* É. Lamotte, *Sur la formation du Mahāyāna*, Asiatica, Festschrift Friedrich Weller, Leipzig 1954, pp. 377–90.

[3] P. Demiéville, *La Yogācārabhūmi de Saṅgharakṣa*, Bulletin de l'École Française d'Extrême-Orient, tome XLIV, Hanoi 1954, p. 381, note 4.

[4] *Cf.* also my essay *Amalavijñānam und Ālayavijñānam*, ein Beitrag zur Erkenntnislehre des Buddhismus, Beiträge zur Indischen Philologie und

in their philosophical views and are unrelated in juxtaposition to one another. It is possible in and of itself that a philosopher may change his views in the course of his life. If, however, the contrast is so stark and, at the same time, tradition traces the works of the one group back to foreign inspiration, it seems justifiable to me to assume actual foreign origin and a different author. In addition, the personal name Maitreyanātha is entirely plausible and has actually been attested to. It is likewise quite possible and understandable that the later tradition saw this Maitreyanātha or, in brief, Maitreya, as the Bodhisattva and that the legend originated in this way.

Finally, I would like to emphasize that the present work restricts itself exclusively to the Buddhist philosophy of India in the classical period. Within that restriction, it is also only a modest sampling of an extensive literature. I hope, however, that it will prove its worth as an initial introduction and that it will enable the reader <8> to gain an initial overview so that, should his interest continue, it will provide him with the prerequisites to delve into the works of the Buddhist philosophers themselves.

Erich Frauwallner

Altertumskunde, Walther Schubring zum 70. Geburtstag dargebracht, Hamburg 1951, pp. 148–59. [*Cf.* Appendix I.]

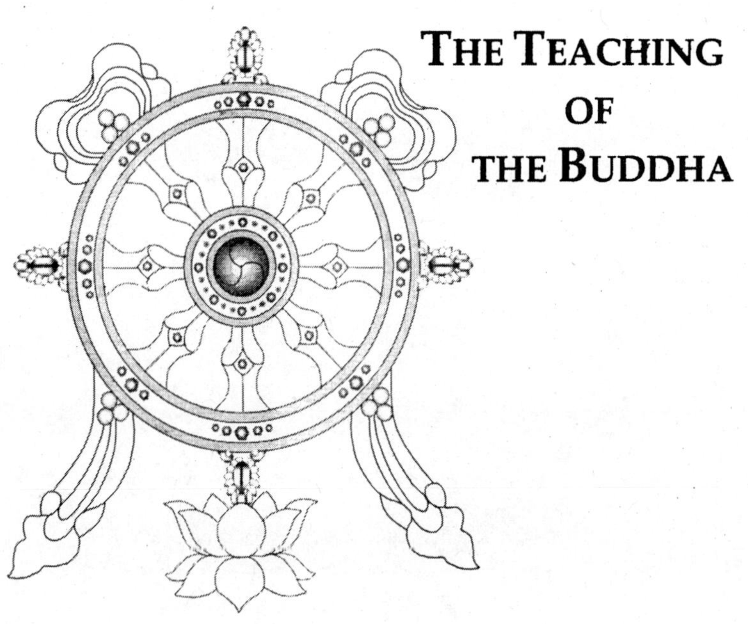

THE TEACHING OF THE BUDDHA

A. # THE TEACHING OF THE BUDDHA

AA. ## *The Buddha (ca. 560–480 b.c.e.)*[1]

Subsequent to the teachings of the *Upaniṣads*, tradition next informs us about the teaching of the Buddha. The Buddha was admittedly not a philosopher in the proper sense, but the proclaimer of a doctrine of liberation. Philosophical matters restrict themselves for him to a few trains of thought and tenets that provide the theoretical foundation for his path of liberation. The impetus that originated from him, however, was so strong, and such important philosophers later joined their systems with his proclamation, that his teaching deserves special consideration.

From a temporal and spatial point of view, the Buddha is not far removed from the most recent doctrines of the *Upaniṣad* period. The country where he was born, lived, and was active was not far from the country of Videha where [king] Janaka, the

---

[1] [The date of the Buddha was the subject of a 1988 conference in Hedemünden near Göttingen (*cf.* the proceedings: Heinz Bechert (ed.), *The Dating of the Historical Buddha.* 3 vols., Göttingen 1991–1998). For a summary of the editor's opinion, *cf.* Heinz Bechert, "The Date of the Buddha Reconsidered," *Indologica Taurinensia* 10, 1982, pp. 29–36. It is nowadays generally accepted that the Buddha's dates as given here by Frauwallner should be changed by approximately 100 years to somewhere between 500 and 350 b.c.e. Contemporary Buddhists celebrated the 2500 year commemoration of the Buddha's Parinirvana in 1956, thus following the seemingly incorrect chronology of the Singhalese histories, which gives the dates of the Buddha as 624–544 b.c.e.]

legendary patron of [the great upaniṣadic sage] Yājñavalkya, had ruled. The temporal separation is also likely not very great. And yet, much had changed in the interval. The momentum and the initial enthusiasm of the *Upaniṣad* period had evaporated. Large numbers of teachers were traversing the country preaching their different doctrines. The squabblings of rival schools had replaced the enthusiastic proclamation of the *ātman*-doctrine. At the same time, however, the period was imbued with a profound striving for liberation, which had the widest circles in its grip and most especially reached the nobility.

Both had a decisive effect on the personality of the Buddha. Above all else, he is imbued with a passionate urge to find liberation from the suffering of existence. The philosophical teaching activities of his time, on the other hand, repelled him. He saw in them a mistaken path leading away from the actual goal of liberation and this determined his attitude toward philosophy for the duration of his life. Thus, he proclaims the path of liberation, which he himself discovered through personal experience. <10> As far as possible, he rejects theoretical discussions, providing only the reasons for entanglement in the suffering of existence and the possibility of liberation in a few formulaic sentences.

AB. *The proclamation of the Buddha*

At the forefront of the proclamation of the Buddha stands the sermon of Benares in which, to use the Buddhist expression, he set in motion the wheel of the teachings. Just as, according to Indian mythology, a miraculous wheel rolls in front of a universal king, showing the path of his victorious advance toward the conquest of the earth, so, through this sermon, the Buddha set in motion the wheel of the teachings, which rolled victoriously over the earth from then on. This sermon is addressed to the five disciples who had accompanied the Buddha during the period of his striving but had then turned away from him when he gave up excessive mortification as useless, accusing him of having turned toward a life of ease. The opening words of the sermon allude to this. The proclamation of the four noble truths, which according to the early view makes up the core of the liberating cognition, then follows. The sermon has the following wording:

ABA. *The sermon of Benares (Dharmacakrapravartanasūtra)*

Thereupon the Exalted One addressed the group of five monks:

"Monks, one who has renounced the world should not adhere to the following two extremes. Which two? On the one hand, with regard to desires, to the devotion to the pleasure of desires, which is low, vulgar, worldly, unworthy of a noble one and which does not lead to the goal, and on the other hand, to the devotion to self-mortification, which is painful, unworthy of a noble one and which does not lead to the goal. Without following either of these extremes, monks, the Perfected One realized the middle way that brings about vision and brings about knowledge and that leads to calming, to special knowledge, to enlightenment, to extinction *(nirvāṇa)*. What, <11> monks, is this middle way, which the Perfected One has realized, that brings about vision and brings about knowledge and that leads to calming, to special knowledge, to enlightenment, to extinction? It is the noble eightfold path, namely, right view, right thought, right speech, right conduct, right livelihood, right striving, right mindfulness, and right concentration. This, monks, is the middle way, which the Perfected One has realized, that brings about vision and brings about knowledge, and that leads to calming, to special knowledge, to enlightenment, to extinction.

Furthermore, monks, this is the noble truth of suffering. Birth is suffering, old age is suffering, sickness is suffering, death is suffering, to be united with what is unpleasant is suffering, to be separated from what is pleasant is suffering, if one wants something and does not get it, that also is suffering; in brief, the five groups of grasping *(upādānaskandha)*[1] are suffering.

Furthermore, monks, this is the noble truth of the origin of suffering. It is the thirst *(tṛṣṇā)* leading to rebirth, which, accompanied by delight and passion, finds enjoyment here and there, namely, thirst for desire, thirst for becoming, thirst for annihilation.

Furthermore, monks, this is the noble truth of the cessation of suffering. It is the cessation of thirst through complete passionlessness, giving up, refusing, emancipation, and not holding on to it.

Furthermore, monks, this is the noble truth of the way leading to the cessation of suffering. It is the noble eightfold path, namely, right view, right thought, right speech, right

---

[1] The five groups that form the worldly personality (*see* S. 26) are so called because the thirst for existence is directed toward them and clings to them.

conduct, right livelihood, right striving, right mindfulness, and right concentration. <12>

'This is the noble truth of suffering, this is the noble truth of the origin of suffering, this is the noble truth of the cessation of suffering, this is the noble truth of the way leading to the cessation of suffering': thus, monks, in regard to things unheard before, there arose in me the sight, there arose in me the understanding, the insight, the knowledge, the seeing.

'Suffering, this noble truth, must be recognized; the origin of suffering, this noble truth, must be avoided; the cessation of suffering, this noble truth, must be realized; the way leading to the cessation of suffering, this noble truth, must be practiced': thus, monks, in regard to things unheard before, there arose in me the sight, there arose in me the understanding, the insight, the knowledge, the seeing.

As long, monks, as I did not possess in full clarity this threefold knowledge and vision with its twelve aspects in regard to these four noble truths, so long, monks, did I not claim to have attained the highest perfect enlightenment in this world with its heavenly gods, lords of death, and Brahma-gods, and among these beings with its ascetics and brahmins, with its gods and humans.

But, monks, since the time when I possessed in full clarity this threefold knowledge and vision with its twelve aspects in regard to these four noble truths, since that time, monks, do I claim that I have attained the highest perfect enlightenment in this world with its heavenly gods, lords of death, and Brahma-gods, and among these beings with its ascetics and brahmins, with its gods and humans. And there arose in me the knowledge and vision: Unshakable is the liberation of my mind; this is my last birth; from now on there is no rebirth." <13>

Thus the Exalted One spoke. The group of five monks joyfully hailed the discourse of the Exalted One.

In view of the great importance tradition accords the four noble truths, this proclamation's lack of content is striking. In it, not much more is said than that existence is full of suffering, that the origin of suffering is desire, and that the cessation of suffering occurs through the annihilation of desire by means of the noble eightfold path. In particular, the explanation of the noble eightfold path is scanty, offering only unelaborated general concepts, nothing clearly graspable. The sermon of Benares is therefore best seen as a kind of programmatic announcement, a framework to be completed and fleshed out through subsequent more detailed teachings. And the Buddha did indeed richly provide such additions in the course of his long teaching activity. First and foremost, a detailed presentation of the path of liberation exists, which is repeated in numerous Buddhist canonical texts and which contains precise, detailed instructions. According to this presentation, the path of liberation appears to be roughly as follows:

ABB.

The Buddhist path of liberation

To begin with, the disciple who renounces the world and goes forth from home into homelessness, trusting in the word of the Buddha, must observe a number of moral precepts. This is followed next by the guarding of the senses, i.e., he should not, through sense impressions, allow himself to become excited and carried away by passion. Thirdly comes the practice of mindfulness and awareness, according to which whatever one does and refrains from doing must always occur with a clear awareness of its meaning and consequences. These are all preparations of a general nature. Only through them does the disciple become able to enter the path of liberation in its stricter sense. This path is—in the Indian tradition—a path of yoga, i.e., through inner concentration, the mind is gradually brought into a state of increased lucidity in which it is able to cognize every intended object through direct vision with complete clarity and certainty. To this end, the disciple sits down in a solitary place with crossed legs in the customary yoga-position and <14> first makes an effort to overcome the five mental hindrances. He then makes his way through the four stages of meditation, through which the Buddha himself originally discovered the liberating cognition, until, at the fourth and last stage, he has gained the desired clear vision. This he then directs first toward his own fate in earlier births, then toward the law of the cycle of existences in general as it rules the entire world. Finally, he directs it toward the four noble truths themselves. He is now able, through his own vision, to recognize them as true with complete certainty through his own vision. As a result of this, passion and ignorance, which have held him in the cycle of existences until now, vanish. Liberation is won and he becomes aware that he is liberated. This most important part of the path of liberation has the following wording:

ABB.1. *From the "Kandaraka Sutta" (Majjhima Nikāya 51)*

Armed with this noble group of moral precepts, with this noble guarding of the senses, and with this noble mindfulness and awareness, (the disciple) seeks out a secluded dwelling, a forest, the foot of a tree, a mountain, a ravine, a mountain cave, a charnel ground, a wilderness, a place in the open air, or a heap of straw. There, on returning from his alms round, he sits down—after his meal—with crossed legs, holding his body erect, while establishing mindfulness.

[1] After he has abandoned greed for this world, he abides with a mind free from greed; he purifies his mind from greed. [2] Having abandoned malice and anger, he abides with a mind free from malice; concerned about the welfare of all living beings, he purifies his mind of malice and anger. [3] Having abandoned rigidity and languidness, he abides [with a mind]

free from rigidity and <15> languidness; with a clear consciousness, mindful and aware, he purifies his mind of rigidity and languidness. [4] Having abandoned agitation and remorse, he remains without agitation; with a mind inwardly calmed, he purifies his mind of agitation and remorse. [5] Having abandoned doubt, he remains free from doubt; not in the dark about the wholesome factors, he purifies his mind of doubt.

After he has abandoned these five hindrances and has recognized the weakening disturbances of the mind, through separation from desires and separation from unwholesome factors, amid contemplation and reflection, he attains the satisfaction and ease born through this separation, and he remains therein. This is the first stage of meditation.

After contemplation and reflection have come to rest, he attains inner calm and one-pointedness of mind and in this way—free from contemplation and reflection—the satisfaction and ease born through this concentration, and he remains therein. This is the second stage of meditation.

After turning away from satisfaction, he remains in equanimity, mindful and aware, and experiences ease through his body. This state is that of which the noble ones say: "He has equanimity, is mindful, and remains at ease." He attains [it] and remains therein. This is the third stage of meditation.

Having abandoned ease and discomfort—contentedness and discontentedness having already previously disappeared—he attains, free from discomfort and ease, pure equanimity and [pure] mindfulness, and he remains therein. This is the fourth stage of meditation.

His mind having thus become collected, purified, cleansed, unblemished, free from disturbances, supple, effective, firm, and unshakable, <16> he directs it to the cognition of the recollection of previous births. He recollects many former births, one birth, two births, three births, four births, five births, ten births, twenty births, thirty births, forty births, fifty births, a hundred births, a thousand births, a hundred thousand births, numerous periods of cosmic destruction, numerous periods of cosmic creation, numerous periods of cosmic destruction and creation. "Here I had this name, belonged to such a lineage and such a caste, had such sustenance, experienced such pleasure and suffering, lived for so-and-so long; here I passed away and there I was reborn. There I had this name, belonged to such a lineage and such a caste, had such sustenance, experienced such pleasure and such pain, lived for so-and-so long; there I passed away and there I was reborn." Thus he recollects many former births with all their circumstances and particulars.

His mind having thus become collected, purified, cleansed, unblemished, free from disturbances, supple, effective, firm, and unshakable, he directs it to the cognition of the passing away and reappearance of beings. He sees with the divine, purified, superhuman eye how beings pass away and reappear, and he recognizes beings that are low and high, beautiful and ugly, that are on the good course and on the bad course, as they return each according to their deeds: "These beings are endowed with bad conduct of body, with bad conduct of speech, with bad conduct of mind, they criticize the noble ones, maintain false views, and perform deeds that are based on these false views. <17> After the disintegration of the body, after death they proceed on the wrong track, on the bad course, to their downfall, to hell. These beings, on the other hand, are endowed with good conduct of body, with good conduct of speech, with good conduct of mind, they do not criticize the noble ones, have right views, and perform deeds based on these right views. After the disintegration of the body, after death they proceed on a good course, to a heavenly world." Thus he sees with the divine, purified, superhuman eye how beings pass away and reappear, and he recognizes beings that are low and high, beautiful and ugly, on the good course and on the bad course, as they return each according to their deeds.

His mind having thus become collected, purified, cleansed, unblemished, free from disturbances, supple, effective, firm, and unshakable, he directs it to the cognition of the vanishing of the negative influxes *(āsrava)*. "This is suffering," he knows in accordance with truth. "This is the origin of suffering," he knows in accordance with truth. "This is the cessation of suffering," he knows in accordance with truth. "This is the way leading to the cessation of suffering," he knows in accordance with truth. "These are the (negative) influxes," he knows in accordance with truth. "This is the origin of the (negative) influxes," he knows in accordance with truth. "This is the cessation of the (negative) influxes," he knows in accordance with truth. "This is the way leading to the cessation of the (negative) influxes," he knows in accordance with truth. By knowing such, envisioning such, his mind is liberated from the (negative) influxes of desire, from the (negative) influxes of becoming, from the (negative) influxes of ignorance. In the liberated one there arises the knowledge of his liberation: "Rebirth is destroyed, <18> the holy life is accomplished, the duty is fulfilled; there is no more returning to this world." Thus he knows.

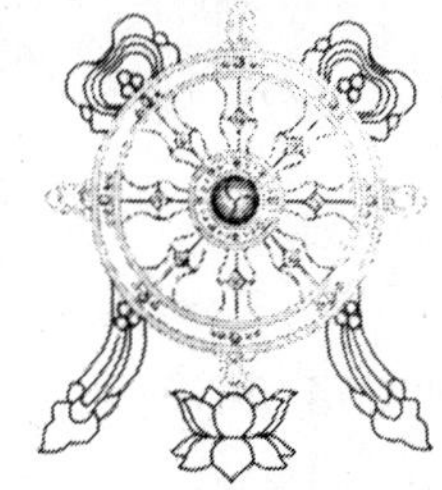

AC. *Questions that the Buddha did not answer*

As we have already noted, the Buddha rejected philosophical questions insofar as they do not immediately concern the path of liberation. This is particularly true in the case of the questions about the existence and nature of the soul, and about one's fate after death. He does not answer these questions in the negative. He does not, for example, deny the existence of the soul and he does not teach that *nirvāṇa* is annihilation. On the contrary, much suggests that he tacitly presupposed views similar to those developed in the final stage of the fire doctrine of the *Upaniṣads*. He does not address these questions, however, remaining silent about them because they "do not lead to turning away (from the mundane), to passionlessness, to cessation (of the transient), to calming, to special knowledge, to enlightenment, to extinction." In the rare cases where he is persuaded to speak, however, he expresses himself to the effect that the nature of the soul and the state of the liberated one are inconceivable and inexpressible. The following two texts may convey some sense of the Buddha's behavior in this regard.

ACA. *Ānanda [Saṃyutta Nikāya 44, 10]*

(On one occasion the Exalted One was dwelling at Rājagṛha in the Bamboo Grove, the Squirrel's Feeding Place.) At that time the wandering monk Vatsagotra betook himself to where the Exalted One resided. Having gone there, he exchanged greetings with the Exalted One and, after having exchanged greetings and friendly words, he sat down to one side. Sitting to one side, the wandering monk Vatsagotra spoke to the Exalted One as follows: "Is there, O Gautama, a self *(ātmā)?*"

When this was said, the Exalted One was silent.

"Then, is there, O Gautama, no self?"

Again, the Exalted One was silent. Then the wandering monk Vatsagotra rose from his seat and departed. <19>

Then, not long after the wandering monk Vatsagotra had left, the Venerable Ānanda said to the Exalted One the following: "Why, O Lord, did the Exalted One not answer the question addressed to him by the wandering monk Vatsagotra?"

"If, Ānanda, in regard to the question, whether there is a self, I had answered the wandering monk Vatsagotra: 'There is a self,' then, Ānanda, I would have sided with the ascetics and brahmins who teach eternality. And if, Ānanda, in regard to the question, whether there is no self, I had answered the wandering monk Vatsagotra: 'There is no self,' then, Ānanda, I would have sided with the ascetics and brahmins who teach annihilation. If then, Ānanda, in regard to the question, whether there is a self, I had answered the wandering monk Vatsagotra: 'There is a self,' would it have helped me to bring forth [in Vatsagotra] the knowledge that all entities are not the self?"

"No, O Lord."

"And if, Ānanda, in regard to the question, whether there is no self, I had answered the wandering monk Vatsagotra: 'There is no self,' then, Ānanda, it would have caused (the wandering monk) Vatsagotra, who is already bewildered, even more bewilderment: 'It seemed that my self existed formerly, but now, does it no longer exist?' "

ACB. *The Discourse of Vatsagotra and the Fire*
(Aggivacchagottasuttanta) [Majjhima Nikāya 72]

Thus have I heard. On one occasion the Exalted One was dwelling at Śrāvastī in Jetavana, the Gardens of Anāthapiṇḍada. At that time the wandering monk Vatsagotra betook himself to where the Exalted One resided. Having gone there, he exchanged greetings with the Exalted One and, after having exchanged greetings and friendly words, <20> he sat down to one side. Sitting to one side, the wandering monk Vatsagotra spoke to the Exalted One as follows:

"How is it, O Gautama? Does the Lord Gautama hold the view that the world is eternal, that alone this is true and everything else is erroneous?"

"No, Vatsa, I do not hold the view that the world is eternal, that this alone is true and everything else is erroneous."

"How is it then, O Gautama? Does the Lord Gautama hold the view that the world will end, that this alone is true and everything else is erroneous?"

"No, Vatsa, I do not hold the view that the world will end, that this alone is true and everything else is erroneous."

"How is it then, O Gautama? Does the Lord Gautama hold the view that the world is limited, that this alone is true and everything else is erroneous?"

"No, Vatsa, I do not hold the view that the world is limited, that this alone is true and everything else is erroneous."

"How is it then, O Gautama? Does the Lord Gautama hold the view that the world is unlimited, that this alone is true and everything else is erroneous?"

"No, Vatsa, I do not hold the view that the world is unlimited, that this alone is true and everything else is erroneous."

This is followed by questions about whether the soul and the body are the same or whether they are different, whether the Perfected One exists after death, whether he does not exist, whether he both exists and does not exist, whether he neither exists nor does not exist, and the Buddha's answer always remains the same. Then Vatsagotra says:

"In regard to the question: 'How is it, O Gautama? Does the Lord Gautama hold the view, that the world is eternal, that this alone is true and everything else is erroneous?' you answer: 'No, Vatsa, I do not hold the view that the world is eternal, that this alone is true and everything else is erroneous.' In regard to the question: 'How is it then, O Gautama? Does the Lord Gautama hold the view that the world will end, <21> that this alone is true and everything else is erroneous?' you answer: 'No, Vatsa, I do not hold the view that the world will end, that this alone is true and everything else is erroneous.' "

The same is repeated regarding all the other questions and then Vatsagotra ends with the following words:

"What defect does the Lord Gautama see in these [speculative] views that, altogether, he does not accept them?"

" 'The world is eternal,' this [speculative] view, Vatsa, is a thicket of a view, a wilderness of a view, a cramp of a view, a shivering of a view, a fetter of a view, it is full of suffering, full of distress, full of despair, full of torment and does not lead to turning away, to passionlessness, to cessation (of all worldly things), to calming, to special knowledge, to enlightenment, to extinction."

Again, the same is repeated regarding all the other [speculative] views, and then the Buddha ends:

"This defect, Vatsa, do I see in these [speculative] views that, altogether, I do not accept them."

"Then does the Lord Gautama hold any [speculative] view?"

"Vatsa, a view is foreign to the Perfected One, for the Perfected One, Vatsa, has understood the following: This is corporeality *(rūpa)*, this is the origin of corporeality, this is the disappearance of corporeality; this is sensation, this is the origin of sensation, this is the disappearance of sensation; this is ideation, this is the origin of ideation, this is the disappearance of ideation; these are the formations, this is the origin of the formations, this is the disappearance of the formations; this is cognition, this is the origin of cognition, this is the disappearance of cognition. Thus, I say, the Perfected One is completely liberated through the vanishing, the refusal, the cessation, the giving up, <22> and rejecting of all the opinions, all the worries, and all the burdens caused by the notions of 'I' and 'mine.' "

"But where, O Gautama, does a monk whose mind is thus liberated arise (again)?"

"Arising, Vatsa, does not apply."

"But then, O Gautama, does he not arise (again)?"

"Not arising, Vatsa, does not apply."

"But then, O Gautama, does he arise and not arise (again)?"

"Arising and not arising, Vatsa, does not apply."

"But then, O Gautama, does he neither arise nor not arise (again)?"

"Neither-arising-nor-not-arising, Vatsa, does not apply."

"In regard to the question: 'But where, O Gautama, does a monk whose mind is thus liberated arise (again)?' you answer: 'Arising, Vatsa, does not apply.' In regard to the question: 'But then, O Gautama, does he not arise (again)?' you answer: 'Not arising, Vatsa, does not apply.' In regard to the question: 'But then, O Gautama, does he arise and not arise (again)?' you answer: 'Arising and not arising, Vatsa, does not apply.' And in regard to the question: 'But then, does he neither arise nor not arise (again)?' you answer: 'Neither-arising-nor-not-arising, Vatsa, does not apply.' Here, O Gautama, I have now fallen into ignorance, here I have fallen into bewilderment, and the clarity that I had gained through the previous conversation with Lord Gautama has now been lost."

"Enough with ignorance, Vatsa, enough with bewilderment! This teaching, Vatsa, is profound, difficult to see, difficult to understand, peaceful, sublime, inaccessible to reasoning, subtle, comprehensible only to the wise; [this teaching] is difficult to understand for you who holds other views, who indulges in other [things] and delights in other [things], who follows another rule and another teaching. Therefore, Vatsa, I will now address counter-questions to you; answer as you see fit. What do you think, Vatsa, if a fire were burning here in front of you, would you then know: 'A fire is burning in front of me'?"

"If, O Gautama, a fire were burning in front of me, I would know: 'A fire is burning here in front of me.' "

"If someone were to ask you now: 'By what means is this fire burning that is burning in front of you?' How would you, Vatsa, answer this question?"

"If, O Gautama, somebody would ask me: 'By what means is this fire burning that is burning in front of you?' I, O Gautama, would answer: 'This fire that is burning in front of me is burning by means of the fuel of grass and wood.' "

"If now, Vatsa, the fire in front of you were to go out, would you know: 'This fire in front of me has gone out.'?"

"If, O Gautama, the fire in front of me were to go out, I would know: 'This fire in front of me has gone out.' "

"If, Vatsa, someone were to ask you now: 'In which direction did the fire that went out in front of you go, to the east, to the west, to the north, or to the south?,' how would you, Vatsa, answer this question?"

"This does not apply, O Gautama, for the fire has consumed the fuel of grass and wood by means of which it was burning, more [fuel] was not supplied and thus, without sustenance, it is defined as having gone out."

"Just so, Vatsa, corporeality, sensation, ideation, formations, and cognition—by means of which one might describe the Perfected One, if one wished to describe him—are given up, uprooted, like a palm tree pulled out of the ground, annihilated, and in future no longer subject to coming into existence. Free from any reckoning in terms of corporeality, sensation, ideation, formations, and cognition, Vatsa, the Perfected One is profound, immeasurable, <24> and difficult to fathom like the ocean. 'Arising' does not apply, 'not arising' does not apply, 'arising and not arising' does not apply, 'neither-arising-nor-not-arising' does not apply."

In answer to this speech, the wandering monk Vatsagotra said the following to the Exalted One: "Just as if, O Gautama, a great *śāla* tree stood near a village or market-town, and, due to impermanence, the branches and the leaves fell off from it, the bark and dry dead bark fell off, and the sapwood fell off, and [the tree] then stood there pure as heartwood, without branches and leaves, without bark and dry dead bark, and without sapwood, just so the proclamation of the Lord Gautama stands there pure as heartwood, without branches and leaves, without bark and dry dead bark, and without sapwood. Wonderful, O Gautama, wonderful, O Gautama! Just as if, O Gautama, one were to set upright what is bent down or were to reveal what has been hidden or were to show the path to one who is lost or were to carry an oil-lamp in the dark so that all those who have eyes can see the forms (of things), just so Lord Gautama has proclaimed the teaching in manifold ways. I take refuge in Lord Gautama, in the teaching, and in the community of monks. May Lord Gautama consider me, from today onward and for the rest of my life, as a lay follower who has taken his refuge in him."

Lastly it should be briefly noted that although as a rule the Buddha adhered strictly to the attitude discussed here and, above all, avoided speaking of a self or a soul, nonetheless, here and there one does also find texts that contradict this. The dispute between the later schools is connected with this. A well-known example of this is the following short sutra, in which the Buddha, contrary to his usual habit, speaks of a personality *(pudgala)*. <25>

ACC. *The Discourse of the Bearer of the Burden (Bhārahārasūtra)*

Thus have I heard. On one occasion the Exalted One was dwelling at Śrāvastī in Jetavana, the Gardens of Anāthapiṇḍada. There the Exalted One spoke to the monks:

I will expound to you, monks, the burden, the taking up of the burden, the laying down of the burden, and the bearer of the burden. So listen and pay thorough and good attention. I will speak to you.

What is the *burden?* The five groups of grasping *(upādānaskandha).* What five? Corporeality as a group of grasping, sensation as a group of grasping, ideation as a group of grasping, formations as a group of grasping, and cognition as a group of grasping.

What is the *taking up of the burden?* It is the thirst that leads to rebirth, which, accompanied by delight and passion, finds enjoyment here and there.

What is the *laying down of the burden?* It is the complete abandoning, the rejecting, the shaking off, the vanishing, the refusal, the cessation, the ceasing, the disappearing of the thirst that leads to rebirth, which, accompanied by delight and passion, finds enjoyment here and there.

Who is the *bearer of the burden?* This should be answered in the following way: the person, i.e., that venerable one who has such and such a name, who is of such and such a family, is descended from such and such a lineage, eats such food, experiences such pleasure and such suffering, whose life lasts so-and-so long, who will live for so-and-so long, and whose lifetime is so-and-so limited. This is what is called the *burden,* the *taking up of the burden,* the *laying down of the burden,* and the *bearer of the burden.*" <26>

Then the Exalted One added the following verse: "If one has laid down the heavy burden, one should not newly take it up again. The heavy burden brings great suffering, the laying down of the burden brings great joy. One must annihilate all thirst, then all formations vanish. If one clearly cognizes the remaining objects, then there is no further rebirth."

Thus spoke the Exalted One. The monks joyfully hailed the speech of the Exalted One.

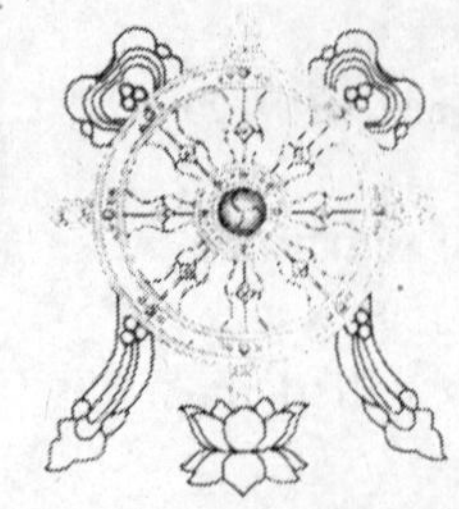

AD. *The tenet of dependent origination*

We turn now to the actual philosophical tenets of Buddhism, namely, the foundation of the path of liberation. In the sermon of Benares, we have not discovered more in this regard than that thirst is the cause of suffering. Later, however, this concept was developed further. First and foremost, a distinction was made between thirst aroused by sense-objects and thirst directed toward one's worldly existence. When, that is, the senses come in contact with their objects, sensations arise and these awaken desire. In this way, the so-called *thirst for [objects of] desire (kāmatṛṣṇā)* arises. The second form of thirst comes into being as follows. Taking the worldly personality to be the true self *(ātmā)* is particularly fateful for one's entanglement in existence. The Buddha, on the other hand, has shown that the worldly personality is in truth only a combination of different kinds of factors *(dharma)*, some material, some mental, all impermanent and all belonging to this world. He distinguished five groups *(skandha)* of such factors, corporeality *(rūpa)*, sensation *(vedanā)*, ideation *(saṃjñā)*, formations *(saṃskāra)*, and cognition *(vijñāna)*. One of the most important points of the Buddha's sermon, therefore, is to demonstrate that these five groups are not the true self. Whoever—as is usual among ordinary human beings—nonetheless takes them to be the self, comes to cling to them. This attachment to the worldly personality is one of the most important causes for constantly being reborn and this is the second form of thirst, the <27> so-called *thirst for becoming (bhavatṛṣṇā)*. Occasionally, as a third form of thirst, the *thirst for annihilation (vibhavatṛṣṇā)* was also placed beside these, since striving for annihilation is just as much a mistaken path for one seeking liberation as is striving for the continuation of life. This third form never gained any great importance, however, and was soon dropped.

The development of the concept of thirst demonstrates some remarkable thinking. Far more important, however, was that a second concept, i.e., that of *ignorance,* was drawn upon in order to explain *entanglement in the cycle of existences,* and that this [concept] was tied to the concept of *thirst.* Beginning with the oldest teachings of the *Upaniṣads*, it was customary to see the means of release, above all else, in knowledge, i.e., in a liberating cognition. What followed naturally from this was to find the cause of entanglement in worldly existence in the lack of this cognition, in *ignorance.* Since Buddhism likewise made liberation dependent on the attainment of a liberating cognition, it also could not avoid this conclusion. Thus it came about that *ignorance* was placed next to *thirst* as a cause of entanglement in the cycle of existences. The two were united when a continuous chain of causes and effects was devised to explain both the arising of entanglement and the ever recurring rebirth. Thus emerged the most important theoretical tenet that Buddhism in its oldest form produced, the famous tenet of *dependent origination (pratītya-samutpāda).* The examples that follow are intended to present this tenet, its interpretation and its development.[1] Here I have chosen examples more generously, not only because of the significance due this tenet itself, but also because it has been dealt with quite often and explained in most diverse ways in Europe. The following examples, on the other hand, are intended, at least to a modest extent, to show how this tenet, and its interpretation, are presented in the Buddhist tradition itself.

---

[1] [See Frauwallner's further general explanations on his presentation of dependent origination, pp. 50f.]

Legend places the discovery of the tenet of dependent origination as early as when the <28> Buddha had only just attained enlightenment, and describes how he spent a long time in contemplation, mulling it over again and again. In view of this, it is said:

ADA. *The Account of Enlightenment (Bodhikathā; Mahāvagga I, 1)*

At that time the Buddha, the Exalted One, was dwelling at Uruvilvā on the bank of the river Nairañjanā at the foot of the tree of enlightenment just after he had attained enlightenment. The Exalted One then sat cross-legged for seven days in one and the same position at the foot of the tree of enlightenment while experiencing the ease of liberation.

Then, in the . . . night, the Exalted One contemplated dependent arising in the forward and in reverse order: Dependent on *ignorance, volitional formations (saṃskāra)* come into being; dependent on *volitional formations, cognition;* dependent on *cognition, name and form;* dependent on *name and form,* the *sixfold sphere;* dependent on the *sixfold sphere, contact;* dependent on *contact, sensation;* dependent on *sensation, thirst;* dependent on *thirst, grasping;* dependent on *grasping, becoming;* dependent on *becoming, birth;* dependent on *birth, old age and death, sorrow and lamentation, pain, distress, and despair.* Thus the origin of this whole mass of suffering comes about.

Through the cessation of *ignorance* due to complete passionlessness, the *volitional formations* cease; through the cessation of the *volitional formations, cognition* ceases; through the cessation of *cognition, name and form* cease; through the cessation of *name and form,* the *sixfold sphere* ceases; <29> through the cessation of the *sixfold sphere, contact* ceases; through the cessation of *contact, sensation* ceases; through the cessation of *sensation, thirst* ceases; through the cessation of *thirst, grasping* ceases; through the cessation of *grasping, becoming* ceases; through the cessation of *becoming, birth* ceases; through the cessation of *birth, old age and death, sorrow and lamentation, pain, distress, and despair* cease. Thus the cessation of this whole mass of suffering comes about.

When the Exalted One had understood this matter, he spoke the following words: "Truly, when the factors *(dharma)* come into view for the striving and pondering brahmin, then all his doubts disappear, since he understands the factors together with their causes."

This text presents the tenet of dependent origination in its customary form. Here, the suffering of existence is traced back through a twelve-membered chain of causes and effects to ignorance as the last cause. Individually, the members of this causal chain are to be understood approximately as follows: The last cause of entanglement in the cycle of existences is, as mentioned, ignorance, i.e., being unaware of the liberating cognition, the four noble truths. In the person who does not possess this cognition, volitional formations directed toward the sense-objects and the worldly personality come into being. Cognition, which like a subtle body is the bearer of rebirth, enters into a new womb after death, driven by these volitional formations. Subsequent to cognition, the body and the factors of the psyche—as this is what is meant by name and form—develop, and finally also the sixfold sphere, i.e., the sense-organs of the new being which thus enters into existence. If this new being is now born, then the <30> fateful contact of the sense-organs with their objects occurs. Sensations of various kinds come into being and rouse the passions, foremost being the thirst that clings to sense-pleasures and to the supposed self, or, as Buddhist texts say, that grasps them, and thereby leads to renewed bondage and new existence. Once again, birth and entanglement in the suffering of existence come about, and so it goes, in an endless chain, for as long as the liberating cognition and the annihilation of thirst do not put an end to the cycle [of existence].

It cannot be denied that this tenet of dependent origination shows some obscurities. Firstly, it is noticeable that two causes of rebirth, *ignorance* and *thirst*, are strung together quite superficially, and accordingly, two descriptions of how worldly existence comes about are given. This tenet has in fact always been considered to be obscure and difficult. Together with the important position that it holds within the proclamation of the Buddha, this has led to the fact that people have occupied themselves with it again and again and have repeatedly attempted to interpret it anew. This [interpretation] has already begun in the oldest parts of the Buddhist canon and continues through the scholasticism of the later schools. Indeed, in the course of time, considerably broader meaning was ascribed to it and fundamental philosophical significance attributed to it. In the following, therefore, at least a few short examples of this development are presented. The first of these comes from the old canon and comprises a conversation between the Buddha and his favorite student Ānanda, in which the Buddha explains the causal chain to him. Noteworthy about this is that in this conversation the causal chain ends with cognition.

ADB. *The Great Discourse of the Foundations of Origination (Mahānidānasuttanta; Dīgha Nikāya 15)*

1

Thus have I heard. On one occasion the Exalted One was dwelling in the land of the Kurus, where there is a market-town of the Kurus <31> named Kalmāṣadamya. Then the venerable Ānanda betook himself to where the Exalted One resided. After arriving there and having greeted the Exalted One, he sat down to one side. Sitting to one side, the venerable Ānanda spoke as follows to the Exalted One:

"It is wonderful, O Lord, it is astonishing, O Lord, how profound this dependent origination is and how profound it appears. And yet it seems to me as if it were clearly right before my eyes."

"Do not say that, Ānanda! Do not say that, Ānanda! This dependent origination, Ānanda, is profound and it appears profound. And because they do not understand and do not penetrate this doctrine, therefore, Ānanda, these beings—tangled like a thread, covered with pustules, and like blades of grass—are not able to pass beyond the wrong track, the bad course, the down-fall, the cycle of existences.

2

If, Ānanda, it is asked: 'Is *old age and death* dependent on anything?' then the answer should be: 'Yes.' And if the person asking says: 'On what is *old age and death* dependent?' then the answer should be: '*Old age and death* is dependent on *birth*.'

If, Ānanda, it is asked: 'Is *birth* dependent on anything?' then the answer should be: 'Yes.' And if the person asking says: 'On what is *birth* dependent?' then the answer should be: '*Birth* is dependent on *becoming*.'

If, Ānanda, it is asked: 'Is *becoming* dependent on anything?' then the answer should be: 'Yes.' And if the person asking says: 'On what is *becoming* dependent?' then the answer should be: '*Becoming* is dependent on *grasping*.' <32>

If, Ānanda, it is asked: 'Is *grasping* dependent on anything?' then the answer should be: 'Yes.' And if the person asking says: 'On what is *grasping* dependent?' then the answer should be: '*Grasping* is dependent on *thirst*.'

If, Ānanda, it is asked: 'Is *thirst* dependent on anything?' then the answer should be: 'Yes.' And if the person asking says: 'On what is *thirst* dependent?' then the answer should be: '*Thirst* is dependent on *sensation*.'

If, Ānanda, it is asked: 'Is *sensation* dependent on anything?' then the answer should be: 'Yes.' And if the person asking says: 'On what is *sensation* dependent?' then the answer should be: '*Sensation* is dependent on *contact.*'

If, Ānanda, it is asked: 'Is *contact* dependent on anything?' then the answer should be: 'Yes.' And if the person asking says: 'On what is *contact* dependent?' then the answer should be: '*Contact* is dependent on *name and form.*'[1]

If, Ānanda, it is asked: 'Is *name and form* dependent on anything?' then the answer should be: 'Yes.' And if the person asking says: 'On what is *name and form* dependent?' then the answer should be: '*Name and form* is dependent on *cognition.*'

If, Ānanda, it is asked: 'Is *cognition* dependent on anything?' then the answer should be: 'Yes.' And if the person asking says: 'On what is *cognition* dependent?' then the answer should be: '*Cognition* is dependent on *name and form.*' <33>

3

Thus, Ānanda, *cognition* is dependent on *name and form,* and *name and form* dependent on *cognition;* dependent on *name and form, contact* comes into being; dependent on *contact, sensation* comes into being; dependent on *sensation, thirst;* dependent on *thirst, grasping;* dependent on *grasping, becoming;* dependent on *becoming, birth;* dependent on *birth, old age and death;* dependent on *old age and death,* sorrow and lamentation, pain, distress, and despair. Thus the origin of this whole mass of suffering comes about.

4

It has been said: 'Dependent on *birth, old age and death* comes into being.' Now, how *old age and death* comes into being dependent on *birth* should be understood in the following way. If, Ānanda, *birth* did not exist, that is, not at all and in no way, of anybody and anywhere, i.e., of gods as gods, of gandharvas as

---

1 The sixfold sphere is skipped here.

gandharvas, of yakṣas as yakṣas, of ghosts as ghosts, of humans as humans, of quadrupeds as quadrupeds, of birds as birds, of reptiles as reptiles, and if *birth* of such and such beings as this and that did not exist, if, then, *birth* did not exist at all, would one, after the cessation of *birth,* observe *old age and death?"* – "No, O Lord."

"Therefore, Ānanda, this here is the ground, this the foundation, this the origin, and this the cause of *old age and death,* namely, birth.

5

Furthermore, it has been said: 'Dependent on *becoming, birth* comes into being.' Now, how *birth* comes into being dependent on <34> *becoming* should be understood in the following way. If, Āṇanda, *becoming* did not exist, that is, not at all and in no way, of anybody and anywhere, namely, a becoming in the sphere of desire, a becoming in the sphere of the material, and a becoming in the sphere of the immaterial, if, then, *becoming* did not exist at all, would one, after the cessation of *becoming,* observe *birth?"* – "No, O Lord."

"Therefore, Ānanda, this here is the ground, this the foundation, this the origin, and this the cause of *birth,* namely, becoming.

6

Furthermore, it has been said: 'Dependent on *grasping, becoming* comes into being.' Now, how *becoming* comes into being dependent on *grasping* should be understood in the following way. If, Ānanda, *grasping* did not exist, that is, not at all and in no way, of anybody and anywhere, namely, grasping after [objects of] desire, grasping after views, grasping after moral behavior and after vows, grasping after the doctrine of a personal self, if, then, *grasping* were not to exist at all, would one, after the cessation of *grasping,* observe *becoming?"* – "No, O Lord."

"Therefore, Ānanda, this here is the ground, this the foundation, this the origin and this the cause of *becoming*, namely, *grasping*.

7

Furthermore, it has been said: 'Dependent on *thirst*, *grasping* comes into being.' Now, how *grasping* comes into being dependent on *thirst* should be understood in the following way. If, Ānanda, *thirst* did not exist, <35> that is, not at all and in no way, of anybody and anywhere, namely, thirst for forms, thirst for sounds, thirst for odors, thirst for tastes, thirst for tangibles, and thirst for things *(dharma)*, if, then, *thirst* did not exist at all, would one, after the cessation of *thirst*, observe *grasping?"* – "No, O Lord."

"Therefore, Ānanda, this here is the ground, this the foundation, this the origin, and this the cause of *grasping*, namely, *thirst*.

8

Furthermore, it has been said: 'Dependent on *sensation*, *thirst* comes into being.' Now, how *thirst* comes into being dependent on *sensation* should be understood in the following way. If, Ānanda, *sensation* did not exist, that is, not at all and in no way, of anybody and anywhere, namely, sensation arisen through contact of the eyes, sensation arisen through contact of the (organ of) hearing, sensation arisen through the contact of the (organ of) smell, sensation arisen through the contact of the tongue, sensation arisen through the contact of the body, sensation arisen through the contact of the mind, if, then, *sensation* did not exist at all, would one, after the cessation of *sensation*, observe *thirst?"* – "No, O Lord."

"Therefore, Ānanda, this here is the ground, this the foundation, this the origin, and this the cause of *thirst*, namely, *sensation*.

9

Thus, dependent on *sensation, thirst* comes into being; dependent on *thirst, seeking;* dependent on *seeking, finding;* dependent on <36> *finding, judgment;* dependent on *judgment, longing and delight;* dependent on *longing and delight, striving;* dependent on *striving, acquiring;* dependent on *acquiring, miserliness;* dependent on *miserliness, defending;* due to *defending,* it comes to many evil, disastrous things, the taking up of sticks, the taking up of weapons, quarrelling and fighting, squabbling and discord, slander and lying."

The listed terms are then explained in the same way as the members of the causal chain. Then the text continues:

19

"Furthermore, it has been said: 'Dependent on *contact, sensation* comes into being.' Now, how *sensation* comes into being dependent on *contact* should be understood in the following way. If, Ānanda, *contact* did not exist, that is, not at all and in no way, of anybody and anywhere, namely, contact of the eye, contact of the (organ of) hearing, contact of the (organ of) smell, contact of the tongue, contact of the body, and contact of the mind, if, then, *contact* did not exist at all, would one, after the cessation of *contact*, observe *sensation?*" – "No, O Lord."

"Therefore, Ānanda, this here is the ground, this the foundation, this the origin, and this the cause of *sensation,* namely, *contact.*

20

Furthermore, it has been said: 'Dependent on *name and form, contact* comes into being.' Now, how *contact* comes into being dependent on *name and form* should be understood in the following way: If, Ānanda, <37> appearances, signs, marks, and indications through which the conglomerate of names is expressed, if these appearances, signs, marks, and indications did not exist, would one then, in regard to the conglomerate of form, observe contact through designation[1]?" – "No, O Lord."

"And if, Ānanda, the appearances, signs, marks, and indications through which the conglomerate of form is expressed, if these appearances, signs, marks, and indications did not exist, would one then, in regard to the conglomerate of names, observe contact through resistance?" – "No, O Lord."

"And if, Ānanda, the appearances, signs, marks, and indications through which the conglomerate of name and the conglomerate of form is expressed, if these appearances, signs, marks, and indications did not exist, would one then observe contact through designation or contact through resistance?" – "No, O Lord."

"And if, Ānanda, the appearances, signs, marks, and indications through which name and form are expressed, if these appearances, signs, marks, and indications did not exist, would one then observe *contact?*" – "No, O Lord."

"Therefore, Ānanda, this here is the ground, this the foundation, this the origin, and this the cause of *contact,* namely, *name and form.*

21

Furthermore, it has been said: 'Dependent on *cognition, name and form* come into being.' Now, how *name and form* come into being dependent on *cognition* should be understood in the following way. If, Ānanda, *cognition* were not to enter into the mother's womb, would then *name and form* mass together in the mother's womb?" – "No, O Lord."

---

[1] In the ancient Buddhist scholasticism not only perception, but also the designating and thinking of an object signifies a contact, which is merely of a different kind than the contact of material objects that mutually resist each other.

"And if, Ānanda, *cognition*, after it has entered into the mother's womb, should leave again, would then *name and form* develop into this being?" – "No, O Lord."

And if, Ānanda, *cognition* were annihilated in the boy or girl, while they are still small, would then *name and form* grow, flourish, and fully mature?" – "No, O Lord."

"Therefore, Ānanda, this here is the ground, this the foundation, this the origin, and this the cause of *name and form*, namely, *cognition*.

22

Furthermore, it has been said: 'Dependent on *name and form*, *cognition* comes into being.' Now, how *cognition* comes into being dependent on *name and form* should be understood in the following way. If, Ānanda, *cognition* did not find any support in *name and form*, would one then in future observe a coming into being of the origin of the suffering of birth, old age, and death?" – "No, O Lord."

"Therefore, Ānanda, this here is the ground, this the foundation, this the origin, and this the cause of *cognition*, namely, *name and form*.

This is, then, Ānanda, that through which one is reborn, ages and dies, passes away and rearises; through which there is a possibility of designation, a possibility <39> of explanation, a possibility of delineation through which knowledge finds a sphere; through which the course of the world proceeds, in order to describe a being—namely, *name and form* together with *cognition*."

With that, the explanation of the causal chain concludes and the text moves on to other subjects.

The next example we provide shows how the tenet of dependent origination is treated in the most ancient scholasticism. The text is presented as a discourse of the Buddha, but by this point this has already become a mere formality. The presentation itself is broken into two parts, the so-called *beginning (ādi),* which expresses the tenet itself, and the *explanation (vibhaṅga).* The explanation is short and dry in the style of the ancient scholasticism. The text, however, was held in high regard and formed the basis for the elucidation of this doctrine in the scholasticism of the classical period.

ADC. *The Discourse of Dependent Origination (Pratītyasamutpādasūtra)*[1]

Thus have I heard. On one occasion the Exalted One was dwelling at Śrāvastī in Jetavana, the Gardens of Anāthapiṇḍada with a great gathering of monks, with twelve hundred and fifty monks. There the Exalted One spoke to the monks:

"I will set forth for you, monks, the *beginning* and the *explanation* of dependent origination. So listen and attend thoroughly and well to this. I will speak.

What is the *beginning* of dependent origination?

Specifically, when this exists, that comes to be; due to the arising of this, that arises. Specifically, dependent on *ignorance, formations (saṃskāra)* come into being; dependent on *formations, cognition;* dependent <40> on *cognition, name and form;* dependent on *name and form,* the *sixfold sphere;* dependent on the *sixfold sphere, contact;* dependent on *contact, sensation;* dependent on *sensation, thirst;* dependent on *thirst, grasping;* dependent on *grasping, becoming;* dependent on *becoming, birth;* dependent on *birth, old age and death, sorrow and lamentation, pain, distress, and despair.* Thus the origin of this whole mass of suffering comes about. This is called the *beginning* of dependent origination.

---

[1] [The full title of this sutra is *Pratītyasamutpādādivibhaṅganirdeśasūtram.*]

What is the *explanation?*

'Dependent on *ignorance, formations* come into being.' Of what type is *ignorance?* Not knowing the past, not knowing the future, not knowing the past and future; not knowing what is inner, not knowing what is outer, not knowing what is inner and outer; not knowing deeds, not knowing their maturation, not knowing deeds and their maturation; not knowing the Buddha, not knowing the doctrine, not knowing the community; not knowing suffering, not knowing the origin, not knowing cessation, not knowing the path; not knowing the causes, not knowing the factors arisen through the causes; not knowing wholesome and unwholesome, blameworthy and blameless, to be attended to and not to be attended to, low and high, black and white dependently originated factors along with their classification; or also [not knowing] the six spheres of contact with regard to their understanding in accordance with truth. Not knowing what is in accordance with truth with regard to this and that, non-seeing, non-vision, darkness, delusion, ignorance, obscurity, this is called *ignorance.* <41>

'Dependent on *ignorance, formations* come into being.' Of what type are the *formations?* There are three formations: formations of body, formations of speech, and formations of mind.

'Dependent on *formations, cognition* comes into being.' Of what type is *cognition?* There are six groups *(kāya)* of cognitions: cognition by means of the eye, cognition by means of the (organ of) hearing, by means of the (organ of) smell, by means of the tongue, by means of the body, and by means of the mind.

'Dependent on *cognition, name and form* comes into being.' What is *name?* The four non-material groups *(skandha)*. Which four? The group of sensation, the group of ideation, the group of formations, and the group of cognition. What is *form?* Everything that is matter, [i.e.,] the four great elements and whatever is based on the four great elements. This *form* and the previously mentioned *name,* bound together as a unit, are called *name and form.*

'Dependent on *name and form,* the *sixfold sphere* comes into being.' What is the *sixfold sphere?* The six inner spheres, the inner sphere of the eye, the inner sphere of the (organ of) hearing, of the (organ of) smell, of the tongue, of the body, and of the mind.

'Dependent on the *sixfold sphere, contact* comes into being.' Of what type is *contact?* There are six groups *(kāya)* of contact: contact of the eye, contact of the (organ of) hearing, contact of the (organ of) smell, of the tongue, of the body, and of the mind.

'Dependent on *contact, sensation* comes into being.' Of what type is *sensation?* There are three sensations: pleasurable sensation, painful sensation, and neither-painful-nor-pleasurable sensation.

'Dependent on *sensation, thirst* comes into being.' Of what type is *thirst?* There are three kinds of thirst: thirst <12> for desires, thirst for the material, and thirst for the immaterial.

'Dependent on *thirst, grasping* comes into being.' Of what type is *grasping?* There are four kinds of grasping: grasping of desires, grasping of views, grasping of moral conduct and vows, and grasping of the doctrine of a self.

'Dependent on *grasping, becoming* comes into being.' Of what type is *becoming?* There are three types of becoming: becoming in the sphere of desire, becoming in the sphere of the material, and becoming in the sphere of the immaterial.

'Dependent on *becoming, birth* comes into being.' What is *birth?* It is the birth of this and that being in this and that group of beings, their being born, their embodiment, their emerging, their becoming visible, the taking on of the groups *(skandha),* the taking on of the elements *(dhātu),* the taking on of the spheres *(āyatana),* the emerging of the groups, the becoming visible of the life-organ.

'Dependent on *birth, old age and death* come into being.' Of what type is *old age?* Baldheadedness, grey hair, being covered with wrinkles, frailty, being stooped, being hunched like a gabled roof, having the limbs covered with black spots, wheezing breath of the body, supporting oneself with a stick, clumsiness, ponderousness, fading away, wasting away, wearing out and decay of the sense-organs, aging and decline of the formations, this is called *old age.* Of what type is *death?* It is the passing away of this and that being from this and that group of beings, their perishing, their disintegration, their disappearance, the fading away of the lifespan, the fading away of the life heat, the cessation of the life-organ, the casting away of the <13> groups *(skandha),* death, the dying; this is called *death.* This *death* and the previously mentioned *old age,* bound together as a unit, are called *old age and death.*

This is called the *explanation* of dependent origination. What I have said to you: 'I will set forth for you the *beginning* and the *explanation* of dependent origination,' this is hereby answered."

Thus spoke the Exalted One. The monks joyfully hailed the Exalted One.

Now, one more short example to illustrate how this text, [i.e., the *Pratītyasamutpādādivibhaṅganirdeśasūtram,*] was explained in the classical period of the Buddhist systems. This explanation comes from a commentary by the famous ecclesiastical master Vasubandhu the Younger, to whom we will later repeatedly refer.[1] Here, I will render a section

[1] [Even though Vasubandhu introduces the *ālayavijñāna* in his *Karmasiddhiprakaraṇa* and his *Pratītyasamutpādavyākhyā,* Muroji (1993, p. 19f.) comments that Vasubandhu's conception of the nature of *pratītyasamutpāda* (without contradicting the doctrines of the Mahāyāna) is also in the *Pratītyasamutpādavyākhyā* fundamentally in accord with the traditional Buddhist view, according to which *pratītyasamutpāda* should explain the arising of rebirth or the cycle of being reborn again and again *(saṃsāra)* without recourse to a substantial self *(ātman).*]

that comprises the explanation of *thirst.* Following a brief elucidation of the concept of thirst, Vasubandhu goes on to discuss various questions; whether sensations of pleasure alone bring about thirst, and similar issues. The text gives one a good idea of the commentarial literature of the classical period in general. In particular, it also shows how sacred texts were drawn on extensively for the purpose of exposition, and how one noted and tried to resolve their contradictions.

ADD.

From Vasubandhu's "Commentary to the Discourse of Dependent Origination" (Pratītyasamutpādavyākhyā)

"Dependent on *sensation, thirst* comes into being. Of what type is *thirst?* There are three kinds of thirst, etc." Here too, the Exalted One taught the classification of *thirst* based on the distinction between (the spheres) of desire, the material, and the immaterial, but [he did not teach] <44> its nature, and that, in consideration of the particular dispositions of those to be instructed; this is as [explained] previously ... *(there follows a brief linguistic-grammatical explanation).* ... Thirst oriented toward the three spheres has been designated in this way. It is a longing, adhering, and attachment, accompanied by the defilements *(kleśa),* in people who are not free from passion related to the sphere of desire, or, respectively, the sphere of the material, or the sphere of the immaterial. Indeed, thirst belongs to the same sphere as sensation on which it is dependent.

(Objection:) Why is it not said of the thirst related to painful sensation, that it is exclusively thirst for that [painful sensation]?[1]

[Answer:] Pleasurable sensation is the cause of thirst to be connected with it and not to be separated from it; painful

[1] The point is to show that painful sensation also brings about thirst for pleasure.

[sensation] is the cause of thirst not to be connected with it and to be separated from it; neither-painful-nor-pleasurable [sensation] is the cause of thirst that delights in this state, or, in the case of a particular meditation, is the condition of thirst to be connected with it and not to be separated from it. In addition, the Exalted One has said: "Contacted by painful sensation, he delights in the pleasure of desire." Painful sensation is therefore also the condition of thirst for pleasure.

Further, thirst for the existence of the self, which, accompanied by the innate afflicted view of a self, indiscriminately dominates the stream of the groups *(skandha)* filled with the threefold sensation, is based on sensation. Indeed, this entire stream of sensations is its dominant cause. Accordingly, it is said in the *Great Discourse of the Foundations* <45> *of Origination:* "Could one, Ānanda, say: 'I am,' where there is no sensation and where one who senses is not observed? – No, O Lord." Dependent on this indiscriminately dominating thirst for the existence of the self, some people then develop an afflicted view of a self based on conceptions. And regarding this [afflicted view of a self], the Exalted One has said: "Dependent on sensation, monks, which has arisen from ignorance and contact, thirst arises and from that, the formations."[1] This [afflicted view of a self] is also equivalent to the grasping of the doctrine of a self, since how, otherwise, could the grasping of the doctrine of a self in dependence on thirst come about? (*Cf.* S. 41f.)

(Objection:) If therefore thirst depends on the threefold sensation, why is it said then: "Passion attaches itself to pleasurable sensation?"

(Answer:) Because [passion] has [pleasurable sensation] as its object-support and occurs in association with it. To be precise,

---

[1] Here, the expression *formations* designates the view of a self based on conceptions, which, immediately following, is equated with the grasping of the doctrine of a self.

this applies to pleasurable sensation belonging to one's own personality-stream.

(Objection:) If thirst is dependent on sensation, then it would follow that the saint is also tainted with thirst because every person has sensations. Further, it would follow that the contentedness that accompanies release from the mundane cannot exist.

(Answer:) It is said: "Rain depends on clouds." Yet, if there is a cloud, must it necessarily rain? In the same way, if there is sensation, then thirst does not necessarily have to appear.

(Question:) Why does it not appear?

(Answer:) <16> Because certain counteragents are there. For instance, its seed is removed from its basis, or destroyed, so that [thirst], in spite of the presence of the condition, does not occur, precisely because the seed is absent or destroyed. Just so, if its seed is absent or destroyed, a shoot does not appear even if the conditions, such as the field, water, etc., are present. Hence the Exalted One gave a more precise explanation in another passage:

> Dependent on sensation, which arises from ignorance and contact, thirst arises.

Further:

> Whoever experiences [the sensation of] pleasure and does not properly discern the sensation, in him passion entrenches itself, because he does not see the way out.

Thus, not every [sensation] is the cause of thirst but only that which is not properly understood.

(Question:) Why then is a more precise explanation not also given in the present case?

(Answer:) Because here in the treatment of the subject it is presupposed that ignorance is the common condition of the formations.

(Objection:) In some places the Exalted One has exclusively pointed out ignorance as the cause of thirst:

> Ignorance, monks, is the ground of thirst, ignorance is the cause, ignorance is the foundation.

Further:

> What, monks, is the nourishment of the thirst for becoming? To that one should answer: "Ignorance."

In some places, again exclusively, contact:

> There are six groups *(kāya)* of thirst, the thirst arisen through contact of the eye, etc.

Further:

> Each group *(skandha)* of sensation, each group of ideation, each group of corporeality is dependent on contact.

Here, though, sensation is exclusively indicated as the cause. How does this not contradict <47> the sacred texts?

(Answer:) Because of the difference in intentions. If, for instance, ignorance is mentioned, then the general cause of thirst is intended. The same applies to contact. With respect to sensation, on the other hand, the special cause is intended. [This is so] since in all three spheres of existence the thirst of that stage to which the sensation belongs appears in the person subject to delusion. Further, in one and the same stage and given the same ignorance, a difference in thirst appears due to a difference in the sensation, its strength and its weakness. Finally, with respect to the occurrence of thirst, the contacts to be experienced as pleasurable, etc., are dependent on the difference in sensation. Therefore, there is no contradiction.

(Objection:) If with the words: "Dependent on *sensation, thirst* comes into being" the intention is to teach the exclusivity of the cause,[1] then the aforementioned faults would follow. In addition, other causes of thirst, that is, the generative cause and the similar and immediately preceding cause would not be possible. If, on the contrary, the intention is to teach the exclusivity of that which is caused, then sensation can be neither the causal nor the similar and immediately preceding cause, nor the object-support cause for other factors. In addition, a contradiction of the following sacred texts would result: "Repugnance attaches itself to painful sensation," etc., and: "In one who is filled with joy the mind collects itself, in one who is filled with joy the factors calm themselves," etc. If the intention is to teach the exclusivity of both, then both faults would follow. Finally, if one assumes no <48> exclusivity whatsoever, then the instruction is meaningless.

(Answer:) Here, there is no such exclusivity. Nonetheless, the instruction is not meaningless since the instruction is given in this form—in accordance with our previous exposition—in order to teach the specific cause of thirst; and also because sensation is the main cause, given that thirst appears due to the connection, etc., with pleasurable sensation, etc.,

This completes the explanation of *thirst*.

> The examples rendered thus far have demonstrated the detailed interpretation and scholastic explanation of the

---

[1] I.e., if with it one wants to say that exclusively sensation causes thirst, or that exclusively thirst is caused by sensation.

tenet of dependent origination. Philosophically much more important, however, is the new meaning that was gradually attributed to it in the course of time. This came about in the following way: Because the tenet of dependent origination follows a series of causes and effects over several births, it came to appear as if it described the worldly personality itself in the different stages of its existence. Thus when, in the course of the development of the doctrine of the impermanence of all entities, the whole worldly personality was dissolved into a stream of perpetually changing phenomena, one no longer saw in the tenet of dependent origination the law according to which entanglement and liberation from the cycle of existences take place. One considered it rather to be the law that rules the entire development of this personality-stream itself and gives expression to its form of existence.

It was, however, not left at that. The impermanence and perpetual change of entities applies not only to the worldly personality but also to the external world, and thus the law of dependent origination was transferred onto it as well. Next to the previous causal chain, which was now designated as the *inner causal chain*, a second, *outer causal chain* was placed. In this way, the tenet of dependent origination became the dominating law of the whole phenomenal world and the philosophical expression of its nature. Hence, when the school of the Mādhyamikas made the first, boldly reasoned, attempt to prove the unreality of the external world, <49> it proceeded from this doctrine and deduced from it not only the impermanence, but also the emptiness, of all worldly entities.

In the following, examples for this development as well will be provided. The tenet of dependent origination as the expression of the worldly personality will be discussed in the section on the denial of the self (S. 77ff.). As an expression of the impermanence and emptiness of the whole phenomenal world it will be dealt with in the section on the Madhyamaka school (S. 171ff.). Here though, we will present just one text that shows how the old causal chain was expanded into a universal law of causality.

The text in question is the so-called *Śālistambasūtra.* Tradition designates it as a Mahāyāna text and, in fact, it is presented as spoken by Maitreya, the future Buddha. In terms of content, however, the Mahāyānistic character of the work is limited to details. The tenet of dependent origination, in particular, does not carry any specific Mahāyāna features. In order not to become too detailed, I have not reproduced the text in its entirety but only the section in which *inner* and *outer* dependent origination are described and contrasted. An introductory general section and an explanation of the old causal chain in the presentation of the *inner* dependent origination have been omitted, although these sections do also contain something of interest.

ADE. *The Discourse of the Young Rice Plant (Śālistambasūtra)*

This dependent origination arises, moreover, because of two. Because of which two? Because of the *connection of causes* and because of the *connection of conditions.* Furthermore, it is to be viewed as twofold: *outer* and *inner.* <50>

What then is the *connection of causes* with respect to *outer* dependent origination? From the seed arises the sprout, from the sprout the leaf, from the leaf the shoot, from the shoot the stalk, from the stalk the node, from the node the bud, from the bud the awn, from the awn the flower, from the flower the fruit. If the seed is not present, the sprout cannot arise, . . . etc., up to[1]

---

[1] Even the old Buddhist texts abbreviate the frequently occurring repetitions in this way.

. . . if the flower is not present the fruit cannot arise. If, however, the seed is present, the development of the sprout occurs, . . . etc., up to . . . if the flower is present, the development of the fruit occurs. In this the seed does not think:[1] "I bring forth the sprout"; and the sprout does not think: "I have been brought forth by the seed," . . . etc., up to . . . the flower does not think: "I bring forth the fruit"; and the fruit does not think: "I have been brought forth by the flower." And yet the sprout develops and manifests if the seed is present, . . . etc., up to . . . if the flower is present, the fruit develops and manifests. The *connection of causes* with respect to *outer* dependent origination is to be viewed in this way.

How is the *connection of conditions* with respect to *outer* dependent origination to be viewed? Through the coming together of six elements. Through the coming together of which six elements? Through the coming together of the elements of earth, water, fire, wind, ether, and the season; so is the *connection of conditions* with respect to *outer* dependent origination to be viewed. <51>

In this, the earth element brings forth in the seed the effect of cohesion; the water element brings forth in the seed the effect of moistening; the fire element brings forth in the seed the effect of maturing; the wind element brings forth in the seed the effect of opening; the ether element brings forth in the seed the effect of not obstructing, and the season element brings forth in the seed the effect of transformation. If these conditions are not present, the emergence of the sprout from the seed does not take place; in other words, if the outer earth element is absent and likewise if the elements of water, fire, wind, ether, and the season are absent. Hence, through the coming together

---

[1] With this it is emphasized that the entirety of worldly events occurs without a thinking subject.

of all [of these], as the seed vanishes, the sprout's emergence from it takes place.

In this, the earth element does not think: "I bring forth the effect of cohesion in the seed"; . . . etc., up to . . . and the season element does not think: "I bring forth the effect of transformation in the seed." The seed also does not think: "I bring forth the sprout"; and the sprout does not think: "I have been brought forth by these conditions." And yet when these conditions are present, as the seed vanishes, the coming forth of the sprout takes place, . . . etc., up to . . . as the flower vanishes, the coming forth of the fruit takes place. Also, this sprout is not created by itself, not created by another, not created by both, not created by god, not transformed by time, not derived from a primal matter, not dependent on a single origin, and also is not arisen without a cause. Nonetheless, through the coming together of the <52> elements of earth, water, fire, wind, ether, and season, as the seed vanishes, the coming forth of the sprout takes place.

The *connection of conditions* with respect to *outer* dependent origination is to be viewed in this way.

In this, *outer* dependent origination is to be viewed in five ways. Which five? Not as eternal, not as annihilation, not as transition *(saṃkrānti),* [but] as the emergence of a great effect from a small cause, and as the succession of something homogeneous.

Why not as eternal? Because the sprout is something other than the seed; for the sprout is not the same as the seed. The sprout, that is, emerges neither from the annihilated seed nor from the not-annihilated seed. Still, the seed vanishes and, at the same time, the sprout arises. Therefore, not as eternal.

Why not as annihilation? Because the sprout arises neither from the previously annihilated nor from the not-annihilated seed. Rather, the seed vanishes and, at the same time, the sprout arises, just as the arms of a scale rise and fall at the same time. Therefore, not as annihilation.

Why not as transition? Because the sprout is something other than the seed; for the sprout is not that which the seed is. Therefore, not as transition.

Why as the emergence of a great effect from a small cause? Because a small seed is sown and brings forth a great fruit. Therefore, as the emergence of a great effect from a small cause.

Why as the succession of something homogeneous? As is the seed that is sown, so is the fruit it brings forth. Therefore, as the succession of something homogeneous. Thus is *outer* dependent origination to be viewed in five ways. <53>

In the same way, *inner* dependent origination arises because of two. Because of which two? Because of the *connection of causes* and because of the *connection of conditions*.

What then is the *connection of causes* with respect to *inner* dependent origination? Dependent on ignorance, volitional formations come into being, ... etc., up to ... dependent on birth, old age and death comes into being. If ignorance did not exist, volitional formations would not be observed, ... etc., up to ... if birth did not exist, old age and death would not be observed. As, however, ignorance is present, volitional formations develop, ... etc., up to ... as birth is present, old age and death develop. In this, ignorance does not think: "I bring forth volitional formations"; and volitional formations do not think: "We have been brought forth by ignorance," ... etc., up to ... and birth does not think: "I bring forth old age and death"; and old age and death do not think: "We have been brought forth by birth." And yet if ignorance is present, volitional formations develop and manifest, ... etc., up to ... if birth is present, old age and death develop and manifest. The *connection of causes* with respect to *inner* dependent origination is to be viewed in this way.

How is the *connection of conditions* with respect to *inner* dependent origination to be viewed? Through the coming together of six elements. Through the coming together of which six elements? Through the coming together of the elements of earth, water, fire, wind, ether, and cognition; so is the *connection of conditions* with respect to *inner* dependent origination to be viewed. <54>

What is the earth element with respect to *inner* dependent origination? That which, through the cohesion of the body, brings about its solidity, is called the *earth element*. That, in the body, which brings forth the effect of a closer consolidation, is called the *water element*. That, in the body, which digests what is eaten, drunk, chewed, and consumed, is called the *fire element*. That, in the body, which brings forth the effect of exhalation and inhalation, is called the *wind element*. That, in the body, which brings about the inner hollowness, is called the *ether element*. That, in the body, which brings forth the sprout of name and form, being like (two) bundles of reeds[1] (leaning against one another), [in other words,] the mental cognition connected with the five groups *(kāya)* of cognition and endowed with (negative) influxes *(āsrava)*, that is called the *cognition element*.

If these conditions are not present, the arising of the body does not take place; just so when the inner earth element is absent; likewise when the elements of water, of fire, of wind, of ether, and of cognition are absent. Therefore, the arising of the body takes place through the coming together of all [of these].

In this, the earth element does not think: "Through the cohesion of the body, I bring forth its solidity"; the water element does not think: "I bring forth in the body the effect of a closer consolidation"; the fire element does not think: "I am

---

[1] *Name and form* are compared to two bundles of reeds that mutually support each other.

digesting what is eaten, drunk, chewed, and consumed"; the wind element does not think: "I bring forth in the body the effect of exhalation and inhalation"; the ether element does not think: "I bring about in the body the inner hollowness"; the cognition element does not think: "I bring forth in the body name and form"; and also the body does not think: "I have been produced through these conditions." And yet, when these conditions are present, the arising of the body takes place.

In this, the earth element is not the self, not the being, not the soul, not the living being, not the human, not the child, not the woman, not the man, not the eunuch, not I, not mine, nor anything else; likewise, the element of water, the element of fire, the element of wind, the element of ether, the element of cognition is not the self, not the being, not the soul, not the living being, not the human, not the child, not the woman, not the man, not the eunuch, not I, not mine, nor anything else.

There follows an explanation of the twelve members of the causal chain. Then the text continues:

Thus, this twelve-membered dependent origination—mutually caused and mutually conditioned, neither impermanent nor permanent, neither created nor uncreated, neither without cause nor without condition, not experiencing, not subject to vanishing, not subject to annihilation, not subject to cessation—flows like a river uninterrupted since beginningless time.

And even though this twelve-membered dependent origination—mutually caused and mutually conditioned, neither impermanent nor permanent, neither created nor uncreated, neither without cause nor without condition, not experiencing, not subject to vanishing, not subject to annihilation, <56> not subject to cessation—flows like a river uninterrupted since beginningless time, still these four members of this twelve-membered dependent origination function as cause for a combined effect. Which four? *Ignorance, thirst, deed [karman]* and *cognition.*

In this, *cognition* is cause, like a seed; the *deed* is cause, like a field; *ignorance* and *thirst* are cause, like defilements *(kleśa).* Thus, deeds and defilements generate the seed of cognition. Thus, the deed brings forth the effect of the field in the seed of cognition, thirst moistens the seed of cognition, and ignorance sows the seed of cognition. If these causes are not present, the development of the seed of cognition does not come about.

In this, the deed does not think: "I bring forth the effect of the field in the seed of cognition"; thirst also does not think: "I am moistening the seed of cognition"; ignorance also does not think: "I am sowing the seed of cognition"; and the seed of cognition also does not think: "I have been brought forth by these conditions." And yet the seed of cognition grows, resting in the field of deeds, moistened by the wetness of thirst, and sown by ignorance, and insofar as it enters here and there into the sphere of arising, it brings forth the sprout of name and form in the mother's womb. Also, this sprout is not created by itself, not created by another, not created by both, not created by god, not transformed by time, not derived from a primal matter, not dependent on a single origin, and also is not arisen without a cause. Nonetheless, as a result of the union of father and <57> mother at the time of readiness to conceive, and through the coming together of the remaining conditions, the seed of cognition, insofar as it—accompanied by lust—enters here and there into the sphere of arising, brings forth the sprout of name and form in the mother's womb. This although the factors are without a master and are not mine, are without attachment, are like the ether, and are in their nature constituted like an illusion. To be precise, because the causes and conditions are not absent.

Next follows the way in which the different kinds of cognition arise through the connection of different conditions. Then the text continues:

Therein, no factor passes over from this world into that world. Yet, deed and fruit are observed, because the causes and conditions are not absent.

Just as when one sees the reflection of a face in the clear disk of a mirror; the face does not thus pass into the disk of the mirror. Still the face is observed because the causes and conditions are not absent. Thus, no one passes away from this world nor do they arise elsewhere, and yet deed and fruit are observed because the causes and conditions are not absent.

Just as when the moon disk moves along four thousand miles high yet one sees the reflection of the moon in a small vessel of water; the moon disk has not thus descended from that position, nor has it passed into the small vessel of water; still the moon disk is observed because the causes and conditions are not absent.

Just as a fire does not burn due to the absence of the causes and conditions, yet with the completeness of the causes and conditions it does burn, in the same way, the seed of cognition generated through deeds and defilements, <58> insofar as it enters here and there into the sphere of arising, brings forth the sprout of name and form in the mother's womb. This although the factors are without a master and are not mine, are without attachment, are like the ether, and are in their nature constituted like an illusion. To be precise, because the causes and conditions are not absent. The connection of conditions with respect to *inner* dependent origination is to be viewed in this way.

In this, *inner* dependent origination is to be viewed in five ways. Which five? Not as eternal, not as annihilation, not as transition *(saṃkrānti),* [but] as the emergence of a great effect from a small cause, and as the succession of something homogeneous.

Why not as eternal? Because the groups *(skandha)* ending with dying are other groups than those involved with arising; since the groups ending with dying are not the same as the groups involved with arising. Rather, the groups ending with dying vanish and the groups involved with arising appear. Therefore, not as eternal.

Why not as annihilation? Because the groups involved with arising appear neither after the previous annihilation of the groups ending with dying nor without their annihilation. Rather, the groups ending with dying vanish, and at the same time the groups involved with arising appear, just as the arms of a scale rise and fall at the same time. Therefore, not as annihilation.

Why not as transition? Since from a dissimilar class of beings there come forth homogeneous groups in another birth. Therefore, not as transition.

Why as the emergence of a great effect from a small cause? Because a small deed is carried out and <59> the maturation of a great retribution is experienced. Therefore, as the emergence of a great effect from a small cause.

Why as the succession of something homogeneous? Just as the deed that is done is to be experienced, so is the maturation that is felt to be experienced. Therefore, as the succession of something homogeneous.

Thus is *inner* dependent origination to be viewed in five ways.

Whosoever, venerable Śāriputra, sees this dependent origination, correctly proclaimed by the Exalted One, in this way, in accordance with reality, with right insight, incessantly as without a soul and free from a soul, truthfully and without error as unborn, unarisen, unfabricated, uncreated, without obstruction, without obstacle, friendly, fearless, not to be snatched away, imperishable, and by nature not coming to rest;

and views it as untrue, hollow, as deception, without a core, as a sickness, as an abscess, as a tumor, as evil, as impermanent, as painful, empty, and without self, that one does not reflect upon the past: "Was I in the past, or was I not in the past? Who was I in the past? How was I in the past?" He does not reflect upon the future: "Will I be in the future, or will I not be in the future? Who will I be in the future? How will I be in the future?" And he does not reflect upon the present: "What is this? How is this? Who are we? Who will we be? From whence has this being come? Where will it end up when it passes away from here?"

The views that some ascetics and brahmins will separately maintain in the world—that are connected with the doctrine of a self, that are connected with the doctrine of a being, that are connected with the doctrine of a soul, <60> that are connected with the doctrine of a personality, that are connected with auspicious signs and sayings—: whatever is done and not done, all of that is given up by him at that time, completely recognized, entirely removed like the top of a palm tree, in its nature no longer appearing, and in the future no longer subject to arising and cessation.

This is followed by several concluding sentences. At the same time, we conclude with this the series of texts intended to elucidate the tenet of dependent origination. In doing so we have already gone far beyond the doctrine of the Buddha himself and have arrived in the midst of the period of the later systems. It is therefore time to break away and to move on to the presentation of those systems. <61>

The Scholasticism (Abhidharma) of the Way of Hearers (Śrāvakayāna)

THE SCHOLASTICISM (ABHIDHARMA) OF THE WAY OF HEARERS (ŚRĀVAKAYĀNA)[1]

In the presentation of the doctrine of the Buddha, we have seen that the Buddha himself refused to answer purely philosophical questions. He occupied himself with theoretical questions only to the extent necessary to establish and support his doctrine of liberation. Anything beyond this he rejected as unnecessary and misleading. He held fast to this attitude throughout his life and certainly his stance with respect to these things continued to have its effect for some time after his death.

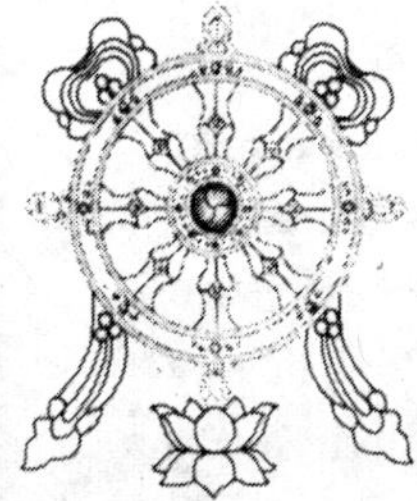

The rise of the Buddhist schools

Then, however, the natural need to penetrate the traditional teaching as thoroughly as possible and to further expand it led to

---

[1] [Frauwallner still used the older terminology of Hīnayāna and Mahāyāna ("Small and Great Vehicle"). The pejorative connotation of the former term was the reason to replace it in more recent literature by the traditional term Śrāvakayāna. But with the use of this term it seems also necessary to decide on the translation of the term *yāna,* which means both "way" and "vehicle." Historically, "way" can be considered to be the meaning better fitting for the period of ancient Buddhism. While in the Mahāyāna the meaning "vehicle" became more prominent with the growing success of the movement, originally the "way of the Bodhisattvas" seems to have been in focus. It is for reasons of balance and terminological consistency that—later on in our book—Māhāyāna is translated as "Great Way."]

the broadening and transformation of the traditional doctrines. At first, a kind of scholasticism of liberation seems to have evolved, which occupied itself in greater detail with the process of liberation and, in Indian fashion, comprehensively listed and classified the related terms. Once this development was under way, however, the actual philosophical questions were also not left untouched. In particular, the questions that the Buddha himself had set aside—questions about the true self and about the nature of liberation [S. 18ff.]—attracted interest and led to serious philosophical discussions. Eventually, under the manifold influences of the contemporary philosophical systems, the doctrine was developed, beyond these first approaches, into a complete system.

This development was immensely rich and diverse, since by that time the Buddhist community had divided itself into numerous schools, each of which, to a greater or lesser extent, made a contribution. Even early on, in Magadha, the homeland of Buddhism, a group by the name of the Great Community (Mahāsāṃghika) had split off from the rest, the so-called Group of the Elders (Sthavira). The Mahāsāṃghikas <62> were centered in the east [of Central India] and they gradually spread along the [eastern] coast far to the south, in the course of which they divided into several, probably mostly local, schools. Far more important was the formation of schools among the large western group of the Sthaviras. In the outskirts, in the farthest north and south, schools of a more conservative character formed. Among them the school of the Tāmraparṇīyas of Ceylon occupies a special position, not least because their literature has to a large extent survived in the original language. Intellectually prominent, however, were the schools of the center. The important school of the Vātsīputrīya-Sāṃmatīyas was based here in western Central India.

By far the most significant, though, was the school of the Sarvāstivādins, also often called Vaibhāṣikas, which spread out from Mathurā over the whole northwest and found strong support in Kaśmīr in particular. It was this school that created the most comprehensive and, in terms of content, the most significant system. Characteristic of this school in particular is a sober, realistic spirit that shoves all mystical aspects into the background. This is evident, as we will see, for example, in the assessment of the four stages of meditation as taught by the Buddha, which here have become almost incidental to [the process of] liberation. Next to this sobriety, on the other hand, stands an incredible boldness of thinking which does not shy away from the most daring assumptions in order to satisfactorily answer the questions raised.

Finally, we must mention the school of the Sautrāntikas, the development and history of which is, however, still largely unclear. From the point of view of doctrine, this school follows the system of the Sarvāstivādins, which it develops along more advanced lines. The Sautrāntikas are above all nominalists, as opposed to the realism of the Sarvāstivādins and also of the Vaiśeṣikas.

BB. *The principal philosophical doctrines of the Sarvāstivāda*

It is quite impossible to present here even an approximate picture of this rich development, which extended over nearly a millennium. To a large extent research has also not yet provided the prerequisites for this. In addition we are dealing here with exceptionally unyielding material. The philosophically meaningful is embedded in a flood of dry scholasticism, <63> which can hardly be of interest to a broader circle of readers. In the following, therefore, I will restrict myself to picking out the essentials. To this end I use the system of the Sarvāstivāda as a basis, it being the most significant, and only occasionally provide a glimpse of the doctrines of the other schools. I begin with a discussion of the principal philosophical thoughts: <S. 63–109>. This is followed by a presentation of the fundamental concepts on which the system of the school is based: <S. 109–26>. A brief description of the doctrine of liberation forms the conclusion: <S. 126–42>.

BBA. *The principal philosophical thoughts*

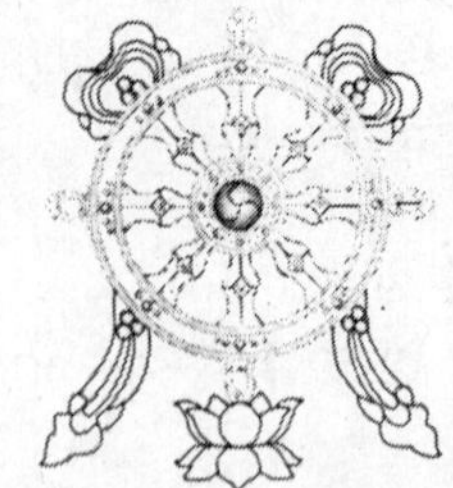

BBA.1. *The denial of a soul, of a self*

The most unique and momentous thought in the system of the Sarvāstivādins is the denial of a soul, of a self. The impetus for this was, after all, provided by the Buddha himself. Precisely, this doctrine of the soul was one of the points on which he persistently remained silent [S. 18f.]. In addition, one of the main points of his sermons was to show that the worldly personality is not the self. He never tires of emphasizing again and again that none of the five groups *(skandha)* that constitute the worldly personality can be held to be the self. It was certainly not his intention though, to thereby completely deny the existence of a soul. After his death, however, no longer faced with the master himself but only the words handed down from him, the one-sidedly negative formulation of his statements began to have an effect, and in the end a denial of the soul was read into them.

This was not, however, a matter of a simple misunderstanding of the master's words. On the contrary, the cause of this development was much deeper. The basic phenomenon from which the proclamation of the Buddha proceeds is the fact of suffering. Everything related to this world is full of suffering and thus it is essential to search for a way out of this suffering, for liberation. Here, however, a very specific feature enters the picture; one that in all probability goes back to the Buddha himself. All earthly things are full of suffering because they are impermanent, and it is from impermanence first and foremost that the Buddha derives the fact of suffering. Of particular significance is the way in which he establishes that the five groups *(skandha)* are not the self. He asks: "What do you think, O monks? Is form permanent or impermanent?" – "Impermanent, <64> O Lord." – "But that which is impermanent, is it suffering or pleasure?" – "Suffering, O Lord." – "So, of that which is impermanent, full of suffering, and subject to change, can one maintain the view: 'This is mine, this is me, this is my self'?" – "No, O Lord." The same questions and answers are asked and given regarding the four other groups. The knowledge of the impermanence of all earthly things is thus the fundamental view from which the Buddha begins and which, after all, provided the impetus for the proclamation of his doctrine.

This knowledge of impermanence, which originally arose from a feeling and an immediate perception, has—as so often happens in the course of development—now gradually been elaborated into a systematic, strictly formulated doctrine. Later [S. 102ff.] we shall have to return to the details of this doctrine. The essential point is that no entity has an eternal existence, rather every entity sooner or later vanishes, while another takes its place. Indeed, the extreme schools of the Sarvāstivādins and the Sautrāntikas go so far as to assert that everything exists for only a moment and then ceases immediately, so that all entities that seem to exist longer are, in reality, only a sequence of such moments that follow one after the other as in a film and, through their similarity, create the appearance of being one and the same entity. The crucial point in this is that there is an actual arising and ceasing and not merely a transformation. The Sarvāstivāda does not accept any duration within change. There is no enduring bearer in which all transformations take place but just a continuous change of impermanent phenomena. The Buddha himself had already strongly emphasized that there is no enduring center to mental events, but only continuously changing processes. This view is now systematically and universally followed through. According to the systems of Buddhism in their heyday, there is no substance but only autonomous, impermanent properties. All entities that appear in our experience have no solid core, but are only a loose conglomeration of such changing phenomena. <65>

From this, according to the classical scholasticism of the Śrāvakayāna, two essential characterizations ensue for all entities of the phenomenal world, namely, their impermanence [S. 102ff.] and closely connected with that, their lack of a solid core, of a substance [S. 96ff.]. This applies quite universally, but also especially to all those factors that are the ultimate causes from which the phenomenal world is constructed. As did all the philosophical systems of the classical period, the scholasticism of the Śrāvakayāna—when it elaborated the old doctrine into a system—had brought these ultimate components of the phenomenal world together, ordered them into groups, and placed the list of them at the head of the system [S. 77ff.]. Specifically, all of these factors were named by the general expression *dharma,* a term used since the early days of Buddhism to indicate all objects of cognition, [and] which is translated into English as *factors* [and into German usually as *Gegebenheiten* or *Daseinselemente*]. According to what has been said thus far, the impermanence of these factors and the fact that they are empty appearances without a solid core, forms one of their essential characteristics. This view of all factors constitutes the so-called *dharma-doctrine* in which it is true we may not see what is central to the classical scholasticism of Śrāvakayāna Buddhism, but certainly one of its characteristic features.

Within this broad framework stands the doctrine of the Sarvāstivādins that a soul or a self does not exist. Here, therefore, the Buddha's teaching that the groups *(skandha)* of the worldly personality are not the self is most strictly followed through. It is philosophically established within the framework of common views. And since a transworldly being, about which the Buddha and his first disciples held a reverent silence, is unknown to the sober realism of the school, in the end, [this doctrine] developed into the consistent denial of any kind of soul.

The oldest work to articulate the denial of the soul in detail and in full clarity is the so-called *Questions of Menandros (Milindapañhā)*. The content of this work consists of a discussion between the Greek king Menandros who, toward the end of the second century b.c.e., starting from Śākala—today's Siālkōt in the Punjab—briefly created a powerful empire, and a Buddhist monk by the name of Nāgasena. The work <66> obviously originates from a time when the memory of Menandros was still vivid, presumably from the first century b.c.e. It was written in a northwest Indian dialect, as were originally also the canonical works of the Sarvāstivādins. All that remains, however, are translations into Pāli, the ecclesiastical language of the Ceylonese school, and into Chinese. With its lively narrative and skillful and interesting treatment of the questions raised, the work is among the best creations of the old Buddhist literature.

Following a historical preamble, possibly a later addition, the account begins with a description of the city of Śākala and then turns to king Menandros (Milinda). Menandros is very experienced in philosophical questions and skillful and clever in disputation. One day, having inspected his army and seeing that the day was still young, he expresses a desire to converse with some monk or ascetic about philosophical questions. His ministers bring him to a Buddhist monk named Yuvala (Āyupāla). But Yuvala is unable to answer the king's questions and Menandros laments disappointedly: "Empty indeed is

India! Empty talk indeed is India! The ascetic or brahman does not exist who would be capable of conversing with me and dispelling my doubts." At this the minister Demetrios (Devamantiya) brings it to the king's attention that a respected Buddhist teacher by the name of Nāgasena has recently arrived in Śākala, and Menandros makes his way to him. Nāgasena is able to address the questions of the king and immediately makes a deep impression on him.

BBA.1.1. *From "The Questions of Menandros" (Milindapañhā)*

II, 1, 1; § 36

Then king Menandros betook himself to where the venerable Nāgasena was residing. Having betaken himself there, he greeted the venerable Nāgasena. And after having <67> exchanged friendly words of greeting, he sat down to one side and also the venerable Nāgasena returned the greeting in a way that put king Menandros in a friendly mood.

Then King Menandros spoke to the venerable Nāgasena as follows: "By what name is the venerable one known? What name does the master bear?"

"I am known by the name of Nāgasena, O great king; my fellow-brethren address me as Nāgasena, O great king. But, even though [one's] father and mother give names such as Nāgasena, Śūrasena, Vīrasena, or Siṃhasena, nevertheless, O great king, if one speaks of Nāgasena, this is only an expression, a designation, an indication, a manner of speech, a mere name, since a personality is not to be observed here."

Then King Menandros spoke as follows: "Listen to me, you five hundred Greeks and you eighty thousand monks! This Nāgasena here speaks as follows: 'A personality is not to be observed here.' Is it right to approve of that?"

Then king Menandros said the following to the venerable Nāgasena: "If, O Nāgasena, a personality is not to be observed, who gives you the necessary supplies, [i.e.,] monastic robes, almsfood, seat and bed, and medicines for caring for the sick? Who uses them? Who holds the moral precepts? Who practices contemplation? Who realizes the path, the fruit, and extinction *(nirvāṇa)*? Who kills? Who steals? Who carries on unchastely? Who lies? Who drinks intoxicating beverages? Who commits the five sins that are immediately followed by retribution? There is thus nothing good, there is nothing bad, there is no doer or initiator of good and bad deeds, there <68> is no fruit or maturation of good and bad deeds and if someone were to kill you, O Nāgasena, then he would commit no murder thereby. There would be among you, O Nāgasena, no teacher, no preceptor, and no admission into the monks' order. And if you say: 'My fellow-brethren address me as Nāgasena, O great king,' who in that case is Nāgasena? . . . Therefore, you speak falsely, a lie, if you say: 'There is no Nāgasena.' "

Then the venerable Nāgasena said the following to king Menandros: "You are, O great king, accustomed to royal luxury, to extremely great luxury. If therefore, O great king, at midday you walk about on the heated ground, on the hot sand, by stepping on the rough gravel, pebbles, and sand, your feet hurt, your body tires, your mind becomes sullen, and a bodily sensation accompanied by pain stirs. So, did you come on foot or in a vehicle?"

"I do not travel on foot, master; I came in a chariot."

"So if, O great king, you came in a chariot, then explain the chariot to me. Is, O great king, the pole the chariot?" – "No, master."

"Is the axle the chariot?" – "No, master."

"Are the wheels the chariot?" – "No, master."

"Is the chariot box the chariot?" – "No, master."

"Is the flag-pole the chariot?" – "No, master."

"Is the yoke the chariot?" – "No, master."

"Are the reins the chariot?" – "No, master."

"Is the goad the chariot?" – "No, master."

"So, O great king, are pole, axle, wheels, chariot box, flag-pole, yoke, reins, and goad the chariot?" – "No, master."

"So, O great king, is the chariot apart from pole, axle, wheels, chariot box, flag-pole, yoke, reins, and goad?" – "No, master."

"So, however I may ask and ask, O great king, I do not see a chariot. What then is the chariot here? Therefore, you speak falsely, a lie, O great king. As you are, O great king, the foremost king in all of India, of whom are you afraid, that you tell a lie? So listen to me, you five hundred Greeks and you eighty thousand monks! This king Menandros here speaks as follows: 'I came in a chariot.' And upon my request: 'If, O great king, you came in a chariot, then explain the chariot to me,' he cannot come up with a chariot. Is it then right to approve of that?"

At these words, the five hundred Greeks shouted their applause to the venerable Nāgasena and said the following to king Menandros: "Now talk, O great king, if you can!"

Then, king Menandros said the following to the venerable Nāgasena: "I speak no lie, O Nāgasena. Based on pole, axle, wheels, chariot box, and flag-pole the expression, the designation, the indication, the manner of speech, the name *chariot* is used."

"Splendidly, O great king, do you understand the chariot. Just so, O great king, in my case, based on the hair of the head, body hair, nails, teeth, skin, flesh, sinews, bones, marrow, kidneys, heart, liver, pleura, spleen, lungs, entrails, intestines, stomach, faeces, bile, phlegm, pus, blood, sweat, fat, tears, lymph, saliva, nasal mucus, synovial fluid, urine, the brain in the head, on corporeality, sensation, ideation, formations *(saṃskāra)*, and cognition the expression, the designation, the indication, the manner of speech, the mere name "Nāgasena" is used. In reality, however, a personality is not to be observed here. The nun Vajrā also expressed this in the presence of the Exalted One with these words: 'Just as the word *chariot* is used when the parts (of a <70> chariot) are put together, so one speaks in everyday life of a *being* when the groups *(skandha)* are present.' "

"Wonderful it is, O Nāgasena! Astonishing it is, O Nāgasena! Brilliant answers have you given to my questions. If the Buddha were here, he would applaud you. Excellent, excellent, Nāgasena. Brilliant answers have you given to my questions."

The king then asks Nāgasena if he would be willing to have a detailed discussion and, when Nāgasena agrees, he invites him home to his palace. Nāgasena comes and a long dialogue develops in the course of which the most diverse points of Buddhist doctrine are discussed, among them once again the question of the denial of a soul. Here, this doctrine already takes its fully developed form. There is no permanent soul. What appears as a worldly personality is only name and form, i.e., the five groups *(skandha)*, which continuously cease and arise anew. From this follows a series of questions, foremost of which is how it is possible to regard the continuously changing groups as the same personality and how, under these circumstances, the responsibility for good and bad deeds and their retribution is possible. Nāgasena answers these questions by means of a number of ingenious allegories. Finally, the stream of the continuously changing groups is related to the tenet of dependent origination, which is the law that governs this unending change.

II, 2, 1; § 55

The king spoke: "Nāgasena, is he who is born (again) the same or another?"

"The elder replied: "He is neither the same nor another."

"Give an example."

"What do you think, O great king, are you, now that you are grown, the same as you were when you were a small tender boy, foolish and lying on your back?"

"No, master, another was the small tender boy, <71> foolish and lying on his back, and another am I now that I am grown."

"If that is so, O great king, then [it would follow that] there is no mother, no father, no teacher, no craftsman, no virtuous one, and no sage. Or is not the mother of the little flake[1] another than the mother of the little bubble;[1] this [one] another than the mother of the little ball;[1] this [one] another than the mother of the little lump;[1] this [one] another than the mother of the small child; and this [one] another than the mother of the adult? Is not he who is learning a craft another than he who has learned it? And is not he who is committing a crime another than he whose hands and feet are being cut off?"

"No, master. But what would you say, O master, if one would ask you in this way?"

The elder spoke: "I, O great king, was the small, tender boy, foolish and lying on my back, and now I am the adult. Based on this same body all these (stages of development) are coalesced into a unity."

"Give an example."

"If, for example, O great king, some man were to light a lamp, would it burn all night?" – "Certainly, master, it would burn all night."

"Now, O great king, is the flame during the first watch of the night the same as that during the middle watch of the night?" – "No, master."

"And is the flame during the middle watch of the night the same as that during the last watch of the night?" – "No, master."

"Was then, O great king, the lamp during the first watch of the night another than during the middle watch of the night, and

---

[1] Different stages of development of the embryo.

this another than during the last watch of the night?" – "No, master; since it burned all night based on the same support."

"Just so, O great king, the stream of the factors <72> continues. The one that arises is another than the one that ceases. Without an earlier or a later, so to speak, [the stream] continues. Thus, [the stream] is neither the same nor another that ends up in the final coalescence of cognition."

"Give another example."

"If, for example, O great king, in the course of time, freshly drawn milk were to transform itself into curdled milk, curdled milk into fresh butter, and fresh butter into clarified butter, if then, O great king, someone were to say: 'The fresh milk is the same as the curdled milk, the same as the fresh butter, and the same as the clarified butter,' would he speak rightly, O great king, if he spoke thus?"

"No, master. Based on the same support, [the milk] turned into them."

"Just so, O great king, the stream of the factors continues. The one that arises is another than the one that ceases. Without an earlier or a later, so to speak, [the stream] continues. Thus, [the stream] is neither the same nor another that ends up in the final coalescence of cognition."

"You are right, Nāgasena" . . .

II, 2, 6; § 60

The king spoke: "Nāgasena, who is reborn?"

The elder spoke: "Name and form, O great king, are reborn."

"Is it the same name and the same form that are reborn?"

"No, O great king, it is not the same name and the same form that are reborn. However, O great king, with this name and this form, one accomplishes good or bad deeds and, through these deeds, another name and another form is reborn."

"If, O master, it is not the same name and the same form that are reborn, then is one not relieved of the bad deeds?"

The elder replied: "If one were not reborn, then one would be relieved of the <73> bad deeds. Since, however, O great king, one is reborn, one is thus not relieved of the bad deeds."

"Give an example."

"If, for example, O great, king, some man were to steal mangoes from another man, and the owner of the mangoes were to seize him and bring him before the king: 'Your majesty, this man has stolen mangoes from me,' and he were to speak as follows: 'Your majesty, I have not stolen this man's mangoes; for the mangoes that he planted are others than the mangoes I have taken; therefore, I do not deserve punishment,' would this man, O great king, indeed deserve punishment?"

"Certainly, master, he would deserve punishment."

"For what reason?"

"Even though he may speak so, the man would, O master, regardless of the first mango, deserve punishment because of the last mango."

"Just so, O great king, with this name and this form, one accomplishes good or bad deeds, and through these deeds another name and another form is reborn. Thus, one is not relieved from the bad deeds." . . .

"Give another example."

"If, for example, O great king, some man were to go up into the attic with a lamp and were to eat there, and the burning lamp were to set the straw on fire, the burning straw were to set the house on fire, and the burning house were to set the village on fire, and the villagers were to seize this man and speak to him as follows: 'Why, fellow, have you set the village on fire?' and he were to answer as follows: 'I have not set the village on fire. The fire of the lamp by whose light I was eating was another than the fire that set the village on fire,' and the quarrelling parties were to come to you, in whose favor, O great king, would you <74> decide the case?"

"The villagers, master."

"Why?"

"Even though he may speak thus, still this fire has indeed arisen from that one."

"Just so, O great king, even though the name and form that end with death may be other than the name and form at birth, yet these have arisen from those. And thus one is not relieved from the bad deeds." . . .

"You are right, Nāgasena." . . .

II, 2, 8; § 62

The king spoke: "Nāgasena, you have spoken of *name and form*. What therein is *name* and what is *form?*"

"The coarse material, O great king, is therein *form*, and the subtle, mind and mental factors, is therein *name*."

"For what reason, Nāgasena, is name alone, or form alone, not reborn?"

"These factors, O great king, are supported by one another and therefore arise only as a unity."

"Give an example."

"If, for example, O great king, the egg-yolk did not arise from a hen, then the egg-shell would not arise, for both egg-yolk and egg-shell are supported by one another and therefore their arising takes place only as a unity. Just so, O great king, if name did not arise, then also form would not arise, for both name and form are supported by one another and therefore their arising takes place only as a unity. This is how this has come about for a long time."

"You are right, Nāgasena."

II, 2, 9; § 63

The king spoke: "Nāgasena, you have spoken of *a long time*. What is it that is called *time?*"

"The past time, O great king, the future time and the present time." <75>

II, 3, 1; § 64

The king spoke: "Nāgasena, what is the root of the past time, what is the root of the future time, and what is the root of the present time?"

"The root of the past time, O great king, of the future time, and of the present time is ignorance; dependent on ignorance, volitional formations arise; dependent on volitional formations, cognition; dependent on cognition, name and form; dependent on name and form, the sixfold sphere; dependent on the sixfold sphere, contact; dependent on contact, sensation; dependent on sensation, thirst; dependent on thirst, grasping; dependent on grasping, becoming; dependent on becoming, birth; dependent on birth, old age and death, sorrow and lamentation, pain, distress, and despair. Thus, an earlier starting point of all of this time is not to be observed."

"You are right, Nāgasena."

II, 3, 2; § 65

The king spoke: "Nāgasena, you have said: 'An earlier starting point is not to be observed.' Give an example of this."

"If, for example, O great king, a man sows a small seed in the earth, and a sprout arises from it, which in turn comes to growth, flourishing, and maturity, and bears fruit, and then he again takes the seed and sows it, and a sprout arises from it, which in turn comes to growth, flourishing, and maturity, and bears fruit, is there an end to this series?"

"No, master."

"Just so, O great king, with respect to time, an earlier starting point is also not to be observed."

"Give another example."

"If, for example, O great king, from the hen the egg, from the egg <76> the hen and again from the hen the egg arises, is there an end to this series?"

"No, master."

"Just so, O great king, with respect to time, an earlier starting point is also not to be observed."

Now we come to the presentation of the form that the doctrine of the non-existence of a soul took on in the fully developed system of the Sarvāstivādins. In so doing, we skip over the older representatives of the school and turn immediately to the man who gave the system its definitive and final form. This is Vasubandhu whom I will call Vasubandhu the Younger to distinguish him from the Mahāyāna teacher Vasubandhu, the brother of Asaṅga [*see* S. 350f.].

BBA.1.2. *Vasubandhu the Younger*[1] *(ca. 400–480 c.e.)*

Vasubandhu the Younger was born about 400 c.e. We have no information about his origins. His teacher was a certain—relatively unimportant—Buddhamitra, but Vasubandhu himself soon gained great esteem. He enjoyed the favor of the Gupta rulers, Skandagupta Vikramāditya (ca. 455–467), and Narasiṃhagupta Bālāditya (ca. 467–473), who summoned him to their court in Ayodhyā. In the end he died in Ayodhyā, at the advanced age of eighty.

Vasubandhu first achieved fame through his successful refutation of Vindhyavāsin, the most famous Sāṃkhya teacher of his time. His greatest achievement, however, is the composition of the *Abhidharmakośa (The Treasury of Scholasticism)* in which he gave the scholasticism of the Sarvāstivāda its final form. In this work the entire system of the school is summarized in just under 600 stanzas with unsurpassed precision and clarity. However, despite the fact that Vasubandhu gave the classical presentation of the scholasticism of the Sarvāstivādins, he himself is not a strict adherent of the school. On the contrary,

---

[1] [See footnote on page 374.]

he leans strongly toward the Sautrāntikas, <77> as is clearly expressed in his own commentary to the *Abhidharmakośa*.

Vasubandhu is the great systematizer of Buddhism. His significance as a philosopher is difficult to judge as yet, since the milieu in which he is found is still too little known. One thing must also not be forgotten, if one wishes to judge him properly: he belongs to the later period of the school. The foundations of the doctrine that he presents are ancient. By contrast, his formulation of it is recent; more recent in fact than those of the great masters of the Mahāyāna, Nāgārjuna and Asaṅga. To lose sight of this will easily lead one to draw wrong conclusions.

The following section, which deals with the non-existence of the soul, comes from the third book of the *Abhidharmakośa* in which the structure of the cosmos and the fate of sentient beings in the cycle of existences is presented. In this context, the question of what it is that wanders in the cycle of existences is raised. The answer is: Not a soul, but merely the five groups *(skandha)*. How these groups move from one existence to another in an uninterrupted stream until liberation is achieved, is set down in the tenet of dependent origination, which is then discussed and explained in detail. The details of the section reproduced here should be clear from what has been said up to now, and calls for no further explanation.

BBA.1.2.1. *A soul does not exist (Abhidharmakośa III, vv. 18–24)*

About this the non-Buddhists, who believe in a self *(ātman)*, say: "If you accept a being *(sattva)* that wanders into the other world, then the self that we assume is established." In order to refute that the author says:

v. 18

The self does not exist.

What is the nature of the self that you accept? A person, an internal agent, who abandons these groups <78> and assumes other groups certainly does not exist, because it cannot be observed like visible form, the eye, etc. Besides this, the Exalted One has said: "Deeds exist and their maturation exists, but a doer who abandons these groups and assumes other groups is not observed apart from the law of factors *(dharmasaṃketa)*. However, this law of factors says: If this exists, then that comes into existence; due to the arising of this, that arises; *(the complete causal chain follows)*."

(Opponent:) Of what kind is the self that you do not reject?

(Answer:)

> The mere groups . . .

If by the name *self* one designates the mere groups, then we do not reject that.

(Opponent:) Should one assume that the groups wander from this world into the other world?

(Answer:) The groups vanish every moment. They are therefore not capable of movement. (However,)

> . . . influenced by deeds and defilements, (they) do enter into the mother's womb through the stream of the intermediate existence *(antarābhavasaṃtati)*; like a light.[1]

Just as with a light, although it vanishes every moment, the stream (of moments) is capable of moving to another place; the same holds for the groups. Thus it is not an error if one speaks of wandering. Hence it is established that, although a self does

[1] The school of the Sarvāstivādins assumes an intermediate existence between two births.

not exist, the stream of the groups enters into the mother's womb through the influence of the defilements and deeds.

v. 19

> In accordance with their projecting cause, the stream (of the groups) grows in sequence and, through the influence of the defilements and deeds, enters again into the other world (i.e., into the next existence).

The streams of the groups induced (by the deeds) are not all the same, in terms of their long or short duration, because the deeds inducing the lifespan differ. In accordance with the great or little strength of the inducing deeds they later then evolve in sequence. What is meant by "in sequence"? As is stated in the holy scripture: "At first the little flake arises, then the little bubble, from this develops the little ball and from the little ball the little lump. Then the limbs develop and after that, in succession, the head- and body-hair, nails, the material sense-organs, and their bearers." That is to say, in the mother's womb there are five different stages of development: first, the little flake; second, the little bubble; third, the little ball; fourth, the little lump; fifth, the body with its limbs. Then the embryo gradually evolves in the womb until the stage of development in which the material sense-organs and their bearers are fully developed. By means of the pressure of the winds that arise through the maturation of the deeds, the embryo now turns in the mother's womb and faces the gate of birth.[1] Sometimes the embryo dies in the mother's womb, either through the mother's inappropriate eating habits or through its own previous bad deeds. Then experienced women insert their hands with small

---

[1] The following sentences, in which the impurity of the womb and the torment of birth are described in Buddhist fashion with painful vividness, are abbreviated.

sharp knives into the mother's womb, cut off limb after limb and pull them out. Or, the birth is without difficulty. Then the mother and other women take [the new-born], wash and dry it. They put butter in its mouth, nurse it with mother's milk, and gradually it becomes accustomed to eating fine and coarse, liquid and solid food. Then it evolves until the state of maturity of its senses. Once again defilements arise and deeds accumulate. Then the body decays. As before, the stream (of the groups) of the intermediate existence arises once again and it enters anew into the other world.

In this way the defilements and deeds are the cause of birth. Birth is again the cause of the coming into being of the defilements and deeds. And from these defilements and deeds birth arises anew.

Thus the wheel of becoming is without a beginning.

If it is assumed that there is a beginning, then the beginning must be without a cause. But if the beginning is without a cause, then everything else must arise also from itself. One sees through the relationship to place and time,[1] however, that sprouts, etc., arise from seeds, etc., as their cause. Just so, the change through heat *(pākaja)*, etc., arises through fire, etc. It is thus certainly not the case that the factors come into being without a cause. The doctrine of an eternal cause (god, etc.,) has, moreover, already been previously repudiated.[2] Consequently, birth and death are certainly without a beginning. There is, on the other hand, an end as a result of the disappearance of the causes, since birth is based on causes. If therefore the causes fall away, birth as an effect must by necessity come to an end. The sentence stands as absolutely justified. <81> In the same way as

---

[1] If they were without causes, they would arise everywhere and at all times.

[2] [See *Abhidharmakośa*, ii. 64 d.]

when the seed perishes, the sprout also by necessity does not arise.

The stream of the groups, of which we are speaking, is spread over three births.

v. 20

> This is the dependent origination, which consists of twelve members and three sections, [i.e.,] two each at the beginning and at the end, and eight in the middle, and this with respect to the complete (person).

The twelve members are: 1. ignorance; 2. volitional formations; 3. cognition; 4. name and form; 5. the sixfold sphere; 6. contact; 7. sensation; 8. thirst; 9. grasping; 10. becoming; 11. birth; 12. old age and death. The three sections mentioned are: i. the *beginning*, ii. the *end*, and iii. the *middle*; and these are three births, namely, the past, the future, and the present. What does it mean that the twelve members are spread over the three sections? Two members each belong to the *beginning* and the *end*, and eight to the *middle*; with that, there are twelve. *Ignorance* and *volitional formations* belong to the *beginning*; *birth, old age and death* to the *end*; and the remaining eight to the *middle*.

(Question:) Are all eight members of the *middle* completely present in each being in a single birth or not?

(Answer:) They are not all present. Why then was it said that there are eight members? With regard to the complete (person). By this is meant: If a person *(pudgala)* passes through all the stages of development, then he is called *complete*; not if, along the way, he dies prematurely; nor [if he abides] in the sphere of the material or sphere of the immaterial. For *The Great Discourse of the Foundations of Origination* (*above* S. 30) teaches only with regard to the person in the sphere of desire <82> that all (members) are present. There it states (S. 38): "The Buddha spoke to Ānanda: 'If *cognition* were not to enter into the mother's womb, . . . etc., . . . would then *name and form* grow, flourish, and fully mature, or not?' – 'No, O Lord.' "

Occasionally, it is said that dependent origination consists of only two sections. The first includes the *beginning* [i.e., members 1 and 2], the second, the *end* [i.e., members 11 and 12]. The *beginning* involves the first seven members, namely, *ignorance* through *sensation.* The *end* involves the last five members, from *thirst* up to *old age and death.* That is to say, both sections then include *beginning* and *end,* with their effect or, respectively, their cause.[1]

What is the nature of these members; *ignorance,* etc.?

v. 21

Ignorance is the state[2] of the previous defilements.

The state of all the defilements in the previous life up to the maturation of the current fruit is summed up by the name *ignorance,* because they constantly occur together with *ignorance,* since they appear through the influence of *ignorance.* Just as when one speaks of the coming of the king, it is in no way stated that his entourage is not coming. One says only, summed up: "The king comes," because the king has precedence.

The *volitional formations* are the state of the previous deeds. <83>

---

[1] That is to say, to the *beginning* [i.e., members 1 and 2] are related those members that represent its effect in the next birth [i.e., members 3 to 7], and to the *end* [i.e., members 11 and 12], those that form its cause in the previous birth [i.e., members 8 to 10].

[2] The word *state* is added because it is always thought that the five groups in this or that state make up the respective member of dependent origination.

The state of the good, etc., deeds in the previous life up to the maturation of the current fruit is summed up by the name *volitional formations*, . . .

> The groups at the time of rebirth *(pratisaṃdhi)* are *cognition*.

The five groups in the state of the single instant of rebirth in the womb are called *cognition*.

> (They are) *name and form* subsequent to that
>
> v. 22
>
> and before the arising of the *sixfold sphere*.

The states in the time after the rebirth of cognition and before the arising of the six spheres are summed up by the name *name and form*. Here it should actually be said "before the arising of the four spheres,"[1] but in view of the fact that they now appear to be in their complete state, six are spoken of.

> This, before the coming together of the triad.

The state in which the eye, etc., has arisen but the sense-organ, object, and cognition have not yet come together, is given the name *sixfold sphere*.

> *Contact*, before the ability to cognize the causes of pleasure, suffering, etc., appears.

The state in which the coming together of the triad has occurred, but in which the different causes of the threefold sensation have not yet been cognized, is summed up by the name *contact*.

---

[1] Because thinking and the body, and thereby also the tactile sense-organ, already exist from the instant of rebirth.

v. 23

Sensation, before copulation.

The state in which the different causes of the threefold sensation have been cognized, but in which <84> the passion for sexual union has not yet arisen, this state is called *sensation*.

Thirst, in the one who desires sensual enjoyments and copulation.

The state in which passion for sensual enjoyments, together with the thirst for copulation, occurs, but in which one does not yet strive for them, this state is called *thirst*.

Grasping, in the person who exerts himself to obtain sensual enjoyment.

If one exerts oneself and runs all over in order to obtain the various objects of sensual enjoyment, then this state is called *grasping*.

v. 24

If one accomplishes deeds that bear their fruit in a future birth, then this is *becoming*.

If, due to this exertion, one accumulates deeds that bring about a fruit in a future birth, then this state is called *becoming*.

The new rebirth *(pratisaṃdhi)* is *birth*.

If, after the passing away from this life, due to the force of these deeds one is reborn again in a new existence, then this state is called *birth*. The future *birth* member therefore corresponds to the current *cognition* [member].

Old age and death reach as far as *sensation*.

The state of gradual maturation after the moment of *birth* up to the future *sensation* is summed up by the name *old age and death*. *Old age and death* thus correspond to the four members, *name and form*, the *sixfold* <85> *sphere*, *contact*, and *sensation* in the present existence. This is the explanation of the nature of the twelve members.

Further explanations of dependent origination follow, then the text moves on to other topics.

In the school of the Sarvāstivāda the denial of a soul has been given its starkest form. Of course, all of the other Buddhist schools also occupied themselves with this question and arrived at a variety of solutions. In sharpest contrast to the Sarvāstivādins stands the southern neighboring school of the Vātsīputrīya-Sāṃmatīya, which even went so far as to assert the existence of a person *(pudgala)*, based on texts such as *The Discourse of the Bearer of the Burden (Bhārahārasūtra)*, rendered above (S. 25). According to the doctrine of the Sāṃmatīyas, besides the three types of conditioned entities *(saṃskṛta)* and the unconditioned entities *(asaṃskṛta)*, there is—as a fifth entity—the *inexpressible (avaktavya)*, otherwise known as the *person*. This person is neither the same as the groups nor different from them; it is neither permanent nor non-permanent, thus inexpressible.

We are informed about the doctrines of the Sāṃmatīyas through a work of their own, preserved in a Chinese translation, the *•Sāṃmatīyanikāyaśāstra (Treatise of the Sāṃmatīya-school)*, which deals mainly with the doctrine of the person. In addition, we have Vasubandhu's polemic at our disposal. Specifically, Vasubandhu composed a small work, the *Refutation of the Person (Pudgalapratiṣedha-*

prakaraṇa), which he appended to the *Abhidharmakośa*. It is meant to serve as a refutation of the different doctrines that accept a soul and is thus directed against the soul-doctrine of the Sāṃkhya and of the Vaiśeṣika, but first and foremost against the Sāṃmatīya-doctrine of the existence of a person. A few brief sections from this work, which will give some idea of the doctrine of the Sāṃmatīyas and at the same time show how the Sarvāstivāda dealt with it, will be translated next.

The first translated section, which is also the beginning of the work, is directed against the definition of the <86> person as inexpressible. Of course, this inexpressibility is not the same as the inexpressibility of the ultimate state of being, which remains inconceivable to all human ways of thinking [S. 147f., 298]. Rather, it was customary at the time to characterize any relationships that one was unable to define clearly, as being neither this nor that and thus as inexpressible. Thus, in the Sāṃkhya and in Kumārila's Mīmāṃsā, it was said that the universal *(sāmānya)* is neither different nor not-different from the particulars. Similarly, the Sāṃmatīyas declared the person to be neither different nor not-different from the groups. In his refutation Vasubandhu now tries to force his opponent to define this relationship more clearly, and demonstrates that any attempt to ascribe a clear meaning to the words is bound to fail.

3BA.1.2.2. *From "Refutation of the Person" (Pudgalapratiṣedhaprakaraṇa)*

Can there be no liberation on another path than this? Certainly not. For what reason? Because the view is obscured by the erroneous belief in a self. All those outside this doctrine (of Buddhism) who assume a self, do not consider it as a designation for the stream of the groups *(skandhasaṃtāna)*, but assume that there is a real self that is distinct from the groups. Through the belief in a self, however, all the defilements arise, the cycle of threefold becoming rolls on, and liberation is not possible.

(Question:) How can one recognize with certainty that the designation *self* indicates only the stream of the groups and not a self as an entity of its own?

(Answer:) Because there is no true [direct] perception or inference with respect to this assumed self that is distinct from the groups. If, namely, <87> the self were by nature a separate real thing like the other factors, then, where no hindrance appears, it would have to be apprehended either through [direct] perception, like the six sense-objects[1] and the mental organ, or it would have to be apprehended through inference, like the five material sense-organs. As for the assertion that the five material sense-organs are apprehended through inference, in general the view prevails that, in spite of ihe presence of the general causes, an effect does not arise if its particular cause is absent, but that it does arise if the latter is not absent as, for example, when a sprout arises from a seed.[2] Likewise, it is observed that in spite of the presence of the causes light, object, attention, etc., perception does not occur among the blind, the deaf, etc., but that it does occur among the not-blind, the not-deaf, etc. From this it can be recognized with certitude that there is a particular cause that is absent or not absent. This particular cause is the sense-organ of the eye, etc. In this sense then, one speaks of the inference of the material sense-organs. But in the case of a self distinct from the groups, both means of knowledge are completely absent. From this we

---

[1] As Buddhism puts the mental organ on equal footing with the sense-organs, it counts six sense-organs and six sense-objects.

[2] Even if a field, water, etc., are present, the sprout arises only if its particular cause, in this case the seed, is also present.

can recognize with certainty that a self as a real entity does not exist.

The school of the Vātsīputrīyas now assumes that a person exists that is by nature neither one with the groups nor distinct from them. Here, one must consider whether (this person) is a thing *(dravya)* <88> or a mere designation *(prajñapti)*. "How is the mark of that which exists as a thing *(dravyasat)* distinguished from the mark of that which exists as a designation *(prajñaptisat)*?" If we are dealing with separate things, then this is the mark of that which exists as a thing, as in the case of visible form, sound, etc. If, on the other hand, we are dealing only with an aggregation, then this is the mark of that which exists as a designation, as in the case of milk, etc.

(Opponent:) What errors ensue if one regards (the person) as a thing or as a designation?

(Answer:) If it is by nature a thing, then it must be distinct from the groups, because it has its own nature as do the different groups themselves. In addition, if it has a real nature, it must necessarily have a cause. Otherwise, it must be something unconditioned *(asaṃskṛta)*, which in turn coincides with the view of the non-Buddhists. It would, moreover, be purposeless.[1] The assumption that [the person] is a thing is therefore meaningless. If, on the other hand, it is by nature (only) a designation, this in turn coincides with our assertion.

(Opponent:) The person of which I speak does not exist, as you explain, either as a real thing or as a designation. Rather, only based on the inner groups—belonging to the present and appropriated *(upātta)*[2]—can one speak of a person.

---

[1] Because, being eternally unchanging, it would be completely detached from the course of the world.

[2] To a Buddhist the [pellucid] organs along with the matter that goes with them, which belong to a personality-stream, are termed *appropriated*.

(Answer:) This is the speech of one who is blind, for whom the subject-matter has not yet become clear, for I still don't understand what you mean by the words "based on" *(upādāya)*. If "based on" means something like *referring to (ālambya)* the groups, and the person thus comes about by referring to the groups, then it is <89> established that the person exists only as a designation, just as [the notion of] milk, etc., comes about by referring to visible form, etc. If, on the other hand, "based on" means something like *[causally] dependent upon (pratītya)* the groups and one thus speaks of a person as being [causally] dependent upon the groups, then the same error follows for that person.[1]

(Opponent:) This is not how we speak about this. "How then?" Just as in everyday life one speaks of fire based on fuel. "Why is it possible, if one is speaking of fire, to say that it is based on fuel?" Because in the absence of fuel, one cannot speak of the presence of fire. Here, the fuel is neither distinct from the fire nor one with it, since if the fire were distinct from the fuel, the fuel could not be hot. And if fire were one with fuel, then that which is burned would also be that which does the burning. In the same way, in the absence of groups, one cannot speak of a person. The person is also neither distinct from the groups nor one with them, since, if it were distinct from the groups, then it would have to be eternal by nature. And, if [the person] were one with the groups, then it would follow that the person is by nature subject to annihilation.

(Answer:) In that case, you must first state clearly what fire is and what fuel is, so that I can understand what it means that the fire is based on fuel.

(Opponent:) What is there to say? If I must say something, however, then *that which is burned* is the fuel and *that which does the burning* is the fire.

---

1 In this case as well, the person exists only as a designation.

(Answer:) But then you would have to explain in turn what *that which is burned* and *that which does the burning* are, which are called *fuel* and *fire.* <90>

(Opponent:) In everyday life everyone knows that the non-blazing object that is consumed is called *that which is burned,* or the fuel, and that the bright, extremely hot, blazing object that consumes is called *that which does the burning,* or the fire. More precisely, this [blazing object] burns or consumes that object since it changes the later moments in its stream relative to the earlier ones.[1] And although both consist by nature of eight things,[2] fire arises in dependence upon fuel, just as sour milk and vinegar arise in dependence upon sweet milk and wine. For this reason, one says in everyday life that the fire is based on fuel.

(Answer:) If the fire is actually based on it, then it is distinct from the fuel because the later fire and the earlier fuel each belong to distinct times. If therefore the person assumed by you is based on the groups as is the fire on the fuel, then it must absolutely be said that it arises dependent upon the groups and is therefore distinct from the groups. In addition, it follows that it is not eternal.

(Opponent:) With regard to the blazing wood, etc., the tangible (named) heat is called *fire,* the other things are called *fuel.*[3]

(Answer:) In that case fire and fuel are indeed simultaneous, but it must stand as established that they are different in nature, and that this is due to <91> the difference in their marks. In which case, what is meant by "based (on fuel)" would once again need to be explained. How then, can you assert that one

---

[1] Under the influence of fire the stream of moments of the wood gradually turns into ashes.

[2] *Cf.* S. 97 what has been said about the doctrine of the elements.

[3] I.e., among the eight atoms that form the molecule of wood, the heat-atom represents the fire, the other seven the fuel.

speaks of the fire based on fuel, since after all, both arise simultaneously. In other words, the fuel cannot serve as cause for the fire, since both arise, at the same time, from their own causes. Neither can the fuel be designated as the *cause of the name "fire,"* since after all, the tangible (named) *heat* is designated as the *cause of the name "fire."*

(Opponent:) The statement that the fire is based on fuel means that both arise at the same time or that (the fuel) is the bearer (of the fire).

(Answer:) Then you must assume that the person arises at the same time as the groups, or that the groups are the bearer (of the person). In addition, you apparently presuppose that it is by nature distinct from the groups. Further, you must assume as a result that, if the groups are absent, the person is by nature also not present; just as when the fuel is not present, the fire is by nature also absent. But, you do not allow these assumptions. Therefore your explanation is also not correct.

With respect to your own assumption, you have, furthermore, raised the objection that the fuel, if it were distinct from the fire, could not be hot. Here, the nature of that which is hot must be clearly stated. If you offer the explanation that that which is hot is the tangible (named) *heat*, then the fuel is not hot because its nature is of a different kind.[1] If, on the other hand, you offer the explanation that that which is hot is that which <92> is connected with heat, then that which is different by nature, must also be given the designation *hot*. Only the tangible (named) *heat* then is designated as the actual *fire*. Everything else connected with heat is given the designation *hot*. With that, however, it is obviously admitted that the fuel is called *hot* although it is distinct from the fire, and this without resulting in an error. How then, can one suggest that there is a problem here?

---

1 Since, according to the above assumption, the fuel consists of the other seven atoms of the wood-molecule.

(Opponent:) The wood, etc., when it blazes brightly, is called *fuel* and, at the same time, *fire*.

(Answer:) In that case you must explain once again what is meant by "based (on fuel)." Further, the person must [then] necessarily be one with the groups of corporeality, etc.; this cannot be refuted by any logic. The assertion that one speaks of the person based on the groups, just as one speaks of the fire based on the fuel, can therefore not be substantiated through argument and counterargument.

The next section that we render is directed against the doctrine of the perceptibility of the person. The Sāṃmatīyas maintain namely that subsequent to the perception of the sense objects the person is also perceived. Vasubandhu, on the other hand, concludes from precisely this that the person has no real existence but only a nominal existence, and that it therefore—as is said in India—does not exist as a real thing *(dravyata)* but only as a designation *(prajñaptita)*. He further shows that impossible consequences follow from the opponent's assumption.

Further, it must be stated which of the six types of cognition[1] cognizes the person.

(Opponent:) All six types cognize it. "How so?" If, at a particular time, the visual cognition <93> cognizes the visible form, it then subsequently apprehends the presence of the person. Therefore one says that (the person) is cognized by the visual cognition. But one cannot say that [the person] is one with the visible form or distinct from it, ... etc., *(through the other types of cognition)* up to: If, at a particular time, the mental cognition cognizes the factors, it then subsequently apprehends

[1] The five types of cognition via the senses and the mental cognition; *cf. below* S. 117.

the presence of the person. Thus one says that (the person) is cognized by the mental cognition. But one cannot say that [the person] is one with the factors or distinct from them.

(Answer:) If that is so, then one can speak of the person assumed (by you)—just as one does of milk, etc.—only as a designation. If, in other words, the visual cognition, at the time that it cognizes the visible form, subsequently apprehends the presence of the milk, etc., then one says that the milk, etc., is cognized by the visual cognition, but one cannot say that [the milk] is one with the visible form or distinct from it, . . . etc. up to: And if the tactile cognition, at the time that it cognizes the tangible, subsequently apprehends the presence of the milk, etc., then one says that the milk, etc., is cognized by the tactile cognition, but one cannot say that [the milk] is one with the tangible or distinct from it. Otherwise it would follow that the milk is nothing but the four (sense-objects), or that it is not comprised of them. Thus it is established that one speaks of the *presence of the person* as a designation based on the totality of the groups, just as in everyday life, based on the totality of visible form, etc., one speaks of *milk, etc.,* as a designation, but not as real.

Moreover, you have said: "If, at a particular time, the visual cognition cognizes the visible form, it then <94> subsequently apprehends the presence of the person." What does this statement mean? Does it mean that the visible form is the cause of the perception of the person, or that, at the time that the visible form is perceived, the person can also be perceived?

If it means that the visible form is the cause of the perception of the (person), and if at the same time one cannot say that [the person] is distinct from the visible form, then one also cannot say that the visible form is distinct from the eye, etc., because the eye, just like light, attention, etc., is a cause of the perception of the visible form.

If, on the other hand, it means that, at the time when the visible form is perceived, the person can also be perceived, is then the perception of the visible form also the perception of the (person), or is it a matter of a distinct perception?

If the perception of the visible form is also the perception of the (person), then one is forced to accept that its nature is precisely this visible form, or that the designation for it refers only to the visible form. In that case, however, there can be no such thoughts as: "Such is the visible form" and "Such is the (person)." How then, can one ascertain the presence of the visible form and of the person without these two sorts of thoughts, since after all the ascertainment of their presence is necessarily dependent upon the thoughts?

If, on the other hand, it is a matter of a distinct perception, then (the person) must be distinct from the visible form because the perception is chronologically separate, just as yellow is distinct from blue, or the earlier from the later, etc.

The same objections can be raised (with respect to the other sense-objects) up to the factors.

(The opponent) says, in order to counter this: Just as one cannot state definitely that the (person) is one with the visible form or distinct from it, the same holds for the <95> examination of the two kinds of perceptions.

(Answer:) In that case, you cannot place perception among the conditioned *(saṃskṛta)*.[1] If you do this, you contravene your own system.

Finally, the third and last section that we present gives a taste of how the two adversaries use the texts of the holy scripture to support their assertions. The Sāmmatīya quotes

[1] If the [above-mentioned] perceptions are neither distinct nor indistinct from each other, then they are inexpressible and belong to the same group as the person, thus not among the conditioned factors.

> *The Discourse of the Bearer of the Burden (Bhārahārasūtra)*, translated above (S. 29). Vasubandhu's reply shows how—since they could not deny the message itself of this widely recognized text—the Sarvāstivādins tried to explain this document away.

(Opponent:) If only the five groups of grasping are called *person*, why then has the Exalted One spoken as follows: "I will explain to you, monks, the burden, the taking up of the burden, the laying down of the burden, and the bearer of the burden"?

(Answer:) For what reason should the Buddha not have spoken in this way?

(Opponent:) Because the burden cannot be called the *bearer of the burden.*[1]

(Answer:) Why not?

(Opponent:) Because such a thing has never been seen before.

(Answer:) In that case, you also cannot speak of any *inexpressible thing*.

(Opponent:) Why not?

(Answer:) Because, similarly, such a thing has never been seen. In addition, the *taking up of the burden* could then also not be included in the groups, because it has never before been seen that a burden takes itself up. It is said in the sutra, however, that thirst is called the *taking up of the burden.* Hence it is included <96> in the groups. And the same holds for the *bearer of the burden.* It must thus be conceded that (the bearer) is to be found in the groups. Besides, the Buddha himself, fearing that the person might be regarded as inexpressible, eternal, and real, explained a little later in the sutra that [the person] designates only—according to the general custom—"that venerable one who has such and such a name," etc., . . . , specifically so that one

---

[1] In the sutra itself, the *burden* is explained as the five groups of grasping. These, therefore, cannot at the same time also be the *bearer of the burden.*

might recognize that the person is by nature expressible, not eternal, and not real. In addition, the five groups of grasping are given the name *burden* because they mutually weigh upon each other. And the earlier moments are called *bearer of the burden* because they entail the later ones. There is therefore no real person.

BBA.2. *General views associated with the doctrine of the denial of a soul*

BBA.2.1. *First general view: All entities lack a solid, permanent core*

We turn now to the general views that appear to be connected with the doctrine of the denial of a soul and that constitute its broader framework. The first of these is the view that all entities lack a solid, permanent core. A tendency toward [this view] is already apparent very early on and probably goes back to the Buddha himself. It is expressed in the endeavor to place fleeting individual phenomena in the foreground and is apparently based on the effort to emphasize the impermanence of all things. The endeavor to make individual phenomena [more] autonomous was encouraged by the ancient method, still prevalent at that time, of considering everything—even properties, when it was a matter of trying to clarify their nature—as real things. It was only later, however, that these first attempts developed into a clearly defined philosophical doctrine, in opposition, specifically, to the Vaiśeṣika system as it created its doctrine of categories. When, that is, the Vaiśeṣika—in a clear philosophical insight—differentiated things and their

properties, i.e., substance and quality, from one another as two different forms of existence, it became necessary to take a stand on this new doctrine. At this point, opinions diverged. With a few exceptions, the Buddhist schools decided to oppose
<97> the Vaiśeṣika doctrine of *substances and their qualities* with the doctrine of the *factors (dharma)*, which so to speak lead an existence of their own, as autonomous attributes without a bearer.

A rough idea of this doctrine is as follows.

BBA.2.1.1. *(A) Discussion of this first general view in the field of material elements*

In the sphere of the elements, the primary concern was with the five properties that, since ancient times, had been held to be the objects of the sense-perceptions, namely: visible form;[1] sound; odor; taste; and tangibility. In the doctrinal discourses of the Buddha, these properties are usually mentioned alone, without reference to the [invisible] elements, since to the Buddha the external world was of interest only insofar as it affects the person and arouses sensations and passions. Now, it was explicitly taught that [visible form, etc.,] are not properties that adhere to the elements, but they are rather autonomous entities. And as the doctrine of atoms—which had been created and propagated in the meantime—was adopted, it was taught that these entities consist of atoms. The things of the external world are therefore not composed of elements but are formed from atoms of color, sound, odor, taste, and tangibility.

Of course, it was also necessary to deal with the old conception of the elements, since elements—specifically the commonly known four elements of earth, water, fire, and wind—are often mentioned in the doctrinal discourses of the

---

[1] Visible form *(rūpa)* includes color and shape.

Buddha. What are these elements then? To explain this, one reverted to the following idea. Since the ancient times, in addition to the five properties that, as objects of the sense-perceptions, correspond to the five sense-organs, a second set of characteristic properties had been attributed to the elements. These were: solidity to earth; wetness to water; heat to fire; and motion to wind. Now it was said that the so-called *four elements* were nothing other than these same properties. With that, these four properties were classified within the *tangible* and of course the theory of atoms was also applied to them. <98> The four elements are therefore atoms of hardness, wetness, heat, and motion.[1]

At the same time, however, according to the commonly held view, the properties of the elements never appear in isolation. The Vaiśeṣika, for example, taught that each element unites several qualities within itself, and all the other systems followed the Vaiśeṣikas in this. Opinions differed only with regard to the number and distribution of these qualities. Buddhism thus also taught accordingly that the atom-like properties of the elements never occur in isolation as single atoms, but always combined into molecules. Each molecule, to be exact, contains one property atom of each type [i.e., visible form, etc.], each of which are joined as support, so to speak, by one atom of each of the four elements. Since sound occurs only occasionally, the molecule therefore consists of a minimum of eight [types of] atoms, which may occasionally be joined by further atoms.[2] The entire material world is built from these atoms and the diversity of individual materials derives from the predominance of this or that property atom. In this way then, against the Vaiśeṣika doctrine of the

---

[1] But, as it was said, these are elements only in the philosophical sense. That which in everyday life is called [*element*, i.e., earth, water, fire, wind,] is a mixture of different atoms, whereby the name [*element*] adheres to the color and shape atoms.

[2] [See *Abhidharmakośa* ii. 22.]

elements, Buddhism set its own doctrine, in which the concept of a [permanent] *substance* was eliminated and a loose association of autonomous property atoms took the place of [permanent] substance atoms with their numerous qualities.

BBA.2.1.2. *(B) Discussion of this first general view in the field of psychology*

The development of the doctrine in the field of psychology was no different. Here the Vaiśeṣika taught that all mental processes are qualities of the soul. Other schools, such as the Sāṃkhya, which transferred all mental processes to the field of matter, saw in them the properties of one or more *mental organs.* The Buddhist view was initially close to that of these schools and we still find clear signs that cognition *(vijñāna)* was originally thought of as such a *mental organ.* But here as well, even the discourses of the Buddha show the unmistakable tendency to make the individual mental processes autonomous. Here as well, the later scholasticism taught precisely and unambiguously that all mental processes <99> are not properties of some kind of *mental organ,* but rather separate autonomous factors that assemble *en masse* into one overall mental process. Nothing remains of the original characterization of cognition, other than that it constitutes the center of this complex, to the extent that cognition must be included in every mental process and that the other factors associate themselves with it. In this case as well, therefore, a loose association of autonomous factors takes the place of the [permanent] mental substance with its numerous qualities, whereby the concept of a *substance* is deliberately eliminated.

This denial of a [permanent] substance is the most important fundamental dictum of Buddhist scholasticism in this field. The same point of view was, however, also extended to all similar cases, wherever a solid core or a permanent nature seemed to show itself in individual entities. This was especially so for the Vaiśeṣika doctrine of the whole *(avayavin)*. In this doctrine the Vaiśeṣika asserted that for all things constituted of atoms—the ultimate components of matter—what exists is not just an accumulation of atoms but that something new, i.e., an undivided whole, arises from their conjunction. This view is also rejected by Buddhism, according to which every whole is a loose aggregation of different factors and nothing more.

In the doctrine of the universal *(sāmānya)*—that general entity that, according to Vaiśeṣika doctrine, is inherent in individual entities and bestows on them their homogeneous character—the Buddhists are influenced by the same attitude [i.e., denial of a solid, permanent core]. Only to a very limited extent did the old schools accept a kind of universal. In later times though, it was categorically denied.

We cannot provide here a detailed sampling of texts for all of these doctrines and their development. And in any case, by Vasubandhu's time this development was already long complete and scholastically fixed. As is usual in India for such a stage of development, the discussion is limited to a polemic in which each party stubbornly holds on to their <100> adopted view and seeks to defend it in every possible way. Although such a polemic often contributed to a clearer view of things and to a more accurate formulation of the doctrines, it makes for difficult and laborious reading and is hardly of interest to broader circles of readers. I thus restrict myself here to rendering a short section of the *Abhidharmakośa,* in which Vasubandhu discusses in a concise way the doctrine of the [permanent] substance. I then immediately move on to the next point, the doctrine of the momentariness of entities.

The section rendered comes from the *Abhidharmakośa*'s third book, specifically from its last part, which gives an account of the periodic destruction of the cosmos. For Buddhists this means a complete destruction of the phenomenal world, whereas according to the Vaiśeṣika doctrine the cosmos merely dissolves into its constituent components, the atoms, which continue to exist as eternal substances. This provides Vasubandhu with an opportunity to briefly discuss the concept of [permanent] "substance." The arguments he advances in doing so are essentially the following:

Although, according to Vaiśeṣika doctrine, the substance can be perceived through the eye sense-organ as well as through the sense of touch, a substance does not exist, because while we do perceive the properties of the elements, we do not perceive a substance apart from them.

Further, when an object is burned, along with its qualities the object itself disappears, which would be impossible if its substance continued to exist unchanged.

Lastly, such a case does indeed seem to occur with the firing of clay pots during which, according to the Vaiśeṣika doctrine, the otherwise unchanging qualities [i.e., color] of the atoms change, while in their substance the pots apparently stay the same. In reality, however, this impression is based on the fact that the appearance, i.e., the arrangement of the parts of the pots, remains the same in the stream of moments. Similarly, for example, given a trail of ants, we believe we are always seeing one [and the same] row of ants, although nothing enduring exists that could be given the name *row*. With this, Vasubandhu breaks off the discussion and returns to his main topic. <101>

BBA.2.1.3. *A substance does not exist (Abhidharmakośa III, ad v. 100)*

Moreover, the name *atom* refers to visible form, etc. Therefore, if visible form perishes, the atoms also perish [at the destruction of the cosmos].

(Opponent:) The atoms are substance *(dravya)* and are distinct in nature from the qualities *(guṇa)*, [i.e.,] visible form, etc. Therefore, they must not necessarily vanish at the same time.

(Answer:) The difference in nature between the two is by no means to be considered as established, since if one observes them, one does not find a separate [substance] earth, etc., apart from the visible form, etc. Thus they are not distinct in their nature. Further, in your own system it is accepted that the earth, etc., is perceived through the eye and the body. How then are visible form and the tangible distinct from it? Since, furthermore—when wool, cotton, opium, etc., are burned—the corresponding cognition no longer exists, the cognition "wool," etc., arises based only on the particular visible form, etc. When the qualities that have been changed through heat *(pākaja)* arise, the cognition "pot" or "bowl" occurs due to the similarity in shape, just as with a row [of ants], since if one does not see the shape, the cognition also does not appear. But who would want to collect their ramblings, which are senseless as those of a fool. So enough with the prolix polemic against this system!

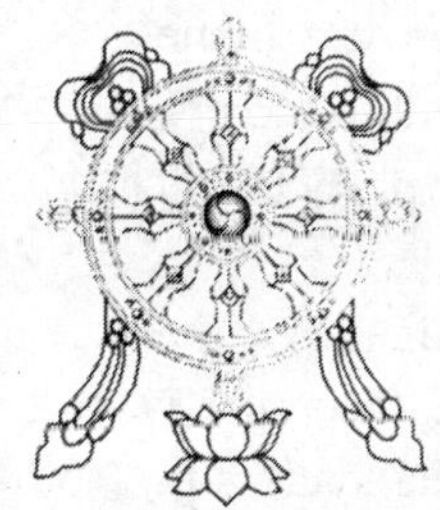

BBA.2.2. *Second general view: The momentariness of all entities*

The second important general view, which is closely connected to the preceding one, [i.e., "All entities lack a solid, permanent core,"] is the idea of the momentariness of all entities. As already noted, the starting point for this was the impermanence of all that is worldly, as emphasized already by the Buddha. As is so often the case, however, the basic conceptions <102> referred to [by the various traditions] were decisive in its development and elaboration.

The Sāṃkhya, in its doctrine of the constant change of all things, had in mind the image of a lump of clay, which becomes a pot and finally breaks into shards. This gave the impression of something that persists through all transformations while the transformations themselves appeared as a mere change in the state [of this something].

Buddhism thought differently. Here the basic conception was the image of wood being consumed by fire. This brought with it, however, the idea of complete annihilation, since the ashes seemed to be something completely different from the wood. The ashes arise while the wood vanishes. The impermanence of all things was thus not perceived as a mere transformation, but as a complete annihilation, in the course of which the annihilated entity is replaced by something completely new. The doctrine was then expressed accordingly. First of all, the distinction was made between things that exist for some time before they are annihilated, such as wood, and things that cease and arise anew with every moment, such as the flame of a lamp, the sound of a bell, and also all mental factors, the impermanence of which had already been particularly emphasized by the Buddha.

Many schools left the doctrine like this, particularly the Vātsīputrīya-Sāṃmatīyas. Others, on the other hand, particularly the Sarvāstivādins and the Sautrāntikas who were the leaders in this development [of the doctrine of impermanence], eventually went so far as to assert the momentariness of all entities. Characteristically enough, these are the same extreme schools that had also formulated the denial of a soul in the starkest terms. The connection is unmistakable, since the more clearly one became aware of the lack of any solid core in things, the more forcibly one was driven also to assert the momentariness of all entities. To one who accepts a [permanent] substance, any change will easily appear as merely a transformation of the state of this substance. The latter was thus the view of the Sāṃkhya, who, despite their emphasis on the eternal flux of all things, nevertheless taught that there was something enduring within change. According to Sāṃkhya doctrine then, it is only the qualities *(dharma)* of things <103> that vanish in all transformations, whereas the bearer of these qualities *(dharmin)*, the eternal primal matter,[1] persists.

On the other hand, for those like the Buddhist schools, who recognize only properties without any bearer as autonomous factors, any transformation of these properties necessarily means a complete ceasing and a new arising, and this must apply to every kind of transformation. Indeed, even growth, aging, and gradual decay must appear as such a succession of annihilation and becoming. The explicit expression of the doctrine of the momentariness of all entities thus signified only a final logical step. With this the conception of the annihilation of things also shifted, since, according to this doctrine, the wood is already ceasing and arising in an uninterrupted sequence before it is consumed by the fire. The fire merely ensures that the stream of moments of the wood does not continue any further. The constant arising and ceasing is therefore not brought about by external causes but lies in the nature of things. The essence of things themselves is impermanence. And the doctrine was then expressed in this way.

This then is the stage of development that the doctrine had reached by Vasubandhu's time. The development itself was essentially complete, with only details remaining in dispute between the Sarvāstivādins and the Sautrāntikas. Otherwise, the discussion basically revolved around the establishment of the momentariness of things in opposition to the Vātsīputrīyas

---

[1] [See Gerald James Larson: *Classical Sāṃkhya. An Interpretation of its History and Meaning*, pp. 7–14.]

and in opposition to the non-Buddhist schools, primarily the Vaiśeṣika.

This state of affairs is thus also reflected in the sample text that we will render in the following, taken from the fourth book of the *Abhidharmakośa*. The occasion for the discussion is provided by the question of movement, because if things are in fact momentary, they cannot move, as every movement takes time. The Sarvāstivāda thus adopts the view that there is in reality no movement. What appears to us as movement is, instead, just the stream of moments that, like the frames of a film, arises in always changing form. This provides the impetus to prove the momentariness of all entities to an opponent who asserts the existence of movement. <104> To this end, Vasubandhu puts forth three inferences, to each of which he appends a refutation of the opposing objections.

The first is as follows: The annihilation of entities cannot be brought about by an external cause, because as a mere non-existence, [annihilation] cannot be the effect of a cause. If, however, impermanence lies in the very nature of entities, then they must immediately vanish, as this nature is present from the outset. To the opponent who appeals to the apparent fact that fire annihilates wood, Vasubandhu responds that this [latter cognition] is not direct perception but an inference, which as such is not necessarily conclusive.

The second inference says: If the annihilation of entities is indeed based on some sort of causes, then such causes would have to be operative everywhere and thus also in the case of mental factors, etc., the momentariness of which the opponent himself accepts. [Vasubandhu] then rejects the causes assumed in these cases by the opponent.

Finally, the third inference is based on the view that fire brings about the gradual transformation of the objects exposed to it. To the Buddhist way of thinking, this occurs in such a way that [fire] constantly brings about new and changed moments, in the stream of moments of those objects. In this way, however, fire is the cause of the arising of these moments and cannot, at the same time, be the cause of their ceasing. This provides an opportunity to clarify the role of fire in such cases. Vasubandhu then closes with a brief summary of the results of his line of argument.

3BA.2.2.1. *The momentariness of entities (Abhidharmakośa IV, vv. 2–3)*

What is a moment? That which ceases immediately after the acquisition of its self *(ātmalābha)*.[1] A factor to which is attributed such a moment is called <105> *momentary* .... All conditioned factors must, after having acquired their self, immediately cease and come to nothing. If they arise in a particular place, then they also cease in this place. Thus, from this location they are not able to arrive at another ....

(Opponent:) If the conditioned factors are momentary, then the view that they cannot arrive at another location can be justified.

(Answer:) The assertion that the conditioned factors are momentary is established,

v. 2 d

because later they definitely cease.

In other words, the ceasing of the conditioned factors has no cause. "Why?" That which has a cause is an effect, but ceasing as a non-existence is not an effect and thus it also has no cause. So since the ceasing has no cause, (the conditioned factors) cease when they have just barely arisen, since if they do not cease right at the beginning, then neither can this occur

---

[1] In Buddhist philosophy of that time, the concept of arising is expressed in this way.

later, since later they are still of the same nature as before. If therefore they later come to an end, it can be seen from this that they are already ceasing earlier.

(Opponent:) They change later and as a result they can then cease.

(Answer:) They cannot be the same and be called *changed*. Thus, it cannot possibly be correct that their nature changes.

(Opponent:) Can it not be observed in everyday life that fire-wood, etc., is subject to annihilation through connection with fire? And certainly there is no other means of valid cognition superior to sensory perception. Therefore, it is not correct that without exception the ceasing of the factors <106> has no cause.

(Answer:) How is it recognized that fire-wood, etc., ceases through the connection with fire?

(Opponent:) Because one no longer sees the fire-wood, etc., after the connection with fire.

(Answer:) In that case the following should be considered: Is the fire-wood, etc., not seen because it ceases through the connection with fire, or is it not seen because the previously arisen fire-wood, etc., ceases by itself and does not arise again later, and is thus no longer present, as is the case with the flame of a lamp or the sound of a bell due to the connection with the wind or with the hand?[1] This matter must therefore be proven by inference.

(Opponent:) How can this be inferred?

(Answer:) As we have said before: The ceasing has no cause because, as non-existence, it is not an effect.

Furthermore, if the ceasing of the fire-wood has a cause,

---

[1] The opponent himself assumes that the light of a lamp or the sound of a bell are momentary and cease by themselves. The wind or the touch of the hand therefore do not annihilate them; rather, a new arising simply does not occur.

v. 3 a

then no ceasing can be without a cause,

just as arising has a cause and is not without a cause. In everyday life, however, it is observed that cognition, flame, and sound cease on their own every moment without a separate cause. Therefore the ceasing of fire-wood has also no cause.

Some (i.e., the Vaiśeṣikas) assume that the earlier cognition and the earlier sound cease through the later cognition and the later sound. This is not correct, <107> because the two [cognitions] do not exist simultaneously. After all, one cannot imagine doubt and certainty, suffering and pleasure, passion and hatred, etc.—which are opposite to each other in their characteristics—existing simultaneously. Or let us assume that, after a clear cognition or a clear sound, an unclear cognition or an unclear sound immediately arises. But how can an unclear homogeneous factor annihilate a clear homogeneous factor? And by what means, again, does a later strong cognition or a later loud sound cease? . . .

If, furthermore, the connection with fire is the cause for the ceasing of the fire-wood, etc., then with respect to the changes brought about through heat *(pākaja)*—which are slight, medium, or great—

v. 3 b

the cause of arising would also have to be the cause of ceasing.[1]

Why? In the case of the changes in fire-wood, etc., caused through the connection with fire and brought forth through

---

[1] The changes brought about through heat gradually become ever greater. The same fire, or if we take momentariness into account, a similar fire to that which brought about the first changes, then also annihilates those changes in order to bring about the next ones.

heat, that which brings about the medium and great changes is also that which annihilates the slight and medium changes. The same thing or something similar to that which is the cause of the arising of the medium and great changes is therefore also capable of being the cause of the ceasing of the slight and medium changes. Thus the cause of the arising would also have to be the cause of the ceasing, or the causes of the ceasing and of the arising could not differ from each other. It is <108> not possible, however, that the existence, as well as the non-existence of something, is based on the same or a similar cause.

In addition, given the arising of the different flames of a fire, one can conceive of a difference in the generating and annihilating causes. How though, in the case of changes in fire-wood, etc., induced by a connection with ashes, snow, caustics, sun, earth, and water, and brought forth through heat, could one conceive of a difference in the causes of arising and ceasing?[1]

(Opponent:) Still, it is observed that boiling water decreases in amount and disappears. What is, in this case, the effect of the connection with fire?

(Answer:) Through the connection with fire, the power of the fire element (present in water) increases. The increase of the fire element makes it so that the mass of water arises in an ever smaller quantity in each of its subsequent states until, having become extremely small, it ceases to renew itself. In this case, this is what is called the *effect of the connection with fire*.

---

[1] In the case of fire, which the opponent also considers to be momentary, he can see the causes of arising and fading away in the different moments of the fire. But as for the other causes of the changes—brought forth through heat—which according to his view are not momentary, this is not possible.

Thus the ceasing of the factors does not have a cause. Rather, the factors cease on their own because they are impermanent. But since they cease on their own, they cease as soon as they have arisen. Through their ceasing as soon as they have arisen, the view of their momentary ceasing is established. So, given that they are momentary, there can of course be no movement. On the contrary, the erroneous idea of movement arises when the factors arise in different places that immediately succeed <109> one another, like the movement of the flames in a prairie fire. Based on this line of proof, there is definitely no movement.

BB. *The fundamental concepts*

BB.1. *The scholasticism of the Sarvāstivāda*

In the previous section, we devoted ourselves to a presentation of the principal philosophical thoughts that dominate the system of the Sarvāstivāda. We now move on to give an overview of the concepts on which the world view of the Sarvāstivāda is based. These concepts are summarized in the list of factors *(dharma)*. As this list is, at its core, typical for all the schools, it illustrates well the ideas with which the philosophical thinking of those days was working. In addition, the factors summarized in this list are repeatedly mentioned here and there [in our book] and thus a brief rendering [of this list] will most certainly be of benefit. The following should, however, be noted about the origin and structure of this list.

The pursuit of systematics, so strongly pronounced among the Indians, had led early on to the fact that different philosophical schools attempted to summarize as lists the basic elements out of which the world—according to their view—is composed. This custom was taken over by the later systems, and thus the Sāṃkhya put forward its series of twenty-five principles *(tattva)*, as did the Vaiśeṣika the list of its categories *(padārtha)*. Thus when the Buddhist schools set out to develop their doctrine into complete systems, they also felt the need to put together such lists, and this they did. In doing so the Sarvāstivādins chose the following division: According to them, all factors are divided into the impermanent and the permanent, for which—following the established Buddhist forms of expression—the designations *saṃskṛta* (the formed) and *asaṃskṛta* (the unformed), which we translate as *the conditioned* and *the unconditioned,* were used. The impermanent or conditioned was further divided into four groups: *matter (rūpa); cognition* or, as one preferred to say in this context, the *mind (citta);* <110> the *factors associated with the mind,* also known as the *mental factors (cittasaṃprayukta dharma* or *caitta);* and the *factors dissociated from the mind (cittaviprayukta dharma).*

This division was, however, not used freely and indiscriminately as it was felt that one needed to somehow rely even here on the words of the Buddha. But since the Buddha had no interest in such things, there was no usable comprehensive division in the canon. At first, the only divisions one could use in a pinch were the five groups *(skandha)* into which the Buddha had divided the worldly personality. Besides this, in speaking of the contact of the sense-organs with their objects, the Buddha had summarized the six sense-organs and their six objects as the twelve spheres *(āyatana)*. And finally, he occasionally placed next to these twelve spheres the six forms of cognition arising from them, and combined all of this into the group of the so-called *eighteen elements (dhātu)*. That was all that could be found and so, in the absence of a better alternative, the list of the factors was forced into the Procrustean bed of these old divisions and in the process their original meaning was broadened as far as necessary. Thus we regularly encounter attempts to establish agreement with these old divisions in works that contain the list of factors.

Our next presentation relies once again on a work of Vasubandhu, the so-called *Pañcaskandhaka,* in particular because of the exemplary clarity and conciseness that distinguish this work. This is, however, a Mahāyāna work. In it Vasubandhu adheres to the list of factors formulated by the famous Yogācāra teacher Asaṅga. Asaṅga, for his part, follows the system of the Śrāvakayāna school of the Mahīśāsakas in his list. Before his conversion to the Mahāyāna, he had originally belonged to this school, and as he later shaped the scholasticism of the Yogācāra school, their system served him as a model. In the end, therefore, the presentation in Vasubandhu's *Pañcaskandhaka* harks back to the scholasticism of the Mahīśāsakas, but the similarity to the scholasticism of the Sarvāstivāda <111> is so great that this presents no problem. It will thus suffice for us to point out the most important deviations.

In this work, as even its title indicates, Vasubandhu primarily discusses the five groups *(skandha).* He then briefly mentions the twelve spheres and the eighteen elements, and clarifies their relationship to the five groups. The conclusion consists of the enumeration of a series of definitions, similar to that in the first book of the *Abhidharmakośa,* and the naming of the factors to which they apply. The discussion of the individual factors is broken into these divisions as follows: The material factors are discussed with the group of corporeality; the mind with the group of cognition; the mental factors and the factors dissociated from the mind—excepting sensation and ideation, which comprise groups of their own—with the group of formations. Lastly, the unconditioned factors are placed amongst the twelve spheres, specifically as part of the *sphere of the factors.* In the following, I translate individual sections of the work and follow them with the necessary explanations.

BBB.1.1. *From the "Treatise on the Five Aggregates" (Pañcaskandhaka)*

As the Exalted One has said in summarizing, there are five groups:

1. the group of matter *(rūpa),*
2. the group of sensation *(vedanā),*
3. the group of ideation *(saṃjñā),*
4. the group of formations *(saṃskāra),* and
5. the group of cognition *(vijñāna).*

What is the *group of matter?* The four great elements and the matter dependent on the four great elements.

What are the *four great elements?* The *earth element,* the *water element,* the *fire element,* and the *wind element.*

What is the *earth element?* Solidity. <112> What is the *water element?* Liquidity. What is the *fire element?* Heat. What is the *wind element?* Easy mobility.

What is the *matter dependent on the four great elements?* The *organ of the eye,* the *organ of the (sense of) hearing,* the *organ of the (sense of) smell,* the *organ of the tongue,* and the *organ of the body; visible form, sound, smell, taste, and one part of the tangible;*[1] and the *matter of non-information (avijñapti).*

What is the *organ of the eye?* The subtle matter that has visible form as its object.

What is the *organ of the (sense of) hearing?* The subtle matter that has sound as its object.

What is the *organ of the (sense of) smell?* The subtle matter that has smell as its object.

What is the *organ of the tongue?* The subtle matter that has taste as its object.

---

[1] The remaining tangibles are the four great elements.

What is the *organ of the body?* The subtle matter that has the tangible as its object.

What is *visible form?* The object of the eye; it is divided into visible form that is color, visible form that is shape, and visible form that is information *(vijñapti).*

What is *sound?* The object of the (sense of) hearing; it is divided into sound caused by the appropriated[1] great elements, sound caused by the non-appropriated great elements, and sound caused by both (kinds of) great elements.

What is *smell?* The object of the organ of the (sense of) smell; it is divided into pleasant smell, unpleasant smell, and neutral (= indifferent) smell.

What is *taste?* The object of the tongue; it is divided into sweet, sour, salty, pungent, bitter, and astringent taste.

What is the *one part of the tangible?* The object of the body; it consists of the other dependent tangibles apart from the four great elements <113> and is divided into that which is soft, hard, heavy, light, cold, hunger, and thirst.

What is the *matter of non-information (avijñapti)?* The matter that arises through information *(vijñapti)* or concentration *(samādhi)* and is neither visible nor impenetrable.

> This presentation of the material factors differs only insignificantly from the doctrine of the Sarvāstivādins and after what we have already said about the doctrine of the elements above (S. 100ff.), it generally needs no further explanation. The ancientness of the list is noteworthy. Its compilation dates back to a very early time and thus it still considers the most diverse things, for example, hunger and thirst, as distinct material entities. The concepts of information and non-information belong to the doctrine of deeds *(karma).* Information is any manifestation of one's

---

[1] *Cf.* p. 94, note 1,

will, through words or actions, that entails merit or demerit. It is a case of non-information when someone accumulates good or bad deeds without at the same time saying corresponding words or performing corresponding actions. In any case, these subtly elaborated ideas fall outside of the scope of this presentation and will thus not be considered further.

The series of the non-material factors follows:

What is the *group of sensation?* The three feelings *(anubhava):* 1. pain, 2. pleasure, and 3. neither-pain-nor-pleasure. *Pleasure* is that at whose fading away the wish to remain connected with it exists. *Pain* is that at whose arising the wish to be separated from it exists. *Neither-pain-nor-pleasure* is that in whose presence both wishes are absent.

What is the *group of ideation?* The apprehending of the various marks of objects. [. . .]

What is the *group of formations?* The *remaining mental factors,* apart from sensation and ideation, and the *formations dissociated from the mind.* <114>

What are the *remaining mental factors?* The *factors associated with the mind.*

And which are these?

1. Contact, 2. attention, 3. sensation, 4. ideation, and 5. will;

1. desire-to-do, 2. conviction, 3. recollection, 4. concentration, and 5. insight;

1. faith, 2. reserve, 3. shame, 4. the root of good, absence of greed, 5. the root of good, absence of hatred, 6. the root of good, absence of delusion, 7. diligence, 8. harmoniousness, 9. attentiveness, 10. equanimity, and 11. non-violence;

1. passion, 2. hate, 3. pride, 4. ignorance, 5. (erroneous) view, and 6. doubt;

1. anger, 2. resentment, 3. hypocrisy, 4. spitefulness, 5. envy, 6. miserliness, 7. deceitfulness, 8. dissimulation, 9. wantonness,

10. malevolence, 11. unrestraint, 12. shamelessness, 13. rigidity, 14. agitation, 15. lack of faith, 16. laziness, 17. negligence, 18. forgetfulness, 19. distractedness, and 20. thoughtlessness;

1. regret, 2. languidness, 3. contemplation, and 4. reflection.

Of these mental factors, [in sequence,] five are all-pervasive, five are bound to specific objects, eleven are good, six are defilements, the next ones are secondary defilements and four are unbound.

Definitions of these [fifty-one] individual mental factors follow. These are of no great interest [in our context] and can thus be omitted. In the section translated, Vasubandhu attempts to give as complete a compilation of all mental phenomena as possible. His list coincides almost completely with that of the Sarvāstivādins; only the way it is divided is different. Vasubandhu first gives the five factors that accompany every mental process, then another five factors, the occurrence of which is conditioned by the objects of the process of cognition, and at the very end, another four that are not bound to a specific moral character of the mental processes, but that can occur alongside good as well as bad or morally undetermined mental factors. <115> In between there are three groups of factors that determine the moral character of the mental processes, specifically, eleven good factors, six defilements, and twenty secondary defilements. By contrast, according to the *Abhidharmakośa*, the system of the Sarvāstivādins distinguishes ten mental factors of the extended domain *(mahābhūmika)* that accompany every mental process and correspond to the first two groups of the *Pañcaskandhaka;* as well as ten good factors of the extended domain; six defilements of the extended domain; two bad factors of the extended domain; a larger number of factors from the sphere of the limited defilements; and finally, as in the *Pañcaskandhaka,* the four unbound factors.

The division of the *Pañcaskandhaka* is distinctly clearer and more advanced. That the prominence of the good factors and of the defilements is common to both divisions is easily understandable, since the whole psychology of these schools is directed toward the goal of liberation and is intended to facilitate the explanation of the process of liberation.

The definitions of the individual mental factors are followed by the discussion of the factors dissociated from the mind. It begins as follows:

What are the *formations dissociated from the mind?* They are mere designations *(prajñapti)* based on various states of matter, of mind, and of the mental factors, and they cannot be clearly determined as either distinct or not-distinct from them [i.e., matter, etc.].

And which are they? Acquisition *(prāpti),* the absorption of non-ideation *(asaṃjñisamāpatti),* the absorption of suppression *(nirodhasamāpatti),* the state of non-ideation *(āsaṃjñika),* the life organ *(jīvitendriya),* homogeneity of beings *(nikāyasabhāga),* birth, aging, duration, impermanence, the group of words, the group of sentences, the group of phonemes, worldliness *(pṛthagjanatva)* and so forth. <116>

Here, again, the definitions of the individual factors follow. The listing itself agrees with that of the *Abhidharmakośa* with the sole exception of *worldliness,* which the Sarvāstivādins do not recognize but consider to be a type of non-acquisition.

This specific group of factors is particularly characteristic of the Sarvāstivādins' way of thinking and of the antiquity of their system. On the one hand, we see the serious effort to trace all the concepts being dealt with back to their factual basis. On the other hand, a primitive realism, which assumes a corresponding reality in the external world for all of these concepts, has not been transcended. I.e.:

- The arising and ceasing of things, their duration and gradual aging are caused by specific factors that combine with them and induce these processes, [i.e., *birth, impermanence, duration,* and *aging*].
- The *absorption of non-ideation* and the *absorption of suppression* refer to two stages of absorption and the *state of non-ideation* to existence in a realm of gods in which the mental processes are suspended. This, too, is explained based on three special factors that prevent the occurrence of the mental factors.
- *Words, sentences,* and *phonemes* are also considered to be separate factors that trigger the corresponding cognitive processes in connection with a specific sound.
- *Acquisition* and *homogeneity of beings* are reminiscent of the Vaiśeṣika concepts, specifically: *acquisition* of the quality of *connection; homogeneity of beings* of the category of the *universal.* In contrast to the Vaiśeṣika, however, they are not forms of existence of a different status; instead they are independent factors, as are also the material or mental factors. In addition, they are restricted only to sentient beings, in relation to which their assumption proved to be particularly necessary. To wit, *acquisition* serves to explain the binding of certain factors to a particular person and the *homogeneity of beings* was intended to explain the fact of belonging to a certain group of living beings.

As for *worldliness,* Buddhism distinguishes between noble ones *(ārya)* who have entered into the path of liberation and worldly individuals for whom <117> this is not the case.

Certain factors, the possession of which constitutes the noble one, are absent in the worldly individual, and this very absence is in turn caused by a specific factor, i.e., *worldliness.*

Vasubandhu does not share these Sarvāstivāda views, however, and he expresses this in the first sentence of this section. For him, in accordance with the view of the Sautrāntikas and Yogācārins, the *formations dissociated from the mind* are not real, autonomous factors; instead they exist only as designations *(prajñaptita).* We will need to discuss this in more detail in what follows [S. 119ff.].

The next section deals with the *group of cognition.* As a start, it includes the six types of cognition that correspond to the different sense-organs and that are thus designated as visual cognition, auditory cognition, olfactory cognition, gustatory cognition, tactile cognition, and mental cognition. In accordance with the Yogācāra doctrine, Vasubandhu also adds the *mind accompanied by defilements (kliṣṭaṃ manas)* and the *fundamental cognition (ālayavijñāna),* and indeed these two types of cognition are the only ones that he treats in greater detail. But as these same two will be brought up in the presentation of the Yogācāra doctrine [S. 328, 358ff.], we can refrain from a discussion of them here.

This concludes the presentation of the five groups. From the discussion of the twelve spheres and the eighteen elements, which comes next, we will select only the section on the unconditioned factors, which alone is of greater interest.

What is the *unconditioned?* Space *(ākāśa),* suppression without knowledge *(apratisaṃkhyānirodha),* suppression through knowledge *(pratisaṃkhyānirodha),* and suchness *(tathatā).*

What is *space?* That which provides space to matter.

What is *suppression without knowledge?* A suppression that is not a separation *(visaṃyoga).* What does this mean? That the groups do not arise at all, [although] a counteragent *(pratipakṣa)* to the defilements is not present. <118>

What is *suppression through knowledge?* A suppression that is separation. What does this mean? That the groups do not arise at all because a counteragent to the defilements is present.

What is *suchness?* The nature of the factors *(dharmatā),* i.e., the essencelessness of the factors.

Of these four unconditioned factors, the Sarvāstivāda recognizes only the first three.

With regard to *space,* we must bear in mind that the Sarvāstivādins hold it to be a truly existing factor. The Sautrāntika and Yogācāra were the first to view it as mere emptiness.

As for the two *suppressions,* the following may be said. [1] It may happen that certain factors do not arise in a personality-stream because the causes for them are not present. [2] Further, the knowledge of the noble truths—as counteragent to ignorance and the rest of the defilements—entails that these defilements no longer occur in the personality-stream and that this stream is finally completely interrupted. According to the doctrine of the Sarvāstivādins, each of these [scenarios] is occasioned by specific factors that, through their connection with the personality-stream, prevent the arising of the mentioned factors. These are called, respectively, *suppression without knowledge* and *suppression through knowledge.* The latter is particularly important, and we will need to discuss it further [S. 130ff.] since it occasions liberation and is therefore also referred to as *extinction,* as *nirvāṇa.*

And *suchness,* finally, signifies the true nature of things and as we will later see, represents the ultimate state of being in the Mahāyāna [S. 148 and *passim*]. It is foreign to the Sarvāstivāda. In his lists, Asaṅga still distinguishes the *suchness of the good [factors]*, the *suchness of the bad [factors]*, and the *suchness of the indeterminate factors* in the manner of the Mahīśāsaka. Vasubandhu was the first to replace them with suchness in general.

We have now had several occasions [S. 76, 114f., 117f.] to note where Vasubandhu deviates from the orthodox doctrine of the Sarvāstivādins and follows the doctrine of the Sautrāntika. It seems appropriate then, in view of the great importance of this latter doctrine to the logico-epistemological school of <119> Buddhism, to say a few words here about this school.

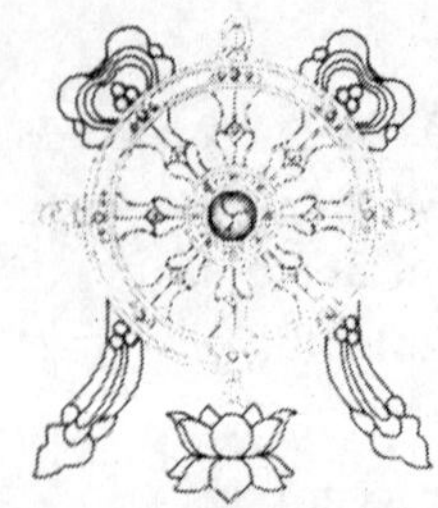

BBB.2. *The scholasticism of the Sautrāntika*

Different reports about the precursors of the Sautrāntika school exist, and its first beginnings seem to reach back a rather long way, however the details of its development remain unclear. The school itself was founded by Kumāralāta who was active in northwestern India in the second half of the third century c.e. His disciple Śrīlāta gave the school its fundamental comprehensive scholasticism and a second disciple, Harivarman, is also worth mentioning as he is the only representative of the school from whom a treatise, the *Tattvasiddhi (Proof of the Truth)*, has survived. In later times, it is most notably Vasubandhu the Younger who tends strongly in the direction of the Sautrāntika.

And even though he shows great independence at the level of details, this tendency is so strongly expressed—especially in his commentary to the *Abhidharmakośa*—that he was just called "the Sautrāntika" by his opponents in the camp of the orthodox Sarvāstivādins. At present we know nothing about a continuation of this school, but it strongly influenced the logico-epistemological school, and a number of its ideas persisted there.

The Sautrāntikas are often called *nominalists*, in contrast to the realism of the Sarvāstivāda. This is justifiable in that they state that many of the Sarvāstivādins' factors exist only as designations *(prajñaptita)*. Of course they by no means deny any real basis for these designations, they simply systematically transcend the primitive realism of the Sarvāstivāda. Space, for example, they see as mere emptiness and the suppressions as mere annihilation. Often, however, they also find the designations to be based in the nature of things, and, especially, the potentials *(śakti)* of things [S. 126] play a role in this, which idea the logical school then further expanded upon.

As a sample of these lines of thought, I will at first present a text that illustrates what it means [from the general Śrāvakayāna point of view] that something exists only as designation. A discussion of acquisition *(prāpti)* then follows [S. 123ff.], as an example of the <120> treatment of terms taught by the scholastics of the Sarvāstivāda. Finally [S. 131–42], within the presentation of the doctrine of liberation, we will discuss the Sautrāntika view of *nirvāṇa*.

The first text is taken from the sixth book of the *Abhidharmakośa* and deals with the question of the seemingly or restricted real *(saṃvṛtisat)* and the truly real *(paramārthasat)*. As we will see [S. 173f., 230, 310], these two concepts are of great importance in the Mahāyāna and they serve to characterize the phenomenal world and true existence. The present text, on the other hand, shows an attempt of the Śrāvakayāna to come to terms with these concepts whereby, of course, one's conception of them differed markedly, depending on its, [i.e., the Śrāvakayāna's] doctrine. Here that is, they are used to make a distinction within the phenomenal world itself; specifically between things that exist only from a conventional stand point and things that are, as such, real. The first of these concerns things that exist as composites, in which case the words and ideas do not have a precise correspondence to a [real] thing. This is thus a case similar to that in the Vaiśeṣika and related systems in which, when dealing with purely external combinations of things, such as a forest or an army, one shied away from assuming a whole or a universal as the basis for the words and ideas in question. Here [in the Śrāvakayāna], however, [this point of view] was taken much further. The same view was extended to all cases of a combination of parts in which the words and ideas are attached to just this combination and its form, and in which, in the event of the dissolution of this combination and the disappearance of this form, the words and ideas no longer apply. As, for example, once a pot is smashed, one speaks only of shards and no longer of a pot. Indeed, this was taken so far as to include all cases where a combination of different things was presupposed, even if one was not able to disassemble them in practice but only theoretically. Such a case was seen, for example, in what are understood in everyday life to be elements: water, fire, etc., <121> but which the Buddhist schools saw as a mixture of various kinds of atoms. In all of these cases then, it was assumed that no real things are present that correspond to the words and ideas. Instead, these things only seemingly exist; only from the point of view of everyday life. Only their constituents are real. In this way, though, a break had been made with the [kind of] fundamental realism that demanded a real correlate for all words and ideas, and the doctrine of things that exist only as designations *(prajñaptisat)* rests on this view [that only the constituents of things are real].

BBB.2.1. *The seemingly and the truly real (Abhidharmakośa VI, v. 4)*

The Exalted One has thus said that there are four truths. Then, in another sutra, he has said that there are two kinds of truths, the restricted truth *(saṃvṛtisatya)* and the highest truth *(paramārthasatya)*. What is the mark of these two truths? The verse text says:

> (v. 4) If the cognition of an object no longer occurs once it is demolished or as soon as one has excluded what is other by means of thought, then it is seemingly real *(saṃvṛtisat)*, just like a pot or water. The opposite of this is truly real *(paramārthasat)*.

If the cognition of an object no longer occurs as soon as it is demolished, then this object is to be considered as seemingly real, as with a pot in regard to which, if it is smashed and only the shards are present, the cognition of the pot no longer occurs. The same applies to a [piece of] cloth, etc. Further, in the case of an object, if as soon as one has excluded what is other by means of thought, its cognition <122> no longer occurs, then it is likewise seemingly real, as in the case of water of which the cognition no longer occurs if one has excluded the form, etc., by means of thought. The same applies to fire, etc. Now, as long as the demolition or the exclusion of the object concerned has not yet taken place, [the object] is designated as such and such, following the usual ways of thinking and speaking, and because it is thus designated, it is called *seemingly real*. If, moreover, in accordance with common usage, one speaks of the presence of a pot, etc., then this is true and not false; and thus one speaks of *seeming truth*.

If an object is the opposite of that, then it is called *truly real*. In other words, the cognition of the object does not vanish when it is demolished and when what is other is excluded by means of thought, the cognition of it continues to occur. This object is thus to be considered as truly real. As in the case of form *(rūpa)*, etc., the cognition of which continues to occur if one splits it down to the atoms or if one excludes what is other—for example, the taste, etc.—by means of thought. The same applies to sensation, etc. So because the (object in question) is completely real, it is called *truly real.* If, moreover, based on the truly real, one speaks of the presence of form, etc., then this is true and not false. And thus one speaks of the *highest truth.*

The ancient masters give the following explanation: Just as the factors are apprehended by supramundane knowledge and the subsequently acquired correct worldly knowledge, so they are called *truly true.* And just as they are apprehended by any other kinds of knowledge, they are called *seemingly true.* With this, the discussion of the truths is finished. <123>

> The next section shows how the concepts of the Sarvāstivādins were given different meaning by the Sautrāntikas, corresponding to their way of thinking. It is taken from the second book of the *Abhidharmakośa* and deals with *acquisition (prāpti).* According to the doctrine of the Sarvāstivādins, this is a distinct entity that binds specific factors—primarily defilements and good factors—to a personality-stream. It thereby causes these factors to occur in this personality-stream at the appropriate time, and at other times—when these factors are not active—it also determines the person's character, so that the latter consequently is considered to be either defiled or virtuous. In contrast to this doctrine and in accordance with the Sautrāntikas, Vasubandhu attempts to show that such an entity, known as *acquisition,* does not exist. In his view, the aforementioned facts rest instead on a specific constitution of the personality-stream that makes up the seed of that particular factor, so to speak, and that enables the personality-stream to produce [this factor] at the

appropriate time. Thus it is also this constitution that is referred to when one speaks of *acquisition,* which therefore exists only as designation and not really as a distinct entity.

BBB.2.2. *The nature of acquisition (Abhidharmakośa II, v. 36)*

How can one assert that a distinct thing *(dravya)* named *acquisition (prāpti)* exists? . . . For since neither its intrinsic nature is observed, as with visible form, sound, etc., or with passion, hatred, etc., nor their effect, as with the eye, the (sense of) hearing, etc., the qualities of a thing are not present and [acquisition] therefore is not possible.[1] <121>

(Opponent:) *Acquisition* is what the cause of the arising of the factors is named.

(Answer:) Then there could be no [acquisition] of the unconditioned.[2] And how then could factors arise that have not yet been acquired or that have been abolished through a change of the sphere [of existence] or through passionlessness?[3]

(Opponent:) The simultaneously arising acquisition is their cause.

(Answer:) In that case, what does birth *(jāti)* or the birth of birth *(jātijāti)* bring about?[4] Further, with individuals who are bound by all the fetters, the diversity of the weak, medium,

---

[1] The means of valid cognition are [direct] perception and inference. *Acquisition,* however, is neither perceived, as is visible form, etc., nor inferred, as is the eye, etc.

[2] According to the doctrine of the Sarvāstivādins, the unconditioned factors, *suppression through knowledge* and *suppression without knowledge,* connect with the personality-stream by means of *acquisition.* However, this would not be possible in the assumed case, as the unconditioned cannot arise.

[3] Since before their arising there also exists no *acquisition* that could cause it.

[4] According to the doctrine of the Sarvāstivādins, the factor *birth (jāti)* is the cause of the arising of things (*see* S. 114f.), and its cause, in turn, is the *birth of birth.*

or strong arising defilements would not be possible, since indeed acquisition (i.e., their cause) does not differ. Or, [these defilements] arise out of that from which this diversity is derived, in which case acquisition is not the cause of arising.

(Opponent:) Who says that acquisition is the cause of arising?

(Answer:) Then what is it?

(Opponent:) It is the cause of the distinction [between states]. If, in fact, there were no *acquisition,* then, with noble ones who entertain worldly thoughts and with worldly individuals, the distinction: "These are noble ones and these are worldly individuals" would not be possible.

(Answer:) This (distinction) can also rest on the difference of whether one has abandoned the defilements or not.

(Opponent:) But how is it possible to say that the former have abandoned the defilements and that the latter <125> have not abandoned the defilements? If, on the other hand, *acquisition* exists, then [the distinction] results from its having disappeared or not disappeared.

(Answer:) It results from the difference in the bearer (i.e., the personality-stream). In the case of the noble ones, for instance, the bearer has been transformed by the path of vision and of contemplation[1] such that the thus to be abandoned defilements can no longer rearise. So if a bearer has in this way—like a grain of rice burned by fire—become such that he can no longer be the seed of defilements, or if, by the worldly path, his capability to be a seed has been impaired, then one says that he has abandoned the defilements; in the opposite case, it is said that he has not abandoned them. Whoever has abandoned them, of him it is said that he does not possess them; whoever has not abandoned them, of him it is said that he possesses them.

Then, as far as the good factors are concerned, they are twofold: *arisen without effort* and *arisen through effort,* i.e.,

---

[1] *Cf.* the presentation of the doctrine of liberation, which follows below.

those that one possesses from birth, and *those that are obtained through exertion.* Here, one says that someone possesses the factors arisen without effort if the capability of the bearer to be their seed is not impaired; if it is impaired, one says that he does not possess them. The roots of good are then cut through. One should know specifically that this occurs through erroneous view. Incidentally, the capability to be the seed of good factors is never completely annihilated in the personality-stream. In the case of the (factors) arisen through effort, on the other hand, one says that someone possesses them once they have arisen and if the capability of the <126> personality-stream to manifest them at will is not subject to any obstruction.

So, the seed that is not completely removed, that is not impaired, and is strong at the time that the capacity takes effect, is that which receives the designation *possession* (= *acquisition*), and not a distinct thing.

(Opponent:) What is this so-called *seed?*

(Answer:) Name and form, insofar as—due to a special transformation of the stream of moments—they are capable of directly or indirectly bringing forth a specific effect.

(Opponent:) What is this so-called *transformation?*

(Answer:) The alteration of the stream of moments.

(Opponent:) And what is this so-called *stream of moments?*

(Answer:) The formations belonging to the three stages of time, insofar as they are related to one another as cause and effect. . . . Therefore, *acquisition* and its negation, *non-acquisition,* are certainly factors by designation only but not factors in the manner of (real) things.

BBC. *The doctrine of liberation of the Śrāvakayāna*

In conclusion [of our discussion of "The scholasticism (Abhidharma) of the Way of Hearers (Śrāvakayāna)"], there remains the task of at least briefly discussing the form that the doctrine of liberation took in the Śrāvakayāna, since with the central position of this doctrine in Buddhism, it is referred to again and again. In addition, the search for the nature of liberation touches upon the most crucial philosophical problems.

For the Sarvāstivādins, in the course of time and through a course of development that we cannot pursue in detail here, the doctrine of liberation assumed the following form: Since beginningless time, living beings have been entangled in the agonizing cycle of existences and they wander restlessly from birth to birth, driven by the power of deeds *(karma)*. Deeds, however, exert their power only if they are morally determined. Otherwise, they have no [maturation] effect. Their being morally determined results from their connection with the good and bad mental factors, above all with the defilements. Whoever strives for liberation <127> from the pain of the cycle of existences must therefore first remove the defilements. Then the deeds lose their power and the cycle of existences comes to an end.

The cessation of defilements is reached by the path of liberation, which culminates in the intuitive clear comprehension of the four noble truths. After various preparatory practices, among them, for example, attentive inhalation and exhalation, one begins with the four awakenings of mindfulness *(smṛtyupasthāna)*, which play an important role in Buddhism even at its earliest. Next come the factors conducive to penetration *(nirvedhabhāgīya)* wherein, in four stages, one considers the revealed four noble truths ever more penetratingly. These flow finally into one's own direct clear comprehension *(abhisamaya)* of these truths. With this the path of liberation in its stricter sense—that which leads to the removal of defilements—begins, commencing with the *path of vision (darśanamārga).*

According to the scholasticism [of the Sarvāstivādins], this process of clear comprehension of the noble truths is divided into sixteen moments. For each truth, that is, first all defilements opposed to its cognition are removed in one moment; then, in a second moment, one obtains the acquisition *(prāpti),* i.e., the firm possession of this cognition. And since for each truth the cognition relative to the lowest world sphere—the sphere of desire—is distinguished from the cognition relative to the two higher spheres—the sphere of the material and the sphere of the immaterial—one comes to a total of sixteen moments in all for all four truths. Noteworthy and characteristic of the sober spirit of the school here is that the path of vision does not necessarily require the practice of the stages of meditation *[dhyāna]* as taught by the Buddha, and that the clear comprehension of the noble truths itself—in spite of its supranatural clear-sighted character—can occur at a preliminary stage *[sāmantaka]* of these stages of meditation.

With the clear comprehension of the noble truths, the most important part of the path of liberation has been traveled. The disciple has now become a noble one *(ārya),* whereas before he was a worldly individual *(pṛthagjana).* <128> With this, however, [complete] liberation has not yet been gained as there are in fact two types of defilements. The first are by nature *imperfect cognition,* and the others are *passions.* This distinction has its original equivalent in the doctrine of the Buddha in which, in the twelve-membered causal chain, suffering is traced back to two roots: ignorance and thirst. Of these two groups, *imperfect cognition* can be eliminated by the clear comprehension of the noble truths; the *passions,* on the other hand, cannot. In other words, it had been recognized that cognition alone is ineffective against the *passions.* They must rather be fought by means of habitual constant influencing. Accordingly, within the path of liberation, along with the *path of vision,* which eliminates ignorance, a *path of contemplation (bhāvanāmārga),* which is supposed to aid in the fight against the *passions,* was discerned.

This *path of contemplation* is itself also twofold. For the noble one who has already envisioned the noble truths, it consists of the repeated contemplation of the noble truths, which then also gradually works on the passions and annihilates them. The fight against the passions is not only possible for the noble one, however. It is true that the removal of ignorance can only occur through the cognition of the noble truths, but the worldly individual can and should also fight against the passions. Aside from the *supramundane (lokottara) path [of contemplation]* taught by the Buddha, therefore, there is also a *mundane (laukika) path of contemplation* on which, for example, [even] independent of the proclamation of the Buddha, one contemplates the pain of existence and turns away from the world. This mundane path of contemplation can, however, also be entered before the path of vision. Indeed, the Buddha himself is the most outstanding example of this, since before his enlightenment he had already completely eradicated all passions on the mundane path of contemplation. Thus, at the moment of enlightenment, the cognition of the noble truths brought him liberation as well.

On this twofold path, the *path of vision* and the *path of contemplation*—whether *mundane* or *supramundane*—it is therefore possible to annihilate all <129> defilements. With the annihilation of the defilements, deeds lose their effectiveness and liberation comes about. Now the question arises, however: What is liberation, or as the Buddha calls it, *extinction, nirvāṇa?* It is precisely in the answer to this question that the sober realistic spirit that characterizes the scholasticism of the Sarvāstivāda now shows itself more clearly than anywhere else. At the same time, however, it also shows the unwavering consistency with which a once-adopted path was adhered to and followed to its end. An *inconceivable ultimate state of being* [S. 147f., 298] remains foreign to the spirit of the school, which turns away from all mysticism. *Nirvāṇa,* like any other object of cognition, must therefore be a factor that exists as a thing, as demanded by the logic of the system.

But how is this factor to be defined more precisely? Here, the numerous scriptural passages characterizing *nirvāṇa* as the cessation of suffering and the vanishing of desire, were once again decisive. *Nirvāṇa* must then be something that eradicates passion from the personality-stream and prevents the arising of other painful factors. With this, however, reasoning could already revert to familiar pathways. The factor *acquisition (prāpti),* which causes the affiliation of specific factors with the personality-stream, was known, and a second factor, *non-acquisition (aprāpti),* was considered to be the cause of non-affiliation. Thus nothing was more obvious than to assume that *nirvāṇa* is a similar type of factor, whose connection with the personality-stream leads to the defilements and all defiled factors being eliminated from it and no longer being able to arise within it. And this indeed was how *nirvāṇa* was then defined. The only difference to come about was the fact that it was classed with the unconditioned factors and not the conditioned ones, but this was necessitated by the numerous scriptural passages that describe *nirvāṇa* as eternal and imperishable. Thus we arrive at the seemingly strange fact that, according to the scholasticism of the Sarvāstivāda, liberation—*nirvāṇa*—is nothing other than a factor like all the others, which connects with the personality-stream and so exerts its effect. <130>

We have already encountered this conception of *nirvāṇa* in Vasubandhu's *Pañcaskandhaka* [S. 119] where it appears among the unconditioned factors under the name *suppression through knowledge (pratisaṃkhyānirodha)*. The same doctrine is also found in the *Abhidharmakośa*. According to this doctrine, *nirvāṇa* is an unconditioned factor, which bears the name *suppression through knowledge* because it occasions the vanishing of the defilements based on the cognition of the noble truths. It is defined as separation *(visaṃyoga)* because it eliminates the defilements and the defiled factors from the personality-stream. Finally, we must note that there is not just one such *suppression through knowledge,* but as many as there are defilements that are to be eliminated from the personality-stream, since otherwise, with the elimination of one defilement, all would be eliminated and hence liberation would already be attained. The passage of the *Abhidharmakośa* that includes the doctrine of *suppression through knowledge,* has the following wording:

BBC.1. *Suppression through knowledge (Abhidharmakośa I, v. 6)*

Suppression through knowledge is separation *(visaṃyoga)*.

Suppression through knowledge is the separation from the contaminated *(sāṣrava)* factors. *Knowledge* refers to the cognition of the noble truths of suffering, etc., thus a form of insight *(prajñā)*. The suppression acquired thereby is *suppression through knowledge* . . .

(Question:) Is *suppression through knowledge* one and the same for all contaminated factors?

(Answer:) No.

(Question:) Then what is it?

(Answer:) (It is)

in each case different.

There are as many separating things as there are connected things, since otherwise the realization of the suppression of all defilements would follow from the realization (13) of the suppression of those defilements that are to be removed by the vision of suffering. In which case, however, the practice of the rest of the counteragents *(pratipakṣa)*[1] would be pointless.

(Objection:) But it is said: Suppression is non-homogeneous *(asabhāga)*. What does this mean?

(Answer:) This statement means that it does not have a homogeneous cause *(sabhāgahetu)*, and that it itself is not the homogeneous cause of something else, but it does not (mean) that nothing at all exists that is homogeneous to it. With this we have discussed the *suppression through knowledge.*

This idiosyncratic Sarvāstivādin conception of the nature of *nirvāṇa* was not, however, shared by the other schools. It is true that—as with the Sarvāstivādin system as a whole—its effects became apparent also outside the school, but the other schools' deviations in the conception [of *nirvāṇa*] were manifold and in some cases considerable. The Sautrāntikas also deviated from the doctrine of the Sarvāstivādins in this point, as in so many other instances. We will now examine their view a little more closely.

The Sautrāntika view of the nature of *nirvāṇa* is a logical extension of their general point of view. They start, as so often, from the Sarvāstivādin view, which they recast in accordance with their own intentions. Thus for them as well, *nirvāṇa* is *suppression through knowledge.* They do not, however, content themselves with the primitive realism of the Sarvāstivāda who sees in this suppression a distinct entity, instead they define it independently after their own fashion. *Suppression through knowledge* thus exists

---

[1] I.e., of the rest of the factors that counteract the defilements.

in the fact that the defilements and the defiled factors no longer arise in the future. A non-arising is, however, a mere non-existence. Thus they concluded that *nirvāṇa* is a non-existence, a mere nothing, and they did not shy away from stating this matter-of-factly. <132>

This doctrine of the Sautrāntika is dealt with in a long discussion in the second book of the *Abhidharmakośa* in which Vasubandhu first briefly states the doctrine of the Sautrāntikas and then defends it against the objections of the Sarvāstivādins. We would like to offer a sampling of this discussion here. As was customary, the opponents are working partly with passages from the sacred scriptures. They have particular difficulty with the problem of how a non-existence can be an object of knowledge and how statements about it are possible.

BBC.2. *Nirvāṇa as non-existence (Abhidharmakośa II, v. 55)*

The Sautrāntika teachers say: Everything unconditioned *(asaṃskṛta)* does not really exist because it is not, like form, sensation, etc., a separate real thing . . . If the already arisen burden *(anuśaya)* and existence is annihilated and, through the power of knowledge, a new one no longer arises, this then is called *suppression through knowledge* . . .

(Objection:) If *nirvāṇa* is a mere non-arising, how can this be reconciled with the wording of the sutra? For the sutra says: "If one practices, maintains, and cultivates the five faculties *(indriya)*, they lead to the casting off of past, future, and present suffering." This casting off is *nirvāṇa*. Only in regard to something in the future, however, can one think of a non-arising, but not in regard to something of the past and present. How then is there no contradiction?

(Answer:) Although this wording does exist, there is still no contradiction in terms of meaning. The meaning the sutra is intended to convey is that one casts off tine defilements that are based on past and present suffering, <133> and for this reason it is called the *casting off of suffering.* Accordingly, the Exalted One has also said: "You should cast off the passion for form. If you cast off passion, then this is called *casting off form* and *[complete] understanding of form,*" etc., in the same way up to cognition.[1] Just so then is the casting off of past and present suffering to be understood . . .

(Objection:) If by nature the unconditioned factors do not exist at all, then why does the sutra say: "Of all the factors that exist, whether conditioned or unconditioned, passionlessness[2] is by far the foremost"? How can one non-existent factor be put forth as foremost among non-existent factors?

(Answer:) We are not indeed saying that by nature the unconditioned factors do not exist at all. Rather, they must exist as we state something (about them). It is said, for example, that a previous non-existence and a later non-existence of sound exists. By contrast, however, one cannot say that the non-existence exists and that, therefore, the view of its existence is established. If therefore one speaks of the existence of the unconditioned, this is to be seen in the same way. One can therefore also praise a non-existence. Passionlessness is in fact called the *complete non-existence of all that is harmful.* And this is the most excellent among every non-existence that there is. It is therefore to be praised as foremost in order to bring forth joy and delight in it in the disciples.

(Objection:) If the unconditioned factors represent a mere non-existence, then *nirvāṇa* cannot be designated as the *noble truth of the cessation (of suffering),* because it does not exist. <134>

(Answer:) What, first of all, does the expression *noble truth*[3] mean? Does this expression not mean something non-erroneous?

---

[1] I.e., the same is said of the other groups in the same wording.

[2] I.e., *nirvāṇa.*

[3] The scholasticism of the Sarvāstivāda usually equates the noble truths with their concrete content.

The noble ones do not see existence and non-existence erroneously. That is, the noble ones see in suffering only suffering and they see in the non-existence of suffering only non-existence. What then is objectionable in this conception of the noble truths?

(Question:) How can this non-existence be put forth as the third noble truth?

(Answer:) Because the noble ones see and teach it immediately after the second, it follows that it is the third.

(Objection:) If by nature the unconditioned factors do not exist at all, then the knowledge of the ether or of *nirvāṇa* would have to be based on a non-existence as object.

(Answer:) In the fact that it is based on a non-existence as object, there is no fault. This will be examined later[1] in the discussion of the past and the future.[2]

(Opponent:) What disadvantage is there if we assume that the unconditioned has its own real existence?

(Answer:) But what advantage does that have?

(Opponent:) If we assume it, then the doctrine of the Vaibhāṣikas is upheld. This is the advantage.

(Answer:) May the gods know whether they wish to uphold (this doctrine), if it can be upheld at all. But if you assume that (the unconditioned) is real, then this is an empty fantasy, and that is the disadvantage. "How so?" Because it has neither a distinct nature that can be perceived, as, [for example,] form, sensation, etc., nor does it produce an effect that <135> can be perceived, like the eye, the ear, etc.[3] . . . . . .

---

1 [See *Abhidharmakośa*, chapter five, verse 25.]

2 The Sautrāntikas, in contrast to the Sarvāstivādins, consider the past and the future not as real, but as mere non-existence.

3 I.e., it can neither be perceived through the senses nor deduced through inference.

(Objection:) As the sutra says, the monk acquires *nirvāṇa* in this life. How [then] can one speak of an acquisition in reference to a non-existence?

(Answer:) One speaks of an acquisition of *nirvāṇa* because one attains the counteragent *(pratipakṣa)*[1] and thereby obtains a bearer (= personality-stream) that is opposed to the defilements and rebirth.

In addition, there is a passage of the sacred scripture that shows that the nature of *nirvāṇa* consists only of a non-existence. A sutra says:

> The complete casting off of existing suffering, the removing, the vanishing, the passionlessness, the annihilation, the appeasement, the sinking; further, the non-rearising of a new suffering, the non-grasping, the non-appearing—that is the peaceful, that is the exalted, the abandoning of all afflictions *(upadhi)* and the complete vanishing of thirst, the passionlessness, the annihilation, the *nirvāṇa*. . . .

From this, the sutra's comparison is easily explained: "Like the extinction *(nirvāṇa)* of a lamp, so was the liberation of the mind."[2] The meaning of this sutra is: Just as the extinction of a lamp is only the fading away of the flame of the lamp, but not a distinct entity, in the same way the mind of the Exalted One attained liberation, i.e., only the groups were annihilated, an existence was no longer present.

> To conclude then, another Sautrāntika—this time Harivarman, the aforementioned student <136> of Kumāralāta [S. 119]—will have his say. He is perhaps even clearer and more precise than Vasubandhu in his statements.

---

[1] I.e., the factors that constitute the noble path and that annihilate the defilements.

[2] The verse refers to the death of the Buddha.

BBC.3. *From "Establishment of the Truth" (Tattvasiddhi)*

(Question:) Is it not the case that *nirvāṇa* really exists?

(Answer:) One speaks of *nirvāṇa* based on the total annihilation of the groups. What is it here that is supposed to exist?

(Question:) (You ask) how one recognizes that *nirvāṇa* is real.

1. The (noble) truth of the cessation (of suffering) is what is called *nirvāṇa*. The truth of suffering, etc., is real. *Nirvāṇa* must therefore also be real.

2. Further, the knowledge of *nirvāṇa* is what is called *knowledge of annihilation.* How can *(nirvāṇa)* bring forth knowledge if it is not a (real) factor?

3. Further, in the sutra the Buddha says to the monks: "There are factors that are born, arisen, brought-about, conditioned, and there are factors that are unborn, unarisen, not-brought-about, unconditioned."

4. Further, the sutra states: "There are only two kinds of factors, conditioned factors and unconditioned factors. The conditioned factors are subject to becoming, passing away, and transformation while they last. The unconditioned factors are not subject to becoming, passing away, and transformation while they last."

5. Further, the sutra states: "Of all factors that exist—whether conditioned or unconditioned—annihilation, vanishing, *nirvāṇa* alone is the most excellent."

6. Further, it states: "Form is not permanent because form is annihilated. <137> *Nirvāṇa* is permanent," etc., in the same way up to cognition.

7. Further, the sutra states: "One should bring annihilation to mind." But if it is not a (real) factor, then what should one bring to mind?

8. Further, the Buddha says in the *Bahudhātukasūtra:* "The sage recognizes the conditioned and the unconditioned in accordance with truth." The unconditioned is *nirvāṇa*. How can

one designate as non-existent, something that is recognized through correct knowledge?

9. Further, there is no passage in the sutras that explicitly states that *nirvāṇa* is not a (real) factor.

- From this it can be seen that it is only a creation of your own thoughts, (if you say) that *nirvāṇa* does not exist.

(Answer:) 1. If, independently of the groups, there is also a specific factor with the name *nirvāṇa,* then one cannot designate the vanishing and the annihilation of the groups as *nirvāṇa.*

2. Further, if there is a *nirvāṇa,* one would have to point out its nature, what it is.

3. Further, the concentration that is focused on *nirvāṇa* is called *signless (ānimittasamādhi).* If the signs of a factor exist, why then is it called *signless?* As the sutra states: "The ascetic observes the abandoning of the signs of visible form," etc., up to "he observes the abandoning of the signs of the factors."

4. Further, the sutras state again and again: "All formations are impermanent, all factors are without a self; annihilation, *nirvāṇa* is peaceful." Here *self* indicates the nature of the factors. If one does not see a nature in the factors, then one says that one sees that they have no self. So if *nirvāṇa* is a (real) factor, then one cannot see that it is without nature, because this <138> factor is not subject to annihilation.[1] As long as a pot exists, for example, there is no factor that embodies the vanishing of the pot.[2] Only once the pot vanishes can one speak of the vanishing of the pot. The same applies to the felling of a tree, etc. Just so, one cannot speak of *nirvāṇa* as long as the formations still exist, since [it is] because the formations are annihilated (in *nirvāṇa*), that it is called *nirvāṇa.*

---

1 For *nirvāṇa* is generally considered to be permanent and unchanging.

2 *Nirvāṇa* is by nature the annihilation of the factors, but according to the doctrine of the opponent, it has existed eternally and thus before the factors have yet been annihilated.

5. Further, the annihilation of suffering is not designated as a further separate factor. The sutra states namely: "Monks, if this suffering falls into annihilation and new suffering does not arise, if a rebirth no longer occurs, then this is the highest abode, the calm, the peaceful [abode], the casting off of afflictions *(upadhi),* the disappearance of thirst, passionlessness, annihilation, *nirvāṇa.*" Here, the annihilation of this suffering and the non-arising of a new suffering is spoken of. What factor exists beyond this that could be called *nirvāṇa?*

6. Further, a separate factor of *vanishing* does not exist. Only if the already arisen thirst is annihilated and the not yet arisen one does not arise does one then speak of *vanishing.* So what factor exists beyond this that could be called *vanishing?* [This factor] cannot be called *real.*

7. In addition, *existence* is only another name for *factor.* The non-existence of the factors of the five groups is called *nirvāṇa.* It is thus impossible to designate non-existence as existence here. It is based on annihilation that one speaks of *nirvāṇa.* If, for example, <139> a robe is annihilated, no separate factor exists from then on, since otherwise, separate factors of the annihilation of the robe, etc., would also have to exist.

8. The *knowledge of annihilation* of which you speak presents no difficulties. In the case of the felling of a tree, for example, knowledge (relating to that) arises, but this does not imply a separate factor *felling.* Incidentally, the knowledge arises in this case based on the formations. Thus, as soon as the formations are no longer present, one speaks of *nirvāṇa.* Just as when a specific object is no longer present, one recognizes the absence of this object.

(Question:) Is there then no *nirvāṇa?*

(Answer:) It is not the case that there is no *nirvāṇa.* It is just not a real factor. Because if there were no *nirvāṇa,* then birth and death would last forever and there would be no liberation at all. In the same way, there is the breaking of a pot and the felling of a tree. These are just not real separate factors. What you have said in regard to the other (noble) truths, etc., has already been answered. "How so?" Since, in fact, an annihilation of suffering exists, one says thus that an unborn, unarisen, not-brought-about, unconditioned factor, etc., exists. Therefore there are no difficulties whatsoever.

So we have seen that according to the Sarvāstivādins liberation—*nirvāṇa*—is *suppression through knowledge*, i.e., a distinct real factor, which combines with the personality-stream and prevents the arising of defilements and thereby a new rebirth. According to the doctrine of the Sautrāntikas, however, *nirvāṇa* is nothing other than this nonarising of the defilements and of rebirth, hence a mere non-existence. Both views are completely clear and understandable <140> from within the respective systems. But the question of the nature of liberation and, in particular, of the state of the liberated one has not really been answered yet, since *suppression through knowledge* is only a factor that leads to liberation, but not liberation itself.

The texts are silent about the state of the liberated one though, whether because the attitude of the Buddha himself on this point continued to have an effect, or because it was a departure from the usual lines of thought to examine things from that perspective. Still a general knowledge of the doctrine makes it possible for us to answer even this question, and in the following way: As we have seen, according to the doctrine of the Sarvāstivādins the worldly personality consists of a stream of factors that constantly cease and arise anew, so long as the deeds *(karma)*, under the influence of the defilements, are active and entanglement in the cycle of existences continues. With the attainment of the liberating cognition, one obtains *suppression through knowledge*, a distinct factor that combines with the personality-stream and prevents any further arising of the defilements. As soon as the defilements no longer arise, however, the deeds lose the power to bring forth new factors. Thus if the present life expires, the personality-stream does not continue. No further rebirth occurs and liberation is attained.

Does this mean then that, since the personality-stream is interrupted, liberation brings annihilation? To answer this, we must call on a doctrine considered to be one of the most characteristic of the Sarvāstivādin school, and after which it is named: the doctrine *(vāda)* that everything exists *(sarvam asti)*. According to this doctrine, not only do the present factors exist, but all do, including those past and future; they are merely at different stages of time. The becoming and fading away of things is thus not a real arising and ceasing, but just a movement of the already existing factors from one stage of time to the other. The seemingly newly arising factors <141> move from the time-stage of the future to the time-stage of the present, and when they cease they move on to the time-stage of the past, just as one shifts a counting stone from the compartment for ones into the compartment for tens and hundreds, whereby its value changes but the stone itself always remains the same. Thus, in the personality-stream as well, the factors do not arise and cease. It is rather an actual stream that flows from the future into the past. Now, according to what has been said thus far, liberation signifies that the personality-stream is interrupted and does not continue any further. This means, given the above assumptions, that it passes once and for all into the past. It ends in a death-like state. It is not annihilated but it is appeased.

The conclusions for the doctrine of the Sautrāntikas, however, are different. Still their view of the nature of *suppression through knowledge* indicates no real fundamental difference, although it is true that for them *suppression through knowledge* is not a factor in its own right. Rather the personality-stream is transformed through the liberating cognition in such a way that the defilements can no longer arise in it, and only this non-arising is regarded as *suppression through knowledge.* But the outcome, the interruption of the personality-stream, is the same. Something else, however, is crucial. In contrast to the Sarvāstivādins, the Sautrāntikas deny the existence of what is in the past and the future. For them only that which is in the present is real. Thus for them, the becoming and fading away of the factors is not a movement from time-stage to time-stage but a real arising and a real annihilation. It follows from this, however, that upon its interruption the personality-stream ceases to exist. According to the Sautrāntika then, liberation is complete annihilation.

Hence we are faced with the strange fact that a doctrine of liberation holds up a death-like state, indeed complete annihilation, as its goal. Stranger still, is that this doctrine was able to win a huge following and achieved unparalleled success. We should not forget, however, that, in the case of the schools of <142> the Sarvāstivādins and Sautrāntikas, we are dealing only with particular trends in Buddhism, and that is, with extreme schools of thought, of which the Sautrāntikas in particular, in spite of their important intellectual accomplishments, were not wide-spread and before long merged with other schools. There were other trends though, that differed strongly from the aforementioned, in some cases even to the point of total direct opposition. It is from these schools of thought then that the movement arose that led Buddhism to its highest flowering and to which we will now turn, the Mahāyāna. <143>

The Schools of the Great Way (Mahāyāna)

C. # THE SCHOOLS OF THE GREAT WAY (MAHĀYĀNA)

The trends of the Śrāvakayāna that we discussed in the last section are characterized first and foremost by the fact that they are ruled by sober, clear, but also cold reason. This is most evident in the relegation of the practices of absorption to the background and the denial of an ultimate state of being (höchstes Sein) [S. 62, 118, 129]. The strong mystical element that was always powerful in Buddhism and that ultimately originates from the Buddha himself [S. 9f., 13ff.], however, could not simply be eliminated. There were always many members of the community for whom the experience of absorption was the essential point and who were more or less indifferent to dogmatic scholasticism. It is from these circles that the Mahāyāna emerged.

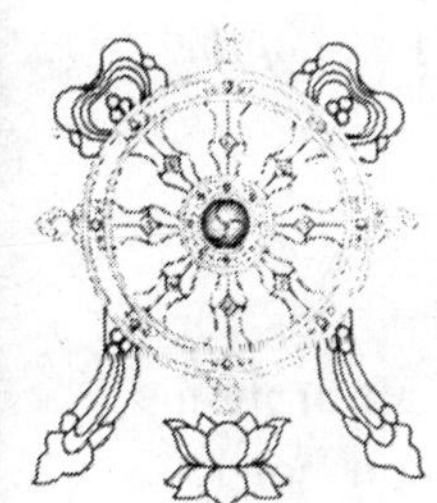

CA. ## *Main elements in the development of the Mahāyāna*

CAA. ### *The new goal of liberation*

There were actually several currents that united into the great movement of the Mahāyāna. The first of these concerns the doctrine of liberation, but we need only mention it briefly, since it is philosophically unimportant. It was, however, all the more important religiously and also gave the whole movement its name. With his teaching the Buddha had shown the path on which one finds liberation from the cycle of existences for oneself, but over time this was not enough for the enthusiastic followers. They wished also to bring salvation to others and they put forth as the highest goal to become a Buddha oneself, indeed even to renounce, at first, one's own liberation and to remain in the cycle of existences in order to be able to save others. It had already become customary to compare the doctrine with a raft that carries the disciple across the dangerous stream of existence to the safe shore of *nirvāṇa*, and thus the new doctrine, which was intended to save many, was designated as the Great Way (Mahāyāna). By contrast, the previous path of liberation was named the Way of Hearers (Śrāvakayāna). This new goal of liberation <144> naturally demanded a capacity for great enthusiasm and a willingness to make sacrifices, which, understandably, were more likely to be found in the circles of mystics than among the sober scholastics. Thus it was primarily the former who became the carriers of the new trend.

CAB. *The philosophical doctrine of an ultimate state of being and of the unreality of the phenomenal world*

The same circles, however, also provided the ground for the development of new philosophical thoughts. The impetus for this was largely twofold. The mystics who practiced absorption and experienced *nirvāṇa* even in this very body would not let go of their belief in an ultimate state of being, which they themselves had experienced in the state of absorption. And in addition, as so readily among mystics, one could see a tendency to consider this [highest] being as being the only true one and to declare everyday life as trivial, by comparison, and as a mere appearance. In this way came about the formation of philosophical doctrines that were centered on the questions of the ultimate state of being and of the reality of the external world. Little attention was paid to the constitution of the phenomenal world itself and with regard to it for the most part the views of the Śrāvakayāna scholasticism were left unchanged and adopted as needed.

The new buddhology

A third and final [element] was that, as a consequence of the new goal of liberation, the view of the personage of the Buddha also shifted. The historical personality became less important than the scholastic concept. The Buddha now appeared as a supranatural being whose activity reaches far beyond the limits of a single worldly existence, as an embodiment of the ultimate state of being. The multiplicity of the Buddhas gained special importance. Thus a specific buddhology developed that was anchored in the new philosophical doctrines.

These then are the three elements that were decisive in determining and dominating the development of the Mahāyāna:

- the new goal of liberation,
- the philosophical doctrine of an ultimate state of being and of the unreality of the phenomenal world and, lastly,
- the new buddhology.

Of these, the new goal of liberation led to the advancement of a new path of liberation that was discussed in a hugely prolific scholasticism of liberation and elaborated down to the smallest detail. <145> The presentation of this new path forms the topic of an entire literature. For the most part this literature is philosophically insignificant and need only occasionally be touched upon. All the more important then are the philosophical doctrines that are among the most significant contributions that Indian philosophy produced and with which we will therefore have to be primarily concerned. The buddhology will be discussed only insofar as it is closely tied to the philosophical doctrines and suitable to complete their depiction.

CB. *The beginnings of the Mahāyāna*

The earliest beginnings of the Mahāyāna developed while still within the framework of the old schools of the Śrāvakayāna, since the new goal of liberation did not represent a fundamental conflict. Any follower of the old schools could resolve to become a Buddha himself without deviating from the doctrine of his school. Only when the Mahāyāna developed complete doctrinal systems that were in some cases in sharp contradiction to the systems of the Śrāvakayāna, did the formation of independent schools of the Mahāyāna come about. Of course, not all Śrāvakayāna schools provided equally favorable possibilities of emergence for the Mahāyāna. Most unfavorable were likely the schools that were the principal upholders of Śrāvakayāna scholasticism, hence primarily the schools of the northwest. Far better were the conditions in the circles of the Mahāsāṃghika in the east. And it is, in fact, here that we find the various rudiments of the new development. In particular, the southern schools in the territory of the Āndhra empire and close to the old capital Dhānyakaṭaka on the lower reaches of the Kṛṣṇā proved to have tendencies toward the new movements. It is this land that could most convincingly claim to be the birthplace of the Mahāyāna.

cc. *The oldest literary documentation of the Mahāyāna*

The oldest literary documentation of the Mahāyāna are sutras. These are discourses whose words are laid in the mouth of the Buddha since, naturally, one sought to connect the new doctrine with the authority of the Buddha. Inwardly and outwardly, however, these sutras differ starkly from the sutras of the old canon. The often quite lively framework narratives have been replaced by formulaic settings. The audience is largely composed of supranatural beings and thousands and millions <146> of future Buddhas, of Bodhisattvas. Instead of sermons intended for a specific audience and circumstance, we find a colorless, uniform lecture. In terms of content, completely new doctrines are being taught, and everywhere the miraculous and the measureless dominate.

As for the difficulties that arose from putting completely different doctrines into the mouth of the Buddha, one then sought to remove them in the following way. Since ancient times the Buddha had been famed for his ability to adapt his teaching to the powers of comprehension of his audience. In reference to this it was now said that only some of the traditional sutras, primarily of course the new sutras, proclaimed the complete truth. The rest are intended for hearers who are not yet capable of grasping the complete truth, and are meant to lead them on the right path. They can therefore not be taken literally, but must rather be interpreted accordingly. This possibility for interpretation was then widely put to use and eventually a whole series of stages of various doctrinal proclamations came to be distinguished.

The sutra literature of the Mahāyāna is exceedingly abundant. From the beginning, new works were constantly created and the old ones expanded and reworked. In this way a nearly unfathomable number of such works was gradually accumulated. It is therefore not possible here to give even an approximate idea of this literature, besides, the present description is intended to primarily introduce the philosophers who are known as actual persons. Consequently, I provide only a few samples, [i.e., sections from the *Aṣṭasāhasrikā Prajñāpāramitā* and *Ratnakūṭa*,] from the oldest period, which are important for the understanding of the origin of the Mahāyāna doctrines, and then I turn right away [S. 170] to the historically known representatives of the different doctrines.

The Prajñāpāramitā literature and its philosophical doctrines

I begin with a group of works that carry the common name *Prajñāpāramitā (Perfection of Insight)*. Occasionally, individual titles also appear, but precisely the oldest and most important works of this group carry just the general name and are distinguished only according to their length. Accordingly, <147> there is first and foremost: a *Perfection of Insight in Eight Thousand Lines (Aṣṭasāhasrikā)*; a *Perfection of Insight in Twenty-five Thousand Lines (Pañcaviṃśatisāhasrikā)*; and a *Perfection of Insight in a Hundred Thousand Lines (Śatasāhasrikā)*. Anyone approaching these works unprepared will initially be taken aback and perhaps disappointed, since the doctrines expressed in them seem strange and nearly unintelligible at first. Their historical importance is, however, extremely great. In them the doctrine of the unreality of the external world [S. 149f.] is expressed for the first time. They had a decisive influence on the emergence of the first important Mahāyāna school, the school of the Mādhyamikas. Moreover, they have always belonged to the most sacred and most esteemed texts of the Mahāyāna. Thus at least a few short samples from one of the oldest texts, from the *Aṣṭasāhasrikā Prajñāpāramitā*, will be presented.

The home of the *Prajñāpāramitā* literature may be the land of Āndhra. Tradition, at least, reports that one of the southern schools of the Mahāsāṃghika possessed a *Prajñāpāramitā* in the vernacular. The founder of the Madhyamaka school, Nāgārjuna, seems to have been of particular importance in the development and propagation [of the *Prajñāpāramitā* literature]. Later as well, much in the old texts was reworked and changed and new texts were created. In terms of content, as with most of the Mahāyāna sutras, the texts dealt primarily with the career of a future Buddha, a Bodhisattva. The philosophical sections, however, take up a relatively large amount of space and form their actual core. Specifically, it is primarily the following thoughts that are present in the oldest texts.

CA.1. *Central philosophical thought: the idea of an ultimate state of being*

The idea of an ultimate state of being is central. This is the age-old idea alive in India since the time of the *Upaniṣads*. But it is not simply adopted here; it has instead been uniquely shaped through personal experience and couched in specific forms of expression.

In accordance with the general state of development in the context of Buddhism, the inconceivability and indeterminability of the ultimate state of being is most strongly emphasized. Only very rarely—in connection with an old view <148> that appears here and there in the canon and that was later taken up by the Mahāsaṃghikas—is it designated as stainless and luminous mind *(prabhāsvaraṃ cittam)*. In general, it is pointed out again and again that no characterizations of any kind apply to it. It is without arising and without ceasing, uncreated *(akṛta)* and unchanging *(avikāra)*, and has not come into existence at all *(anabhinirvṛtta).* It is unthinkable, unweighable, unmeasurable, uncountable, and unequalled. It is boundless, i.e., without start, without center, and without end, and thus spatially unbounded. It is, however, also without beginning, without present, and without finish, and thus exists outside of the three periods of time. In brief, it is by nature pure *(viśuddha)* and apart *(vivikta)* from all characterizations. It is therefore also unimaginable *(avikalpa)* and in it no processes of cognizance take place. Due to its boundlessness and inconceivability it is readily compared to empty space.

A further consequence of this is that it is also untouched by all events within the phenomenal world. It is not bound and not released, not stained and not purified, and also does not, for its part, produce any effect. Whether it is recognized or not, does not affect it. It does not flourish if it is taught, and does not decline if it is not taught.

The expressions *nature of factors (dharmāṇāṃ dharmatā), element of the factors (dharmadhātu),* and also *pinnacle of the real (bhūtakoṭi),* often appear as designations for the ultimate state of being. More characteristic and also very popular is the designation *suchness (tathatā),* which first appears in canonical scriptures, and which here seems to express the inconceivable nature of the ultimate state of being equal only to itself and which later was seen as an expression for its unchangingness. Finally, the designations *emptiness (śūnyatā), signless (ānimitta),* and the *wishless (apraṇihita)*—all already used in the Śrāvakayāna, albeit in a different sense—although rarer, are even more distinctive, since the indeterminability of the ultimate state of being is most strongly emphasized in these concepts. Their importance is accentuated <149> by the fact that they and their contemplation are known as the *gates to liberation (vimokṣamukha).*

As the nature of all entities, this ultimate state of being is also the nature of the Buddha *(tathāgatatva).* It is omniscience *(sarvajñatā)* and the perfection of insight *(prajñāpāramitā).*

CCA.2. *The unreality of the phenomenal world and its relationship to the ultimate state of being*

In contrast to this stands the phenomenal world, which is not real. This is not further explained [S. 171] since this view apparently rests on the sense—so alive among mystics—of the vanity of everything worldly, as compared to the true state of being that they have experienced in the state of absorption. This non-reality of the phenomenal world is expressed quite sharply and starkly. Things do not exist and cannot be established, that is, not at all and in no way. They are namely free *(virahita)* and apart *(vivikta)* from any intrinsic nature *(svabhāva),* from the intrinsic nature of that which characterizes *(lakṣaṇa)* and that which is characterized *(lakṣya).*. They are therefore nothing, and their nature *(prakṛti)* is a non-nature *(aprakṛti).* That which we believe we have recognized is mere words *(nāmadheyamātra)* and resembles a magical illusion *(māyā),* a dream and a mere echo.

But as the things are unreal and apart from all signs, no characterizations of any kind apply to them. They are unborn and uncreated, without arising and ceasing. They are unthinkable, unweighable, unmeasurable, uncountable, and unequalled. And they are unlimited and without past, future, and present. In this way the statements about the phenomenal world coincide with those about the ultimate state of being, and the things seem themselves to be the ultimate state of being, as it were. Thus it is necessary to determine the relationship between the two, but this presents difficulties. At every attempt it can only be said that they are different and yet not different. The characterizations attributed to the ultimate state of being such as, for example, non-arising and non-ceasing, are not [the same as] the five groups [that arise and fade away]. And yet [these characterizations] and the five groups are not two. In the same way, the ultimate state of being itself is not the same as the five groups, but it is also not to be sought outside of them. <150>

Now since, as mentioned above, the phenomenal world is not real and all characterizations related to it are invalid, there is also no bondage and no liberation, and all concepts connected with liberation are futile. For this reason there is no attainment and beholding of the truth. Even the turning of the wheel of the teachings by the Buddha does not apply.

How then under these circumstances does the phenomenal world come about, and how are we supposed to deal with it? The answer is: [The phenomenal world] is based on an illusion, on the false ideas of worldly individuals. As already mentioned, it resembles a magical illusion, and when, for example, a Bodhisattva liberates beings, this is the same as when a magician allows his self-created illusions to disappear. In order to free oneself from this illusion, one should not entertain it. One should not cling to it, support oneself with it, and tarry within it. Every grasping to words *(nāman)* and signs *(nimitta)*, indeed their mere usage, is, however, already clinging. Even the thought that entities are natureless and empty, any attempt to capture the ultimate state of being in concepts and words, entails entanglement and should be abandoned. The only correct conduct is to remain in complete apartness *(viviktatā)* and non-perception *(anupalambha)*, as it occurs in the state of absorption. The enormously difficult task of a Bodhisattva consists in remaining in the phenomenal world in order to fulfill his task and yet to maintain this apartness.

These are in essence the philosophical doctrines of the older *Prajñāpāramitā* texts. These doctrines are, however, not presented in a coherent manner; they appear as fragmentary single thoughts and points of views, according to their relevance to the conduct of a Bodhisattva, since this is and remains the principal subject of the texts. This naturally makes the thoughts more difficult to comprehend. There is in addition a certain archaic quality [to these texts]. There is still a sense of wrestling with the thoughts and their expression. In the end, mysticism always loves the mysterious. And here this finds expression in the manner of lapsing into stark formulations that surprise the hearer and <151> remain at first incomprehensible to him. This explains the oddity and the difficulty of these texts. A good example of this is provided by the very beginning of the *Aṣṭasāhasrikā Prajñāpāramitā.* The text is as follows:

CA.3. *From the "Perfection of Insight in Eight Thousand Lines" (Aṣṭasāhasrikā Prajñāpāramitā)*

From chapter I

Thus have I heard. Once the Exalted One was dwelling at Rājagṛha on Gṛdhrakūṭa [Vulture Peak] Mountain together with a great gathering of monks, with twelve hundred and fifty monks, all saints *(arhan),* whose (negative) influxes had vanished, who were free of defilements, masters of themselves, with a liberated mind, liberated insight, like well-trained horses, like great serpents, who had done what was to be done, who had accomplished what was to be accomplished, who had cast off the burden, who had attained their goal, in whom the fetters [binding them] to existence had vanished, whose minds were liberated through right knowledge, who had attained the highest perfection of control of the entire mind, with the exception of one single person, that is, the venerable Ānanda.

Then the Exalted One spoke to the venerable elder Subhūti: "Recall, Subhūti—regarding the perfection of insight of the Bodhisattvas, the great beings—how the Bodhisattvas, the great beings, arrive at the perfection of insight." . . .

Then the venerable Subhūti, through the power of the Buddha, spoke to the Exalted One as follows: "The Exalted One

<152> spoke in the following way: 'Recall, Subhūti—regarding the perfection of insight of the Bodhisattvas, the great beings—how the Bodhisattvas, the great beings, arrive at the perfection of insight.' Here, O Exalted One, the expression *Bodhisattva* is used. For what factor, O Exalted One, does the expression *Bodhisattva* serve as designation? I do not see, O Exalted One, any factor called *Bodhisattva*. I also do not see, O Exalted One, any factor by the name *perfection of insight*. Therefore, since I neither find, nor observe, nor see a Bodhisattva or a factor called *Bodhisattva*, nor find, nor observe, nor see a perfection of insight, to what kind of Bodhisattva should I instruct or teach and about what kind of perfection of insight?

If, moreover, O Exalted One, with respect to such words, teaching, and instruction, the mind of a Bodhisattva does not founder, does not collapse, become alarmed, fall into dismay, if the backbone of his thinking is not removed, not broken, if he does not tremble, shake, and begin to quiver, then this Bodhisattva, this great being, is to be taught the perfection of insight. This is to be understood to be the perfection of insight of this Bodhisattva, of this great being. This is the instruction in the perfection of insight. If he abides in this way, then this is his instruction and his teaching.

If, moreover, O Exalted One, a Bodhisattva, a great being, engages in the perfection of insight and practices in the perfection of insight, then he should train himself in such a way that, in the course of this training, he also does not entertain an opinion with respect to the thought of enlightenment *(bodhicitta)*. For what <153> reason? Because this thought is no thought;[1] for the nature of mind *(citta)* is luminously pure *(prabhāsvara)*."

---

[1] The thought of enlightenment *(bodhicitta)* is a moment of cognition *(citta = vijñāna)*. But since cognition in its apparent form is not real, it is no real cognition, hence, non-cognition.

Then the venerable Śāriputra spoke to the venerable Subhūti as follows: "Does, venerable Subhūti, this thought of which (you say) that it is no thought, exist at all?"

In answer to these words, the venerable Subhūti said the following to the venerable Śāriputra: "Can one, venerable Śāriputra, with respect to this *being no thought (acittatā)*, find or observe an existence or non-existence?"

Śāriputra spoke: "No, venerable Subhūti."

Subhūti spoke: "But if, venerable Śāriputra, with respect to this *being no thought*, an existence or non-existence cannot be found or observed, then is your question justifiable, when you ask: 'Does this thought of which (you say) that it is no thought, exist at all?' "

In answer to these words the venerable Śāriputra said the following to the venerable Subhūti: "Of what kind, venerable Subhūti, is this *being no thought?*"

Subhūti spoke: "Unchanging, venerable Śāriputra, and unimaginable *(avikalpa)* is the *being no thought.*"

Then the venerable Śāriputra applauded the venerable Subhūti: "Splendid, venerable Subhūti, you have demonstrated this splendidly, you who have been designated by the Exalted One as the most excellent among those who abide in the state without quarrel."

Now I will provide a few more examples of how the ideas presented above [S. 147–50] are dealt with in the same text. The first section [chap. II] discusses the perfection of insight, and in particular its infinity, in the same terms as the ultimate state of being, since the perfection <154> of insight is identical in nature with the ultimate state of being. After that, the concept of a being *(sattva)* is discussed in addition and it is shown to be empty and vain.

From chapter II

In answer to these words, Śakra, the ruler among gods, spoke to the venerable Subhūti as follows: "This perfection of insight, noble Subhūti, is a great perfection. [This perfection of insight, noble Subhūti, is an immeasurable perfection.] This perfection of insight, noble Subhūti, is a limitless perfection. This perfection of insight, noble Subhūti, is an infinite perfection."

The elder, Subhūti, spoke: "Thus it is, Kauśika, thus it is. This perfection of insight, Kauśika, is a great perfection. This perfection of insight, Kauśika, is an immeasurable perfection. This perfection of insight, Kauśika, is a limitless perfection. This perfection of insight, Kauśika, is an infinite perfection. "For what reason?" The perfection of insight, Kauśika, is a great perfection due to the greatness of form. In the same way, the perfection of insight, Kauśika, is a great perfection due to the greatness of sensation, of ideation, of formations, and of cognition. The perfection of insight, Kauśika, is an immeasurable perfection due to the immeasurability of form. In the same, way, the perfection of insight, Kauśika, is an immeasurable perfection due to the immeasurability of sensation, of ideation, of formations, and of cognition. The perfection of insight, Kauśika, is a limitless perfection due to the limitlessness of form. In the same, way, the perfection of insight, Kauśika, is a limitless perfection due to the limitlessness of <155> sensation, of ideation, of formations, and of cognition. The perfection of insight, Kauśika, is an infinite perfection due to the infinity of form. In the same way, the perfection of insight, Kauśika, is an infinite perfection due to the infinity of sensation, of ideation, of formations, and of cognition. At the same time, Kauśika, one does not entertain the thought: '[The perfection of insight] is a great perfection.' One does not entertain the thought: 'It is an immeasurable perfection,' 'It is a limitless perfection,' and 'It is an infinite perfection.' Therefore, Kauśika, the perfection of insight is a great perfection, an immeasurable perfection, a limitless perfection, and an infinite perfection.

The perfection of insight, Kauśika, is an infinite perfection due to the infinity of the object-support *(ārambaṇa)*. The perfection of insight, Kauśika, is an infinite perfection due to the infinity of beings *(sattva)*. Why, Kauśika, is the perfection of insight an infinite perfection due to the infinity of the object-support? Since for all factors, Kauśika, no beginning, no middle, and no end are to be observed, therefore, Kauśika, the perfection of insight is an infinite perfection. The perfection of insight due to the infinity of the object-support, Kauśika, is, in this way, an infinite perfection. Further, since, Kauśika, all factors are infinite and unlimited, and as a beginning, a middle, and an end are not to be observed in them, therefore, Kauśika, the perfection of insight <156> is an infinite perfection. For what reason? With respect to form, Kauśika, a beginning, a middle, and an end are not to be observed. Just so, Kauśika, with respect to sensation, ideation, formations, and cognition, a beginning, a middle, and an end are not to be observed. The perfection of insight due to the infinity of the object-support, Kauśika, is, in this way, an infinite perfection. Further, Kauśika, beings are infinite and unlimited. For what reason? With respect to beings, a beginning, a middle, and an end are namely not to be observed. Therefore, Kauśika, the perfection of insight due to the infinity of beings is an infinite perfection."

Then Śakra, the ruler among gods, spoke to the venerable Subhūti as follows: "In what respect, venerable Subhūti, is the perfection of insight due to the infinity of beings an infinite perfection?"

The elder, Subhūti, spoke: "Not because of the impossibility of counting, Kauśika, nor because of the magnitude of counting is the perfection of insight due to the infinity of beings an infinite perfection."

Śakra spoke: "Then in what respect, noble Subhūti, is the perfection of insight due to the infinity of beings an infinite perfection?"

The elder, Subhūti, spoke: "What do you think, Kauśika, for what factor does the term *being* serve as a designation?"

Śakra spoke: "For no factor, noble Subhūti, and for no non-factor does the term *being* serve as a designation. The term *being* is used as an adventitious designation, it is used as a baseless designation, it is used as an essenceless designation, it is used as a designation without an object-support.

The elder, Subhūti, spoke: "What do you think, Kauśika,
<157> did any kind of proclamation of beings take place here?"

Śakra spoke: "No, noble Subhūti."

Subhūti spoke: "Where no proclamation of beings took place, Kauśika, what kind of infinity of beings is there? If, Kauśika, the Perfected One, the Saint, the perfectly Enlightened One should utter the word *being* with the sound of infinite speech, with a sonorous voice for as many cosmic aeons as the Ganges river contains grains of sand, [then] has, because of that, any kind of being arisen, will it arise, or is it arising, has it been annihilated, will it be annihilated, or is it being annihilated?"

Śakra spoke: "No, noble Subhūti. For what reason? Because beings are pure from the beginning and purified from the beginning."

Subhūti spoke: "In this way then, Kauśika, the perfection of insight due to the infinity of beings is an infinite perfection. And so, Kauśika, is the infinity of the perfection of insight due to the infinity of beings to be understood."

The next section (chap. XXII) deals with the question of the coming about of the phenomenal world and tries to show that it is based only on a fallacy.

From chapter XXII

Subhūti spoke: "If all factors, O Exalted One, are apart [from characterizations] and all factors are empty, how is it then, O Exalted One, that the idea of the pollution of beings comes about, how is it then, O Exalted One, that the idea of the purification of beings comes about? For something that is apart, O Exalted One, cannot be polluted, something that is apart, O Exalted One, cannot be purified. Something that is empty, O Exalted One, cannot be polluted, something that is empty, O Exalted One, cannot be purified. Something that is apart <158> or something that is empty does not attain the highest perfect enlightenment. Except for [apartness and] emptiness, O Exalted One, there is, however, no factor to be observed that has attained, will attain, or is attaining the highest perfect enlightenment. Or how should we, O Exalted One, understand the meaning of these words? Explain it, O Exalted One, explain it, O Perfected One!"

In answer to these words, the Exalted One spoke to venerable Subhūti as follows: "What do you think, Subhūti, do beings walk for a long time in the belief in an 'I' and in the belief in a 'mine'?"

Subhūti spoke: "Thus it is, O Exalted One, thus it is, O Perfected One. Beings walk for a long time in the belief in an 'I' and in the belief in a 'mine.' "

The Exalted One spoke: "What do you think, Subhūti, is the belief in an 'I' and the belief in a 'mine' empty?"

Subhūti spoke: "They are empty, O Exalted One, they are empty, O Perfected One."

The Exalted One spoke: "What do you think, Subhūti, do beings travel in the cycle of existences due to the belief in an 'I' and due to the belief in a 'mine'?"

Subhūti spoke: "Thus it is, O Exalted One, thus it is, O Perfected One. Beings travel in the cycle of existences due to the belief in an 'I' and due to the belief in a 'mine.' "

The Exalted One spoke: "Then the idea of the pollution of beings comes about in this way. If one assumes beings and clings to them, then the pollution takes place, and yet no one is defiled by this. If, on the other hand, Subhūti, one assumes nothing and clings to nothing, then the idea of a belief in an 'I' and a belief in a 'mine' does not come about. The idea of the purification of beings, Subhūti, comes about in this way. If one does not assume beings and does not cling to them, then purification takes place, and yet no one is purified by this. <159> A Bodhisattva, Subhūti, a great being who walks in this way, walks in the perfection of insight. The idea of the pollution and the purification of beings, Subhūti, comes about in this way, even though all factors are apart and all factors are empty."

The following section (chap. I) presents the comparison of the phenomenal world and also especially of the process of liberation to a magical illusion.

From chapter I

Then the venerable Subhūti spoke to the Exalted One as follows: "It is said, O Exalted One, 'armed with a great armor, armed with a great vehicle.' In which manner, O Exalted One, is a Bodhisattva, a great being, *armed with a great armor?*"

The Exalted One spoke: "A Bodhisattva, a great being, Subhūti, has the thought: 'Immeasurable beings are to be led by me to liberation, innumerable beings are to be led by me to liberation.' And yet there is no one by whom they are to be led to liberation, and no one who is to be led to liberation. Still he leads these many beings to liberation. Nevertheless, there is no being that is liberated, and no being by whom it is led to liberation. For what reason? This nature of things *(dharmatā dharmāṇām)*, Subhūti, is based on the nature of a magical illusion. Say, for example, Subhūti, a skilled magician or magician's apprentice at a great crossroad creates a great crowd of people, and after he has created them, he makes this crowd of people disappear again. What do you think now, Subhūti? Has anybody thereby been killed, died, <160> been destroyed, or been made to disappear by anyone?"

Subhūti spoke: "No, O Exalted One."

The Exalted One spoke: "Just so, Subhūti, does a Bodhisattva, a great being, lead immeasurable and innumerable beings to liberation. And yet there is no being that is liberated and no being by whom it is led to liberation. If then, a Bodhisattva, a great being, when he hears the exposition of this teaching, does not tremble, shake, and begin to quiver, then, Subhūti, this Bodhisattva, this great being, is to be regarded as *armed with a great armor.*"

In conclusion, I will render a last section [chap. VIII], which deals with clinging to objects of the phenomenal world and which finishes with valuable remarks about the nature of things and the ultimate state of being.

From chapter VIII

Then the venerable Śāriputra spoke to the venerable Subhūti as follows: "Of what type, venerable Subhūti, is this clinging *[saṅga]?"*

Subhūti spoke: "The thought, venerable Śāriputra, that form is empty is clinging. In the same way, venerable Śāriputra, the thought that sensation, ideation, formations, and cognition are empty is clinging. If one thinks of past factors that they are past factors, then this is clinging. If one thinks of future factors that they are future factors, then this is clinging. If one thinks of present factors that they are present factors, then this is clinging. And if one thinks that an individual who is within the vehicle of the Bodhisattvas earns such and such an amount of merit due to the first arousing of the thought (of enlightenment), then this is clinging. <161>

Then Śakra, the ruler among gods, spoke to the venerable Subhūti as follows: "How, noble Subhūti, is it clinging?"

Subhūti said: "If, Kauśika, one thinks about the thought of enlightenment: 'This is the first thought of enlightenment,' then it is directed (toward the highest perfect enlightenment) with the thought: 'I direct it toward the highest perfect enlightenment.' But the nature of mind cannot be directed, be it by the noble son, be it by the noble daughter, who are within the Great Way. Therefore, Kauśika, if one teaches another about the highest perfect enlightenment, tries to lead, rouse, and inspire him, then one has to teach, lead, rouse, and inspire him in accordance with the truth. For in this way, the noble son or noble daughter does not harm him- or herself and leads others in the manner approved by the Buddha (to the highest perfect enlightenment). At the same time, he avoids all these millions of types of clinging."

Then the Exalted One applauded the venerable Subhūti: "Splendid, splendid, Subhūti, you who teaches the Bodhisattvas, the great beings, about these millions of types of clinging! I wish therefore to proclaim to you yet other, more subtle types of clinging. So listen and pay good and close attention! I will speak to you."

"Good, Exalted One," the venerable Subhūti answered the Exalted One.

The Exalted One spoke as follows: "Here, Subhūti, a faithful noble son or noble daughter observes the Perfected One, the Saint, the Perfectly Enlightened One based on a mark *(nimitta)*. But for as many marks as exist, Subhūti, there are so many types of clinging. For what reason? Because clinging, Subhūti, results from the mark. By thinking: 'I rejoice <162> in the uncontaminated qualities of the past, future, and present exalted Buddhas,' with the thought: 'I will direct this root of good toward the highest perfect enlightenment,' he directs this (root of good)—accompanied by rejoicing and by the object of rejoicing—(toward the highest perfect enlightenment). The nature of the factors, Subhūti, is, however, neither past, future, nor present. But that which is neither past, future, nor present, is apart from the three time periods. And what is apart from the three time periods cannot be directed, cannot serve as a mark or as an object-support. And it is neither seen, nor heard, nor thought of, nor cognized.

Subhūti spoke: "Profound, O Exalted One, is the nature of the factors."

The Exalted One spoke: "Because of their apartness, Subhūti."

Subhūti spoke: "The perfection of insight, O Exalted One, is profound by nature."

The Exalted One spoke: "The perfection of insight, Subhūti, is profound by nature, because it is pure by nature, because it is apart by nature."

Subhūti said: "The perfection of insight, O Exalted One, is apart by nature. I pay my respect, O Exalted One, to the perfection of insight."

The Exalted One spoke: "All factors, also, Subhūti, are apart by nature. And this apartness by nature of all factors is the perfection of insight. For what reason? Because all factors, Subhūti, have been seen as uncreated by the Perfected One, the Saint, the Perfectly Enlightened One."

Subhūti spoke: "Therefore, O Exalted One, all factors have not been seen by the Perfected One, the Saint, the Perfectly Enlightened One." <163>

The Exalted One spoke: "Because, Subhūti, the factors are by nature nothing. [This is so] for their nature is a non-nature and the non-nature is their nature, because all factors have only one characteristic *(lakṣaṇa)*, that is, characteristiclessness. Therefore, Subhūti, all factors have not been seen by the Perfected One, the Saint, the Perfectly Enlightened One. For what reason? Because, Subhūti, there are not two natures of factors, for the nature of all factors, Subhūti, is only one. And this nature of all factors, Subhūti, is a non-nature, and this non-nature is their nature. In this way, Subhūti, all of these millions of types of clinging have been avoided."

These examples will suffice to give at least a brief glimpse of the rich literature of the *Prajñāpāramitā* texts. From the wealth of the remaining old Mahāyāna sutras I select as a sample only a single work, the *Jewel Heap (Ratnakūṭa).*[1] This work owes its special significance to the fact that in it, for the first time, an idea that was of decisive importance to the appearance of the Madhyamaka system is developed in detail, that is, the idea of the middle way. The Buddha himself had called his doctrine the *middle way*, as it steers the middle course between the extremes of a life of ease and of excessive asceticism. This concept was also quickly buttressed by philosophical ideas. Even early in the canon we find a discourse, the *Instruction of Kātyāyana (Kātyāyanāvavāda)*, in which the Buddha rejects as extremes the views that everything exists and that nothing exists, and confronts these with his doctrine as the middle doctrine. Similar ideas also appear in the *Prajñāpāramitā* works. In itself this is nothing new. The rejection of opposites is widespread in the philosophical world of thought in India <164> and especially since the time of the *Upaniṣads* it is common, in attempts to define the ultimate state of being, to reject all definitions based on opposed concepts. In the *Ratnakūṭa,* however, this thought is accorded its full significance and deliberately made the central point. The right contemplation of the ultimate state of being consists precisely of the fundamental negation

[1] This is the name of the old sutra. In later times an entire group of sutras was brought together under this name and within this group the old text was given the title "Kāśyapa-section" *(Kāśyapaparivarta).*

of all opposing characterizations, and this alone is the right doctrine, the middle way. The idea of the middle way therefore decisively determines the entire formation of the doctrine here. In addition, next to this basic idea, the non-involvement of the ultimate state of being in any process of the phenomenal world is also emphasized in the strongest terms. The stern exhortation is also spoken not to adhere to conventional concepts, since exactly this essencelessness of entities, when taken as a doctrine in the conventional sense, brings about the most fateful bondage.

The *Ratnakūṭa* belongs to the oldest Mahāyāna sutras. It was translated into Chinese as early as the second century c.e. and therefore still falls within the period before the creation of the Madhyamaka system by Nāgārjuna. In comparison to the works of the *Prajñāpāramitā* literature, however, it represents a fundamental advance. In contrast to the disjointed and mysteriously abruptly expounded teachings of the *Prajñāpāramitā,* we find here a train of thought that is systematically followed through, and the thoughts themselves are more deeply developed and better elaborated. It should also be noted in passing that a large part of the work deals with questions about the doctrine of liberation, which are, however, of no import for us here.

From the "Jewel Heap" (Ratnakūṭa)

§ 52

"A Bodhisattva, Kāśyapa, who wishes to train himself in this proclamation of the doctrine, the great *Jewel Heap,* must apply right effort toward the doctrine. What, Kāśyapa, is right effort toward the doctrine? <165> The regarding of all factors in accordance with truth. What, Kāśyapa, is the regarding of all factors in accordance with truth? If, Kāśyapa, they are not regarded as a self, if they are not regarded as a being, nor as a soul, nor as humans, nor as a person, nor as a man, nor as a human being, then, Kāśyapa, this is called the *middle way, the regarding of factors in accordance with truth.*

§ 53

This also, Kāśyapa, is the middle way, the regarding of factors in accordance with truth. If form is not regarded as permanent nor as non-permanent, if sensation, ideation, formations, and cognition are not regarded as permanent nor as non-permanent, then, Kāśyapa, this is called the *middle way, the regarding of factors in accordance with truth.*

§ 54

If the element of earth is not regarded as permanent and not as non-permanent, if the element of water, the element of fire, and the element of wind are not regarded as permanent nor as non-permanent, if the element of space and the element of cognition are not regarded as permanent and not as non-permanent, then this, Kāśyapa, is called the *middle way, the regarding of factors in accordance with truth.*

[. . .]

§ 56

Permanent, Kāśyapa, that is one extreme. *Non-permanent*, Kāśyapa, that is a second extreme. What lies in the middle between these <166> two, the permanent and the non-permanent, is formless, unshowable, without appearing image, without cognizance, without support, and without sign. This, Kāśyapa, is called the *middle way, the regarding of factors in accordance with truth.*

§ 57

Self (ātman), Kāśyapa, that is one extreme. *Non-self (nairātmya)*, Kāśyapa, that is a second extreme. What lies in the middle between these two, the self and the non-self, is formless, unshowable, without appearing image, without cognizance, without support, and without sign. This, Kāśyapa, is called the *middle way, the regarding of factors in accordance with truth.*

§ 58

Correct cognition (bhūtacitta), Kāśyapa, that is one extreme. *Incorrect cognition,* Kāśyapa, that is a second extreme. Where there is, Kāśyapa, no mind *[cetanā]* and no thinking *[manas]* and no cognition *[vijñāna],* that, Kāśyapa, is called the *middle way, the regarding of factors in accordance with truth.*

§ 59

Likewise, Kāśyapa, with respect to all factors, [whether] wholesome and unwholesome, mundane and supramundane, blameworthy and blameless, contaminated and uncontaminated, conditioned and unconditioned, *pollution* is one extreme, *purification* a second extreme. Not-adopting, not-communicating, and not-expressing these two extremes, that, Kāśyapa, is called the *middle way, the regarding of factors in accordance with truth.* <167>

§ 60

Existence, Kāśyapa, that is one extreme. *Non-existence,* Kāśyapa, that is a second extreme. What lies in the middle between these two extremes is called, Kāśyapa, the *middle way, the regarding of factors in accordance with truth.*

§§ 61–62

That which I have also told you, Kāśyapa—that dependent on ignorance, volitional formations *(saṃskāra)* come into being; dependent on volitional formations, cognition; dependent on cognition, name and form; dependent on name and form, the sixfold sphere; dependent on the sixfold sphere, contact; dependent on contact, sensation; dependent on sensation, thirst; dependent on thirst, grasping; dependent on grasping, becoming; dependent on becoming, birth; dependent on birth, old age and death, sorrow and lamentation, pain, distress, and despair; and that thus the origin of this whole great mass of suffering comes about; that, further, through the cessation of ignorance the volitional formations cease; through the cessation of the volitional formations, cognition; through the cessation of cognition, name and form; through the cessation of name and form, the sixfold sphere; through the cessation of the sixfold sphere, contact; through the cessation of contact, sensation; through the cessation of sensation, thirst; through the cessation of thirst, grasping; through the cessation of grasping, becoming; through the cessation of becoming, birth; through the cessation of birth, old age and death, sorrow and lamentation, pain, distress, and despair; and that thus the cessation of this whole great mass of suffering <168> comes about—in this, Kāśyapa, knowledge and ignorance are not two things and do not constitute a duality. And this cognition, Kāśyapa, is called the *middle way, the regarding of factors in accordance with truth.*

Likewise, formations and the non-formations *(asaṃskṛta);* the cognition and the cessation of cognition; name and form and the cessation of name and form; the sixfold sphere and the cessation of the sixfold sphere; contact and the cessation of contact; sensation and the cessation of sensation; thirst and the cessation of thirst; grasping and the cessation of grasping; becoming and the cessation of becoming; birth and the cessation of birth; old age and the cessation of old age are not two things and do not constitute a duality. And this cognition, Kāśyapa, is called the *middle way, the regarding of factors in accordance with truth.*

§ 63

This also, Kāśyapa, is the *middle way, the regarding of factors in accordance with truth:* that one does not make the factors empty through emptiness but, rather, the factors themselves are empty; that one does not make the factors signless through the signless but, rather, the factors themselves are signless; that one does not make the factors wishless through the wishless, but, rather, the factors themselves are wishless; that one does not make the factors unformed through non-formation, but, rather, the factors themselves are unformed; that one does not make the factors unarisen through non-arising, but, rather, the factors themselves are unarisen; that one does not make the factors unborn through not being born, but, <169> rather, the factors themselves are unborn; and that one does not make the factors essenceless through essencelessness *(asvabhāvatā)*, but, rather, the factors themselves are essenceless. This regarding, Kāśyapa, is called the *middle way, the regarding of factors in accordance with truth.*

§ 64

Further, Kāśyapa, emptiness does not lead to the destruction of the person. Emptiness is, rather, itself empty. It is empty at the beginning, empty at the end, and empty in the present. Turn toward emptiness, Kāśyapa, and not toward the person *[pudgala]!* Those, however, Kāśyapa, who turn toward emptiness by conceiving of emptiness, those, Kāśyapa, I call lost and completely lost to this doctrine. The profession of the belief *(dṛṣṭi)* in a person—may this [belief] be as large as Sumeru, mountain of gods—is better than the belief in emptiness in a person who entertains this afflicted view. For what reason? For all types of beliefs, Kāśyapa, emptiness is indeed the way out. Whosoever believes in emptiness, however, Kāśyapa, how will he find the way out?

§ 65

If, for example, Kāśyapa, a man were sick and the physician were to give him a medicine and this medicine were to drive out the agents of disease yet itself remained in the stomach and did not come out—what do you think, Kāśyapa, would this sick person be freed from sickness?"

He said: "No, Exalted One. The sickness of this man in whom the medicine drives out all agents of disease yet itself remains in the stomach and does not come out would be even more serious."

The Exalted One spoke: "Just so, Kāśyapa, <170> emptiness is the way out for all types of beliefs. Whoever believes in emptiness, however, Kāśyapa, him I call incurable."

These examples from the old sutra literature show how far the philosophical development of thoughts in the Mahāyāna had already advanced by the beginning of the common era. The views about the unreality of the external world and about the nature of the highest reality had already taken shape and different fundamental lines of thought were clearly and systematically followed through. With this, however, no philosophical system has yet been created. This task was first undertaken by a man who is one of the most important figures in Buddhism and in Indian philosophical history as a whole: Nāgārjuna.

CD. *The Madhyamaka school*

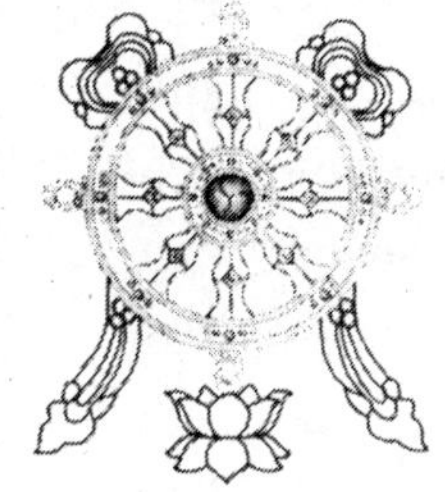

CDA. *Nāgārjuna (ca. 200 c.e.)*

The life of Nāgārjuna, the founder of the first philosophical school of the Mahāyāna, the school of the Mādhyamika, is so overgrown with legends that it is difficult to peel it down to a historical core. It is not only that legend has made him into a magician and alchemist, but reports about other persons of the same name are also merged with the traditional accounts of him, so that only by conjecture can we sift out the little that is genuine. So if we are to trust tradition, his home was Vidarbha, today's Berār in Central India, but he seems to have spent the greatest part of his life in South India, in the Āndhra empire, where he enjoyed the favor and friendship of one of the last kings of the Śātavāhana dynasty. He spent the last days of his life on [mount] Śrī Parvata on the banks of the Kṛṣṇā (Kistna).

CDA.1. *The works of Nāgārjuna*

Just as uncertain as the reports about his life are those about his literary activity. In the course of time an entire literature has been put under his name, which includes not only works that wrongly bear his name, but also works of other <171> authors with the same name. The basic text of the Madhyamaka school, the *Madhyamakakārikā (Mnemonic Verses of the Middle Doctrine)*, is generally considered to be his work. Next to it stand a number of works whose genuineness is highly probable. Far greater though is the number of works whose authorship remains questionable and must still be clarified. In the following selection I will therefore present primarily sections from the *Madhyamakakārikā*. In addition, I provide samples only from two works, [the *Vigrahavyāvartanī* and the *Ratnāvalī*,] whose genuineness seems assured to me. The following brief presentation of Nāgārjuna's doctrine is also based exclusively on the *Madhyamakakārikā*.

CDA.2. *The philosophical system of Nāgārjuna*

As we have already noted, Nāgārjuna was the first to create a Mahāyāna philosophical system, but this does not mean a system in the later sense. It is not a systematically presented complete edifice, as the time was not yet ripe for such system. He did try, however, to give an exact proof of the unreality of the external[1] world, which had merely been asserted in the *Prajñāpāramitā* [S. 149f.]. He also developed and defined the decisive fundamental concepts of the Madhyamaka school. Systematically arranged, the views that he maintained look roughly like this:

CDA.2.1. *The unreality of the external world*

His main goal is the proof of the unreality of the external world. To this end he replaces the mere assertions of the *Prajñāpāramitā* with proper inferences by demonstrating with bold logic that the most ordinary concepts of daily life are impossible, and that the phenomenal world as it presents itself to us—precisely because it rests on these concepts—is impossible. In his principal work, the *Madhyamakakārikā*, he pours out a whole abundance of such

---

1 [Here, and occasionally also below, Frauwallner uses the term external world in a more general way as referring to the entirety of the phenomenal world. However, later when starting to discuss differences between the Madhyamaka and Yogācāra, as for example on S. 248, he distinguishes more clearly between external world and phenomenal world.]

inferences before the reader, such that their initial impact is bewildering. Still, there is no lack of a core of solid views underlying this bewildering abundance.

CDA.2.1.1. *The phenomenal world as dependent origination*

Before all else, Nāgārjuna laid down a definite fundamental view of the nature of the phenomenal world. When the subject of the phenomenal world came up, the *Prajñāpāramitā* had usually spoken of the five groups. Nāgārjuna replaces this with dependent origination *(pratītyasamutpāda).* <172> When considering the external world, since the time of the Buddha himself, its impermanence had stood in the foreground [S. 63ff., 101ff.]. The nature of the world was seen above all in the continuous becoming and ceasing that is governed by the law of dependent origination [S. 26–60]. For Nāgārjuna then, this very law of dependent arising appeared to be the appropriate formula through which to express the nature of the phenomenal world. His inferences thus also address this dependent origination.

CDA.2.1.2. *The relativity of opposing terms and the middle way*

As for the concepts on which our conception of the phenomenal world is based and whose impossibility Nāgārjuna tried to prove, the *Prajñāpāramitā* had selected such concepts rather arbitrarily. Nāgārjuna, following the example of the *Ratnakūṭa,* prefers to choose opposed pairs of concepts [S. 165ff.]. Dependent origination is unreal to him since neither of the opposing possibilities of becoming and ceasing, of permanence and impermanence, etc., applies. The true doctrine consists rather in the rejection of both opposites, in the middle way. With this, Nāgārjuna makes a link to the proclamation of the Buddha who himself designated his doctrine as the middle way [S. 10f.], and asserts that he is proclaiming the genuine doctrine of the Buddha. For this reason then, his system is also called the *middle doctrine*, Madhyamakadarśana.

The fundamental inference from which he begins is meant to show that neither an arising nor a passing away is possible. Then follows a long series of similar inferences that at first bewilder and nearly stupefy. On closer inspection, however, solid fundamental views appear here as well, being reiterated again and again. One of the views with which Nāgārjuna prefers to work is the relativity of opposed concepts. Such concepts are, in other words, mutually dependent on one another since the one is possible only if the other is also given. From this though, Nāgārjuna draws the conclusion that the corresponding entities cannot really exist, because the existence of the one always presupposes the existence of the other. A cause, for example, is a cause only with respect to an effect. A cause can therefore not exist as long as the effect does not exist. Without a cause, <173> however, an effect also cannot exist. Neither [Nāgārjuna] nor his contemporaries were able to recognize the error underlying this conclusion.[1] [See S. 176, 221, 224, 247].

---

[1] [Frauwallner actually never explained in writing what he thought was the error underlying Nāgārjuna's conclusion. It can only be assumed that he considered this error to be along the lines of some classical sophistic arguments (*cf.*, in a similar vein, Richard Robinson: "Some Logical Aspects of Nāgārjuna's System." *Philosophy East and West* 6, 1957, pp. 291–308; Richard Hayes: "Nāgārjuna's Appeal." *Journal of Indian Philosophy* 22, 1994, pp. 299–378). The present error is basically due only to an assumed congruence between language and reality, which in Nāgārjuna's time, however, had still not been clearly understood as a silent presupposition underlying such arguments (*cf.* Johannes Bronkhorst: "The Correspondence Principle and its Impact on Indian Philosophy." *Indo-Shisōshi Kenkyū* 8, 1996, pp. 1–19). Nāgārjuna's arguments and their often surprising logic and style have been subject to a great number of studies recently. Examples of closer analyses of Nāgārjuna's arguments can be found so far only in some papers by Claus Oetke, a good one being his "On some non-formal aspects of the proofs of the Madhyamakakārikās," in: *Earliest Buddhism and Madhyamaka*. Eds. David Seyfort Ruegg – Lambert Schmithausen,

CDA.2.1.3. *Nāgārjuna's concept of intrinsic nature (svabhāva) and the emptiness of the phenomenal world*

Still more important is Nāgārjuna's uniquely developed concept of an intrinsic nature *(svabhāva)*. For Nāgārjuna, in accordance with the Indian meaning of the word, *intrinsic nature* means a being in and of itself and conditioned by only itself, independent of everything else. From this, however, it follows that such an intrinsic nature has not arisen because it cannot be caused, and that it is not subject to passing away because its existence is not dependent on anything else. It is therefore permanent and imperishable. And so Nāgārjuna draws the conclusion that entities of the phenomenal world, because they are subject to constant becoming and ceasing, cannot possess an intrinsic nature. They are therefore without a nature, i.e., unreal.

At the same time, this argument of the unreality of entities enables him to bring the nature of the phenomenal world as he sees it into sharper focus. The unreality of the phenomenal world does not mean that it does not exist [at all]. It just does not exist intrinsically. With this, a characterization comes to the fore, which in the *Prajñāpāramitā* was still only one among many, but which for Nāgārjuna became the decisive expression for the nature of the phenomenal world: emptiness *(śūnyatā)*. The things of the phenomenal world are empty, are natureless. We can therefore neither say that entities exist nor that they do not exist. Both are mistaken. Both are opposites. The truth lies in the middle, in the middle way, in emptiness.

Leiden 1990, pp. 91–109. A good survey and balanced summary is in Tom J. F. Tillemans: *Trying to be Fair to Mādhyamika Buddhism*. (The Numata Yehan Lecture in Buddhism, Winter 2001). Calgary, The University of Calgary, 2001, pp. 1–29.]

CDA.2.1.4. *The highest and the restricted truth*

That it is so constituted, however, makes the phenomenal world as we know it possible in the first place. If things possessed an intrinsic nature, they could, as noted, neither arise nor cease. Only because of their unreality can the entire course of the world unfold in accordance with the law of dependent origination. The phenomenal world therefore does exist and it exists in accordance with its own fixed laws. Thus also a certain truth is allowed to it. Not truth in terms of the highest reality, however, but a restricted truth *(saṃvṛtisatya)*. In terms of the restricted truth then, the events of the world, and in particular the Buddhist path of liberation <174> and the proclamation of the Buddha, have validity. From the point of view of the highest truth *(paramārthasatya)*, which applies exclusively to the highest reality, though, there is neither a Buddha, nor a doctrine, nor a community, since these all belong to the phenomenal world.

CDA.2.1.5. *The nature of the phenomenal world is diversity (prapañca)*

A second view of the nature of the phenomenal world is worth mentioning. While it does not come fully into play with Nāgārjuna, it appears as significant for the first time. The nature of the phenomenal world is *diversity (prapañca)*, a concept not further analyzed by Nāgārjuna. The world of dependence is based on manifoldness, which *diversity* provides. Most importantly, however, all our conceptions, which feign the phenomenal world for us, but which do not apply to the highest reality since this is free of all diversity, rest on diversity. And here lies one of the germs of the later doctrine that sees in the phenomenal world a creation of cognition.[1]

---

1 [*Cf.* 221, 229, 268, 282, 299f., 329ff., 354f.]

DA.2.2. *The highest reality*

DA.2.2.1. *Distinction from the phenomenal world: free from diversity, extinction, peace, etc.*

When it came to the highest reality, Nāgārjuna had less that was new and original to say than about the phenomenal world. In particular, he avoids the positive expressions and designations that appear in the *Prajñāpāramitā.* He does not speak of an *element of the factors (dharmadhātu),* of a *suchness (tathatā),* but only of *extinction (nirvāṇa).* The latter is without arising and passing away, without ending, and also is not permanent. Most importantly, it is neither existent nor non-existent, since existence and non-existence, as opposing concepts, belong to the world of dependence. Furthermore, *nirvāṇa* is free from all diversity and so offers no basis for our concepts and is thus unimaginable and inexpressible. In it the manifoldness of appearances and the law of dependent origination are thus set aside. It is by nature peaceful *(śānta).*

DA.2.2.2. *Identity in nature of the phenomenal world and nirvāṇa*

In this way, however, the same statements ensue about *nirvāṇa* as about the nature of the phenomenal world. And so it is that Nāgārjuna, just as does the *Prajñāpāramitā* [S. 149], comes to assert the unity of the phenomenal world and *nirvāṇa.* The same characterizations that are <175> valid for the nature of things *(dharmatā)* are also valid for *nirvāṇa. Nirvāṇa* and phenomenal world are, so to speak, just two forms of appearance of the same nature. That which in conditionality and dependency constitutes the phenomenal world is, free from conditionality and dependency, *nirvāṇa.* Nāgārjuna is also not afraid to emphasize this sameness of nature most emphatically and most sharply. The phenomenal world and *nirvāṇa* are one and the same. There is not the least difference between them. From this it follows, however, that *nirvāṇa* is nothing separate *per se* that one attains by freeing oneself from the phenomenal world. It consists rather only in the fact that the deception of the phenomenal world is no longer perceived, as the diversity on which it is founded is appeased.

CDA.2.3. *Doctrine of liberation*

At the same time, this tells us wherein liberation lies according to Nāgārjuna's doctrine. It remains only to briefly add how the process of liberation presents itself within the phenomenal world. Nāgārjuna solved this question very simply. According to the old Śrāvakayāna doctrine, rebirth depends on deeds, and the efficacy of the deeds on the defilements—in particular on the mistaken belief in an 'I', in a soul. Nāgārjuna now says that with the abolition of diversity, resulting from the emptiness of all entities, the bottom falls out of all ideas concerned with the entities of the phenomenal world. With this, however, the belief in an 'I' is also invalidated, and with it the efficacy of deeds vanishes and rebirth comes to an end. Thus, in the end, the cognition of the emptiness of all entities is the cause of liberation and provides the impetus for an unfolding of the process of liberation as it has been conceived of thus far.

These are the essential features of Nāgārjuna's views as they appear in the presentation of the *Madhyamakakārikā*.

CDA.3. *Introduction to sections of the Madhyamakakārikā*

CDA.3.1. *Chapter I: Examination of causes (pratyayaparīkṣā)*

We turn now to Nāgārjuna's works themselves, beginning with his principal work, namely the *Madhyamakakārikā*. Here we begin with the first chapter, which contains the basic proof of the impossibility of any *arising*. The chapter is, at the same time, <176> a good example of Nāgārjuna's logic, which, it is true, is based to a great extent on sophisms, but which, like the sophisms of the Eleatic Zeno, made a deep impression because of its surprising boldness.

As with most Buddhist works, this one is prefaced with a stanza of homage to the Buddha which, however, at the same time briefly presents what constitutes the essential content of the work: namely, the true teaching of the Buddha, i.e., dependent origination *(pratītyasamutpāda)* as the nature of the phenomenal world as it is in truth, free from all opposing characterizations; and therewith also the ending of the diversity of appearances and hence, liberation.

The actual presentation begins [v. 1] with the fundamental assertion that there is no *arising*, neither from itself, nor from something other, nor from both, nor from neither.

The next verse [v. 2] provides a brief proof. Things cannot arise from themselves because their own nature, as presupposed for the moment, is not present in the causes. As long as their own nature is not present, however, another nature cannot exist, since any other nature is only possible in contrast to one's own nature. Consequently, things also cannot arise from something other. Nāgārjuna thus bases himself here on the relativity of opposing concepts, which makes the occurrence of one dependent on the occurrence of the other.

Then [v. 3] he moves on, in order to prove the impossibility of an arising, to refute the opponent's doctrine of causes; here first of all, the doctrine of the Śrāvakayāna scholasticism. According to this doctrine there are four kinds of causes: The cause *(hetu)* or generative cause; the object-support *(ālambana)* or the object of knowledge; the immediately preceding cause *(samanantara-pratyaya)*. By this latter is to be understood—according to the Buddhist doctrine of the momentariness of all entities—that moment in the stream of moments of a thing, which immediately precedes the moment considered to be the effect, and which therefore is to be seen as its cause. Finally, the dominant cause *(adhipatipratyaya)*, to which belong all things that enable the arising of an effect through their mere existence. <177> To begin, Nāgārjuna presents general objections to this doctrine.

An effect, as he says [v. 4], can neither have causes nor can it be without a cause, and *vice versa:* the causes can neither have an effect nor be without an effect.

As proof of this statement, he again uses [v. 5] the relativity of concepts. *Cause* is what one calls that on which an effect depends. But as long as the effect does not exist, it also cannot depend on anything. And thus before the arising of the effect no cause can exist.

The cause, on the other hand [v. 6], can have neither something existent nor something non-existent as its effect, since as the cause of something non-existent, it would, as stated, not be a cause. And as the cause of an already existing effect, it would be useless.

Nāgārjuna then [vv. 7–10] turns briefly, in one verse each, against the different kinds of causes accepted by the Śrāvakayāna scholasticism. Against the *cause* or *generative cause,* he notes [v. 7]—in connection with the aforementioned—that if the effect, i.e., that which is produced, can be neither existent nor non-existent, nor existent-and-non-existent, then of course a generative cause is also impossible. With respect to the *object-support,* he refers [v. 8] to a saying of the Buddha in the *Prajñāpāramitā* texts, according to which the factors are without object-support. As refutation of the *immediately preceding cause,* he bases himself [v. 9] on the definition of the opponent who designates the passing away of the preceding moment as cause of the following one. The passing away, however, cannot take place before the following moment has arisen. But if it has arisen, then nothing exists any longer that could be a cause. Finally [v. 10], concerning the *dominant cause,* he refers to the essencelessness of all things (he substantiates this later in more detail), which does not permit one to speak of their existence, such that it is impossible to assert that the existence of one thing depends on the existence of another.

The following verses (vv. 11–14) appear to be directed against the doctrine of causality of the Sāṃkhya and the Vaiśeṣika, who had primarily the material cause in view, and of which the Sāṃkhya taught that <178> the effect already pre-exists in the cause, whereas the Vaiśeṣika asserted the opposite. Nāgārjuna now first [v. 11] adopts the point of view that the effect exists neither in the combined nor in the individual causes, and poses the question as to how something can arise from causes in which it is not contained. And even if this should take place, why does it then, he asks further [v. 12], arise only from certain things as causes and not also from others. If [v. 13] on the other hand, one assumes that the effect is contained in the causes and thus has their nature, then the same applies equally to these causes. They themselves thus have no intrinsic nature of their own, so how then can one assert that the effect has their nature? Nāgārjuna then concludes [v. 14]: If therefore the effect is neither contained nor not contained in the causes, then there is no effect at all. And if there is no effect, then there is also no cause.

CDA.3.1.1. *From the "Mnemonic Verses of the Middle Doctrine" (Madhyamakakārikā)*

Chapter I:
[Examination of causes]

To the Buddha who has proclaimed dependent origination as being without annihilation and without arising, without cessation and not eternal, without unity and without manifoldness, without coming and without going, as the peaceful appeasement of diversity *(prapañca)*, to Him, the most excellent of teachers, I pay homage.

1

Neither from itself, nor from something other, nor from both, nor without cause, have any things whatsoever ever arisen anywhere.

2[1]

For the intrinsic nature of entities is not present in the causes, etc. If, however, no intrinsic nature is <179> present, then also no extraneous nature is present.

3

There are four causes: the cause [or generative cause], the object-support [cause], the immediately preceding [cause] and the dominant cause. There is no fifth cause.

4

The effect has no cause. But the effect also does not exist without a cause. The causes likewise are not without an effect, but they also do not have an effect.

5

Whatever the arising of a (thing) depends upon, those are considered to be its causes. But as long as [this thing] does not arise, why, for so long, should these not be non-causes?

6

A cause is appropriate to neither an existent nor a non-existent object. For of what is it the cause, if (the object) is non-existent? If, however, (the object) does exist, of what use then is the cause?

7

If neither an existent [factor] nor a non-existent [factor], nor an existent and non-existent factor arises, how then is a productive cause possible?

8

About the existing factor, it is taught that it is without object-support. But if it is without object-support, from whence should an object-support then come? <180>

---

1 [Frauwallner switched stanzas 2 and 3.]

9

As long as the factors have not arisen, annihilation does not come about. The immediately preceding cause is therefore not possible. If, on the other hand, annihilation has taken place, then what is supposed to be the cause?

10

Since for things without intrinsic nature there is no existence, it is inadmissible to say: When this exists, that comes to be.

11

Neither in the individual [causes] nor in all the causes is the effect contained. But how should that which is not contained in the causes arise from the causes?

12

But if the effect, even without being present, arises from the causes, why then does it not also arise from non-causes?

13

If the effect consists of the causes, then the causes do not consist of themselves. How then can the effect, which originates from the causes that do not consist of themselves, consist of the causes?

14

There is therefore no effect that consists of causes, and none that does not consist of causes. But if there is no effect, then how can there be causes and non-causes?

CDA.3.2. *Chapter XV: Examination of intrinsic nature (svabhāvaparīkṣā)*

From the numerous following chapters, in which Nāgārjuna tries to prove the most diverse concepts of common life to be contradictory and impossible, <181> I select only one, the fifteenth, because in it a particularly important concept comes up for discussion: the concept of intrinsic nature *(svabhāva)*. For the Indian, in the concept of intrinsic nature or own-being lies, as we have already stated, the idea that something exists only in itself and through itself. This means that it is dependent on and conditioned by nothing else. And, for Nāgārjuna, it further follows from this that it can neither arise nor cease. From this, however, it necessarily follows that in the phenomenal world—the basic law of which is represented by dependent origination—an intrinsic nature is impossible.

In the chapter before us, Nāgārjuna starts from the concept of intrinsic nature and asserts, first of all [v. 1], that an intrinsic nature cannot arise and hence cannot exist in the phenomenal world. Then [v. 3], from the opposition of concepts, he draws the further conclusion that without an intrinsic nature there also cannot be an extraneous nature *(parabhāva)*. But [v. 4] without an intrinsic and extraneous nature, any existence *(bhāva)* at all is impossible, and without existence, there is also no non-existence. The rejection of existence as well as of non-existence [v. 5] is, however, the core of the proclamation of the Buddha with respect to the phenomenal world. And as confirmation of this, Nāgārjuna cites [v. 7] a famous sutra from the old canon, the so-called *Instruction of Kātyāyana (Kātyāyanāvavāda)*.

This sutra mentions the two opposed statements: "It exists" and "It does not exist," and this occasions a few further comments, since these two statements are keywords in the canon for the two views that the Buddha branded as the worst heresies, the doctrine of eternality *(śāśvatadṛṣṭi)* and the doctrine of annihilation *(ucchedadṛṣṭi)*, in particular, of the self. Nāgārjuna therefore briefly examines these two doctrines.

First [v. 8], he notes that from the existence of an intrinsic nature its eternality follows, because the intrinsic nature cannot change. Indeed [v. 9], in the case of an existing intrinsic nature, no transformation is at all possible because it is unchanging, and in the absence of an intrinsic nature, because nothing is there that could change. Then he concludes [v. 10]: Both, existence and non-existence, must be <182> rejected because the heresies of eternality and annihilation result from them. For [v. 11] if one assumes that something exists by nature, then eternality follows from that. If, on the other hand, one says that something was and is no more, then the heresy of annihilation results.

Chapter XV:
[Examination of intrinsic nature]

1

An arising of intrinsic nature through causes and conditions is not possible. For, if intrinsic nature were to arise from causes and conditions, then it would be created.

2

But how could a created intrinsic nature exist? For intrinsic nature is nothing created and is not dependent on something other.

3

How could there be an extraneous nature if there is no intrinsic nature? For the intrinsic nature of an extraneous nature is called *extraneous nature.*

4

Further, how could there be an existence without an intrinsic nature and extraneous nature? For only if an intrinsic or extraneous nature is present, does an existence come about.

5

But if there is no existence, then non-existence also cannot be. For people call *non-existence* the being-different of an existence.

6

Those who see an intrinsic nature and an extraneous nature, an existence and a non-existence, do not see the truth in accordance with the teaching of the Buddha. <183>

7

In the *Instruction of Kātyāyana*, the Exalted One, who knows existence and non-existence, has rejected both statements: "It exists" and "It does not exist."

8

If existence exists by nature, then there is no non-existence of the (thing in question). For a being-different of the nature *(prakṛti = svabhāva)* can never come about.

9

If there is no nature, of what should the being-different then come about? And if there is a nature, how then is a being-different possible?

10

"It exists," from this results the belief in eternality. "It does not exist," from this results the view of annihilation. A judicious person should, therefore, affirm neither existence nor non-existence.

11

Because what exists by its intrinsic nature cannot not exist; consequently it is eternal. If on the other hand one says: "It does not exist now, but existed previously," annihilation follows from this.

CDA.3.3. *Chapter XVIII: Examination of the self (ātmaparīkṣā)*

I now present a few more chapters in which, along with the refutation of various concepts, other important topics come up for discussion. The first of these is the eighteenth chapter, which is devoted to the refutation of the concept of *ātman* and which also contains valuable statements about the proclamation of the Buddha and the true doctrine. The reasoning begins [v. 1] in Nāgārjuna's customary manner. There cannot be an *ātman,* a self, because it can neither be identical with the groups *(skandha)* nor <184> different from them.

But [v. 2] if there is no self, then there is also no mine, and with this, the fateful belief in an 'I' and in a 'mine'—the principal cause for entanglement in the cycle of existences—is invalidated.

Nāgārjuna quickly interjects [v. 3] that of course one must also not believe in a person freed from a belief in an 'I' and in a 'mine.'

He then continues [vv. 4–5]: With the vanishing of the belief, the defilements and deeds are abolished, birth no longer comes about, and liberation takes place. This corresponds, as far as the establishment of liberation is concerned, with the old Śrāvakayāna doctrine. He [v. 5] now connects this with his own view. The belief in an 'I' and in a 'mine' rests on conceptions. The conceptions themselves rest on the deceptive diversity of the phenomenal world *(prapañca).* The latter is abolished through the knowledge of its emptiness. Thus the doctrine of the emptiness of all things is the final cause of liberation. We will encounter the same line of thinking—as hinted at here—in more detail in the first chapter of the *Ratnāvalī (Garland of Jewels),* to be rendered later [S. 208ff.]. This concludes the actual line of reasoning within the eighteenth chapter.

Next [v. 6], Nāgārjuna makes a few comments on the proclamation of the Buddha. The Buddha speaks in various ways, here of a self, there that there is no self, there again that a self neither exists nor does not exist. The statements are intended for different hearers who, according to their power of comprehension and the stage that they have attained, are to be gradually led to true cognition of the nature of the self.

This true nature itself [v. 7] is, however, not expressible since the actual nature of things, no different from *nirvāṇa,* lies beyond the sphere of human cognition and can therefore also not be captured in words.

Nāgārjuna then [v. 8] repeats the same thoughts in a general form. With respect to the things of the phenomenal world, the proclamation of the Buddha includes all four statements, affirmation, negation, affirmation and negation, and neither affirmation nor negation, and these are matched with the mental capacity of the hearers.

The true nature of things is [v. 9], however, free from the diversity that <185> characterizes the phenomenal world, and is therefore unimaginable and cannot be communicated.

Then [v. 10] he summarizes the cognition of the nature of the phenomenal world briefly once again in the only form in which it can be expressed and in which it was already expressed in the introductory verse of the entire work, that is, in the form that presents the true teaching of the Buddha.

Then [v. 12] he concludes with the comment that this eternal doctrine—even during times when no Buddha appears and the tradition is extinct among the disciples—survives among the Pratyekabuddhas, who have found enlightenment for themselves alone.

Chapter XVIII:
[Examination of the self]

1

If the *self* is the same as the *groups,* then it is subject to arising and fading away. If it is distinct from the groups, then it does not have the characteristics of the groups.

2

If there is no *self,* whence should there be a *mine?* As a result of invalidation of self and mine one is freed from the belief in a 'mine' and the belief in an 'I'.

3

There is, however, no one present who is free from the belief in a 'mine' and the belief in an 'I'. Whoever believes that they see someone who is free from the belief in a 'mine' and an 'I', sees falsely.

4

If the ideas of 'mine' and 'I' have vanished outwardly and inwardly, then grasping is abolished, and with its disappearance, birth disappears. <186>

5

Through the disappearance of deeds and of defilements, liberation occurs. Deeds and defilements originate from conceptions. These [originate] from diversity. But diversity is abolished through emptiness.

6

That there is an 'I' has been proclaimed. That there is no 'I' has been taught. That there is neither an 'I' nor not an 'I' has been taught by the Buddha.

7

Where the sphere of cognition ends, the nameable also ends. For the nature of the factors *(dharmatā)* is, like *nirvāṇa,* without arising and without annihilation.

8

That everything is true, not true, both true and not true, and neither true nor not true, that is the teaching of the Buddha.

9

Not to be recognized through extraneous help, peaceful, not diversified through diversity, unimaginable, and without manifoldness, that is the characteristic of reality *(tattva).*

10

What arises dependent on another is not the same as the other and is also not distinct from it. Thus it is not annihilated, but it is also not eternal.

11

No unity and no multiplicity, without annihilation and also not eternal, that is the nectar of the teaching of the protector of the world, the Buddha. <187>

12

If no Buddhas appear and the disciples have vanished, then the cognition of the Pratyekabuddhas appears of its own accord.

CDA.3.4. *Chapter XXIV: Examination of the noble truths (āryasatyaparīkṣā)*

The following chapter contains Nāgārjuna's doctrine of the twofold truth. It begins [v. 1] with an attack by the opponent who raises the objection that the assertion of the emptiness of all things undermines the foundation of the Buddhist doctrine. This opponent says: If there is no arising and fading away, then the four noble truths, that is, suffering, the origin of suffering, the cessation of suffering, and the path leading to the cessation of suffering, cannot exist. Of these four truths [v. 2], suffering should be recognized, its origin should be avoided, its cessation realized, and the path leading to it practiced. All this is not possible if the four noble truths do not exist. With this [v. 3], the fourfold reward promised to the disciple also fails to appear, namely that he enters the stream leading to liberation *(srotaāpanna)*, that he returns only once more to the cycle of existences *(sakṛdāgāmin)*, that he no longer returns *(anāgāmin)*, and that he becomes a perfect saint *(arhan)*. As a result of that, however, there are also no disciples who are striving for this reward or who have already attained it. And if there are no such disciples [v. 4], then there is no Community. In addition, without the four noble truths, there is no Doctrine. And without a Community and a Doctrine [v. 5], there is no Buddha. With this, the threefold foundation on which Buddhism rests is destroyed.

Nāgārjuna answers [v. 7] that all this is based only on a misunderstanding on the part of the opponent who understands the doctrine of emptiness wrongly. Two types of truths [v. 8] must be distinguished, the restricted truth and the real truth. The path of liberation [v. 10] belongs to the sphere of the restricted truth and has its validity therein. This provides the occasion to point out [v. 11] the dangers that are entailed by a wrong understanding of the doctrine, and that thus also made the Buddha at first hesitant about the proclamation of his doctrine. Next Nāgārjuna himself goes on the offensive [v. 13]. All of the opponent's objections <188> are actually turned back on him. Only if entities are empty, i.e., without an intrinsic nature, is an arising and ceasing and, with it, everything else possible [v. 14]. An intrinsic nature, on the other hand [v. 15], can neither arise nor cease. Emptiness and dependent origination are thus one and the same and are mutually dependent [v. 18]. Nāgārjuna then shows [vv. 20–39] in detail that everything set forth by the opponent, beginning with the four noble truths, is possible only because of emptiness. After what has been said already, these discussions are easily understandable and do not require any further explanation. Finally [v. 40], he concludes with the statement that only a correct understanding of dependent origination makes the understanding of the noble truths possible.

Chapter XXIV: [Examination of the noble truths]

1

(Opponent): If all this is empty and there is no arising and passing away, then the non-existence of the four noble truths would ensue for you.

2

Due to the non-existence of the four noble truths, recognizing, avoiding, practicing, and realizing are not possible.

3

Since this does not exist, the fourfold reward of the noble ones does not exist. And if the reward is absent, then there are no abiders in the reward and no strivers toward it.

4

If these eight kinds of persons do not exist, then there is no Community. And resulting from the absence of the noble truths, the noble Doctrine does also not exist. <189>

5

But if there is no Doctrine and no Community, then how shall there be a Buddha? Therefore, if you assert emptiness, you deny the three jewels (the Buddha, the Doctrine, and the Community).

6

And you make impossible the presence of the reward, of right and wrong, and, in general, everything that people do and do not do.

7

(Answer:) To this we say: You do not know the purpose of emptiness, emptiness, and the meaning of emptiness. Therefore you object.

8

The doctrinal proclamation of the Buddha is based on two truths: on the restricted truth of ordinary life and on the real truth.

9

A person who does not understand the difference between these two truths does not understand the profound truth *(tattva)* in the teaching of the Buddha.

10

If one does not base oneself on ordinary understanding *(vyavahāra)*, the real cannot be taught. And if one does not apprehend the real, then *nirvāṇa* cannot be attained.

11

Wrongly understood, emptiness brings the fool to ruin, like a snake unskillfully seized or a wrongly cast spell. <190>

12

Thus also the sage (the Buddha) shied away in his mind from proclaiming the doctrine because he considered how difficult this doctrine is for the foolish to understand.

13

Further, as for the criticisms you raise against emptiness, the faults that ensue do not apply to us and they also do not appear with respect to that which is empty.

14

For one who accepts emptiness, everything proves to be possible for him. For one who does not accept emptiness, nothing proves to be possible for him.

15

By transferring your own faults onto us, you are like someone who, while sitting on a horse, has forgotten the horse.[1]

16

If you are of the opinion that things exist by their intrinsic nature, then you view the things as being without causes and without conditions;

17

you deny effect and cause; agent, action, and deed; arising, ceasing, and reward.

18

It is dependent origination that we designate as emptiness. [Emptiness] is a mere designation dependent on some foundation *(upādāya prajñapti)* and it is the middle way. <191>

19

Because there is no factor that is not dependently arisen, there is also no factor that is not empty.

20

If all of this is not empty and there is no arising and ceasing, then the non-existence of the four noble truths results for you.

---

[1] ["Here is the idea behind this image, a standard trope in classical Indian rhetoric: A man with a herd of horses thinks that he is missing one and accuses you of having stolen it. As he rides around and counts his horses, he always comes up one short. But you point out to him that the one he is accusing you of stealing is in fact the very one he is riding but has forgotten to count." *The Fundamental Wisdom of the Middle Way: Nāgārjuna's Mūlamadhyamakakārikā*. Translation and commentary by Jay L. Garfield; Oxford University Press, 1995.]

21

How can there be suffering that is not dependently arisen? For *suffering* is what one calls the impermanent. But in the presence of an intrinsic nature, [the impermanent] does not exist.

22

Further, how should something arise that is present by its intrinsic nature? Thus for the person who denies emptiness, there is also no origin (of suffering).

23

There is no cessation of suffering if it exists by its intrinsic nature. Therefore, if you assert the intrinsic nature, you make cessation (of suffering) impossible.

24

If there is an intrinsic nature of the path, then it is not possible to practice it. But if the path is practiced, then for you there can be no intrinsic nature.

25

If there is no suffering, no origin, and no cessation, to what cessation of suffering should the path lead? <192>

26

If (suffering) is not recognized in its intrinsic nature, how can it then later be recognized? Or does intrinsic nature perhaps not remain?

27

In the same way as recognition, however, avoidance, realization, and practice are also not possible, and likewise the fourfold reward of the noble one.

28

After all, how is it possible for the person who assumes an intrinsic nature to later attain a reward that by its intrinsic nature is not attained.

29

But if there is no reward, then there are no abiders in the reward and no strivers toward it. If these eight kinds of persons do not exist, then there is no Community.

30

And due to the absence of the noble truths, the noble Doctrine does also not exist. But if there is no Doctrine and no Community, then how shall there then be a Buddha?

31

Further, it follows for you that the Buddha is independent of enlightenment, and it follows for you that enlightenment is independent of the Buddha.

32

For you, no one who is not enlightened by nature will attain enlightenment on the path of the Bodhisattva, <193> even if he strives for enlightenment.

33

Further, no one will ever do right or wrong. For how shall one act on something non-empty? After all, an intrinsic nature cannot be created.

34

In addition, for you there is a reward even without right and wrong, and for you there is no reward that is induced by right and wrong.

35

Or, if there is a reward for you that is induced by right and wrong, then how is the reward that is arisen from right and wrong not empty?

36

Further, you make everything that people do and do not do impossible, if you deny the emptiness of dependent origination.

37

For the person who denies emptiness, there is nothing to do, there is action even without it having begun, and there is an agent even without him doing anything.

38

In the presence of an intrinsic nature, the world would have to be not arisen and not ceased, unmoved *(kūṭastha)* and free from all varying states. <194>

39

If (everything) is not empty, then there is no acquisition of the non-attained, no putting an end to suffering, and no abandonment of all defilements.

40

Whoever sees dependent origination (correctly), sees suffering, the origin, the cessation, and the path.

CDA.3.5. *Chapter XXV: Examination of nirvāṇa (nirvāṇaparīkṣā)*

Lastly, I will present the twenty-fifth chapter, which deals with *nirvāṇa,* that is, with the highest reality. Similar to the previous chapter, it begins [v. 1] with the objection that if all entities are empty there is nothing through the cessation of which one attains *nirvāṇa.* Nāgārjuna responds [v. 2] again that this difficulty arises precisely in the instance that things are not empty because precisely then a becoming and ceasing is not possible. He [v. 3] then proceeds to determine the nature of *nirvāṇa.*

After provisionally establishing what tradition says about *nirvāṇa,* namely that it can neither be given up nor attained, is neither impermanent nor permanent, and neither arises nor ceases, he begins [v. 4] to investigate whether it is to be viewed as existence, non-existence, both as existence and non-existence, or as neither existence nor non-existence. The examination leads to the result that none of the four possibilities applies. As existence, *nirvāṇa* would be subject to old age and death, it would arise from causes, and it would not be independent, which contradicts tradition.

Nirvāṇa [v. 7] cannot be considered as non-existence because non-existence presupposes existence, and because in that case it would likewise not be independent.

Here, Nāgārjuna interjects [v. 9] the important comment that *nirvāṇa* is simply the other aspect of the phenomenal world, in which conditionality and dependency have been abolished.

Then he adds [v. 10] that *nirvāṇa* can neither be existence nor non-existence because the Buddha taught that there is no becoming and ceasing in *nirvāṇa*.

In similar fashion [v. 11], the refutation of the views that *nirvāṇa* is both existence and non-existence and neither existence nor non-existence follows. In the first case, liberation would be, at one and the same time, existence and non-existence; <195> *nirvāṇa* would not be independent [v. 12]; would arise from causes [v. 13]; and finally [v. 14], two opposites such as existence and non-existence cannot come together to form a unity.

Nirvāṇa [v. 15], however, cannot be considered neither as existence nor as non-existence, if neither an existence nor a non-existence that can be negated has been established. So [v. 16] by what means shall a *nirvāṇa* that is neither existence nor non-existence be established? Nāgārjuna then refers [v. 17] to the proclamation of the Buddha in confirmation of his assertion. In the texts of the old canon, it is already stated (*cf. above* S. 19ff.) that it cannot be said of the Liberated One that he exists, that he does not exist, that he at one and the same time exists and does not exist, or that he neither exists nor does not exist, and that, indeed [v. 18], these statements do not even apply when he is still alive. This is thus established.

Next follows [vv. 19–20] the decisive statement about the relationship of *nirvāṇa* to the phenomenal world: Both are one and the same. Not the least difference exists between them.

Nāgārjuna then [v. 21] quickly rejects the other heretical doctrines that are dismissed in the canon, along with the views about the existence and non-existence of the Liberated One. That the world is limited or unlimited, permanent or impermanent, all these views are wrong and meaningless given that all things are empty, that is, unreal.

And now one last question [v. 22]: Of what does liberation consist if there is no *nirvāṇa* that can be attained, but rather *nirvāṇa* and the cycle of existences are one? Nāgārjuna answers [v. 24]: In the mere vanishing of all perceptions and in the ending of the deceptive diversity of the phenomenal world, since the Buddha's path of liberation is also not real. In reality, a doctrine has never been proclaimed by the Buddha.

Chapter XXV: [Examination of *nirvāṇa*]

1

(Opponent:) If all this is empty and there is no arising and ceasing, then, in your opinion, through the abandonment or annihilation of what, does *nirvāṇa* result? <196>

2

(Answer:) If all this is not empty and there is no arising and ceasing, then, in your opinion, through the abandonment or annihilation of what does *nirvāṇa* result?

3

Not abandoned and not attained, not interrupted and not eternal, not annihilated and not arisen—this is called *nirvāṇa*.

4

Nirvāṇa is, first of all, no existence, because it would follow from this that it bears the characteristics of old age and death. For there is no existence without old age and death.

5

If *nirvāṇa* were an existence, then *nirvāṇa* would be something conditioned *(saṃskṛta)*. For nowhere is there an existence that is not conditioned.

6

If *nirvāṇa* were an existence, then how would *nirvāṇa* be independent? For there is no existence that is independent.

7

If *nirvāṇa* is not an existence, then how could it be a non-existence? For where there is no existence, there also is no non-existence.

8

If *nirvāṇa* were a non-existence, then how would *nirvāṇa* be independent? For there is no non-existence that exists independently. <197>

9

Conditioned and dependent coming and going (in the cycle of existences) is, insofar as it is unconditioned and independent, designated as *nirvāṇa*.

10

For the master (the Buddha) has called it the *abandonment of becoming and ceasing*. From this it results that *nirvāṇa* is neither an existence nor a non-existence.

11

If *nirvāṇa* were both existence and non-existence, then liberation would be existence and non-existence. And this is not possible.

12

If *nirvāṇa* were both existence and non-existence, then *nirvāṇa* would not be independent. For those are both dependent.

13

How could *nirvāṇa* be both existence and non-existence? For *nirvāṇa* is not conditioned, and existence and non-existence are conditioned.

14

How could *nirvāṇa* be both existence and non-existence? For the two cannot be united in one place, like light and darkness.

15

The assumption that *nirvāṇa* is neither an existence nor a non-existence is possible if an existence and non-existence is established. <198>

16

If there is a *nirvāṇa* that is neither existence nor non-existence, then by what means does one recognize that it is neither existence nor non-existence?

17

It cannot be recognized that the Exalted One exists after death, it cannot be recognized that he does not exist, that both are the case, and that neither of the two is the case.

18

Even when he is still alive, it cannot be recognized that the Exalted One exists, and it cannot be recognized that he does not exist, that both are the case, and that neither of the two is the case.

19

The cycle of existences is not different from *nirvāṇa* and *nirvāṇa* is not different from the cycle of existences.

20

The limit of *nirvāṇa* is also the limit of the cycle of existences. Not the slightest thing exists that separates the two from each other.

21

The views about (the state) after death, the limit (of the world), etc., and about its eternity, etc., are based on a *nirvāṇa*, a beginning and an end.

22

If, however, all factors are empty, what is then limited, what is unlimited, what is both limited and unlimited, and what is neither limited nor unlimited? <199>

23

What is the same and what is different, what is eternal and what is not eternal, what is both eternal and not eternal, and what is neither of these two?

24

All perception ceases, the diversity is appeased, and peace prevails. Nowhere has the Buddha proclaimed any doctrine to anyone.

CDA.4. *Introduction to sections of the Vigrahavyāvartanī*

I now follow with two brief samples from two of Nāgārjuna's other works. His inexorable logic, which stops at nothing and proves everything to be without intrinsic nature, has brought on the criticism that he thereby cuts away the ground beneath his own feet. After all, if everything is empty and without intrinsic nature, then the proofs that he brings forward are also empty and therefore prove nothing. Nāgārjuna opposes these criticisms in a separate work, the *Vigrahavyāvartanī (Averting of Quarrels)*. It is one of his best works and shows him at his most idiosyncratic, in particular in his unwavering logical consistency. It consists of a verse-text with Nāgārjuna's own commentary and is divided into two parts, the first of which comprises the attacks of the opponent, the second their refutation. The following samples are taken only from the second part. There was no need to render the corresponding sections of the first part since, for every new point to which he turns, Nāgārjuna briefly reviews the opponent's objection. His fundamental attitude toward the questions raised can be drawn from these samples. All his lines of argument, so he says, conform only to the world of illusion and serve to refute it alone. They do not comprise any positive assertions of his own. All of the opponent's attacks are therefore invalidated because they could only apply to such assertions.

The first objection [v. 1] of the opponent says that given the absence of an intrinsic nature for all things, Nāgārjuna's line of arguments is also without intrinsic nature, and therefore proves nothing.

Nāgārjuna replies [v. 21] that the absence of intrinsic nature in his words only <200> confirms the absence of intrinsic nature for all things. Then he accuses his opponent of not correctly understanding the doctrine of the emptiness of things. Emptiness is identical in nature with dependent origination [v. 22]. Only through the emptiness of all things are dependent origination, whatever we do and do not do, and thus any line of argument at all possible. And as the entities of the phenomenal world, in spite of their emptiness, are able to bring forth their various effects within the phenomenal world, so his line of argument, in spite of its emptiness, is also effective. He elucidates this [v. 23] through comparing it to a man created by means of a magical illusion. who stops the action of a second man likewise created through a magical illusion.

The opponent's next objection [v. 4] anticipates a [possible] reply by Nāgārjuna, for to the [opponent's] objection that [Nāgārjuna's] refutation of the intrinsic nature of all things is empty and therefore not conclusive, Nāgārjuna might answer that the same applies to the refutation of this refutation through the opponent, [i.e., it is empty and therefore not conclusive]. According to the opponent, however, this is not correct, since the assertion that all entities are empty is exclusively Nāgārjuna's statement, and hence only abolishes his refutation but not the refutation of the opponent, who does not admit this thesis.

Nāgārjuna replies [v. 29] that he does not put forward any positive thesis at all, including the thesis that all things are empty. No statement can therefore be regarded as his thesis. And neither can the faults arising therefrom apply to him.

CDA.5. *From the "Averting of Quarrels" (Vigrahavyāvartanī)*

You have said at first:

[v. 1]

> If, for all entities everywhere, there is no intrinsic nature, then your own words *[vacana]* are without intrinsic nature and not capable of refuting an intrinsic nature.

To this we reply: <201>

v. 21

> If my words are not present in either the causes, conditions, and their totality, nor in a separate state, then the emptiness of things is indeed established precisely because of its being without intrinsic nature.

If my words are not present in the causes, that is, in the great elements, whether associated or dissociated; if they are not present in the conditions, that is, in the chest, the throat, lips, tongue, teeth, palate, nose, skull, and so forth, and in the exertions *(prayatna)*; if they are not present in the totality of these two; and if they are also not present separately, that is, distinct from the causes, conditions, and their totality, then they are without intrinsic nature and due to their being without intrinsic nature, empty. The emptiness of my words is thus established by reason of their being without intrinsic nature. But just as my words are empty by reason of their being without intrinsic nature, so are all things empty by reason of their being without intrinsic nature. If you therefore have said: By reason of the emptiness of your words, the emptiness of all things does not apply, then this is not correct. Further:

v. 22

> To wit, the dependent origination of things is called *emptiness,* for a thing that arises dependently is without intrinsic nature.

Without understanding the emptiness of things and without knowing the meaning of emptiness, you have undertaken to present a criticism, (by saying): "By reason of the emptiness of your words, your words are without intrinsic nature. But a refutation *[pratiṣedha]* of the intrinsic nature of things is not possible with your natureless words." The dependent origination of things is in fact their emptiness. How so? By reason of their being without intrinsic nature. Things that are dependently originated <202> are without an intrinsic nature because they lack an intrinsic nature. How so? Because they are dependent on causes and conditions. If entities were to exist by their intrinsic nature, then they also would exist regardless of causes and conditions. But this is not the case. Therefore they are without intrinsic nature. And since they are without intrinsic nature, they are called *empty.* Thus it is established that my words also are without intrinsic nature, because they are dependently originated, and because they are without intrinsic nature, that they are empty. But just as a cart, pots, clothes, etc., although they are dependently originated and therefore empty of an intrinsic nature, nevertheless exert their different effects—that is, hauling wood, [grass,] and earth; holding honey, water, and milk; protecting against cold, wind, and heat, etc.—likewise these words of mine, although they are dependently originated and are therefore without intrinsic nature, nevertheless prove the lack of intrinsic nature of things. Thus, if you have said: Your words are by reason of their being without intrinsic nature empty, and by reason of their emptiness it is not possible to refute the intrinsic nature of all things by means of them, then this is not correct. Further:

v. 23

> Just as a person created through miraculous power *(nirmitaka)* fends off *[pratiṣedhayeta]* a person created through miraculous power, or as a magical person *[māyāpuruṣa]* fends off a person brought forth through his own magic, so it is with this refutation.

Just as a person created through miraculous power fends off another person created through miraculous power who comes along for a particular purpose, or as a magical person brought forth by a magician fends off another magical person [brought forth through his own magic] who comes along for a particular purpose—in all this, the person created through miraculous power <203> who is fended off is empty, and the person who fends him off is likewise empty; the magical person who is fended off is empty, and the person who fends him off is likewise empty—just so it is possible to refute the intrinsic nature of all things by means of my empty words. Thus if you have said: By reason of the emptiness of your words, the refutation of the intrinsic nature of all things is not possible, then this is not correct.

. . .

You have also said:

[v. 4]

> "One [i.e., Nāgārjuna] might think that the same holds true for the refutation of [his] refutation. That is not correct. In this way, based on the characteristic

of the thesis, [your] objection applies to you but not to me."[1]

To this we say:

v. 29

If I were to advocate any kind of thesis, then this fault would result from it for me. But I do not advocate any thesis. Therefore no fault applies to me.

If I were to advocate any kind of thesis, then the characteristic of that thesis could apply to me, and the fault arising from it would, as you have said, result for me. But I advocate no thesis. How, if all entities are empty, completely appeased, and apart by nature, can there be a thesis? How could the characteristic of the thesis apply to it? And how could the fault produced by the applicability <204> of the characteristic of the thesis ensue? Thus if you have said: The fault applies only to you because (for you) the characteristic of the thesis applies, then this is not correct.

CDA.6. *Introduction to the sections of the Ratnāvalī*

Lastly, I present a sample from a more easily understandable work of Nāgārjuna. As we have already mentioned, tradition informs us that Nāgārjuna was friends with a king from the South-Indian ruling house of the Śātavāhana. And in fact, among the works attributed to him we find two that constitute admonitory letters to a king, composed in verse, the *Suhṛllekhaḥ (Letter to a Friend)* and the *Ratnāvalī (Garland of Jewels)*. The following text sample is taken from the much more extensive and more important of the two works, the *Ratnāvalī*.

---

[1] Since the statement, that all things are empty, is, by definition, considered to be your [i.e., Nāgārjuna's] assertion.

The *Ratnāvalī* is not a systematic presentation of Nāgārjuna's doctrines. It proceeds from one topic to another without strict organization of the subject matter, and in it, moral admonitions in particular are given much attention. But also interspersed are purely philosophical sections, which are highly significant in terms of content and which form a valuable complement to the portrayal of his other works. It is one such section from the first chapter of the work that I render in the following.

To begin a few introductory words [vv. 1–3] are offered. Then [v. 4] a twofold goal of the doctrine is established: well-being through piety; and liberation. The means for this are faith and insight [v. 5].

First [vv. 6–24], the ethical life of the believer, which brings him happiness and well-being, is described.

The presentation then moves on to the doctrine that leads to liberation, and with this the philosophical part of the chapter begins. The opening consists of the observation (v. 25) that the fool experiences fear if he hears that a self and a mine neither exist nor will exist. And indeed [v. 27], the belief in an 'I' and in a 'mine' is the principal cause of entanglement in the cycle of existences. This is explained in more detail, for it is this very belief that leads to the accomplishment of deeds and to rebirth. On the other hand [v. 29], the belief itself <205> in turn rests on the external world that one thinks one perceives, in other words, on the five groups. For just as [v. 31], based on a mirror, one believes that one sees one's reflection—which is, however, nothing real—in the same way, based on the groups, one believes in a self. In this way [v. 35] the cycle in which continuous rebirth occurs in mutual dependence, is closed. Liberation takes place [v. 37] through recognition of the unreality of dependent origination, because with this the belief in an 'I' vanishes, and deeds and birth come to an end. The unreality of dependent origination and thus of the external world results, however, from the fact that an arising of things either from itself, or from something other, or from both is not possible. This indicates the basic reasoning with which Nāgārjuna introduces his principal work (*see above* S. 176ff.).

At the same time [v. 38], he takes this opportunity to point out that unreality is not non-existence but signifies neither-existence-nor-non-existence. Then he returns [v. 39] to his initial remark that upon hearing the true doctrine, the fool experiences fear. That [v. 40] a self and the groups do not exist for the liberated one has already been acknowledged. Why then, he asks, should one experience fear in the face of the fact that they are also not really present in this world?

Next comes a new line of thinking (v. 42) in which the most peculiar feature of this doctrine of liberation is discussed, i.e., that it teaches neither an existence nor a non-existence. It was already indicated in the preceding verses that the unreality of the external world does not signify a non-existence. Likewise, *nirvāṇa* is to be considered as neither existence nor non-existence. The true doctrine steers clear of these opposites. Nāgārjuna now briefly points out the moral significance of the different views. The doctrine of non-existence [v. 43] denies the reality of good and bad deeds and leads to punishment in an unfavorable rebirth. The doctrine of existence [v. 44] admits the effectiveness of the deeds and leads to reward in a favorable rebirth. The doctrine of neither-existence-nor-non-existence, on the other hand [v. 45], avoids both and leads to liberation.

Then follows a more thorough discussion of the question of how the phenomenal world is <206> to be regarded neither as existent nor as non-existent. Since [v. 46] it arises from causes, its non-existence cannot be asserted. And since, along with the causes, it ceases, its existence cannot be asserted. At the same time [v. 47], the arising from causes is not real because the cause cannot be a cause, whether it exists prior to the effect or simultaneous with it. Its prior existence contradicts the relativity of the opposed concepts, while its simultaneity makes a bringing forth impossible. The old sutras [v. 48] had expressed dependent origination in the words: "When this exists, that comes to be; due to the arising of this, that arises" (*cf. above* S. 39). Nāgārjuna relates the first phrase to the relativity of the opposed concepts: something short can only exist relative to something long. The second phrase he relates to the arising of one thing from something other, just as light arises due to a lamp. In the first case, however, the long is also not possible without something short because the two mutually condition each other. And therefore, the cause cannot exist prior to the effect because the concept of the cause also presupposes the effect (*cf. above* S. 176f.). On the other hand, no light can arise as long as the lamp is not there. Thus the simultaneity of cause and effect is also impossible. Finally [v. 50], however, in the phenomenal world as it appears to us, an arising is indeed present, and if one takes this into consideration, then one will not believe in non-existence. And [v. 51] as the arisen things within this phenomenal world cease again, one will also not believe in existence.

Following this (v. 52), Nāgārjuna uses an example to elucidate how neither existence nor non-existence applies with respect to the phenomenal world. The phenomenal world resembles a mirage that appears to be water. Whereas something real is seen more accurately on closer inspection, the water of the mirage cannot be perceived from close up. Likewise [v. 53], on closer inspection, the phenomenal world proves to be different than it appears on first sight. Both [i.e., the water of the mirage and the phenomenal world] [v. 54] are therefore an illusion and unreal. But [v. 55] just as in the case of the mirage, although there is no water there, one cannot speak of non-existence since the deception of the mirage as <207> such is present, so likewise [v. 56] in the case of the phenomenal world, one can no more speak of non-existence than of existence. It is noted in passing (v. 58) that from the denial of existence and non-existence one should not deduce any type of negativism, since, if from the denial of existence one were to derive a belief in non-existence, one would likewise have to infer a belief in existence from the denial of non-existence. Nāgārjuna then concludes [v. 62] this section with the remark that this doctrine, which goes beyond existence and non-existence and which alone leads to liberation, belongs exclusively to the proclamation of the Buddha.

Next comes another new line of thinking (v. 63). Nāgārjuna now offers new proofs of the unreality of the phenomenal world. With respect to entities, the old Buddhism distinguishes three characteristics *(lakṣaṇa)* or stages of time: *arising, abiding,* and *ceasing.* These correspond to birth, old age, and death, and thus *abiding* is also defined as becoming-different during abiding. Nāgārjuna now asserts that these three stages of time are not real, and that the phenomenal world also, because it lies outside of the three stages of time, cannot be real and is, therefore, [v. 64] identical in nature with *nirvāṇa.*

He proves this in the following way [v. 65]. *Arising* and *ceasing* cannot be real because there is no *abiding.* However [v. 66], *abiding* is excluded due to the momentariness of things (*cf. above* S. 102f.), since all things are subject to continuous change, because only in this way is the presupposed becoming-different during abiding possible. On the other hand [v. 67], however, momentary things also cannot be real, since they cease either completely or partially in every moment. In the case of a *partial ceasing* the contradiction arises that the same thing ceases and does not cease at the same time. A *complete ceasing,* on the other hand, cannot be observed. In addition [v. 68], in the case of a *complete ceasing* there is no aging, just as in the case of an *unchanging abiding.* Finally though [v. 69], the concept of the *moment* itself presents difficulties as well, because the *ceasing* of a *moment* presupposes a preceding *arising* and *abiding.* In that case <208> the *moment* would split into three parts and would no longer be a *moment.* And [v. 70] what is more, the same deductions could be drawn for each of its parts. In addition, *beginning, middle,* and *end* are relative concepts and, as such, impossible. Further [v. 71], due to the multitude of its parts, the *moment* would not be a unity. On the other hand, nothing partless exists. *Unity* and *multitude* are themselves again relative concepts, just like *existence* and *non-existence.* This last remark allows Nāgārjuna to make the statement [v. 72] that *non-existence* is possible only through the destruction of an *existence* or in opposition to it. *Existence* and *non-existence* are therefore relative concepts as well and thus not real. Consequently [v. 73], also with respect to *liberation,* no real destruction of worldly existence takes place. It is thus with good reason and complete justification that the Buddha responded only with silence to the question of whether the world has an end, since this question proceeds from completely false assumptions. With that, this discussion is finished and the chapter concludes [v. 74] with a few general remarks about the significance of this doctrine and about the danger of a false understanding by fools.

CDA.7. *From the "Garland of Jewels" (Ratnāvalī)*

Chapter I

1

After I have paid homage to the sole friend of all beings (= the Buddha), who is freed from all faults, adorned with all virtues, omniscient,

2

so that your merit may increase I will present to you, O king, the exclusively good doctrine, for the doctrine bears fruit in a worthy recipient of the good doctrine. <209>

3

Where merit first flourishes, later, the highest good comes about, for if flourishing has been attained, then one later arrives at the highest good.

4

Well-being is considered as flourishing, liberation as the highest good. The means for this are, briefly summarized, faith and insight.

5

Through faith one obtains merit, through insight one cognizes in accordance with truth. Insight is, however, the more important of the two, although faith precedes it.

Next follows a brief description of the virtuous life that should be lead based on faith. Then the text continues:

25

Of the doctrine that leads to the highest good and that is subtle and profound to see, the Victorious Ones (= the Buddhas) have said that it causes trembling in the fools who are unable to hear it.

26

The thought: "I do not exist and will not exist, nothing is mine and nothing will be mine," means fear for the fool, the vanishing of fear for the wise.

27

He who proclaims exclusively that which is wholesome for the creatures has said that the creatures are brought about through the belief in an 'I' and are accompanied by belief in a 'mine.' <210>

28

"There is an 'I', there is a 'mine' "; this is erroneous from the point of view of the highest truth, since, in terms of true knowledge, both do not exist.

29

From the belief in an 'I' the groups arise. This belief in an 'I' is, in truth, false. But how can something, the seed of which is false, truly rise up?

30

If one has seen that the groups are untrue, the belief in an 'I' vanishes. But if the belief in an 'I' vanishes, then the groups no longer come about.

31

Just as, based on a mirror, the reflection of one's own face is seen, and like this [reflection] is, in fact, nothing,

32

so, based on the groups, the belief in an 'I' is observed, but it is, in fact, nothing, exactly as with the reflection of one's own face.

33

And just as without the help of the mirror, the reflection of one's own face is not seen, so without the help of the groups, (the conception) of an 'I' is not observed.

34

After the noble Ānanda had attained the eye of the doctrine through hearing this fact, he himself repeatedly proclaimed this fact to the monks. <211>

35

As long as the belief in the groups exists, so long also does (the conception) 'I' exist. But if the belief in an 'I' exists, deeds and birth again arise from it.

36

This wheel of the cycle of existences, consisting of three sections, having no beginning, no end, and no middle, circles by mutually causing itself, like a firebrand whirled around in a circle.

37

Since it (= the dependent becoming of the cycle of existences) cannot come about from itself, from something other, and from both, and this in all three time periods, the belief in an 'I' becomes invalid and thereby deeds and birth also.

38

In that one views the arising of causes and effects and likewise their fading away in this way, one recognizes that the world, in reality, neither exists nor does not exist.

39

If somebody who is thoughtless hears this doctrine, which leads to the vanishing of all suffering, then he trembles in his ignorance, being afraid of the state of fearlessness.

40

That this will all not exist in *nirvāṇa,* does not frighten you. Why then does it cause you fear if one says that it does not exist here?

41

In the case of liberation there is no 'I' and no groups. If such a liberation is welcome to you, why then is an elimination of the 'I' or of the groups undesired by you? <212>

42

Nirvāṇa is, however, also not a non-existence, much less an existence. The vanishing of the conceptions of existence and non-existence is called *nirvāṇa.*

43

The view of non-existence says, in brief, that there is no reward for deeds. [This view] is non-meritorious and leads along a bad path (to an unfavorable rebirth), and is designated as a *false view.*

44

The view of existence says, in brief, that there is a reward for deeds. [This view] is meritorious and entails the good path (i.e., a favorable rebirth), and is designated as a *correct view.*

45

Through knowledge one transcends sin and merit, since existence and non-existence are appeased. And thus this is called by the good ones *liberation from the bad (path) and from the good path.*

46

If one sees the causally dependent arising, one transcends non-existence. And if one sees the cessation together with its cause, existence is not asserted.

47

The cause is, in fact, no cause, though it may have arisen earlier or it may have arisen at the same time, <213> because neither the designation nor a real arising is observed.

48

If this exists, that exists, just as the short [exists], if the long exists. Due to the arising of this, there is the arising of that, just as light [arises] due to the arising of the lamp.

49

But as long as the short does not exist, the long is by nature not present. And if the lamp has not arisen, the light also does not arise.

50

If one sees the arising of cause and effect in this way, non-existence is not asserted in that one accepts the actuality *(yāthābhūtya)* of this world sprung from diversity.

51

And in that one, in accordance with actuality, accepts its ceasing, which results from diversity, one does not assert existence. One is thus liberated since one no longer clings to either.

52

A form glimpsed from a distance is seen clearly when it is near. If the mirage were water, why is it not seen when it is near?

53

The way this world is seen from far off, is not how it is seen when it is near, because it is signless *(animitta)* like the mirage. <214>

54

Just as the mirage resembles water but is not water and is not real, so the groups resemble the 'I' but are not the 'I' and are not real.

55

If someone thinks of the mirage: "This is water," walks toward it and then once he is there, holds that the water [as the mirage] does not exist [at all], then he is a fool.

56

Likewise it is a delusion if one thinks of the world, which resembles a mirage, that it exists or that it does not exist. So long as the delusion exists, however, one is not liberated.

57

One who believes in non-existence walks the bad path. One who believes in existence, walks the good path. One who does not cling to either, because he recognizes how it really is, arrives at liberation.

58

If someone who rejects existence and non-existence, because he recognizes how things really are, succumbs to (the belief in) non-existence due to delusion, why does he not succumb to (the belief in) existence?

59

One might think that, from his dismissal of existence, non-existence would implicitly ensue. But why does existence not ensue from the dismissal of non-existence? <215>

60

If the belief in non-existence implicitly ensues for those who know of no thesis, no engagement, and no thought in reliance on enlightenment, then why are they not, (just as well,) designated as *followers of the belief in existence?*

61

Ask people, including the Sāṃkhyas, Vaiśeṣikas, and Jainas, the followers of the doctrine of a person and [the followers] of the groups, whether they teach such a transcendence of existence and non-existence.

62

Know then that this elixir of deathlessness of the teaching of the Buddha, which transcends existence and non-existence, is designated as the *gift of the doctrine* and as *profound.*

63

The world does not cease, does not come, and does not remain even for a moment. How then should it be real, since by nature it is outside of the three time periods?

64

What difference is there in truth, therefore, between the world and *nirvāṇa,* since in both there is, in fact, no coming, no going, and no abiding?

65

As there is no abiding, there is, in fact, also no arising and no annihilation. How should there in truth be something arisen, remaining, and annihilated? <216>

66

How should there be a non-momentary thing, if a change is continually occurring? If no change occurs, how in truth should there be a being-different?

67

Something can be momentary because it ceases partially or entirely. It is, however, impossible in both cases because it contains a contradiction and is not to be observed (?).

68

If a thing is entirely momentary, then how is there an aging? But if it is not momentary due to its constancy, then how is there an aging?

69

If a moment has an end, so also a beginning and a middle must be assumed. Since the moment consists therefore of three parts, the world cannot last for just a single moment.

70

Further, beginning, middle, and end are to be considered in the same way as the moment. Also, the being beginning, middle, or end is not possible either through itself or through something other.

71

Nothing can be single, if it contains several parts. But something without parts does not exist. There also is no multitude without singularity, just as there is no non-existence without existence. <217>

72

A non-existence can only exist through the destruction of or in opposition to an existence. But how is the destruction or the opposite possible if there is no existence?

73

Consequently, with respect to extinction, a ceasing of the world does not in truth apply. Thus the Victorious One (= the Buddha) chose to remain silent on the question of whether the world has an end.

74

The Omniscient One is recognized as truly omniscient by the informed because he has not imparted this profound doctrine to unsuitable people.

75

Of this doctrine that leads to the highest good, that is profound, and does not hold onto anything, the enlightened ones who have seen the truth, have said that it is free of anything to which one could cling *(anālaya)*.

76

Of this doctrine that is free from anything to which one could cling, foolish people who gladly cling to something and who have not transcended existence and non-existence, are afraid and therefore come to ruin.

77

And since they come to ruin because they fear the state of fearlessness, they also bring others to ruin. Therefore, O king, act in such a way that you are not brought to ruin by those who are lost. <218>

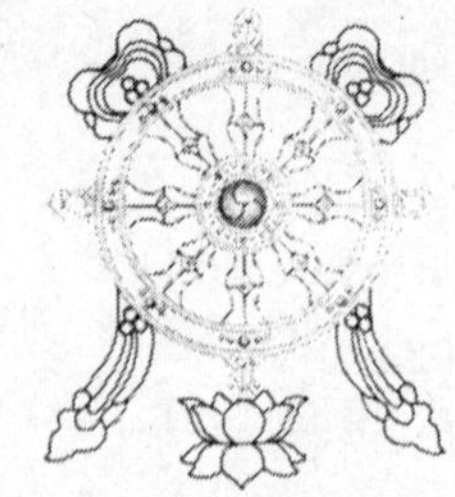

CDB. *Āryadeva (beginning of third century c.e.)*

Next to Nāgārjuna stands his great student Āryadeva, also called Deva for short. According to tradition, Āryadeva came from Ceylon. What is reported about his life is completely legendary. [With Āryadeva] we have the rare case that a significant student appears to be in complete agreement with his teacher and complements him most successfully. He agrees with Nāgārjuna in all essential views, but goes beyond him in his style of presentation. Whereas, especially in his basic treatise, Nāgārjuna works with generalized abstract inferences, Āryadeva examines the disputed views very closely and deals with them in great detail. For this reason he is an important source of the views of the opposing schools of his time. But since in a philosophical sense he presents nothing fundamentally new, and in consideration of the limitations of space, a brief sample of his style should suffice here. To this end I select a few verses from his most extensive work, the *Catuḥśataka (The Treatise in Four Hundred Stanzas);* specifically, the refutation of the doctrine of atoms.

CDB.1. *Introduction to the sample from the Catuḥśataka*

In this treatise Āryadeva opposes the Vaiśeṣika's doctrine of atoms according to which all material entities are composed of atoms. At the same time, according to the Vaiśeṣikas, these entities are not simply an aggregation of atoms. Instead the atoms form a new *whole* that is different from them; specifically, the substance and the qualities of the *whole* are formed from the substance and the qualities of the atoms [*cf.* S. 360]. Āryadeva now states [v. 13] that the atoms do not make up with their entire nature the *whole* that represents their effect. In particular, the minute sphericity *(pārimāṇḍalya)* that distinguishes the atoms does not apply to the *whole.* But [v. 12] that which with one part of its nature is a cause, and with another, on the other hand, is not, is by nature combined. And that which is combined, so he infers, cannot be eternal. With this the eternality of atoms, assumed by the opponent, is refuted.

Incidentally [v. 14], that the atoms as cause and the whole as effect cannot have the same extension <219> results from the fact that one atom cannot occupy the same place as another atom.

A further reason [v. 15] why the atoms themselves must consist of particles is that with each attempt to conceive of an atom, we must necessarily assume different sides of this atom facing the different directions. But that which has several sides also has several parts.

A further reason [v. 16] ensues from the Vaiśeṣika doctrine of movement, according to which the movement of an entity consists in the fact that with its anterior parts, it establishes new spatial connections, while with its posterior parts, it dissolves earlier connections. This, however, again presupposes the presence of parts.

In addition [v. 17], a perfect partlessness would render the atom completely invisible, whereas according to the Vaiśeṣika doctrine, at least to the supranatural perception of a yogin, it is visible.

Finally [v. 18], Āryadeva—against the Vaiśeṣika conception of atoms and of the whole that they form—also calls on the Buddhist doctrine of causality according to which the arising of an effect presupposes the annihilation of its cause (*cf. above* S. 101ff.), which likewise contradicts the assumed eternality of the atoms. In addition [v. 18b], cause and effect, atoms and whole, could not, as the Vaiśeṣika doctrine assumes, occupy the same place.

He concludes [v. 19] therefore with the statement that eternal, materially impenetrable atoms such as the opponent accepts, cannot be proven and that consequently the doctrine of the Buddha also speaks of no such atoms.

CDB.2. *From the "Treatise in Four Hundred Stanzas" (Catuḥśataka)*

Chapter IX:
[Refuting permanent entities]

12

That of which one part is a cause, while another part is not a cause, is thus manifold, and something manifold cannot be eternal. <220>

13

The sphericity of the cause is not present in the effect. Thus the atoms cannot combine with their entire nature (into the whole).

14

It is not accepted that the place of one atom is also the place of another. Thus it is also not accepted that both, cause and effect, have the same extension.

15

That which has an eastern side has also an eastern part. Because the atom thus has parts, therefore the atom is designated as a non-atom.

16

Seizing what is in front and abandoning what is behind—one for whom these two do not take place cannot be going (= moving).

17

That which has no beginning, that which has no middle, and that which has no end, is invisible. Who can see it?

18

The cause is destroyed through the effect, thus the cause is not eternal. Further, the effect is not there where the cause is to be found.

19

An impenetrable eternal thing is nowhere to be observed. Thus the Buddhas have never designated atoms as *eternal.* <221>

As far as the further development of the Madhyamaka doctrine after Nāgārjuna and Āryadeva, we find here no development of the same type as with the other schools. After all, unlike the other schools, the Madhyamaka system did not present a complete world view that could be amended and corrected. Instead, at its core it confined itself rather to a few metaphysical fundamental views that remained unchanged after Nāgārjuna's time. If in spite of this, a sort of development did take place within the school, it was determined by external circumstances. There were, in effect, two things that initiated this: The advances made in the meantime in the field of logic, and the blossoming of the second great Mahāyāna school, the school of the Yogācāra.

The advances in the field of logic necessitated that in lieu of Nāgārjuna's deductions, which proved for the most part to be disputable fallacies [*see* S. 173, 176], more tenable proofs be put forth. The Yogācāra school had gone beyond the Madhyamaka most notably in explaining the coming about of the phenomenal world by means of a kind of epistemological idealism and thereby answering the most important question that the Madhyamaka had left open. The great successes of the Yogācāra school forced the older school to take a stand on this new doctrine.

Under these circumstances the later development of the Madhyamaka school is best portrayed by showing how their most important representatives related to these two points: how they took into account the advances of logic; and how they dealt with the Yogācāra doctrine.

CDC. *Buddhapālita (ca. fifth century c.e.)*

After Āryadeva, the first important personality of the Madhyamaka school to break new ground, was Buddhapālita who probably dates to about the fifth century c.e. It was Buddhapālita who was the first to take into account the advances in logic, in that he composed a commentary on Nāgārjuna's *Madhyamakakārikā* in which he tried to support the latter's assertions through more thorough and more tenable <222> reasoning. In doing so he held himself on principle to Nāgārjuna's approach of advancing no assertions of his own, and confined himself to proving the opponent's assumptions to be impossible. He did this by showing that undesired conclusions follow *(prasaṅga)* from the assertions of the opponent, hence, *via deductio ad absurdum*. A brief example from his commentary will suffice to illustrate his method. I select for this purpose the commentary to the first verse of the *[Madhyamaka]kārikā* (*see above* S. 178), since the establishment of the impossibility of any arising increasingly became the foremost proof on which the refutation of the external world by the Madhyamaka school was primarily rested.

CDC.1. *Introduction to the sample from the Mūlamadhyamakavṛtti*

The details of his presentation is clear and it requires no extensive explanation. One after the other he discusses the four possibilities of arising rejected by Nāgārjuna: from itself; from something other; from both; and without cause. Things do not arise from themselves, because it would be pointless for something already existent to arise a second time, and because otherwise they would have to arise all the time since the cause—i.e., their own selves—would indeed always be present. Things do not arise from something other, because then everything could arise from everything since one extraneous thing is just as much something else as another. They do not arise from both, because then the objections brought forth against the above individual assumptions would apply to both. And they do not arise without cause, because then everything could arise from everything at any time, since indeed no cause whose occurrence must be awaited is necessary; and because then all effort would be pointless, since even without cause everything would still come about.

DC.2. *From the "Commentary to the Mnemonic Verses of the Middle Doctrine" (Mūlamadhyamakavṛtti)*

Chapter I

(Opponent:) First, it needs to be shown how it is a mere manner of speaking *(vyavahāramātra)* when one speaks of <223> an arising.

(Answer:) To this, the first thing to be said is:

v. 1

> Neither from itself, nor from something other, nor from both, nor without cause, have any things whatsoever ever arisen anywhere.

If namely, some thing arises, then the arising of this thing takes place from itself, from something other, from itself and something other, or without cause. If one now examines (these four possibilities), it proves in all four cases to be impossible. How so? From itself means the same as from one's own self. Now, first of all, things do not arise from their own selves because their arising would be pointless, and because an endless arising would result. That is, there is no need for things that in themselves are already existent to arise again. If, however, something already existent were nonetheless to arise, then it would never not arise. And this [conclusion] is undesired. Thus, first of all, things do not arise from themselves. But they also do not arise from something other. How so? Because it would follow from this that everything could arise from everything. Further, they do not arise from themselves and something other at the same time since both faults would ensue. And finally, they also do not arise without cause since it would follow from this that everything could always arise from everything, and since the fault would ensue that all efforts would be pointless. Since therefore the arising of entities is not possible in any way, they do not arise. And hence if one speaks of their arising, it is a mere manner of speaking. <224>

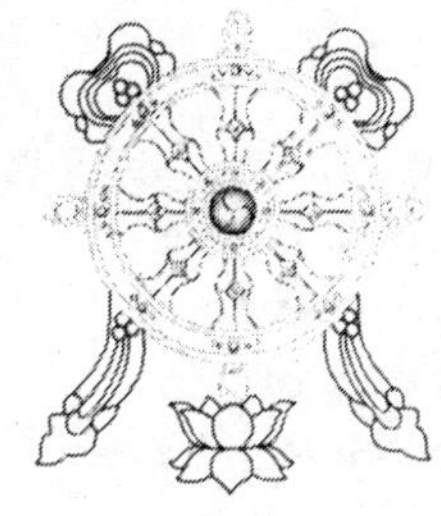

CDD. *Bhāvaviveka (middle of sixth century c.e.)*

The next Madhyamaka teacher of note is Bhāvaviveka or Bhāviveka, the greatest innovator in the history of the school. He lived in the middle of the sixth century c.e. and was a contemporary and opponent of Dharmapāla [S. 394ff.], at that time the most famous representative of the Yogācāra school in Nālandā. Bhāvaviveka innovated both by considering the logical advances of his time as well as by making use of Yogācāra ideas. The decisive impetus for his logical innovations came from the fact that Dignāga had shortly before led Buddhist logic to its full height and had precisely laid down, out of what members an inference must consist and what conditions the individual members must fulfill. Bhāvaviveka took advantage of this, and to be precise by proceeding as follows. He sought to extract the members for such an inference from Nāgārjuna's words, and from this he put together a formal inference that conformed to all of the required conditions and that he defended against all possible objections. Thus in contrast to Buddhapālita—who was content to lead the opponent *ad absurdum*—he advanced autonomous *(svatantra)* inferences, and this earned his school the name of the Svātantrika-Mādhyamikas. The followers of Buddhapālita, on the other hand, were designated as Prāsaṅgikas [Consequentialist].

He also dealt with the doctrines and objections of other, and by no means only Buddhist schools, thoroughly and in detail. As an example of his methodology, I present a sample from his principal work, his great commentary on Nāgārjuna's *Madhyamakakārikā, Prajñāpradīpa (Shining Light of Insight);*

specifically, just as for Buddhapālita, the explanation of the first verse of the *[Madhyamaka]kārikā*. I render only the first section of this explanation though, i.e., the refutation of the arising of entities from themselves, since Bhāvaviveka is incomparably more detailed than Buddhapālita and since this section sufficiently exemplifies his way.

CDD.1. *Introduction to the sample from the Prajñāpradīpa*

Like Buddhapālita, Bhāvaviveka first cites the verse of Nāgārjuna that he will discuss, and adds <225> to it a few explanatory details. Whereas Buddhapālita, however, then puts forward his consequences in full independence, Bhāvaviveka begins even here to prepare his inferences and to derive them from Nāgārjuna's words. In the statement that things do not arise from themselves, he reads into the words *from themselves* that they are already present beforehand, which he regards as a reason. As he notes, any thing in which the quality that proves and the quality to be proven—i.e., reason and consequence—appear connected, can serve as an example. He then proceeds to present the formal inference; he actually divides it properly into *thesis, reason,* and *example.* Things—he names as an example the inner spheres—do not in truth arise from themselves because they are already present, like the cognitive capacity. There follows, as the custom of the logicians demands, a defense of the individual members of the inference against possible objections. The most important condition that the reason must fulfill is that it is absent from that which is dissimilar *(vipakṣa).* This is self-evident in the case in question since something dissimilar—i.e., something that is in truth arisen—does not exist.

Bhāvaviveka then rejects an objection by the Sāṃkhya. According to Sāṃkhya doctrine, the existent arises from the existent, i.e., the effect is already present in the cause.

The Sāṃkhya then says: No one is asserting that things, insofar as they are an effect, arise from themselves. So if that is what your proof is saying, that is like breaking down an open door. If on the other hand you wish to prove that, insofar as they are a cause, they do not arise from themselves, then you entangle yourselves in a contradiction. This is namely actually the case and this is also what our doctrine says.

Bhāvaviveka rejects this objection with the remark that his inference is meant to be general and without the alternative put forward by the opponent, and that besides, a refutation of an arising from the nature of the cause—whether it has its own or another nature—is yet to come (*cf.* vv. 2 and 3 of Nāgārjuna). Finally, he also justifies the use of *cognitive capacity* as an example, since in accordance with the Yogācāra doctrine he has adopted, in the stream of cognition every cognition already exists as a seed, i.e., as a latent impression, before its <226> arising. If this is taken into consideration, cognition thus indeed already exists before its arising. And since therefore the reason, i.e., the already being existent, is present in [cognition], it can serve as an example.

With this Bhāvaviveka's own line of argumentation is concluded and he proceeds to reject Buddhapālita's line of argumentation as being inadequate. His reasons are that Buddhapālita does not present a formal three-membered inference; that he does not deal with the objections of the opponent; and lastly that every *deductio ad absurdum* implies that the opposite of what is proven to be impossible is true.

How Buddhapālita's followers faced up to these criticisms we will see in the discussion of Candrakīrti (*see below* S. 241f.). This then, is the manner in which Bhāvaviveka explains Nāgārjuna, and he also deals in the same way with all other assertions put forward in Nāgārjuna's verses.

CDD.2. *From the "Shining Light of Insight" (Prajnāpradīpa)*

Chapter I

Of those who assert an arising, some say that the entities arise from themselves; others, from something other; some, from both; others, without cause. However, if (these views) are examined in accordance with logic and tradition, then it becomes clear that an arising in each mode is impossible. In this sense, (Nāgārjuna) says:

v. 1

> Neither from itself, nor from something other, nor from both, nor without cause, have any things whatsoever ever arisen anywhere.

With this, the general thesis is put forward.

(Opponent:) First of all, what does "neither from itself" signify here?

(Answer:) The words "have any things whatsoever ever arisen anywhere" are to be related to the individual (parts of the thesis). "From itself" means the same as *from one's own self.* Since the intended subject is not proven by a mere thesis, the existence is to be considered as reason here, since with the words "from itself" it is stated that one's own self already exists. The example is based on the quality to be proven and the quality that proves. For a bearer of qualities, proven to possess the quality to be proven and the quality that proves, is an example. The negation "not from itself" is to be understood in the sense of a simple [or non-affirming] negation *(prasajyapratiṣedha)*, because in this the negation is the essential point and the intention there is to call forth—through the removal of the net of all conceptions—the nonconceptual knowledge *(nirvikalpaka jñāna)* that includes all objects. If, on the other hand, [the negation] also implied an exclusion *(paryudāsa)*, then the words "things have not arisen" would teach non-arising in positive form, since with this [negation] the affirmation is the essential point, and through this there would be a deviation from one's own system. For it follows from tradition that he who engages in the non-arising of form *(rūpa)* does not engage in the perfection of insight . . .

To that end the formal inference reads as follows: These inner spheres *(āyatana)* do not arise, in truth, from themselves, because they already exist, like cognitive capacity.

(Opponent:) The reason, i.e., the existence, is no reason, because it is not proven that it is not present in the dissimilar [cases] *(vipakṣa).*

(Answer:) The not-being-present needs not to be considered, since (something dissimilar) does not exist. Thus here, and <228> in all (like cases), there is no fault.

Against this some Sāṃkhyas object: "What is the sense of this thesis? Does it mean that (things do not arise) from themselves insofar as they have the nature of the effect, or insofar as they have the nature of the cause? What follows from this? If it means insofar as they have the nature of the effect, then only something already proven is proven. If on the other hand, it means insofar as they have the nature of the cause, then this is a contradiction with regard to content, since everything that arises does so after it has already existed in the form of the cause."

[Answer to the Sāṃkhyas:] This is not valid because we oppose this very arising from itself, and because also as far as the nature of the cause is concerned—whether this (cause) now has its own or another nature—we reject an arising. The existence of the cognitive capacity is incontestable because it is also included here, insofar as it bears the characteristic of force (i.e., in the potential state).

To this, others (= Buddhapālita) give the following explanation: Things do not arise from their own selves because their arising would be pointless and because an endless arising would result.

[Answer:] This is off the mark, because no reason and no example are stated and because the objections advanced by the opponent are not rejected. Further, since [Buddhapālita's explanation] consists of an undesired consequence *(prasaṅga)*, there ensues—in contrast to the statement in question—a thesis and a reason of opposing content, that is: Things arise from something other, because their arising has a point and because their arising comes to an end. And that would mean a contradiction to one's own system.

Philosophically far more important than Bhāvaviveka's logical innovations is his discussion <229> of the doctrine of the Yogācāra. To understand this discussion the following should be considered. In their fundamental views the Mādhyamika and the Yogācāra are—by nature—not necessarily opposed. The idea of considering the phenomena of the external world as conceptions can already be found in Nāgārjuna. And since this idea was systematically elaborated by the Yogācāra school and made the fundamental idea of the edifice of their teachings, then no clear break was thus made vis-à-vis the Mādhyamikas. The same goes for the richly developed psychology and the doctrine of liberation based on it, which were created by the Yogācārins in compliance with this fundamental idea. These were also conceivable for the Mādhyamika and, given their greater advancement, they offered several advantages, so that the thought of making use of these advantages readily suggested itself. And this is just what Bhāvaviveka did. He adopted the Yogācāra school's psychology and the doctrine of liberation based on it, albeit with certain alterations. In this way he achieved a considerable enrichment of his own doctrine with valuable concepts, and he could do this without infringing on the principles of his own doctrine.

This did not, however, come about entirely without difficulties, and there was one point in particular around which these difficulties set in. For every doctrine that considers the world to be a conception, the idea of ascribing the character of cognition to the highest reality suggests itself, and this is what the Yogācārins did. But it was not easy to bring this into harmony with the sharply emphasized ungraspable nature of the highest reality, which stands above all worldly determinations. And as we will see,[1] there were a number of different opinions about this within the Yogācāra school. In principle though, the opinions were favorable. – The situation was different for Bhāvaviveka. In the Madhyamaka system, since Nāgārjuna's time, the inconceivability and indeterminability of the highest reality had been so strongly and uncompromisingly developed and emphasized, that it was impossible to reconcile with it the character of cognition. Bhāvaviveka's decision was thus made accordingly. For him cognition belongs to the sphere <230> of the phenomenal world. To express this in the terminology of the schools, according to the Yogācāra school, cognition belongs to the dependent characteristic *(paratantralakṣaṇa)* and therefore a certain degree of reality accrues to it. For Bhāvaviveka, on the other hand, cognition belongs to the sphere of restricted truth *(saṃvṛtisatya)* and has nothing to do with the highest reality. On this point, therefore, Bhāvaviveka differed from the Yogācārins. A dispute arose about this, and on this he was thus most vehemently attacked by the representatives of the Yogācāra school. On this question, however, he decided in favor of his own doctrine and thereby remained a faithful follower of Nāgārjuna.

---

[1] [*Cf.* 396f., and also Frauwallner's *Amalavijñāna and Ālayavijñāna*.]

As an example of these views, I render in the following a piece from an original work of Bhāvaviveka's, i.e., from the *Jewel in the Hand (Tschang tschen).* This work briefly summarizes the doctrines of the Madhyamaka school as understood by Bhāvaviveka. The main part consists of the refutation of the reality of the external world in two broadly discussed formal inferences, one of which proves the unreality of the conditioned factors *(saṃskṛta [dharma]),* the other the unreality of the unconditioned factors *(asaṃskṛta dharma).* The conclusion consists of a description of the path of liberation and of the highest knowledge. I render the better part of this section, since it offers an unusually good presentation of the principal philosophical thoughts of the Mahāyāna path of liberation from the point of view of the Madhyamaka doctrine, and at the same time clearly shows the difference between the views of Bhāvaviveka and the Yogācārins.

To understand it, the following should be noted. For Bhāvaviveka, the starting point is the cognition of the unreality of the external world, gained through instruction, but more importantly through the two preceding inferences. According to the old view, however, such cognition alone does not suffice for liberation. Contemplation *(bhāvanā)* must still be joined with it (*cf. above* S. 128f.).

According to Yogācāra doctrine, this path of contemplation has as its purpose the gradual removal of all the conceptions that make up the content of <231> worldly cognition. The same goes for Bhāvaviveka, only for him, the path of contemplation with regard to the conceptions that are to be removed is adapted to the Madhyamaka doctrine, and likewise the sutras to which he refers are those that were esteemed by the Madhyamaka school most of all.

The first stage [part one, subsection 1 (S. 232)] of this path of contemplation consists in that the practitioner contemplates all phenomena of the phenomenal world as unreal, i.e., as empty. Specifically, he must hold in this to the definitions of emptiness as given in the *Prajñāpāramitā* texts. The outcome of this contemplation is that finally all coarse external phenomenal forms and the conceptions tied to them disappear.

In the second stage [subsection 2] of the contemplation the practitioner comes to the knowledge that knowledge of the emptiness of all entities is also a conception that, as such, impedes the highest liberating knowledge and must therefore be removed. Consequently—again following the *Prajñāpāramitā* texts—he also contemplates things no longer as empty and he continues this contemplation until the conception of emptiness vanishes as well. By thus contemplating things neither as empty nor as not empty, he enters the middle way *(madhyamā pratipat)* as described in the *Ratnakūṭa Sūtra* [S. 163ff.].

This knowledge, however, that rejects both opposites, emptiness and non-emptiness, existence and non-existence, this knowledge, as a knowledge, is also a conception and must be overcome. And so [subsection 3] the practitioner arrives at the third stage of contemplation in which any content of knowledge is eliminated. With this he attains the last and highest stage, nonconceptual knowledge *(nirvikalpaka jñāna)*.

[In part two (S. 236)] the Yogācārins also speak of this nonconceptual knowledge. But here opinions differ. According to the Yogācāra doctrine, nonconceptual knowledge also bears the character of knowledge, but according to Bhāvaviveka, this is not the case. According to him, nonconceptual knowledge has shed even the character of knowledge and is, as he says elsewhere, designated as knowledge only in a figurative sense. Nonconceptual knowledge is therefore no knowledge, even <232> though one speaks of knowledge. Just as, with respect to the saint on this stage, there is no movement (i.e., engagement) even though one speaks of movement. As stated already in the sacred texts, this final knowledge consists rather in the absence of any knowledge, just as the engagement of the saint consists in the absence of any engagement. And this is the highest, the emancipation from any error, the silence of the saints.

CDD.3. *From the "Jewel in the Hand" (Tchang tchen) (T 1578, pp. 276a3–377b11)*

[*Prajñā* without movement]

[Part One: Contemplation *(bhāvanā)* of the emptiness of the conditioned and unconditioned factors:]

After the practitioner has removed all objections in this way, he apprehends, by means of correct inference, the emptiness of the unconditioned (factors) assumed by himself and by others. But although he may have apprehended emptiness on the ladder of knowledge won through hearing, so long as the power of contemplation *(bhāvanā)* is absent, he is still not capable of clearing away the obstructions *(āvaraṇa)* that must be removed. Thus, he now makes an effort to practice the power of contemplation.

1

In doing so, as long as a conditioned or unconditioned image *(nimitta)* of any kind is present, which appears with interruption or without interruption, he must remove this image through truthful contemplation of its emptiness, so that it no longer appears. (In doing so,) he apprehends all factors (in the following way): Since they are without an intrinsic nature, they are by nature empty. Since they are empty, they possess no real sign *(nimitta)*. They are therefore signless. Since they are signless, they are nothing <233> for which one yearns. Thus they are unwished for. Since they are free from contamination by a sign, they are apart. Since they are apart, the defilements that attach themselves to them do not arise at all. Thus they are peaceful. Since their intrinsic nature does not arise, they are not arisen. Since they are not arisen, they are not impermanent. They are not painful. They are not without a self. Since they are not arisen, they are, further, without a sign. Since they are without a sign, the non-duality of all factors can be apprehended through contemplation, the sole sign of which is signlessness.

In this form [the practitioner] endeavors to practice contemplation. In that the power of contemplation grows in this way, he removes the coarse images so that they no longer appear. Thus there is no longer any appearing form to occupy his mind. In other words, he apprehends the conditioned and unconditioned appearing forms as does someone with an eye disease *(taimirika)* whose eyes have been freed and cleared of the coarse cloudiness caused by the eye diṣease. That is, he no longer sees the appearing images that he previously apprehended.

2

Although he has now come to the point of not abiding in these (images), the stream of his mind—because the conceptions of emptiness, etc., still appear—remains nevertheless connected with a certain striving *(ābhoga)* and thus does not yet attain immovability.[1] Since he recognizes thus that the occurrence of conceptions of emptiness, etc., prevents the supramundane, nonconceptual insight, he wishes to remove them. He makes a sincere effort, therefore, to consider the following [i.e., first reasoning]: "From the standpoint <234> of the highest truth, the conceptions of emptiness, etc., concerning objects that are by nature empty are likewise not real since they arise from causes,

---

[1] [La Vallée Poussin comments that this means that the practitioner has not yet obtained the eighth stage *(acalābhūmi)* of the Bodhisattva. *See Siddhi*, p. 616.]

like a conjuror's illusion, etc." In practicing contemplation in this way, he is now able to remove the conceptions of emptiness, etc. And by removing these, he avoids the two extremes of emptiness and non-emptiness, etc. Thus, he no longer sees the factors under the form of their emptiness.

Accordingly it is said in the *Perfection of Insight (Prajñā-pāramitā)* [i.e., second reasoning]: "If he engages himself correctly, he views corporeality neither as eternal nor as non-eternal; he sees it neither as pleasurable nor as painful; he sees it neither as self nor as non-self; he sees it neither as peaceful nor as non-peaceful; he sees it neither as empty nor as non-empty; he sees it neither as sign nor as non-sign; he sees it neither as wished for nor as unwished for; and he sees it neither as apart nor as non-apart. Likewise, he sees sensation, ideation, formations, and cognition, all visible forms, sounds, odors, tastes, all tangibles, and all factors, the eye, the ear, the nose, the tongue, the body, and the mind, the perfections of generosity, of moral conduct, of patience, of vigor, of absorption, and of insight, the awakenings of mindfulness, the right efforts, the constituents of miraculous power, the faculties, the powers, the members of enlightenment, the members of the [noble] path, the meditations, the absorptions of the formless sphere, the supranatural knowledges, the ten powers, the certainties, the unlimited knowledges, the qualities unique to the Buddha, the concentrations, <235> the gates of retention, and omniscience, neither as eternal nor as non-eternal, etc., etc."

Since in this way the (practitioner) is capable of removing both extremes, he is able to bring about and to further the middle way. This middle way, free of both extremes, is called *formless [arūpin]* because—due to the two reasonings above rendered—the forms of the conditioned and the unconditioned no longer appear. Because it is formless and because the conceptions of existence, etc., are absent from it, there is no factor at all whose characteristic could be demonstrated by saying: "This is so, thus that is likewise so." [The middle way] is therefore called *undemonstrable [anidarśana]*. Because it is essenceless, there is nothing on which to base oneself, and nothing that is based upon it. Therefore, because it knows of no abiding, it is called *without support [apratiṣṭha]*. Whether it be the image of the conditioned or the image of the unconditioned, whether it be something conceived or non-conceived, conception or non-conception—a knowledge that shows such an image does not occur [in this path]. Hence it is called *without image [anābhāsa]*. Since it is free of any image of existence or non-existence, no knowledge arises that has this [image] as its object, and therefore it is called *without cognizance [avijñaptika]*. Because it is formless and shapeless, and there is no determination or mark in it, it is called *without mark [aniketa]*.

Accordingly, the Exalted One said to Kāśyapa (*cf. above* S. 165f.): "*Eternal*, that is one extreme. *Non-eternal*, that is a second. What lies in the middle between these two, that is formless, undemonstrable, without support, without image, without cognizance, and without mark. <236> That is called the *middle way*, the truthful consideration of the nature of all factors," etc., up to "*existence*, that is one extreme. *Non-existence*, that is a second," etc.

Further, the Buddha said to Kāśyapa (*above* S. 167f.): "Knowledge *[vidyā]* and ignorance *[avidyā]* are not two things and do not constitute a duality. The correct understanding of this is called the *middle way*."

3

While the (practitioner) is able in this way to remove both extremes, he abides in the conception that arises with regard to the view of non-duality. Now he recognizes that this view of non-duality is also an obstacle to peaceful abiding in the supramundane, nonconceptual insight. He therefore quickly removes the causes mentioned. Because he removes them, such or such a conception no longer appears, the twofold speaking *[jalpa]* of the voice and of the mind simultaneously comes to a standstill, and he becomes aware of the true nature of the factors: unmoving; without image; without sign; and free from any diversity. Thus, based on that [awareness], he attains an unmoving realization and he abides in the stream of the knowledge of the intrinsic characteristic *(svalakṣaṇa).* Thus although he makes an effort to practice the unmistaken view of emptiness, nevertheless, he does not bring the nature of emptiness into consciousness at all.

Another long citation from a sutra follows and then the text continues:

[Part Two: Nonconceptual knowledge *(nirvikalpakajñāna)*:]

[1. The Yogācāra doctrine:]

The Yogācārins hold the following view: "If all conceptions of something grasped and a grasper are removed, then this is the <237> supramundane, nonconceptual knowledge. A firm view of reality arises in him [i.e., the practitioner] and he makes an effort to practice the contemplation."

Others, who examine this correctly, say: [1] If this knowledge arises, then indeed, the above mentioned conceptions are not present. It arises, however, in connection with the image of a signless object, is accompanied by the conception according to its intrinsic nature *(svabhāvavikalpa)*,[1] is caused, and therefore—just like the other knowledges that are sensory perception *[pratyakṣabuddhi]* and are accompanied by conceptions—cannot be considered to be supramundane, nonconceptual knowledge. [2] Likewise, the highest reality *[paramārtha]*

---

1 Buddhist scholasticism distinguishes several kinds of conceptions. Of them, the conception according to its intrinsic nature *(svabhāvavikalpa)* is the basic form that also appears in other processes of knowledge, which are otherwise considered to be nonconceptual.

assumed by them, the signless and designationless suchness *(tathatā)*, is the object-support (of knowledge) and, as such—just like the other object-supports—cannot be considered to be the highest reality. For these reasons both (assumptions) are not incontestable.

Accordingly, it is said in the sutra: "What is in all of this the truth in the highest sense? – To this, knowledge has no access." Further, in the *Question of Mañjuśrī (Mañjuśrīparipṛcchā)* it is said: "What is it that the eye of insight *(prajñācakṣu)* regards?" The answer states: "If something were present that it regards, then it would no longer be the eye of insight. Since this eye of insight is free from conceptions, it does not regard the conditioned and also does not regard the unconditioned since everything unconditioned does not fall into the sphere of this eye of insight." <238>

According to these reasons and these sacred texts, the above mentioned view must be discarded.

Further, those who correctly examine, say: According to the truth in the highest sense, such a supramundane, nonconceptual knowledge is not real because it has arisen from causes, like a person created by magic. All difficulties and faults, whatever they may be, are to be removed due to correct contemplation. But if it is a knowledge that removes such views, then just like them, it is faulty. Thus one makes no further effort to examine and to explain. With that, all such views are destroyed.

[2. Apprehension in accordance with truth:]

With respect to the signless nature of the objects, which is the subject matter of knowledge *[jñeya]*, there is no direct apprehension. And since the causes and conditions are absent, no other types of knowledge arise either. Because there is, however, no direct apprehension, one speaks of *apprehension in accordance with truth*.

Accordingly, the Exalted One has said: "What is called *apprehension in accordance with truth?* – The complete non-apprehending of all factors: that is called the *apprehension in accordance with truth.*" Further, a sutra says: "The Exalted One does not see enlightenment at all." In addition, in the *Question of Mañjuśrī (Mañjuśrīparipṛcchā)* it is said: "What does he see who sees the (noble) truths?" – The answer states: "There is no factor of any kind that can be seen. Why? Everything that is seen is false. If there is nothing that is seen, then one speaks of seeing the truths *[satyadarśana]*." Further, it is asked: "How does one make an effort to practice clear comprehension *[abhisamaya]*?" – The answer states: "If one knows that there is no factor of any kind and thinks and reflects in this way, then one is making the effort to practice clear comprehension." Further, it is <239> asked: "When has one realized clear comprehension?" – The answer states: "If one contemplates the equality of all factors." Further, it is asked: "Is there someone who sees the equality *[samatā]* of all factors?" – The answer states: "There is no one who sees the equality. For if there is something that is seen, then the result is that equality is not seen." The expressions "apprehension in accordance with truth," "seeing the truth," and "clear comprehension" all have one and the same meaning.

[3. Absence of movement:]

In one who practices contemplation, neither mind *[citta]*, nor thinking *[manas]*, nor cognition *[vijñāna]*, nor knowledge *[jñāna]* moves. This is called *correct movement in nonconceptual insight*. If he is able to move without movement in this way, then he attains the true prediction *[bhūtavyākaraṇa]* of the Perfected Ones, the Perfectly Enlightened Ones.

Accordingly, a sutra says: "Exalted One, how should a Bodhisattva practice so that he attains—about the highest, perfect enlightenment—the true prediction of the Perfected Ones, the Perfectly Enlightened Ones? – O brahman, if the

Bodhisattva at that time moves, i.e., engages neither in the arising nor in the ceasing; if he engages neither in the good nor in the bad; if he engages neither in the mundane nor in the supramundane; if he engages neither in the contaminated nor in the uncontaminated; if he engages neither in the blameworthy nor in the blameless; if he engages neither in the conditioned nor in the unconditioned; if he engages neither in the connection nor in the non-connection; if he engages neither in the apartness nor in the non-apartness; if he engages neither in birth and death *[saṃsāra]* nor in extinction *[nirvāṇa]*; if he engages neither in what is seen nor in what is heard, what is thought, and what is cognized; if he engages neither in generosity and renunciation nor in moral <240> conduct and discipline; if he engages neither in patience nor in vigor; if he engages neither in absorption nor in concentration; if he engages neither in insight nor in understanding; and if he engages neither in knowledge nor in calling to mind; if the Bodhisattva engages, i.e., moves without movement in this way, then he attains—about the highest perfect enlightenment—the true prediction of the Perfected Ones, the Perfectly Enlightened Ones."

[4. Silence:]

Such an engagement in insight is called the *silence of the saints [ārya tūṣṇīmbhāva]*. Accordingly, a sutra says: "The true proclamation of the thirty-seven factors conducive to enlightenment, just as the Buddha taught them is called the *preaching of the doctrine*. If, further, (the practitioner) realizes these factors with his body, then he does not regard them as separate from the body, and he does not regard the body as separate from the factors. Rather, he regards them in the way that he sees them, neither as duality nor as non-duality. And while he regards them in this way, he also does not, subsequently, regard the knowledge and vision by way of sensory perception. And because he does not regard them, this is called the *silence of the saints*.

From these reasonings and sacred texts results—if one examines them accurately—that it is impossible to make the intrinsic nature of all that is conditioned and unconditioned into the intrinsic nature of the objects of mind or of insight, be they accompanied by conceptions or free from conceptions. If one recognizes this, then the sunshine of clear insight chases away all the darkness of delusion. <241>

With the innovations discussed here, Bhāvaviveka had gone far beyond anything that had hitherto existed and this led to a backlash. He was attacked more vehemently by the Yogācāra teachers than any other representative of his school. And within the [Madhyamaka] school itself as well, a countercurrent arose, the principal representative of which was Candrakīrti.

CDE. *Candrakīrti (seventh century c.e.)*

Candrakīrti is the most significant personality of the Madhyamaka school in the seventh century. His principal effort was directed at reestablishing Nāgārjuna's doctrine in its purity, free from all the more recent expansions and distortions. He drew support therefore from Buddhapālita, whom he saw as his role model, while he most vehemently opposed Bhāvaviveka. From this fundamental approach, however, ensues that we should not expect to find in him something significant, new, and original. And it is characteristic of him that, in contrast to most of the great Madhyamaka teachers, his activity was confined almost exclusively to the composition of commentaries. He did, however, represent the school with all the know-how of his time and with great success, and since he belongs among the best known and most oft-mentioned representatives of the school, he is entitled to a place here.

CDE.1. *The works of Candrakīrti*

The most important of Candrakīrti's commentaries is his great commentary on Nāgārjuna's *Madhyamakakārikā,* called *Prasannapadā (The Clearly Worded).* Aside from this, an original work, the *Madhyamakāvatāra (Introduction to the Madhyamaka Doctrine),* is most worthy of mention. One sample from each shall be presented, which will illuminate Candrakīrti's approach to logic and his relationship to the Yogācāra school at the same time.

Firstly, as for his approach to the question of logic, he saw in the formulation of formal inferences by Bhāvaviveka an aberration and an offense against Nāgārjuna's principle that Mādhyamikas should not advance any thesis of their own. <242> In his opinion, the correct method is that of Buddhapālita who does indeed refute the opponent by means of *deductio ad absurdum,* but in doing so avoids any assertion of his own. He deals with this question in detail in his commentary to the first verse of the *Madhyamakakārikā* [S. 179], in which he defends Buddhapālita against Bhāvaviveka's attack, and from this broad discussion is taken the brief selection that I present as an example.

CDE.2. *Introduction to the sample from the Prasannapadā*

The text does not offer any difficulties. Candrakīrti first makes a few explanatory remarks about Nāgārjuna's verse; and for a detailed proof of the theses put forward therein, he refers to his own *Madhyamakāvatāra.*

He then immediately cites Buddhapālita's explanation and defends it against Bhāvaviveka's attacks. These attacks encompass three points.

First, Bhāvaviveka criticizes Buddhapālita for not stating a reason and an example, as is demanded by a proper inference. Candrakīrti responds that the *deductio ad absurdum* is entirely sufficient for the refutation of the opponent and thus a proper inference is unnecessary.

In addition, according to the testimony of Āryadeva and Nāgārjuna, a Mādhyamika should put forward no thesis of his own. With this, Bhāvaviveka's second criticism is also invalidated, that is, that Buddhapālita does not refute the opponent's objections. Since Buddhapālita does not put forward a thesis of his own, the opponent also cannot advance any objections that would need to be refuted.

Bhāvaviveka's third criticism states that from a *deductio ad absurdum* it follows that the opposite of the refuted thesis is correct. Candrakīrti replies that, in such cases, the Mādhyamika starts from the assumptions of the opponent and not from his own views, and that therefore the resulting consequences also apply only to the opponent and not to himself.

The answers clearly show Candrakīrti's fundamental stance. The further extensive discussions that he ties to this are without general interest and are therefore not rendered. <243>

DE.3. *From the "Clearly Worded" (Prasannapadā)*

Chapter I

The arising that the opponents assume could be conceived as from itself, could be conceived as from something other, from both, or without cause. But in no mode is it possible. With this in mind, (Nāgārjuna) says:

v. 1

> Neither from itself, nor from something other, nor from both, nor without cause, have any things ever arisen anywhere.

... (Opponent): If one states that they do not arise from themselves, then the undesired consequence follows that they arise from something other.

(Answer:) This does not follow since a simple [or non-affirming] negation *(prasajyapratiṣedha)* is intended to be expressed, and since in addition, the arising from something other has yet to be refuted. The line of argumentation according to which an arising from itself is impossible is found in the *Introduction to the Madhyamaka Doctrine (Madhyamakāvatāra)*, etc., where it is said (chapter VI, v. 8):

> With respect to the arising of same from same, there is no advantage. In addition, a renewed arising of something already arisen, is nonsensical, etc.

The Master Buddhapālita says on the other hand (*see above* S. 223): "Things do not arise from themselves because their arising would be pointless, and because the error of consequences that are too far reaching would result. That is, there is no need for things, which in themselves are already existent, to arise again. If, however, something already existent were nonetheless to arise, then it would never not arise." <244>

In opposition, some (= Bhāvaviveka) raise the following objections (*see above* S. 228). This is off the mark, because no reason and no example are stated and because the objections advanced by the opponent are not rejected. Further, since it is a matter of an undesired consequence *(prasaṅga)*, there results in contrast to the statement in question, a thesis and a reason of opposing content. Specifically: things arise from something other, because their arising has a point and because their arising comes to an end. And that would mean a contradiction to one's system.

We regard all of these objections as unjustified. How so? If you say, first of all: "Because no reason and no example are stated," then this is not appropriate. Why? Because we ask the opponent who assumes an arising from itself, what point it would serve if something already existent were to arise again. Since after all, "from itself" is given as a cause, this means that the same arises. We see no point in the renewed arising of something already existent, but rather see (that) an infinite regress *(anavasthā)* results. But the renewed arising of something already arisen also appears unwanted by you, and likewise, an infinite regress is unwanted. Therefore, your assertion is impossible and contradicts your own assumptions. Is it not the case that the opponent now agrees, when he is challenged [in this way,] so that there is still reason to state a cause and an example? If, however, the opponent does not admit defeat even when shown that he contradicts his own assumptions, then he in his shamelessness will also not admit defeat when reason and example are given. But we will not debate with a madman. <245>

The good master thus only shows his fondness for inferences when he advances an inference even where it is not appropriate. It is not fitting, however, for a Mādhyamika himself to formulate an autonomous inference of his own since he does not admit any thesis. Accordingly, Āryadeva says (*Catuḥśataka* XVI, v. 25):

> Whoever holds no thesis, be it existence, non-existence, or both existence and non-existence, to refute him is not possible however long [one tries].

It is also said in *Averting of Quarrels (Vigrahavyāvartanī)* (*see above* S. 203f.):

v. 29

> If I were to advocate any kind of thesis, then this fault would result from it for me. But I do not advocate any thesis. Therefore no fault applies to me.

v. 30

> If I were to apprehend anything, then I would put forward and refute theses based on objects observed through sensory perception, etc. Since this is not the case, no reproach applies to me.

However, if the Mādhyamika does not put forward any autonomous inference, then what has he to do with the autonomous inference (*see above* S. 227f.): "The inner spheres do not arise from themselves," against which the Sāṃkhyas bring forth their objections by saying: "What is the sense of this thesis?

Does it mean that (things do not arise) from themselves insofar as they have the nature of the effect, or insofar as they have the nature of the cause? <246> What follows from this? If it means insofar as they have the nature of the effect, then only something already proven is proven. If on the other hand, it means insofar as they have the nature of the cause, then this is a contradiction with regard to content, since everything that arises does so after it has already existed in the form of the cause." What do we have to do with the reason (*see above* S. 227): "Because they already exist"? This [reason] only proves what is already proven, or it contains a contradiction with regard to content, so that we then have the work of invalidating this proving of what has been proven or this contradiction with regard to content. So since no objections brought forth by the opponent ensue for the Master Buddhapālita, he also does not have to invalidate them. . . .

The view opposed to the undesired consequence concerns only the opponent, but not us, since we do not put forward any thesis of our own, and thus no contradiction to our own doctrine results. If on the other hand, the various objections apply to the opponent because the opposite of the undesired consequence holds true, then this is fine with us. Indeed, why should the Master Buddhapālita, who follows the unmistaken doctrine of the Master Nāgārjuna, make contestable statements so that the opponent would be able to find an opportunity to attack? And why should the view opposed to the undesired consequence result for the proponent of the doctrine of the essencelessness (of things), if he holds up un undesired consequence to the follower of the doctrine of an intrinsic nature (of things)? After all, words are not persecutors that rob the speaker of his freedom. Rather, insofar as they have the appropriate capacity for expression, they depend upon that which the speaker wishes to express. Therefore, since bringing forward an <247> undesired consequence has the sole purpose of refuting the thesis of the opponent, the view opposed to the undesired consequence in no way necessarily results from it.

> As for Candrakīrti's relationship to the Yogācāra school, in accord with his fundamental attitude his stance is one of a fundamental rejection of any adoption of Yogācāra ideas. In this respect then, he goes beyond Bhāvaviveka. On the main question though, as to whether cognition is to be regarded as real or whether it belongs to the unreal phenomenal world, he agrees with him. As this question is central to the dispute with the Yogācāra school, he sees no need to take up a position against Bhāvaviveka. And indeed in the section that disputes the Yogācāra doctrine, there is no polemic against Bhāvaviveka.

CDE.4. *Introduction to the sample from the Madhyamakāvatāra*

The section that I render in the following comes from Candrakīrti's great original work, the *Introduction to the Madhyamaka Doctrine (Madhyamakāvatāra)*. This work discusses the career of a Bodhisattva with reference to the old doctrine of the ten stages *(bhūmi)* that a Bodhisattva must pass through. Philosophically most important is the sixth chapter, which deals with the sixth of these stages, on which the Bodhisattva gains the perfection of insight. As befits its importance, this chapter makes up more than half of the entire work. It is divided into three parts. The first contains the proof of the unreality of the external world. The second combats the false belief in a self. The third, finally, discusses the sixteen kinds of emptiness, which are already enumerated in the *Prajñāpāramitā* texts and also otherwise often dealt with. The proof of the unreality of the external world shows the same development that we could see in Bhāvaviveka's *Jewel in the Hand*. The bewildering wealth of in many ways questionable inferences—as advanced by Nāgārjuna—is given up, and in their place we find a single, but thoroughly elaborated line of argument. Specifically, it is in Candrakīrti the <248> proof—which also stands at the beginning of Nāgārjuna's principal work—that indeed any kind of arising is in reality impossible. Various digressions are woven into this line of argument, among them a broad refutation of the Yogācāra doctrine. It is from this that the following brief sample is taken.

The selection is prefaced [vv. 45–47], according to general custom, by a brief rendering of the tenets of the opponent that are to be refuted. I have translated only the verses of this part without Candrakīrti's explanation, since they are easily understandable on the basis of the later presentation of the Yogācāra doctrine [in our book].

Next [v. 48], Candrakīrti's polemic begins. In order to prove the unreality of the external world, the Yogācārins could not use Nāgārjuna's line of argument, since it serves as proof that the entire phenomenal world is unreal, whereas the Yogācāra school asserts only the unreality of the external world while accepting the processes of cognizance as real. This made it necessary for them to find a different way. In doing so they used above all various examples that were intended to show that cognition is also possible without really existing external objects. Among these examples the most popular was once again the dream. They said: Just as cognition in a dream displays the most diverse objects, which do not in reality exist, so also the objects that we believe we see in the waking state are not real. At this point Candrakīrti's polemic begins and in accordance with the aforementioned fundamental view of the Mādhyamikas, he tries to show that not only the external world but the entire phenomenal world is unreal. Hence he says: Your example proves nothing because in a dream not only the seen objects but cognition as well is unreal.

The Yogācāra replies [v. 49]: Cognition in a dream is real because we can remember it.

Candrakīrti answers: We can also remember the objects seen in a dream.

Now [v. 50], the Yogācārin formulates his doctrine more precisely: In a dream it is not a matter of [sensory] perception but of mental cognition *(manovijñāna)*, whereby the image is erroneously projected as external; and the same applies for cognition during <249> the waking state.

In contrast to this, Candrakīrti holds fast [v. 51] to the view that in this case also, cognition is just as unreal as its object. He elaborates this further as follows: According to the Buddha's doctrine—as it holds true for all Buddhist schools—perception does not arise due to the fact that someone sees, but because the perceived visible form and the eye jointly bring about a visual cognition. Now, if the visible form and the eye are not real, then of course the cognition cannot be real.

This is valid for all six types of cognitions, including the mental cognition [v. 52]. And nothing changes in this regard even if one points out that only as a constituent of the sphere of the factors *(dharmāyatana)* is the visible form an object of the mental cognition. For if one were to infer from this that, just like the visible form and thinking *[manas]*, the mental cognition of the dream is also real, then the entire example loses its meaning. The unreality of the objects of waking awareness can namely no longer be proved by it, since the object [of the example] itself is presupposed to be real.

Next Candrakīrti cites a few references from the sacred scripture and then he concludes by interpreting and making use [v. 53] of the opponent's example from his own perspective: Just as in a dream all three factors on which the processes of cognizance are based appear as real, whereas upon waking they are recognized as unreal, just so in the case of cognition during the waking state, the same factors appear at first as real.

One who wakes from the dream of ignorance, however, realizes that these too are unreal. With that, this line of thinking comes to an end and Candrakīrti moves on to the next arguments of his opponent. These follow in a long series, from whose rendering we must, however, refrain.

CDE.5. *From the "Introduction to the Madhyamaka Doctrine" (Madhyamakāvatāra)*

[Chapter six]

45

The Bodhisattva abiding within insight, who has reached the understanding that reality <250> is only cognition, understands, since he does not see a grasper without something grasped, that the threefold existence (= the triple world) is only cognition.

46

Just as waves arise out of the great ocean through the impetus of the wind, in the same way, mere cognition arises out of the so-called *fundamental cognition* that contains all seeds through its own power *(śakti)*.

47

Hence, the dependent nature *(paratantrarūpa)*, which forms the foundation of all things that exist merely as designation, exists. It arises without something external that is grasped, it exists, and it lies by nature outside the sphere of all diversity *(prapañca)*.

To this is to be said:

48 a

The mind exists without something external – as where?

This is to be examined in detail.

(The opponent) says:

> As in a dream. (48 b)

If one sleeps in a tiny room, one dreams—deceived by sleep—of a herd of raging elephants within the house. But they are not [actually] present in any way. Since therefore no external object exists, this cognition [without the existence of an external object] must of necessity be accepted.

In order to show that this is also not sound, the (author) says:

> This is to be investigated. (48 b)

How so?

(In answer) he says:

> Since according to our view the mind in a dream also does not exist, your example is not valid. (48 c–d) <251>

According to our view, the cognition that bears the form of the raging herd of elephants exists no more than the object, because it is not arisen. But if this cognition does not exist, then there is no example accepted by both parties, and it is therefore not correct that cognition exists without an external (object).

Now, one might think that if there were no erroneous cognition in the dream, then, upon waking, one could not remember what was perceived in the dream. But this is also not correct, since:

49 a–b

> If mind exists because a dream is remembered in the waking state, then it is the same for the external object.

How so?

> Just as you remember: "I have seen," just so there is also the memory of the external object. (49 c–d)

As the mind exists due to the memory of the perception in the dream, likewise, the object must necessarily exist due to the existence of the memory of the perception of the object, or the cognition also does not exist.

(Opponent:) If the visible form *(rūpa)* of the elephants, etc., existed in the dream, then, in order to apprehend it, the visual cognition would also have to exist. But this is not the case since within the bewilderment of sleep the groups of the five (sense-) cognitions cannot come about.

In other words

50

> if you [i.e., the Yogācāra] hold: Because a visual cognition is not possible in sleep, no (object) exists. <252> But the mental cognition exists. And just as its appearing form in the dream is conceived as external, so it is also the case here (in the waking state).

In a dream, a visual cognition does not exist in any way, and because it does not exist, the form of the elephants, etc., which could be apprehended as the visual sphere *(āyatana)*, also does not exist. But the mental cognition is there. Even if therefore an external visible form *(rūpa)* does not exist, nevertheless, there can be no objection to the appearing form of cognition being conceived as external. Therefore, just as in a dream, only the cognition arises without anything external existing, so it is also the case here.

(Answer:) It is not like this, because in a dream, a mental cognition cannot arise. Since

51 a–b

> just as for you [i.e., the Yogācāra] no external object arises in the dream, so also no mind arises.

Thus

> all three, the eye, the object of the eye, and the cognition arising out of them, are untrue. (51 c–d)

Just as in the perception of a visible form the eye, the visible form, and the cognition—these three—appear together, so also in the apprehension of an object in a dream, these three are perceived to occur together. And as here the eye and the visible form do not exist, so also visual cognition does not exist.

And like these three, so

52 a

> also the other groups of three, the ear, etc., do not arise.

With the words "ear, etc.," are the sound, auditory cognition, etc., up to thinking, the sphere of the <253> factors, and mental cognition included. Thus in a dream, all these groups of three are untrue. Therefore it is also impossible that mental cognition exists in a dream.

(Opponent:) The visible form belonging to the sphere of the factors is recognized by the mental cognition, and this does exist in a dream. Therefore it is not at all correct that the cognition is without an object.

(Answer:) This is also not correct because in sleep the three do not exist in any case. If, however, we were to accept it in order to refute the doctrine of the opponent, then the example of the dream loses its meaning, since with an example whose subject-matter is not established as untrue, a real subject-matter cannot be established as untrue. Thus because in dreams these three are altogether untrue, it follows from this—since through that which is proved the non-proved is proved—that also in the waking state all factors are without intrinsic nature. Hence, (the author) says:

> Just as in a dream, so also here in the waking state things are untrue and the mind does not exist; and also the sense faculties do not exist, since they do not have an [existing] object. (52 b–d)

Just as in a dream the object, sense faculties, and cognition are untrue, so are they also in the waking state. This is to be understood in this way. Hence it is also rightly stated:

> Just as living beings created through a magical illusion appear to be perceived, but in truth are not real, so—as the Perfected One has taught—are the factors, like a magical illusion and like a dream.

Further:

> The entire course of existence is like a dream. No one is born and no one dies. No being, no soul, and no individual are to be apprehended. <254> All of these factors are like foam or a (hollow) bamboo reed.

And so forth.

Thus we have said that, with regard to the cognition in the waking state, the entire triad is not arisen. In a dream then—with regard to the cognition of the one dreaming the dream—

53 a–b

> just as here in the waking state, as long as he does not awaken, the triad exists.

Just as for someone who is considered to be awake—although he is submerged in the sleep of ignorance—because he is free from the sleep that is different from that [sleep of ignorance], this triad—although by its intrinsic nature not arisen—exists since he observes it, because due to the sleep of ignorance he dreams a dream; so for those who are not free from sleep and who have not arisen from the dream state, the corresponding triad exists.

> Just as this triad does not exist upon waking, just so it is the case when one awakens from the sleep of delusion. (53 c–d)

Just as for one who has awakened from sleep the triad seen does not exist, so for those who have completely shaken off the sleep of ignorance and who have brought to mind the element of the factors *(dharmadhātu)* in direct perception, the triad does not exist. Thus, it is not correct that cognition (alone) exists without external (objects).

With this we conclude our overview of the development of the Madhyamaka school. Of their better-known representatives from the later period, Śāntideva (around 700 c.e.) is more significant as a poet than as a philosopher. <255> Tibet's great apostle Śāntirakṣita (middle of the eighth century) deserves particular mention along with his student Kamalaśīla, who attempted, in the style of Bhāvaviveka, a blending of the Madhyamaka- with the Yogācāra-doctrine. After him the school produced no further significant personalities and gradually became extinct on Indian soil.

It should still be mentioned, however, that the tantric schools of Buddhism, with their mystical cults and magical rites, are based to a great extent on the ideas of the Madhyamaka school.

CE. *The school of Sāramati*

Before we proceed to the examination of the second great Mahāyāna school, the school of the Yogācāra, we must at least briefly mention a small school, which I call the school of Sāramati, after its most important representative. It deserves mentioning not just because it is itself noteworthy and demonstrates the multiplicity of currents in the Mahāyāna, but most importantly because it strongly influenced the actual founder of the Yogācāra school, Maitreyanātha. Among the works of the Sāramati school, the *Mahāyānaśraddhotpādaśāstra (The Treatise on the Development of the Mahāyāna Faith),* attributed to an Aśvaghoṣa, is the most well-known in Europe. But historically, Sāramati is more significant. He had a long lasting effect whereas—in India at least—the *Mahāyānaśraddhotpādaśāstra* soon disappeared. Indeed, it is not impossible that this work actually originated in China. Therefore only Sāramati will be briefly taken into account here.

CEA. *Sāramati (ca. 250 c.e.)*

According to tradition, Sāramati came from Central India and lived not long after Nāgārjuna. We are in possession of two of his works. The more important is the *Ratnagotravibhāga (Elucidation of the Germ of the [Three] Jewels),* <256> mostly called *Uttaratantra (The Ultimate Doctrine).* The title of the second, which is preserved only in Chinese translation, is usually rendered as *Dharmadhātvaviśeṣatāśāstra (Treatise on the Non-difference of the Element of the Factors).*

The doctrine that is set down in these works stands in stark contrast to the *Prajñāpāramitā* and to Nāgārjuna. Whereas in these latter, the unreality of the external world is the focus of interest [S. 149, 171ff.] and the inconceivability of the ultimate state of being is so strongly emphasized that it finally recedes entirely into the background and disappears almost into nothingness [S. 147f., 174], Sāramati deals primarily with the ultimate state of being, which has for him a decidedly positive character and a strong similarity to the world soul of the Vedānta. This ultimate state of being is stainless *(amala)* or luminous mind *(prabhāsvaraṃ cittam)*. It is also designated as *suchness (tathatā)*. But usually, it is called *element (dhātu)* or, more precisely, *true element (paramārthadhātu), element of the factors (dharmadhātu),* and *element of the Buddhas (buddhadhātu)*. It is not at all inconceivable, but is characterized by clearly distinctive qualities, that is, by stains *(mala)* [or faults *(doṣa)*] as well as by virtues *(guṇa)*. First and foremost, the four perfections—purity, self, bliss, and permanence—are attributed to it. But whereas the faults are adventitious *(āgantuka)* and do not affect its nature, the virtues are inseparably connected with its nature, like light rays with the sun.

The ultimate state of being is the foundation of the entire phenomenal world. Through incorrect thinking *(ayoniśomanaskāra)* the deeds and defilements *(karmakleśa)* arise and through these the groups *(skandha)*, spheres *(āyatana)*, and elements *(dhātu)* out of which the phenomenal world is composed. Since the ultimate state of being is omnipresent, it is also innate in all living beings and they all, therefore, possess the germ *(gotra)* of buddhahood. In ordinary individuals, though, it is impure, in noble ones, partly pure and partly impure, and completely pure only in Buddhas. In its completely pure form it is thus buddhahood *(buddhatva)*, <257> the noble truth *(āryasatya)*, and extinction *(nirvāṇa)*.

The true nature of the Buddha, therefore, is the ultimate state of being. This is [the Buddha's] body of the doctrine *(dharmakāya),* which alone is genuinely true *(paramārthakāya).* His worldly body *(rūpakāya),* which appears in twofold form, is on the other hand only seemingly (true) *(samvṛtikāya)* and relates to the body of the doctrine as the [moon's] reflection in water does to the moon. The bodies of the Buddha possess the various characteristics and virtues, which are ascribed to it by scholasticism. Through them the Buddha brings about the liberation of beings, but without striving *(ābhoga)* and without the ultimate state of being—which makes up his body of the doctrine—moving [in any way] or suffering any kind of change. All of this is elaborated on in great length; yet this brief indication must suffice here.

The translated samples that follow are taken from various parts of the *Ratnagotravibhāga* and are meant to illustrate the doctrines outlined above. A continuous translation of longer sections is not advisable due to the affected and unmethodical arrangement of the text. In terms of the details, few explanations are necessary. The first series of verses (I, vv. 49–63) deals with the arising of the phenomenal world out of the ultimate state of being, which is compared with the creation of the world, wherein, according to Buddhist doctrine, first the wind arises, then the water and, finally the earth. The second series of verses (I, vv. 40–47) deals with the ultimate state of being as the germ of buddhahood, innate in all living beings; more specifically, in worldly persons in impure [form], in the noble ones in partly pure [form], and in the Buddhas in completely pure form. In its pure form the ultimate state of being thus also constitutes buddhahood as well as liberation, which two are therefore identical in nature (I, vv. 84 and 87). The next series of verses (II, vv. 3–7) describes buddhahood as the ultimate state of being. The two obstructions mentioned here—obstruction of defilements and obstruction to what is to be known—and the two forms of liberating knowledge [—nonconceptual knowledge and subsequently attained knowledge—] recur in the doctrine of the Yogācāra school and will be explained there (S. 267 and 300f., etc.). Next comes a description of the two bodies of the Buddha (III, vv. 1–4). The body of the doctrine is attained through the freeing of the ultimate state of being—innate in beings—from all adventitious stains. <258> Scholasticism attributes to it ten powers, four fearlessnesses, and eighteen qualities unique to the Buddha. The worldly body arises in the cycle of existences through the maturation of deeds. It possesses the thirty-two marks that distinguish a great man in Indian mythology. Lastly, the final series of verses (IV, vv. 53–64) deal with the activity of the Buddha whose uniqueness is elucidated through comparison with the activity of the god Brahman and of the sun.

CEA.1. *From the "Elucidation of the Germ of the (Three) Jewels" (Ratnagotravibhāga)*

Chapter I

49

Just as space, by nature free from conceptions, pervades everywhere, so the element, consisting of the natural stainlessness of the mind, pervades everywhere.

[. . .]

51

Since it is connected in an adventitious way with faults and endowed by nature with virtues, the constitution of unchangingness accrues to it, before and after.

52

Just as, due to its subtlety, the omnipresent space does not become soiled, so this (element) that exists everywhere in beings, is not soiled.

53

Just as worlds arise and vanish everywhere in space, so the sense faculties vanish and arise in the unconditioned element. <259>

54

Just as space has never yet been consumed by fires, so the fires of death, sickness, and old age do not consume this [element].

55

Earth is based on water, water on wind, wind on space. Space, however, is not based on the elements of wind, water, and earth.

56

Likewise, the groups, elements, and sense faculties are based on deeds and defilements. Deeds and defilements are always based on incorrect thinking.

57

Incorrect thinking is based on the purity of mind. The nature of mind, however, is not based on all the factors.

58

Groups, spheres, and elements are to be seen as akin to the element of earth. Deeds and defilements of embodied beings are to be seen as akin to the element of water.

59

Incorrect thinking is to be seen as akin to the element of wind; the nature (of mind), which is without root and without foundation, is akin to the element of space.

60

Incorrect thinking adheres to the nature of mind. Defilements and deeds originate from incorrect thinking. <260>

61

The groups, spheres, and elements originate from the "water" of deeds and defilements. They arise and vanish, just as this ["water" of deeds and defilements] is created and destroyed.

62

The nature of mind, just like the element of space, knows no cause, no condition, and no totality (of causes and conditions), no arising, no vanishing, and no abiding.

63

This luminous nature of mind, just like the sky, never suffers any change. Through the adventitious stain of passion, etc., which arises from false conceptions, it does, however, experience pollution.

[... ...]

40

If the element of the Buddhas did not exist, then there would be no weariness with suffering and there would be no wishing, no desire, and no aspiration for extinction.

41

If the germ *(gotra)* exists, the faults and the suffering of existence as well as the virtues and the bliss of extinction are seen. In (those) in whom the germ is absent, this is not the case.

[...]

45

Since the suchness of worldly individuals, noble ones, and enlightened ones is not different, the beholders of <261> truth have proclaimed that this germ of the Buddhas *(jinagarbha)* is present in (all) living beings.

46

Worldly individuals are trapped in error. For those who have seen the truth (the noble ones), it is the other way around. Truly free from error and free from diversity are the perfected ones.

47

The element of beings, of Bodhisattvas, and of the perfected ones is designated, respectively, as *impure, impure and pure,* and *completely pure.*

[...]

84

Since this is the body of the doctrine, the perfected one, the noble truth, and true extinction, there is no extinction apart from buddhahood because its qualities are inseparable from it, like the light rays from the sun.

[. . .]

87

Enlightenment, in all aspects, and the removal of stains along with their permeation, [i.e.,] buddhahood and extinction, are thus in truth one and the same.

[. . .]

Chapter II

3

Buddhahood—which, as is taught, is luminous in nature; which, like the sun and space, is covered by the adventitious obstructions of defilements and <262> to what is to be known, as by the cloak of a dense veil of clouds; which, endowed with all the stainless qualities of a Buddha, is permanent, steadfast and eternal—is attained due to knowledge that consists of the nonconceptual distinction of the factors.

4

Buddhahood is conditioned by inseparable bright factors and is characterized, like the sun and space, by two [features:] knowledge and abandonment.

5

It is endowed with all the luminous qualities of a Buddha, which outnumber the [grains of] sand on the banks of the Ganges, are uncreated, and are inseparably attached to him.

6

The obstructions of the defilements and to what is to be known, because they are unreal by nature, all-pervading and adventitious, are thus designated as being like clouds.

7

The two knowledges, the nonconceptual [knowledge] and the subsequently attained knowledge, are considered to be the cause of the removal of both obstructions.

[. . .]

Chapter III

1

The true body and the seemingly [real] body based on it serve the benefit of oneself and the benefit of others. This fruit is divided into sixty-four qualities, according to whether it is based on separation or on the maturation (of deeds). <263>

2

The true body of the sage (= the Buddha) is the foundation of one's own fortune. The foundation of the fortune of others is the body of the worldly truth *(sāṃketika).*

3

The first body is connected with the qualities based on separation, the powers, etc., the second with the marks—based on maturation—of a great man.

4

Through the possession of the powers, in relation to the hindrances of ignorance, the sage is like a thunderbolt. Through the possession of the fearlessnesses, in the assemblies he is like a lion. Through the qualities unique to the Perfected One, he is like the air; through his twofold appearing [as visible bodies], [he is like] the moon in water.

[. . .]

Chapter IV

53

Just as Brahman—without departing his Brahman abode—effortlessly shows his appearance in all the worlds of the gods,

54

so the sage (= the Buddha)—without departing from the body of the doctrine—is effortlessly visible in all realms to those worthy of instruction by means of his created (appearances).

55

Just as Brahman does not depart his palace, yet still the gods see him always in the sphere of desire and the sight of him takes away their delight in sense objects, <264> so the Perfected One does not depart from the body of the splendid doctrine, and yet those worthy of instruction see him always in all worlds and the sight of him removes all of their stains.

[. . .]

59

Just as the sun, free of conceptions, wakes the lotuses and ripens other [crops] by means of its simultaneously radiated rays,

60

so the sun of the Perfected One, free of conceptions, affects the lotuses of those worthy of instruction by means of the rays of the splendid doctrine.

[. . .]

63

Since the sun of the Buddha always spans the entire vault of the sky of the element of the factors, its (rays) fall on the "mountains" of those worthy of instruction, according to what they deserve.

64

Just as, in this world, the sun as it rises, illuminates the whole world with the span of its thousand rays, and shines, in turn, on the highest, the middle, and the lowest mountains, so the sun of the Buddha shines in turn on the crowds of beings.

CF. *The Yogācāra school*

We turn now to the most important Mahāyāna school, the school of the Yogācāra. It bears this name because the practice of yoga played a special role in the circles from which it arose. <265> Here yoga is understood in a general sense as the entire striving, the practice, and activation of all virtues demanded of a future Buddha, a Bodhisattva. Naturally, the description of the path that a Bodhisattva has to travel was always the central interest to all the Mahāyāna schools. In this case, however, it was elaborated on and depicted in a wildly imaginative way that surpasses anything else of its kind. But even early on, various philosophical lines of thought emerge alongside this, although at first to a modest extent. These were later fused with and expanded through a wide variety of other ideas from important teachers. In this way a great, all-encompassing system finally arose.[1]

---

1 [For a brief overview of the development of the doctrines of the Yogācāra (Mahāsaṃghikas, Sāramati, Maitreyanātha, Asaṅga), see Frauwallner's discussion of the bearer of cognition and the relationship of highest reality to phenomenal world in Buddhism in his *Amalavijñāna and Ālayavijñāna*, S. 151–59, in Appendix I.]

CFA. *The beginnings of the Yogācāra school: the Yogācārabhūmiśāstra*

The most characteristic work produced by the older Yogācāra school is the *Yogācārabhūmiśāstra (Treatise of the Stages of the Application of Yoga).* It is one of the typical gigantic works that Indian excessiveness so readily created. Tradition names the heads of the school, Maitreya and Asaṅga, as its authors, but it is probably a work (of the school), whose development extended over several generations. The oldest part may be the *Bodhisattvabhūmi (The Stage of the Bodhisattva).* In this the career of the Bodhisattva is described with inexhaustible imagination in all its details and with bewildering and nearly stupefying elaborateness, wherein the philosophical completely recedes behind the tropically proliferative scholasticism of liberation. A few isolated sections that are also of philosophical significance are, however, inserted. And since they give a good idea of the lines of thought from which the development of the Yogācāra system began, I will render a sample from them.[1] In doing so, I abridge them and render only the philosophically most important pieces, since in and of itself, the work is written in a peculiar, complicated, and longwinded style. And since on top of this it is also broadly elaborated what significance the philosophical insights in question have for the career of the Bodhisattva, such abbreviations seem to be called for. <266>

---

1 [Later, S. 306, in the context of introducing chapter VI of the *Mahāyānasūtrālaṃkāra,* Frauwallner comments that this chapter corresponds to the section of the *Bodhisattvabhūmi* that is partially translated here.]

CFA.1. *The divisions of reality (sections 1–8)*

The subject of the rendered segment is reality *(tattvārtha* or *tattva).* In accordance with the overtly scholastic manner that characterizes the entire work, it begins with various divisions of reality.

The first is superficial and insignificant. It distinguishes the [true] existence *(bhūtatā)* of the factors and their totality *(sarvatā),* by which [distinction] apparently the extent of the sphere of reality is meant.

More important, although still peripheral, is the second division. According to this, there is a fourfold reality or truth, respective to the mode of cognition of which it is the object. Specifically, the first [reality] is the object of the view of all ordinary individuals, thus of the *opinio communis;* the second is the object of rational knowledge. This is simple and nothing special.

Noteworthy, however, is the distinction between the third and the fourth realities, for the third is the object of knowledge through which the obstruction of defilements is removed, and the fourth is the object of knowledge through which the obstruction to what is to be known is removed.

This distinction is based on an important further development of the doctrine of liberation. In the Śrāvakayāna (*cf. above* S. 126ff.), the process of liberation had been conceived in such a way that the defilements are removed through the cognition of the four noble truths, and that through this the deeds lose their power and the chain of rebirths comes to an end. In other words, one was strongly inclined to see the core of the liberating cognition in the non-existence of a worldly personality. Now, however, a new fundamental understanding had been reached, to which much importance was attached: the understanding of the essencelessness of the phenomenal world. Thus it was only natural that a role in liberation was attributed also to this understanding. Nāgārjuna had done this, as we have seen above

(S. 175f.), in that he made the cognition of the non-existence of a worldly personality dependent on the cognition of the essencelessness of the phenomenal world.

In the long run though this did not suffice. Both cognitions, each of which seemed so important, had to be brought out equally as causes of liberation, and this was done in the following way. Two causes <267> of entanglement in the cycle of existences were distinguished. The first, in accordance with the views existing up until then, is the defilements, and so one spoke of the *obstruction of defilements (kleśāvaraṇa).* In addition to this, however, a second obstruction, which prevents the correct cognition of that which is to be cognized, was now adopted, and this was called the *obstruction to what is to be known (jñeyāvaraṇa).* For its removal, however, this double hindrance naturally demanded a twofold liberating cognition, and so it was taught that the obstruction of defilements is removed by recognizing the essencelessness of the worldly personality *(pudgalanairātmya),* while on the other hand, the obstruction to what is to be known is removed by becoming aware of the essencelessness of the factors *(dharmanairātmya).* This twofold establishment of the bondage and liberation gradually gained general acceptance, and it is this [establishment] that forms the basis for the present distinction of the third and fourth realities, which we thus encounter for the first time here.

:FA.2. *The determination of the nature of reality: non-duality & the middle way & the constitution of the nature of reality {sections 9–13}*

Next follows the actual determination of the nature of reality and, with this, the philosophically most important part of this section. It is explained that the nature of reality is based on non-duality. With this an old idea is taken up, with which we have already become acquainted in the *Ratnakūṭa* [S. 167f.]

and in Nāgārjuna [S. 174ff.]. But here [in the *Bodhisattvabhūmi*] it is given a new meaning. The duality, of which reality is free, is existence and non-existence, which is also Nāgārjuna's primary concern. – Nāgārjuna had stated that existence does not apply because the diversity that is ruled by the law of dependent origination is not real, but that non-existence also does not apply because [this diversity] is not completely non-existent [S. 171f., 174]. – Here [in the *Bodhisattvabhūmi*, however,] the same fundamental thought, [i.e., that reality is free of existence and non-existence,] is given a different form. Existence does not apply [to reality] because our conceptions of things, which we project onto them, are unreal. But non-existence, likewise, does not apply, because the ungraspable thing in itself *(vastumātra)*, on which the conceptions are based, is real. – According to Nāgārjuna, the things of the phenomenal world are unreal because they do not conform to the demands of logic [S. 171f., 175f.]. In addition, the thought appears that these things are the objects of our conceptions, whereas the ultimate state of being remains inaccessible to all conceptions. <268> – Here [in the *Bodhisattvabhūmi*], it is now maintained that the appearances themselves are conceptions and as such unreal. The ultimate state of being, on the other hand, is that which stands behind these conceptions and is their basis, but it is itself free from all of the conceptions.

With this, an important shift has taken place. The deception of a phenomenal world as taught by Nāgārjuna [S. 206f.] has been replaced by the world as conception. The doctrine of non-duality is now elaborated upon with this in mind. We should not regard reality as existent, because our conceptions are unreal. But we should also not declare it to be non-existent, because the entity in itself on which the conceptions are based is real and is not to be denied. This view, which avoids both extremes of existence and non-existence, is the middle way and the correct doctrine, which helps Bodhisattvas to achieve the highest enlightenment.

CFA.3. *The proof of the unreality of the phenomenal world {section 14}*

Next there follows an attempt to prove the supposed nature of reality, specifically through the proof of the unreality of the phenomenal world. This proof conforms to the new view and proceeds quite differently than Nāgārjuna [S. 171ff.]. In order to understand it, the following should be kept in mind.

In the discussion of Śrāvakayāna doctrines we have seen (S. 119f.) that, at that time, one had come to understand that not all objects of our cognition are real. The Sautrāntikas in particular taught that we also speak of things that do not have a corresponding entity in the real world, and they called such things *existent only by designation (prajñaptisat).* We must therefore assume that these lines of thought were already known at the time [of the *Bodhisattvabhūmi*]. But to this we must also add the following: In those days, in spite of a few noteworthy attempts, one [the early Yogācārin][1] was not yet able to distinguish between perception and conceptual thinking as two [clearly] distinct forms of cognition. They were rather considered as processes of cognition that belong together and are similar. One then believed to observe that every process of cognition is accompanied by "words," in the sense of either actual speaking or mental speech *(manojalpa).* From this it was concluded that all cognition is not only necessarily connected with "words," but also conditioned by them. <269> And since

[1] [See S. 330 for Asaṅga's view that not every cognition is conception, but only mental cognition. – See in this context also Frauwallner's comment in his *Amalavijñāna and Ālayavijñana,* S. 155, that "it is one of the most characteristic features of the earliest Mahāyāna that it is without a philosophically clearly defined terminology and a systematics comparable to the Śrāvakayāna Abhidharma."]

it is we who [falsely] attribute the designations in the form of "words" [as actually belonging] to the things, it was concluded that the appearing forms expressed through the designations were also only [falsely] attributed to the things by us, but that in reality they are our own conceptions.

Accordingly, and more clearly expressed, the nature of reality being discussed here is depicted in the following way. Underlying all appearances there is a thing in itself *(vastumātra)*, which is, however, completely ungraspable and inexpressible. We impute onto it the various designations *(prajñaptivāda)* and thereby the related appearing forms. This imputation *(samāropa)* of designations is thus false. But it would be equally false to deny *(apavāda)* everything, since the thing in itself, which underlies the designations and makes the imputation possible in the first place, is real.

CFA.4. *The two proofs of the unreality of the designations {sections 15–16}*

That the designations are in fact not real and cannot be real is established in two ways.

Firstly, we impute a whole variety of designations to each thing and, with it, a whole variety of appearing forms. But they cannot all belong to the nature of the thing, because a thing cannot have all sorts of natures. But we have no grounds and hence no justification for seeing the nature of the thing in only one of these appearing forms. Therefore, we must regard all of them as unreal.

The second reason is the following. If the designations and appearing forms that we attribute to the things constituted their nature, then before this imputation occurs the things would be essenceless, hence non-existent. Thus also the imputation would be impossible, since any basis for it is absent. If, on the other hand, we were to assume that the things already possess the appropriate nature before we make the imputation, then the conceptions connected with the appropriate designations would have to already appear before we have yet imputed these designations to the things and have thereby connected them with each other. But this is not the case.

Consequently, the designations and the appearing forms connected with them cannot belong to the nature of the things and are thus not real. <270>

CFA.5. *The two errors & the false and correct view of reality {sections 17–19}*

Next comes another longer section, which, however, after what has been said so far is easily understandable and needs no further explanation.

This section also proceeds from thoughts already found in the *Ratnakūṭa* and in Nāgārjuna (*cf. above* S. 169f. and 180ff.) and merely reshapes them in accordance with the new views. We are concerned here with the two errors that one may make with respect to the view of reality if one misses the correct middle way: the error of one-sided affirmation and the error of one-sided negation. The first error, in which one believes exclusively in existence, consists, according to the new view, in the fact that the appearing forms imputed upon the thing in itself are regarded as real. The second, in which one believes exclusively in non-existence, consists in the fact that one also regards the thing in itself as unreal. And just as in the *Ratnakūṭa* and in Nāgārjuna, here too it is explained that the second error is by far the more fatal, because it is impervious to correction.

Finally, the false and correct views of reality are discussed as the false and correct views of emptiness. This idea as well is elaborated according to the new way of thinking, but already the very expressing of it by using the word *emptiness* shows the connection with the old.

In conclusion an attempt is made to support the doctrine presented by means of passages from the sacred scripture.

This is not rendered here. The presentation then moves on to other topics.

CFA.6. *From the "Stage of the Bodhisattva" (Bodhisattvabhūmi)*

[From] part 1, chapter IV

{1} What is reality? In brief, it is twofold. With respect to the manner of existence of the factors, [it is] their [true] existence *(bhūtatā)*. With respect to the extent of their existence, [it is] the totality *(sarvatā)* of the factors. In this way, [true] existence and totality <271> are, in brief, to be considered as reality.

{2} Further, reality is—divided according to its varieties—fourfold: that which is accepted in the [ordinary] world *[loka]*; that which is accepted based on rational arguments *[yukti]*; the sphere of knowledge *[jñānagocara]* purified of the obstruction of defilements; and the sphere of knowledge purified of the obstruction to what is to be known.

{3} [As for the first,] when all ordinary people, based on knowledge that is in accordance with convention, custom, habit, or tradition, have a shared view with respect to any given thing: for example, with respect to the earth: "This is earth and not fire"; and just as with earth, so with respect to fire, water, wind; with respect to visible forms, sounds, odors, tastes, tangibles; with respect to food and drink, vehicles, ornaments . . .; with respect to pleasure and pain: "This is pain and not pleasure" and "This is pleasure and not pain"; in brief: "This is this and not something else; this is so and not some other way"; – this thing then—which is the object of a very particular view, which is accepted by all ordinary people by means of their own conception as based on an opinion handed down by means of a continuous tradition, and which is accepted without having been pondered, weighed and investigated—that is called *reality accepted in the [ordinary] world.*

{4} [As for the second,] what is the *reality that is accepted based on rational arguments?* A recognizable thing that by sensible people who are skilled in what is reasonable, who are smart, who know logic, are versed in methodical investigation, and belong to a stage governed by logic on which their own flashes of insights are valid and which is connected with the sphere of worldly people and with methodical investigations, (thus a thing that, by such people,) is proven and established—with the help of <272> the means of valid cognition, that is, sensory perception, inference, and authoritative tradition—as an object of clearly determined knowledge through demonstrations, proofs, and rational arguments, this is called *reality accepted based on rational arguments.*

{5} [As for the third,] what is the *reality that is the sphere of knowledge purified of the obstruction of defilements?* (That reality) that is the sphere and object of uncontaminated *[anāsrava]* knowledge,[1] of the knowledge that brings about uncontaminated knowledge, and of the worldly knowledge of all Hearers *(śrāvaka)* and Solitary Buddhas *(pratyekabuddha)* attained subsequent to the uncontaminated knowledge, that is called *reality that is the sphere of knowledge purified of the obstruction of defilements.* By means of this object-support, knowledge is purified of the obstruction of defilements and henceforth remains in this state of unobstructedness. Thus one speaks of a *reality that is the sphere of knowledge purified of the obstruction of defilements.*

{6} What, then, is this reality? The four noble truths: suffering, the origin, the cessation, and the path. Whoever clearly distinguishes and comprehends these four noble truths, in him arises this knowledge [purified of the obstruction of defilements] as soon as he clearly comprehends them. This clear comprehension of the truths in turn arises in Hearers and Solitary Buddhas, when—through insight connected with the

---

[1] The vision of the noble truths is designated as uncontaminated knowledge.

arising and ceasing of the dependently arisen formations, <273> based on the constant consideration of the non-existence of a person apart from the groups—they perceive only the groups and do not perceive a self as an object distinct from the groups.

{7} [As for the fourth,] what is the *reality that is the sphere of knowledge purified of the obstruction to what is to be known?* A hindrance to knowledge with respect to what is to be known is called *obstruction.* (That reality, then,) which is the sphere and object of knowledge freed from the obstruction to what is to be known, is to be regarded as the *reality that is the sphere of knowledge purified of the obstruction to what is to be known.*

{8} What, then, is this reality? (It is that reality) that is the sphere and object of the knowledge of the Bodhisattvas and exalted Buddhas, (that knowledge) that is aimed at penetrating into the essencelessness of factors, that is completely pure, and that, in view of the inexpressible nature of all factors, realizes the nature of designations free of conceptions as completely the same (?). That is that highest suchness *(tathatā)*, the unsurpassable [suchness], which forms the limit of the knowable, in the face of which the correct distinguishing of all factors retreats and to which it does not extend.

{9} Further, with regard to the characteristic of reality, it should be understood—in light of its determination—as being called forth by non-duality. Existence and non-existence are designated as *duality [dvaya].*

{10} Therein, *existence [bhāva]* is that which is determined as the nature of designations *(prajñaptivādasvabhāva)*, that which has been conceived by people in this way for a long time, and that which is, for the people, the root of the diversity of all conceptions *[sarvavikalpaprapañcamūla]*: e.g., corporeality [i.e., visible form, etc.] or sensation, ideation, formations, and cognition; the eye or the ear, nose, tongue, body, and mind; earth or water, fire and <274> wind; visible form or sound, odor, taste, and the tangible; the good, the bad, or the undetermined; arising or ceasing; the dependently arisen; what is past, future, or present; the conditioned or the unconditioned; this world or that world; both, sun and moon; what is seen, heard, thought of, and cognized; what is acquired and searched for, or what is contemplated and reflected in the mind; up to, finally, *nirvāṇa*. The nature of the factors that is constituted in this way and that is—for the people—firmly attached to designations is called *existence*.

{11} Therein, *non-existence [abhāva]* is the thinglessness and signlessness of the designation "corporeality," etc., up to, finally, the designation "*nirvāṇa*"; the entire and complete non-existence and non-presence of a basis for the designations, based on which the designations could be used. That is called *non-existence*.

{12} That thing *[vastu]* included within the characteristic of the factors that is free from the above-mentioned existence and from this non-existence, from both of these, from existence and non-existence, that is the *non-duality [advaya]*. This *non-duality* is the middle way, is free from both extremes and is designated as the *unsurpassable [niruttara]*. The completely pure knowledge of the exalted Buddhas is to be regarded as being aimed at this reality. The knowledge of the Bodhisattvas, brought about on the path of training, is [also] to be regarded as being aimed at this reality.

{13} For the Bodhisattva, this insight is a precious means for the attainment of the highest perfect enlightenment . . .

{14} Through what kind of rational arguments, then, can the nature of all factors be recognized as *inexpressible [nir-abhilāpya]?* Every designation of the intrinsic characteristic *(svalakṣaṇa)* of the <275> factors, e.g., "corporeality" or "sensation," etc., – as above, up to, finally – or "*nirvāṇa*," is to be regarded as a mere designation, [i.e.,] not as the intrinsic nature [of the factors itself] and not as a sphere or object of speech that is [completely] separate and distinct from [the intrinsic nature].

That being the case, the nature of factors does not exist in the way it is expressed. But it is also not completely absent. But how does it exist if it does not exist in the way [it is expressed] and yet is not completely absent? Free from the false view that consists of the affirmation of something unreal, and free from the false view that consists of the denial of something real, it exists. This true nature of all factors is, further, to be regarded exclusively as the sphere of nonconceptual knowledge.

{15} If, further, all factors *[dharma]* and each thing *[vastu]* were so constituted as the expression used for these factors and that thing, in this case a single factor and a single thing would have many and different intrinsic natures. For what reason? Since many and different designations are attributed *(upācāra)*, by means of many expressions, to a single factor and a single thing. With respect to these many and different designations, however, a fixed rule cannot be found according to which a particular single designation belongs to the nature, constitution, and intrinsic nature of this factor and this thing, but not the other remaining designations. Hence, all designations do not belong, either as wholly or in part, to the nature, to the constitution, and to the intrinsic nature of all factors and all things.

{16} If, further, the above-mentioned factors, corporeality, etc., had the designation as their nature, in this case, at first the thing would be present, and <276> then the designation would be attributed to it at will. Thus before the attribution of the designation and for as long as the attribution of the designation has not yet taken place, this thing and this factor would be without an intrinsic nature. But if the intrinsic nature is absent, then the designation—for which (in this case) the thing is lacking—would not be possible. And if no attribution of the designation takes place, then it is also not possible that the factor or the thing has the designation as its nature.

If, on the other hand, before the attribution of the designation, corporeality already had the nature of corporeality and subsequently this nature of corporeality were to be additionally attributed to corporeality by means of the designation, in this case even without this attribution of the designation "corporeality" with respect to the factor designated as corporeality and the thing designated as corporeality, the cognition of corporeality would appear. But it does not appear.

Thus, for this reason and because of these rational arguments, the nature of all factors is to be recognized as *inexpressible.* And just as for corporeality, this also applies to the rest of the factors mentioned: sensation, etc., up to, finally, *nirvāṇa.*

{17} About the two that follow, one should know that they have fallen away from the rule of this doctrine *[dharmavinaya]:*

[1] he who—with respect to factors, such as visible form, etc., and with respect to a thing, such as corporeality, etc.—clings to their intrinsic characteristic, which is by nature only a designation, by attributing something unreal to them, and [2] he who invalidates the thing—which as the foundation is the occasion for the designation, which as the support is the occasion for the designation, and which in its inexpressible self is truly real—by denying it and saying: "It does not exist at all."

As for the errors, firstly, <277> that follow from attributing something unreal, these have already been described, made known, clarified, and explained previously: i.e., the errors due to which one is to be regarded as having fallen away from the rule of this doctrine, because one attributes something unreal to a thing such as corporeality, etc. Why, on the other hand, he who overturns everything by denying the thing in itself *[vastumātra]* in factors such as visible form, etc., has fallen away from the rule of this doctrine, this I will now state.

For him who, with respect to factors such as visible form, etc., denies the thing in itself, both are not possible, neither reality *[tattva]* nor designation *[prajñapti]*. Because, namely, just as the designation of *person* is possible if the groups, corporeality, etc., exist, but not if they do not exist, since then the designation of *person* would be without a thing; in the same way, the bestowing of the designation of *factor,* such as visible form, etc., is possible if, with respect to the factors visible form, etc., the thing in itself exists but not if it does not exist, since then the bestowing of the designation would be without a thing. For indeed when a thing does not exist for the designation, then the designation also does not exist, since it has no foundation.

If therefore, after having heard the sutras belonging to the Mahāyāna—which are difficult to understand, profound, connected with emptiness, and intended with a specific meaning—some people, because they do not correctly understand and do not correctly ascertain the meaning of what is taught, advocate—as a result of a mere unskillful attempt at reasoning—the following view and the following doctrine: "All of this is mere designation; that is the truth, and whoever sees thus, sees correctly," then for these (people), this designation too does not exist at all since the thing in itself as the foundation of the <278> designation is absent. How then is reality supposed to be mere designation? In this way, they thus deny both reality and designation, and also both together. Hence, because (such a person) denies designation and reality, he is to be regarded as an arch-denier. And because he is such a denier, intelligent fellow disciples should not talk to him and should not associate with him, for he plunges himself into ruin, and those people who approve of his views are also plunged into ruin. In this sense the Exalted One has said: "Better that someone here believes in a *person* than that someone wrongly comprehends *emptiness.*"

For what reason? If a person believes in a *person,* then he merely deludes himself about that which is to be known, but he will not deny all that is to be known. For this reason he will therefore not be reborn in bad forms of existence. He will not oppose and will not delude another who seeks the doctrine and who seeks liberation from suffering, but he will help him toward the doctrine and the truth. And he will not be lax in the observation of the precepts.

Through a wrong comprehension of *emptiness,* on the other hand, one is deluded about the thing that is to be known. Indeed, one even denies all that is to be known. For this reason one is reborn in bad forms of existence. One plunges another, who adheres to the doctrine and seeks liberation from suffering, into ruin. And one is lax in the observation of the precepts. In this way then, he who denies the real thing has fallen from the rule of the doctrine.

{18} But in what way is emptiness *wrongly comprehended [durgṛhīta]?*

If a particular ascetic or brahmin does not accept that of which something is empty and also does not <279> accept that which is empty, then this type of emptiness is called *wrongly comprehended.* For what reason? If that of which something is empty is not present, but on the other hand, that which is empty is present, then emptiness is possible. If, on the other hand, everything is absent, what is then supposed to be empty, where and of what? Also, the emptiness of something [being empty] of itself is not possible. In this way then is emptiness *wrongly comprehended.*

{19} But, in what way is emptiness *correctly comprehended [sugṛhīta]?*

If something is regarded as empty of that which is not present in it, yet that which is then left over is truthfully recognized as being present here, then this is called *truthful, unerring penetration of emptiness.* For example, a factor that is by nature the designation of visible form, etc., is not present in a thing designated as visible form, etc., as we have called it above. Therefore, this given thing designated as visible form, etc., is empty of the nature of the designation of visible form, etc. So then what is left of this thing designated as visible form, etc? That which forms the basis of the designation of visible form, etc.

Now, if one truthfully recognizes these two, namely, the present thing in itself and the mere designation of the thing in itself, if the unreal is not attributed and the real is not denied, if nothing is added and nothing taken away, nothing is inserted and nothing eliminated, then true suchness, the inexpressible nature, is truthfully understood. This is called *correctly comprehended emptiness, well-discerned through correct insight.*

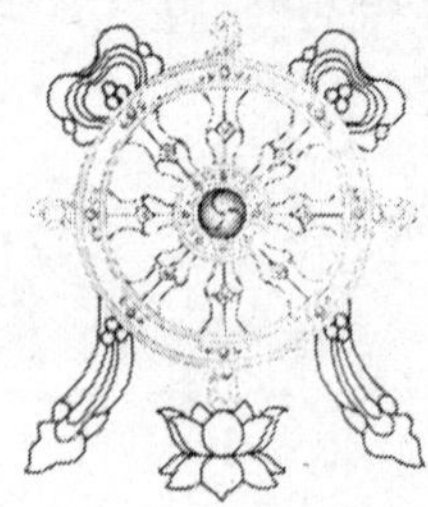

CFB. *The Saṃdhinirmocanasūtra*

As with the Madhyamaka school [S. 145ff., 163f.], the sutra literature also plays a great role in the Yogācāra school, particularly in the earlier period, and we find several important thoughts first expressed in sutras. A sample of this should thus also be given, and I choose for this purpose a work that was especially esteemed <280> and that most strongly influenced the development of the school, the *Saṃdhinirmocanasūtra (Elucidation of the Secret Meaning).* With regard to this work, it is also interesting that it still clearly shows traces of its gradual formation and so, to a certain extent, reflects the course of the general development of the school. Its oldest parts fully adhere to the manner of the *Prajñāpāramitā* texts, while in the more recent ones the new philosophical thoughts and the scholasticism of liberation of the Yogācāra school find expression.

CFB.1. *The doctrine of the threefold nature of things in chapter VI*

The section rendered in the following contains a doctrine that was characteristic of the Yogācāra school throughout the entire duration of its existence. This is the doctrine of the threefold nature or the threefold characteristic of things, and connected with that, the doctrine of their threefold essencelessness. With the doctrine of the nature of reality, as we have come to know it in the *Bodhisattvabhūmi,* one of the fundamental doctrines of the system was created. It had, however, not yet assumed the form in which it was to find lasting acceptance. This first occurred with the doctrine of the threefold characteristic.

The *Bodhisattvabhūmi* had taught [S. 267ff.] that the phenomenal world is mere conception, but that an ungraspable and inexpressible thing in itself underlies it, and it had clothed this view in the form of the old doctrine of the middle way.

The *Saṃdhinirmocanasūtra* chose another form for this. It distinguished first and foremost between *things [insofar] as they appear to us* and *things as they really are.* This was important from the point of view of the doctrine of liberation, since on the view of things as they appear rests entanglement in the cycle of existences; on the knowledge of how they really are, liberation. Now, this twofold nature of things is caused by the fact that in the first case, the appearing forms that actually belong to conception are attributed to the things, whereas in the second case, things are free from [the appearing forms]. The *appearing forms belonging to conception* are thus the factor whose presence or absence brings about the twofold nature of things. Thus they were placed as a third [nature] next to [this twofold nature], thereby distinguishing a threefold nature <281> *(svabhāva)* or a threefold characteristic *(lakṣaṇa)* of things: first, the appearing forms that we attribute to things; second, the things insofar as they present themselves to us in these appearing forms; and, third, the things insofar as they are free from these appearing forms. The first nature was called the *imagined nature (parikalpita svabhāva)* because these appearing forms are mere conception; the second, the *dependent nature (paratantra svabhāva)* because the phenomenal world presents itself to us in this form and its most essential characteristic is dependent origination; and finally the third, the *perfect nature (parinișpanna svabhāva)* because it represents the ultimate state of being in its pure form.

That is the doctrine of the threefold nature of things as the *Saṃdhinirmocanasūtra* presents it. It superseded the doctrine of the nature of reality from the *Bodhisattvabhūmi* and became a firm tenet of the Yogācāra system. The threefold break-down of reality it gives, however, is askew unbalanced and has presented difficulties time and again. The *Saṃdhinirmocanasūtra* itself does not completely succeed in clearly following the idea through, but the systematic found therein conformed to the Indian style of tending toward numerical categorization, particularly strongly pronounced in the Yogācāra school. And thus, this doctrine quickly gained irrevocable acceptance [within the Yogācāra school].

In the first part of the section of the *Saṃdhinirmocana* (= chap. VI) translated below then, this doctrine of the threefold nature of things is expounded. First the doctrine itself is briefly formulated [vv. 1–6]. Then [vv. 7–10] it is explained using examples. As its conclusion [vv. 11–12], the threefold nature is finally considered from yet another point of view: with respect to the doctrine of liberation. It is stated that—through correct insight into the imagined nature—the factors are recognized as being without characteristic or without a sign, since the appearing forms belonging to conception are without essence; that—through correct insight into the dependent nature—the factors in the state of pollution *(saṃkleśa)* are recognized, since the dependent nature represents the nature of the phenomenal world and hence the cycle of existences; and that—through correct insight into the <282> perfect nature—the factors in the state of purification *(vyavadāna)* are recognized, since the perfect nature corresponds to the ultimate state of being and hence liberation. This threefold assumption [with respect to the doctrine of liberation] did not survive for long. Only the view of the phenomenal world as a state of pollution and of the ultimate state of being as a state of purification were incorporated into the lasting views of the [Yogācāra] system.

CFB.2. *The doctrine of the threefold essencelessness of things in chapter VII and its relation to the doctrine of the Prajñāpāramitā and of the Mādhyamikas*

The subsequent second part of the translation (= chap. VII) deals with the counterpart to the doctrine of the threefold nature of things, i.e., the doctrine of the threefold essencelessness, wherein the threefold nature of things is considered from the viewpoint of a threefold essencelessness. This doctrine as well has its special significance and its deeper background. In spite of all outward connections to and all reliance of the old Yogācāra school on the doctrine of the *Prajñāpāramitā* and of the Mādhyamikas, inwardly there is a deep contrast.

Thus far we have only pointed out [S. 268] the difference that lies in the fact that the Yogācārins replaced Nāgārjuna's doctrine of the deception of the phenomenal world with the view of the world as conception.

Far more essential is, however, the difference in the view of the highest reality. In Nāgārjuna [S. 174] this [highest reality] is beyond all conceptions and determinations and indeed cannot even be described as existent or non-existent. This position of Nāgārjuna's is then followed through and held onto with a logical consistency never again achieved, so that, cloaked in silence, the highest reality nearly disappears into nothingness. In the school of the Yogācāra, however, despite all the emphasis on its inexpressibility, [the highest reality] retains a decidedly positive character. Nothing is more typical than the way [1] the concept of *emptiness (śūnyatā)*—which dominates everything in Nāgārjuna—is completely relegated into the background here and [2] the highest reality is described using other terms such as, first and foremost, *suchness (tathatā)*. It is also explicitly stated that only in the form in which it appears to us does the highest reality not exist and that on the other hand, it does exist as a thing in itself. Important consequences ensue from this for the relationship of <283> the highest reality to the phenomenal world. No unbridgeable gap exists, and a firm, clearly conceivable connection takes the place of the mystical unity of the cycle of existences *[saṃsāra]* and *nirvāṇa*, as Nāgārjuna had taught it [S. 174f.]. This separates the schools of the Mādhyamikas and the Yogācārins more clearly than anything else and also determines their very dissimilar development.

For the Yogācārins, however, this dissimilarity brought with it a significant problem. The numerous sutras, particularly the *Prajñāpāramitā* works, which were closely connected with the Madhyamaka school, and which the Yogācārins also recognized as the Buddha's words, spoke explicitly of the emptiness and essencelessness of all things. How then was this to be reconciled with their own positive stance toward the phenomenal world and its underlying reality? In order to circumvent this problem, they resorted to the favorite assumption (*cf. above* S. 146) that with these works one is dealing with texts that do not proclaim the full truth, but that were rather revealed by the Buddha with a particular purpose in mind, for a specific audience. It was said that in this case the Buddha was thinking not of a complete essencelessness, but only of an essencelessness from a particular perspective, namely, that of a threefold essencelessness, corresponding to the threefold nature of things:

The first essencelessness is essencelessness in terms of a characteristic or of a sign *(lakṣaṇaniḥsvabhāvatā)*. This corresponds to the imagined nature as this has no intrinsic characteristic *(svalakṣaṇa)* and hence no essence.

The second is essencelessness in terms of arising *(utpattiniḥ-svabhāvatā)*. It relates to the dependent nature and is based—apparently in reliance upon Madhyamaka thinking—on the fact that things arise not from themselves but from other causes.

The third essencelessness, finally, is essencelessness in terms of the highest truth *(paramārthaniḥsvabhāvatā)*. As the name indicates, it is related to the ultimate state of being. And since the ultimate state of being is connected with the dependent as well as with the perfect nature—since these two represent the ultimate state of being in the states of pollution and of purification—essencelessness <284> in terms of the highest truth is also connected with both. More precisely, in the case of the dependent nature one can speak of an essencelessness in terms of the highest truth since only the ultimate state of being in the state of purification is to be regarded as the highest truth. The perfect nature, in turn, can be considered as essencelessness in terms of the highest truth since the highest truth consists precisely in the selflessness or essencelessness of the factors *(dharmanairātmya)*.

By means of this doctrine of the threefold essencelessness, the essencelessness of all things as expounded in the *Prajñāpāramitā* [S. 149f.] was explained from the point of view of the Yogācāra. While it is true that this doctrine did not prove fruitful for the development of the ideas of the system, it was still, with only a few alterations, continually preserved and remained firmly connected with the doctrine of the threefold nature. In the following translation [of chapter VII] the question is first raised as to why the Buddha taught the doctrine of the essencelessness of all things. Then the doctrine of the threefold essencelessness is expounded and briefly explained, and following that, how the Buddha leads beings to liberation through this doctrine is elaborated upon in detail.

CFB.3. *From the "Elucidation of the Secret Meaning" (Saṃdhinirmocanasūtra)*

Chapter VI

1

At this, the Bodhisattva Guṇākara asked the Exalted One: "Exalted One, one speaks of *Bodhisattvas who are experienced in the characteristic (lakṣaṇa) of the factors.* In what way, O Exalted One, are the Bodhisattvas experienced in the characteristic of the factors? And for what reason does the Perfected One designate the Bodhisattvas as *experienced in the characteristic of the factors?"* <285>

2

When he had said this, the Exalted One spoke as follows to the Bodhisattva Guṇākara: "Guṇākara, you ask the Perfected One about this matter for the welfare of many individuals, for the well-being of many individuals, out of compassion for the world, for the benefit, for the welfare, and for the well-being of creatures, including gods and humans. Excellent, excellent! Then listen, Guṇākara, I will explain *experience in the characteristic of the factors* to you.

3

Guṇākara, there are three characteristics of factors. What are these three? The imagined characteristic *(parikalpitalakṣaṇa),* the dependent characteristic *(paratantralakṣaṇa),* and the perfect characteristic *(pariniṣpannalakṣaṇa).*

4

In this, Guṇākara, what is the *imagined characteristic* of the factors? It is any attribution of a name and a convention[1] for the factors in terms of their nature or distinction, in order to indicate them in day to day language.

---

[1] According to the Buddhist view, the connection between word and object rests on human convention *(saṃketa).*

5

What, Guṇākara, is the *dependent characteristic* of factors? It is the dependent origination of the factors, that is, when this exists, that comes to be; due to the arising of this, that arises; that is, dependent on ignorance, formations come into being, etc., up to: thus the origin of this whole great mass of suffering comes about. <286>

6

What, Guṇākara, is the *perfect characteristic* of factors? It is the suchness of factors, the recognition of [this suchness] by the Bodhisattvas as a result of their energy and correct observation *(yoniśomanasikāra)*, and finally, the establishment of the highest perfect enlightenment through establishment of the practice of this recognition.

7

Just as [the defect of] an eye disease, Guṇākara, in the eye of a person who suffers from an eye disease, so is the *imagined characteristic* to be seen.

Just as the images of strands of hair, bees, sesame seeds, of blue, yellow, red, or white appear to such a (person) due to the eye disease, so is the *dependent characteristic* to be seen.

And just as the natural sphere, [i.e.,] the errorless object of the same eye when the eye of the same person has been cleared and freed of the [defect of] the eye disease, so is the *perfect characteristic* to be seen.

8

It is the same, Guṇākara, as with a transparent crystal. If this [crystal] comes in contact with something blue, it appears like a sapphire, and in that it is mistaken for a sapphire, it fools beings. If it comes in contact with something red, it appears like a ruby, and in that it is mistaken for a ruby, it fools beings. If it comes in contact with something green, it appears like an emerald, and in that is mistaken for an emerald, it fools beings.

If it comes in contact with something yellow, <287> it appears like gold, and in that it is mistaken for gold, it fools beings.

9

Guṇākara, just as in the case of the transparent crystal, the contact with the color [is to be seen,] so in the case of the dependent characteristic, permeation[1] through the use of language—which belongs to the imagined characteristic—is to be seen.

Just as in the case of the transparent crystal, the erroneous apprehension of it as sapphire, ruby, emerald, or gold, so in the case of the dependent characteristic, the [erroneous] apprehension of it as the imagined characteristic is to be seen.

Just as the transparent crystal itself, so the dependent characteristic is to be seen.

Just as the transparent crystal, in terms of its characteristic as sapphire, ruby, emerald, or gold, is not permanently and perpetually given and is without essence, so the perfect characteristic is to be seen, insofar as the dependent characteristic, in terms of the imagined characteristic, is not permanently and perpetually given and is without essence.

10

In this, Guṇākara, the imagined characteristic is recognized in that one relies on the names connected with the images.

The dependent characteristic is recognized in that one relies on taking the dependent characteristic as being the imagined characteristic.

And the perfect characteristic is recognized in that one relies on no longer taking the dependent characteristic as being the imagined characteristic. <288>

---

[1] The underlying view is that all conceptions and words leave imprints in the cognition, from which, later, corresponding conceptions again arise. These imprints, called *permeation (vāsanā)*, take the place of words and conceptions. *Cf.*, in regard to this, *below* S. 328f.

11

Now, Guṇākara, in that the Bodhisattvas recognize the imagined characteristic [attributed falsely to] the dependent characteristic in accordance with truth, they recognize the factors without characteristic in accordance with truth.

In that Bodhisattvas recognize the dependent characteristic in accordance with truth, they recognize the factors in the characteristic of pollution *(saṃkleśa)* in accordance with truth.

And in that Bodhisattvas recognize the perfect characteristic in accordance with truth, they recognize the factors in the characteristic of purification *(vyavadāna)* in accordance with truth.

In that Bodhisattvas recognize the factors without characteristic in the dependent characteristic in accordance with truth, they abandon the factors in the characteristic of pollution. And in that they abandon the factors in the characteristic of pollution, they attain the factors in the characteristic of purification.

Thus, Guṇākara, because the Bodhisattvas—by recognizing the imagined characteristic, the dependent characteristic, and the perfect characteristic in accordance with truth—recognize the absence of the characteristic, the characteristic of pollution, and the characteristic of purification in accordance with truth; because they—by recognizing the factors without characteristic in accordance with truth—abandon the factors in the characteristic of pollution; and because they—by abandoning the factors in the characteristic of pollution—attain the factors in the characteristic of purification, therefore the Bodhisattvas are experienced in the characteristic of the factors, and if the Perfected One designates the Bodhisattvas as *experienced in the characteristic of factors*, then he does so because of this. <289>

12

After that, the Exalted One at that time spoke the following stanzas:

If one recognizes the factors without characteristic,
then one abandons the factors in the characteristic of

pollution. If one abandons the factors in the characteristic of pollution, [then] one attains the factors in the characteristic of complete purity.

People who are lazy and overcome by heedlessness, who do not appreciate the faults of the formations and are lost in the unstable, by nature fluctuating factors, are pitiable.

Chapter VII

1

Then the Bodhisattva Paramārthasamudgata said the following to the Exalted One: "Exalted One, once when I was dwelling alone in solitude, the following reflection came to my mind: The Exalted One has proclaimed the intrinsic characteristic *(svalakṣaṇa)* of the [five] groups in many ways. He has proclaimed the characteristic of arising, the characteristic of perishing, the avoiding and the recognizing. Just as with the groups, so he has proclaimed [the intrinsic characteristic, etc., of] the spheres, dependent origination, and the sustenances *(āhāra)*.

The Exalted One has proclaimed the intrinsic characteristic of the truths in many ways. He has proclaimed recognizing, avoiding, realizing, and practicing.

The Exalted One has proclaimed the intrinsic characteristic of the [sense-]elements in many ways. He has proclaimed the variety of the [sense-]elements, the manifoldness of the [sense-] elements, the avoiding, and the recognizing. . . .

And yet the Exalted One has proclaimed that all factors are without essence, that all factors are unborn, unceasing, <290> peaceful from the very beginning, and completely extinct by nature. With what hidden intention has the Exalted One proclaimed that all factors are without essence, that all factors are unborn, unceasing, peaceful from the very beginning, and completely extinct by nature? I ask the Exalted One about this matter: 'With what hidden intention has the Exalted One proclaimed that all factors are without essence, that all factors are unborn, unceasing, peaceful from the very beginning, and completely extinct by nature?' "

2

When he had said this, the Exalted One said the following to the Bodhisattva Paramārthasamudgata: "Paramārthasamudgata, your reflection is good and has come about correctly. Excellent, excellent! Paramārthasamudgata, you ask the Perfected One about this matter for the welfare of many individuals, for the well-being of many individuals, out of compassion for the world, for the benefit, for the welfare, and for the well-being of creatures, including gods and humans. That also is excellent. Listen then, Paramārthasamudgata, I will explain to you with what hidden intention I have proclaimed that all factors are without essence, that all factors are unborn, unceasing, peaceful from the very beginning, and completely extinct by nature.

3

Paramārthasamudgata, with respect to the threefold essencelessness *(niḥsvabhāvatā)* of the factors, I have proclaimed that all factors are without essence; that is, with respect to the essencelessness in terms of characteristic *(lakṣaṇa-niḥsvabhāvatā)*, to the essencelessness <291> in terms of arising *(utpattiniḥsvabhāvatā)*, and to the essencelessness in terms of the highest truth *(paramārthaniḥsvabhāvatā)*.

4

In all of this, Paramārthasamudgata, what is *essencelessness of the factors in terms of characteristic?* It is the imagined characteristic.

For what reason? – Because in terms of its characteristic, this [imagined characteristic] is based on names and convention and is not based on an intrinsic characteristic *(svalakṣaṇa)*, thus it is called *essencelessness of the factors in terms of characteristic*.

5

What, Paramārthasamudgata, is *essencelessness of the factors in terms of arising?* It is the dependent characteristic of the factors.

For what reason? – Because this [dependent characteristic] arises through the power of extraneous conditions and not from itself, for this reason it is *called essencelessness of the factors in terms of arising.*

6

What, Paramārthasamudgata, is *essencelessness in terms of the highest truth?* The dependently arisen factors, which are without essence due to the essencelessness in terms of arising, are also without essence due to the essencelessness in terms of the highest truth.

For what reason? – That which, with regard to the factors, is the object-support *(ālambana)* of purification,[1] this I have proclaimed as the *highest truth.* The dependent characteristic is not the object-support of purification; therefore it is called *essencelessness of the highest truth.*

Further, the perfect characteristic <292> of the factors is also called *essencelessness in terms of the highest truth.*

For what reason? – With regard to the factors, the selflessness of the factors *(dharmanairātmya)* is designated as their *essencelessness.* And this [selflessness] is the highest truth. Thus because the highest truth emerges from the essencelessness of all factors, it is called the *essencelessness in terms of the highest truth.*

7

Just as a skyflower,[2] Paramārthasamudgata, so is the *essencelessness in terms of characteristic* to be seen.

---

[1] I.e., to which the process of purification of liberation applies.

[2] The favorite Indian example of something completely unreal is the skyflower, i.e., a flower that grows in empty space from nothing.

Just as a magical illusion, so is the *essencelessness in terms of arising* to be seen and so is one part of the *essencelessness in terms of the highest truth* to be seen.

And just as space, which emerges from the mere essencelessness (= the non-existence) of matter and extends everywhere, so is one part of the *essencelessness in terms of the highest truth* to be seen, insofar as it emerges from the selflessness of the factors and extends everywhere.

8

With respect to this threefold essencelessness, Paramārthasamudgata, I have proclaimed that all factors are without essence.

In so doing, with respect to the *essencelessness in terms of characteristic,* I have proclaimed that all factors are unborn, unceasing, peaceful from the very beginning, and completely extinct by nature.

For what reason? – Because that which in terms of an intrinsic characteristic does not exist, has also not been born. But that which has not been born has also not <293> ceased. That which has not been born and has not ceased is peaceful from the very beginning. That which is peaceful from the very beginning is completely extinct by nature. In that which is by nature completely extinct, there is nothing that must still be brought to complete extinction. Thus, with respect to the *essencelessness in terms of characteristic,* I have proclaimed that all factors are unborn, unceasing, peaceful from the very beginning, and completely extinct by nature.

9

Further, Paramārthasamudgata, with respect to the *essencelessness in terms of the highest truth,* which emerges from the selflessness of factors, I have proclaimed that all factors are unborn, unceasing, peaceful from the very beginning, and completely extinct by nature.

For what reason? – Because the *essencelessness in terms of the highest truth*—which emerges from the selflessness of factors—is permanently and perpetually given. As the nature of the factors *(dharmadharmatā),* it is, in addition, unconditioned and completely free from the defilements. But that which is permanently and perpetually given as the nature of the factors and is unconditioned, that, because it is unconditioned, is also unborn and unceasing. And because it is free from all defilements, it is also peaceful from the very beginning and completely extinct by nature. Thus with respect to the *essencelessness in terms of the highest truth,* which emerges from the selflessness of factors, I have proclaimed that all factors are unborn, unceasing, peaceful from the very beginning, and completely extinct by nature. <294>

10

I have not, Paramārthasamudgata, proclaimed the threefold essencelessness because the beings in the realm of beings see the imagined nature, in terms of its nature, as something distinct [from the dependent and perfect nature] and because they see the dependent nature and the perfect nature, in terms of their nature, as something distinct [from the imagined nature]. On the contrary, beings attribute the imagined nature onto the dependent and the perfect nature, and thus designate—according to linguistic usage *(vyavahāra)*—the dependent and the perfect nature according to the characteristic of the imagined nature.

As they now designate [the dependent and the perfect nature] according to linguistic usage, their mind becomes permeated by these designations according to linguistic usage. And through the connection with the designations according to linguistic usage and through the imprints *(anuśaya)* of the designations according to linguistic usage, they cling—with respect to the dependent and perfect nature—to the characteristic of the imagined nature. As they now cling to this [characteristic of the imagined nature], then due to this cause and this condition—i.e., that they cling to the imagined nature with respect to the dependent and perfect nature—a dependent nature is produced (again) in the future.

And this forms the foundation so that they become polluted by the pollution *[saṃkleśa]* of the defilements *[kleśa]*, that they become polluted by the pollution of deeds and by the pollution of birth, and that they roam around for a long time in the cycle of existences, wandering either among hell beings, among animals, among ghosts, among gods, among demons, or among humans, since they have not succeeded in leaving the cycle of existences.

A long description of how beings reach liberation through
the doctrine of the threefold essencelessness of the <295>
factors follows. It ends with the words:

24

Then at that time the Exalted One spoke the following stanzas:

The factors are without essence, the factors are unborn, the factors are unceasing, the factors are peaceful from the very beginning, all factors are extinct by nature: What sensible person would speak in such a way without a hidden intention?

Essencelessness in terms of characteristic, essencelessness in terms of arising, and essencelessness in terms of the highest truth, this I have proclaimed. The sensible person who recognizes the hidden intention in this does not travel the path to ruin.

This is the one path of purification. There is only one purification, there is no second. For this reason I proclaim this one vehicle. Yet this is not to say that there are not beings of various lineages *(gotra)*.

The beings who, in this realm of beings, attain *nirvāṇa* for themselves alone, are innumerable. However, those who—although they are extinct—steadfastly and compassionately do not abandon beings are difficult to find.

The uncontaminated realm of the liberated ones is subtle, inconceivable to thought, equal, and undifferentiated. It is the fulfillment of all wishes, the casting away of suffering and defilements. It is without duality, inexpressible, the lasting treasure.

Then in conclusion the Bodhisattva Paramārthasamudgata speaks up and once more summarizes the doctrine as he has understood it. <296>

Maitreyanātha (ca. 300 c.e.)

Thus far we have discussed the beginnings of the Yogācāra school and in doing so, we have pointed out the lavishly developed scholasticism of liberation. In addition, however, we have become acquainted with valuable philosophical lines of thought. These did show several points of contact with the beginnings of the Madhyamaka school, but above and beyond that, they contained much that was new and significant. Nevertheless, we are dealing here only with the initial stages of a development of philosophical thoughts that completely recede behind the theory and practice of liberation. By no means can we speak in this connection of a philosophical system. As was the case with the Madhyamaka school, this was first created through the activity of a significant personage. Here this personage appears to have been Maitreyanātha.

Tradition records that the head of the Yogācāra school, Asaṅga, received teachings from the Bodhisattva Maitreya in Tuṣita heaven and that Maitreya also revealed various works to him. Similar traditions are quite common. In the present case, however, it is striking that the works attributed to Maitreya are not sutras, as one would expect, but philosophical works like any others. Asaṅga cannot, however, be the author of these works since the doctrines expounded in them show a clearly pronounced originality and distinguish themselves noticeably from Asaṅga's own works. We are therefore justified in seeing in their author a historical personage other than Asaṅga, who was probably known by the oft handed down name of Maitreyanātha, and who was only later seen as the well-known Bodhisattva.

CFC.1. *The works of Maitreyanātha*

Maitreyanātha's most frequently mentioned works are:

- the *Abhisamayālaṃkāra* (The Ornament of Clear Comprehension)
- the *Mahāyānasūtrālaṃkāra* (The Ornament of the Discourses of the Mahāyāna)
- the *Madhyāntavibhāga* (Elucidation of the Middle and of the Extremes)

Buddhists designated as *alaṃkāra* ("ornament") works that, written for the most part in verse and loosely connected with authoritative texts, provided explanations and augmentations to these. <297> The first two above-mentioned works are such *alaṃkāras*. Specifically, the *Abhisamayālaṃkāra* seeks to systematically and lucidly summarize the path of liberation as described in the *Pañcaviṃśatisāhasrikā Prajñāpāramitā* (*The Perfection of Insight in Twenty-five Thousand Lines*; *see above* S. 146f.), whereas the *Mahāyānasūtrālaṃkāra*, while closely following the structure of the *Bodhisattvabhūmi* (*The Stage of the Bodhisattva*; *see above* S. 265), yet otherwise with great latitude, discusses the subjects treated therein. Both works thus represent an attempt to bring order to the jumble of the older scholasticism of liberation, but this attempt met with only limited success. Maitreyanātha has only partially forged the immense and in many ways reluctant mass of material into a unity. For the most part, he simply arranged them according to an external division and thereby gave the thoughts a clearer form.

The third work, the *Madhyāntavibhāga*, is of a similar type, even though it does not rely externally on an older text, as do the two *alaṃkāras*. Here as well, important subjects of the doctrine are treated in such a way that the traditional views are arranged into the schema of an external division, without achieving a real unity.

In addition to these incomplete attempts to master the recorded mass of the scholasticism of liberation, Maitreyanātha, however, also developed clear philosophical views; a real philosophical system, in fact. Even though in his works—which indeed deal essentially with the scholasticism of liberation—philosophical views are only raised occasionally and in a few disconnected sections, it still becomes apparent that the same underlying views are always present, which are readily connected to each other and joined together to form one great whole. And this whole we can then see as the doctrine of Maitreyanātha and as the first philosophical system of the Yogācāra school.

CFC.2. *The first philosophical system of the Yogācāra: the doctrine of Maitreyanātha*

Seen on a large scale, Maitreyanātha's doctrine is an ingenious edifice in which all sorts of older doctrines along with valuable thoughts of his own have been forged into a unity. <298> Sāramati's doctrine [S. 256f.] of the ultimate state of being, together with his buddhology, forms one essential constituent. To this are added the philosophical views of the older Yogācāra school, in particular the doctrine of the three characteristics, augmented and enriched through Maitreyanātha's own thoughts. Lastly, all kinds of ideas have also been taken from the Madhyamaka school. In particular, Maitreyanātha again and again makes an effort to give his statements the form of the middle doctrine and, in this way, to establish his doctrine, instead of the Madhyamaka doctrine, as the true middle way.

CFC.2.1. *The ultimate state of being as the center of the system*

In the center of his system stands the ultimate state of being, which he most often calls the *element of the factors (dharmadhātu)* and less frequently, *suchness (tathatā)*. He speaks of *emptiness (śūnyatā)* only in connection with the Madhyamaka doctrine. This ultimate state of being is the only thing in the world that really exists, and it is also the basis of the deception of the phenomenal world. It is itself inexpressible *(anabhilāpya)* and without diversity *(aprapañcātmaka)*. To these views, which are also common to the Madhyamaka school, are added the fundamental doctrines of Sāramati; primarily the doctrine of the pure mind. As for Sāramati, so also for Maitreyanātha the ultimate state of being is mind *(citta)* and is brightly luminous *(prabhāsvara)*. First and foremost, however, it is pure by nature *(prakṛtiviśuddha)*, like water, gold, or space. All pollution, which the deception of the phenomenal world entails, is merely adventitious *(āgantuka)* and cannot touch its essence. And thus [the ultimate state of being] is also not changed in its nature through the purification of pollution. Nevertheless, its pollution and purification are of fundamental importance, since on these are based bondage and liberation, and the entire deception of the phenomenal world in general.

CFC.2.2. *The ultimate state of being and the phenomenal world*

The phenomenal world encompasses all of the factors *(dharma)*. According to Maitreyanātha, these are based on the ultimate state of being and cannot exist separately. Rather, the ultimate state of being constitutes the nature of the factors *(dharmatā)*. Specifically, their relationship is such that they are neither distinct nor not distinct. The character of the phenomenal world itself is best elucidated, in Madhyamaka <299> style, through comparison to a magical illusion *(māyā)*. Just as, on some sort of basis, such [an illusion] simulates something that does not exist in reality, so it is also with the phenomenal world. The latter is thus unreal with respect to what it simulates, but it is real as semblance. Consequently, it can be designated neither as existent nor as non-existent, instead it is at once existence and non-existence. Other comparisons that elucidate its nature are the illusion that a good painting produces, or a dream.

CFC.2.3. *The false conception and the deception of the phenomenal world, etc.*

In order to explain the deception of the phenomenal world, Maitreyanātha says, as did the older Yogācāra school, that it is conception, i.e., a creation of our cognition. He is not content with this, however, but goes significantly further, and here he develops his most valuable original thoughts. Up to this point, the questions of who the bearer of the conception is and how it comes about had not been asked. Maitreyanātha asked this. In doing so he focused on the idea of false conception[1] *(abhūta-parikalpa),* i.e., of a cognition that conceives of something that is not real. For Maitreyanātha this false conception is the foundation of the entire phenomenal world and comes about in the following way. As already stated, the ultimate state of being is itself mind and is inherent in all beings as a seed or element *(dhātu).* From this element, the false conception emerges. In this it displays the image of the various things of the phenomenal world. Among Buddhist schools, it is namely widely held that the cognition of a thing comes about through the mind taking on its form. Thus the false conception also reflects the various things of the phenomenal world. No real

---

1 [Obviously, *unreal conception* would be the literal translation of "unwirkliche Vorstellung," but even though Frauwallner qualifies this term at once and in the next paragraph, the "unreal" in this literal translation could be read as a statement about the status of the conception itself.]

things correspond to these reflections in the conception, however. On the contrary, all factors are just such reflections. Real things outside of cognition do not exist at all.

The false conception not only reflects the objects of the seeming external world, however, it also reflects the subject. It displays, as Maitreyanātha expresses it, the apprehended *[grāhya]* as well as the apprehending *(grāhaka)*. It is thus one of its characteristic marks that <300> it continually simulates a duality *(dvaya)*. Occasionally, Maitreyanātha makes the attempt to further structure this duality. Hence he says that conception reflects, on the one hand, objects and beings; on the other hand, the self and cognition. In other passages it is stated, however, that it appears on the one hand, as words, objects, and bodies; on the other hand, as thinking *(manas)*, view *(udgraha)*, and conception *(vikalpa)*. He does not seem to have formed firm views in this respect.

His views concerning the constitution of the mental organism are also fragmentary. While he usually speaks only of the false conception, he occasionally distinguishes—as do most Buddhist schools—between mind *(citta)* and mental factors *(caitta)*. But he does not elaborate on this any further. It is noteworthy, however, that he occasionally states explicitly that the defilements *(kleśa)*, which are usually counted as mental factors, are mere appearing forms of the mind.

Maitreyanātha also clothes all of these views of the phenomenal world and the ultimate state of being in the form of the doctrine of the three characteristics, as we have encountered it in the *Saṃdhinirmocanasūtra* [S. 280f.]. Accordingly, the images that are reflected as duality in the conception are the imagined characteristic. The false conception itself, which displays these images, is the dependent characteristic. And lastly, the absence of duality, in other words the ultimate state of being underlying the false conception in its pure form, is the perfect characteristic. At the same time, it is clearly noticeable that for Maitreyanātha the adoption of this doctrine of the three characteristics is only a concession to the tradition of the school without in any way fruitfully influencing his own lines of thought.

CFC.2.4. *The doctrine of liberation*

CFC.2.4.1. *Nonconceptual knowledge and liberation*

As far as the doctrine of liberation is concerned, Maitreyanātha dealt with the traditional scholasticism of liberation of the Yogācāra school in great detail. In addition, however, he also developed his own clear views about the decisive mental processes pertaining to liberation, and <301> these views are also philosophically significant. According to these views, liberation occurs in the state of absorption by means of nonconceptual knowledge *(nirvikalpakaṃ jñānam)* once the Bodhisattva has obtained the necessary merit and knowledge and, in particular, has heard and correctly comprehended the Mahāyāna doctrine. Here the Bodhisattva first recognizes that all objects of cognition are accompanied by words and conditioned by words, and can therefore not be real. From this, the knowledge next results that cognition [itself] also cannot be real, because without an object, there can be no cognition. And once the unreality of object and subject has thus been recognized, the mind gathers itself in the element of the ultimate state of being that is its basis *(cittasya svadhātau sthānam),* all duality of conception vanishes, and the element of the factors itself is seen. This is the so-called *nonconceptual knowledge.* What is important here most especially, is that thereby also the sameness *(samatā)* of the element of the factors in all beings is recognized. This nonconceptual knowledge—gained in the state of absorption—is further followed, as a result, by another knowledge *(pṛṣṭhalabdhajñāna),* which remains in the ordinary state of consciousness as well. And while the first brings about one's own liberation, the second makes possible the teaching and thereby the liberation of other beings.

Liberation itself consists in the fact that, through nonconceptual knowledge, the pollution that occasions entanglement in cyclic existence is removed so that the element of the factors, which is inherent in all beings, attains its own natural purity. This process is called *transformation of the basis (āśrayaparāvṛtti).* It is not an all at once process but one that takes place in stages over long periods of time. Maitreyanātha ties it, as indeed he does all the processes leading to liberation, to the numerous stages of the path of liberation as elaborated by the old scholasticism of liberation. This complicated schema is, however, philosophically insignificant and need not be taken into consideration here.

CFC.2.4.2. *Buddhology and the ultimate state of being*

With the last and final transformation of the basis, liberation is gained and at the same time—corresponding to the goal <302> of the Mahāyāna—omniscience and buddhahood. Thus for Maitreyanātha, the doctrine of the state of the Liberated One is connected with buddhology. Since liberation consists of the purification of the element of the factors, which is inherent in all beings, of the adventitious pollution of worldly existence, the Liberated One belongs to the pure ultimate state of being. Our presentation thus returns to the point from which it started. From the point of view of buddhology, however, features other than those we have first discussed [S. 298ff.] emerge with respect to the ultimate state of being. As buddhahood, it does not appear as brightly luminous mind but rather as similar to a world soul, which pervades everything in its activity. It is eternal and omnipresent. Its activity is uninterrupted and all-encompassing. If it does not manifest everywhere in its activity, this is due to the corruptness of beings. Further, its activity is manifold and inexhaustible, like a light that shines without becoming exhausted. What is noteworthy here, is that its activity occurs without striving *(yatna)*, without effort *(ābhoga)*, and without egotism, in other words, without anything that could signify a bondage.

A special question arises as to how the personage and the multiplicity of the Buddhas is to be reconciled with the buddhahood that is based only on the ultimate state of being. Here on the one hand, Maitreyanātha professes the logically consistent view that, with respect to the unity of the stainless element of the factors, no multiplicity is possible, and that a multiplicity can be spoken of only in consideration of a previous embodiment. He does, on the other hand, actually reckon—in practice—with the multiplicity of Buddhas and explains their combined activity using the analogy of the combined activity of sunbeams. Likewise, he explains the significance of this combined activity using the analogy of rivers, whose value as dwelling-places for beings first fully comes into being when their waters unite in the ocean.

Maitreyanātha also refers several times to the good or white qualities, which according to the old doctrine, are the marks of the Buddha and are unique to him.

Finally, it must be noted that Maitreyanātha is also acquainted with the doctrine of the three bodies of the Buddha, so widespread in the Mahāyāna, <303> but this is more theologically than philosophically interesting and hence need not be considered here.

CFC.2.5. *The doctrine of Maitreyanātha and the Madhyamaka doctrine*

In broad strokes, this is the doctrine of Maitreyanātha. A final essential feature is the fact that he tried as far as possible to fuse the views of the Madhyamaka school with his doctrine and in this way sought to replace and supersede the Madhyamaka doctrine. This he does by adopting and incorporating—wherever an opportunity presents itself—the concepts of the Madhyamaka system; for example, by equating his ultimate state of being with emptiness *(śūnyatā)*, in spite of all the differences in these views. First and foremost, however, he does so by seeking to give his doctrine the form of the middle way. In this, unlike the Madhyamaka school originally, he does not deny the respective extremes on the principle that both are not in any way applicable. Instead, he denies their one-sided affirmation, since in a certain sense their opposite is also applicable, i.e., with a view of their relativity. Such a middle view through the negation of the two extremes is applied—in his doctrine—at every possible opportunity and with respect to the most varied of concepts. The most systematic attempt of this application of the middle way is found, however, in chapter I of the *Madhyāntavibhāga,* translated below. This chapter can serve as a good example of this entire way of looking at things and so it seems good to make particular reference to it.

CFC.3. *Introduction to the samples from the Mahāyānasūtrālaṃkāra*

The first of the following translated samples is taken from the *Mahāyānasūtrālaṃkāra*. Here I have selected verses from different chapters of the work and arranged them in a meaningful order in order to elucidate the most significant tenets. A translation of continuous sections was out of the question, since Maitreyanātha himself does not give a continuous presentation and too much that is philosophically insignificant is woven in. I have refrained from a more thorough sequential explanation and elucidate [in the following] only a few points where it seems necessary, since after the preceding presentation, most of this should be readily understandable.

The first series of verses (XIII, vv. 16–19) deals with the nature of the phenomenal world and the highest reality. The phenomenal world is perceived, although in reality it does not exist. This is elucidated using the examples of a magical illusion [*māyā*] and of the illusion produced by a good painting. The highest reality is purified, although in reality it is not polluted. Space and clear, merely outwardly cloudy water serve as examples.

The second series of verses (XI, vv. 13–23) begins with a short description of the nature of the highest reality. Here, the statement that it must be recognized, abandoned, and purified, refers to the doctrine of the threefold characteristic and is easily understandable from the previously translated sections from the *Saṃdhinirmocanasūtra* (VI, 11, *above* S. 288). Next [vv. 14–18], the emergence of the deception of the phenomenal world is elucidated using the example of a magical illusion. The last two of these verses (vv. 17–18) allude to the supranatural power gained by the ascetic subsequent to the liberating cognition about the phenomenal world, as soon as—with the purification of the element of the factors—the so-called *transformation of the basis (āśrayaparāvṛtti)* takes place. By way of explanation it is pointed out that even those people who have been deceived by a magical illusion are, after the illusion has vanished, able to deal with its origins just as they please. The magician, after all, does not bring forth the illusion out of nothing. Instead he takes some real object, e.g., a piece of wood, as a support and simply causes it to appear in a different shape, perhaps as an elephant. Following that [vv. 19–21], Maitreyanātha applies the middle doctrine's way of seeing things to this view of the phenomenal world. A magical illusion exists as an appearance, it is true, but not as a real thing. Hence one should neither state one-sidedly that it exists, nor that it does not exist. And the same applies to the phenomenal world.

The next series of verses (XI, vv. 31–35) deals with conception and how it comes about. First, the entire sphere of the phenomenal world, which is indeed nothing but conception, is classified as follows: [1] false conception, by which is meant the ordinary processes of cognition; [2] neither true or false conception, by which is understood the processes of cognition that prepare for the liberating cognition; [3] non-conception, i.e., the nonconceptual <305> knowledge *(nirvikalpaka jñāna)* that brings liberation; and finally, [4] the resulting knowledge belonging to the ordinary state of consciousness, which is to be seen neither as conception nor as non-conception. Ordinary conceptions emerge from their element, i.e., from the element of the factors, which is inherent—as a germ—in all beings. They display the appearance of duality without containing an actual duality. If they are turned toward the highest object accessible to them, by directing them toward their element, then the appearance of duality vanishes, i.e., they lose the character of a conception. This is illustrated through the example of leather, which, given appropriate treatment, loses its hardness and becomes soft; or through the example of a bent rod, which becomes straight under the influence of heat. In addition, the good and bad mental factors are mentioned, in particular, the defilements of which it is said that they are not independent factors but only appearing forms of the mind.

The subject of the next three verses (XI, vv. 39–41) is the doctrine of the threefold nature of things; specifically, they give a brief definition of this threefold nature according to Maitreyanātha's view.

Hence the *imagined characteristic* is the conceived image in which object-referent *[artha]* and name *[nāma]* mutually condition each other.

The *dependent characteristic* is the false conception, which displays the twofold appearance of object and subject, whereby each of these appears to be triply divided: the object into word *[pada]*, object-referent *[artha]*, and body *[deha]*; the subject into mind *[mana]*, taking notice *[udgraha]*, and conception *[vikalpa]*.

The *perfect characteristic,* finally, the nature of which consists in the absence of the duality of object and subject, is defined here according to the middle doctrine (*cf.* the section from the *Madhyāntavibhāga* translated below, S. 324ff.). It is non-existence, since this duality does not exist, and it is existence, since this non-existence exists. Thus, it unites in itself existence and non-existence. Further, it is not peaceful, since it is polluted through adventitious stains, and it is peaceful, since it is pure by nature. Lastly, in spite of its nature as mind, it lacks the nature of conception. <306>

The next series of verses [vv. 1–10] forms the VIth chapter of the *Mahāyānasūtrālaṃkāra.* I present this brief chapter in full because it corresponds to the section of the *Bodhisattvabhūmi* partially translated above, and shows how Maitreyanātha follows this work only superficially and very freely expresses his own thoughts in the comments related to it. Furthermore, the chapter presents in concise terms a good summary of the essential features of the processes of liberation according to Maitreyanātha's view.

The first five verses lean heavily on lines of thought from the Madhyamaka. First [v. 1], a definition of the highest reality is given, which retains the style of the *Prajñāpāramitā* texts. Only the statement that the highest reality is not purified and yet does become purified, refers once again to the fact that it is pure by nature and merely adventitiously stained. Next [v. 2], the belief in a self, as the cause of entanglement in the cycle of existences, is discussed in nearly as broad a manner as in Nāgārjuna. This belief is merely an error, since neither it nor the five groups are the self, and something else that could be the self does not exist. Nevertheless [vv. 3–4], under the influence of this belief, people are unable to recognize that things are full of suffering and thus cannot be the self, and that all things, including the factors of the psyche, are called forth by each other only in accordance with the law of dependent origination, without an active self being behind them. These are old lines of thought that reach all the way back to the canonical texts. In between are interspersed comments from the perspective of the middle way. People experience suffering because they feel it, and they do not experience it because they do not understand it. They are tormented by it but also not tormented because, indeed, there is no self, since they consist only of factors. Yet even that is not the case since the factors are also not real. To the thought that the belief in a self is merely an error, and that liberation thus consists simply of the extinction of this error,[v. 5] is then also joined the doctrine that liberation and the cycle of existences are in reality one and the same, even though the attainment of liberation by means of the path shown by the Buddha is taught. <307> This too corresponds to the doctrine of the *Prajñāpāramitā* and the Madhyamaka school.

This is followed (v. 6) by the presentation of the process of liberation itself and here Maitreyanātha begins once again to expound his own views. First, he mentions the preparatory stages, which consist of the Bodhisattva obtaining the necessary accumulation of good deeds and knowledge, and also his hearing and correctly comprehending the Mahāyāna doctrine. The decisive process of cognition begins with his becoming aware that all conceived images—hence, all objects of cognition—are accompanied by "words" [S. 268f.] and are conditioned by "words" and are thus unreal. Through this he comes to the insight [v. 7] that nothing exists but the cognition that displays the appearance of the objects, and subsequently, by freeing himself from the duality of subject and object, he arrives at a direct seeing of the highest reality. Explained in detail [v. 8], this last step takes place in such a way that, with the disappearance of the object, the subject as well is rendered invalid. With this, insight into the unreality of duality is gained and the highest cognition, which consists of the direct clear comprehension of the nondual highest reality, appears. This highest cognition brings with it [v. 9] the recognition of the sameness of the element of the factors, which is one and the same in all beings, and in removing all of the stains that cause entanglement in the cycle of existences, this same cognition leads to liberation. As a kind of addendum, the last verse [v. 10] mentions, that at this stage the Bodhisattva also recognizes the doctrine of the Buddha as mere conception, which is based on the element of the factors, and that he henceforth rapidly acquires the countless virtues that make him a Buddha.

As a last sample from the *Mahāyānasūtrālaṃkāra,* several groups of verses from chapter IX, which deals with buddhahood, follow. First (vv. 11–12), buddhahood is praised as the refuge for all beings and its attainment is briefly described. Thereby the following [three] points are emphasized: [i] The prerequisite is the removal of both of the obstructions, the obstruction of defilements and the obstruction to what is to
be known. This occurs gradually through numerous <308>
processes of elimination. [ii] Buddhahood itself is based on the transformation of the basis, which brings about the purification of the element of the factors, and it is distinguished through the qualities unique to the Buddhas, which, in accordance with their moral character, are called *white factors.* [iii] The path to this is, finally, nonconceptual knowledge unafflicted by stains, which brings with it omniscience.

The remaining groups of verses are easily understood and need no detailed explanation. They deal with (vv. 15–17) the omnipresence of buddhahood, and explain through examples why buddhahood does not become apparent everywhere. Then it is mentioned that the activities of the Buddhas are without effort *(ābhoga),* in other words, without inner bondage (vv. 18–19), and that they occur uninterruptedly (vv. 20–21). Following this, (v. 26) the reason why one can speak neither exclusively of a unity nor of a multiplicity of the Buddhas, and hence why in a certain sense both apply, is established. Further, using the analogy of sunbeams, there is an explanation of the uniformity of the activity of the Buddhas (vv. 29–31), which is without any selfishness (v. 32) and which extends to everything, so long as the wickedness of beings does not stand in its way (vv. 33–34). One verse (v. 37) shows that buddhahood, as the pure form of the element of the factors, is inherent—as a germ—in all beings. A further series of verses deals once more with the activity of a Buddha. It describes (v. 51) how the one Buddha displays a thousandfold activity in numberless world spheres and yet by his actual nature remains immovable. It emphasizes again (vv. 52–53) how the activity of the Buddha takes place without inner involvement and effort. Using the example of a lamp, it illustrates (v. 54) how the nature of the Buddha, in spite of all that it radiates, does not exhaust itself. Finally, using the analogy of the ocean, it explains (v. 55) how the element of the factors, as the sphere of the Buddha, does not become full and does not increase, in spite of the influx that results from the continual purification and liberation of so many beings. The last series of verses, finally (vv. 82–85), and again by means of an example, shows how the activity of the Buddha comes into full effect only through <309> its unity in buddhahood.

CFC.3.1. *From the "Ornament of the Discourses of the Mahāyāna" (Mahāyānasūtrālaṃkāra)*

Chapter XIII:

[The nature of the phenomenal world and the highest reality.]

16

Perception, without existing factors, and purification, without existing pollution, are to be regarded like a magical illusion, etc., and like space, [respectively].

17

Just as in a properly painted picture, there exists no height and depth and yet they are seen, so in false conception, there is never and in no way a duality, and yet it is seen.

18

Just as with water that has been churned up and then calmed again, the clarity does not arise from elsewhere, but rather a separation of the dirt takes place; this same principle applies also to the purification of one's own mind.

19

The opinion is accepted that the mind is by nature continually clear [luminous *(prabhāsvara)*] and becomes clouded only through adventitious faults. Apart from the mind that is based on the nature of the factors *(dharmatācitta)*, there is no other mind whose natural clarity [luminosity] is taught.

Chapter XI:
[The nature of the highest reality]

13

Reality is continually free from duality; it is, however, the foundation of error. It cannot be <310> expressed in any way and is by nature without diversity. It must be recognized, abandoned, and purified; is considered to be stainless by nature; and its purification from defilements is considered to be similar to space, to gold, and to water.

14

There is nothing in the world [of beings] that could be other than it, and still the entire world [of beings] is deluded about it. Why does this peculiar kind of delusion of people, which clings to the non-existent and completely disregards the existent, occur?

15

Like a magical illusion [as cause], so the false conception *(abhūtaparikalpa)* is explained. Like the effect of the magical illusion, so the deception [error] of duality is explained.

16

Like the non-existence of the one [i.e., the effect of the magical illusion] in the other [i.e., magical illusion as cause], so the highest truth is accepted. Just as with the perception of this [effect of the magical illusion], however, so (it is with) the restricted truth.

17

Just as with the vanishing of the ([effect of the] magical illusion) the (true) state of its cause *(nimitta)* is apprehended, so with the transformation of the basis *(āśrayaparāvṛtti)* (the true constitution) of the false conception is apprehended.

18

And just as people, when they are freed from error, deal with this cause just as they please, so, if the error has vanished due to the transformation, <311> it is in the power of the ascetic to proceed just as he pleases.

19

The corresponding shape [e.g., elephant] is there, yet [real] existence is not present. Thus, with respect to a magical illusion, etc., one speaks of existence and non-existence.

20

In this, existence is not non-existence and non-existence is not existence. However, with regard to a magical illusion, etc., one asserts the non-difference of existence and non-existence.

21

Likewise the appearance of duality is there, yet [real] existence is not present. Thus, with respect to visible form, etc., one speaks of existence and non-existence.

22

In this, existence is not non-existence and non-existence is not existence. However, with respect to visible form, etc., one asserts the non-difference of existence and non-existence.

23

This [non-difference] is assumed in order to reject the two extremes of affirmation and negation and in order to reject the way of the small vehicle (Hīnayāna).

[. . .]

[Conception and how it emerges]

31

The entirety of the knowable is explained as false conception, as neither-true-nor-false[-conception], as non-conception, and as neither-conception-nor-non-conception.

32

From their element *(dhātu)* emerge the conceptions, which show the appearance of duality, are accompanied—in their working—by ignorance and defilements, <312> and are free from a real duality *(dvayadravya).*

33

They, [i.e., those conceptions,] attain their most excellent object-support if one practices directing them toward their element, since they then appear without thc appearance of duality, like a piece of leather or a rod.

34

It is maintained that the mind that displays the appearance of duality also displays the appearance of passion, etc., and the appearance of faith, etc. A defiled or good factor distinct from this does not exist.

35

The mind thus becomes apparent in that it displays manifold appearances and manifold appearing forms. Existence and non-existence thus concerns the image, and not the factors.

[. . .]

[The doctrine of the threefold nature of things]

39

The appearance of the object-referent and of the name corresponding to the name and object-referent, which is the object *(nimitta)* of the false conception, that is the imagined characteristic.

40

The false conception, which is characterized by the apprehended and the apprehending, and displays respectively a threefold appearance, that is the dependent characteristic.

41

Non-existence and existence, the equality of existence and non-existence, not peaceful and peaceful, and non-conception, that is the perfect characteristic. <313>

Chapter VI:

[Bondage and essential features of the processes of liberation]

1

It is not existent and not non-existent, it is not so and not otherwise, it does not arise and does not pass away, it does not decrease and does not increase, it is not purified and yet is purified, that is the mark of the highest truth.

2

The belief in a self does not itself have the mark of the self; just as little as does the world of suffering *(duḥsaṃsthitatā)*, since [the latter] is of another type [than the self]. Something other than these two does not exist, however. Thus, [the belief in a self] is an error. Consequently, liberation is the mere extinction of this error.

3

Why do people who are merely in error, not recognize the eternally painful nature (of things)? They experience it and they do not experience it. They are tormented and not tormented by suffering. They consist of the factors and they do not consist of them.

4

Why do people, even though they have the dependently originated before their eyes, believe that it has arisen through something else? What peculiar kind of blindness is this, that they do not see that which exists and see that which does not exist?

5

In reality, there is also no difference here at all between peace (i.e., *nirvāṇa*) and birth *[saṃsāra]*. And yet, for those who perform good deeds, the attainment of peace through the extinction of birth is taught. <314>

6

After he has collected an unlimited accumulation of knowledge and merit, the Bodhisattva, having attained full clarity through reflection on the doctrinal texts, recognizes that the apprehension of the object-referents is dependent on speech.[1]

7

After he has recognized the object-referents as mere speech, he abides in the mere mind that displays their appearance, and the element of the factors becomes apparent to him. Through this, he is liberated from the characteristic of duality.

8

For in that, through his intellect, he recognizes that something other than the mind does not exist, he thereby also recognizes the non-existence of the mind. And having recognized the non-existence of duality, the intelligent person abides in the element of the factors, which is not affected by [duality].

9

Through the power of nonconceptual knowledge—which everywhere and always accompanies sameness *(sama)*—the dense heap of faults that has collected in the intelligent person is removed; as is poison by a strong antidote.

---

[1] [On speech, see Frauwallner's comments, S. 268, on the parallel section in the *Bodhisattvabhūmi*.]

10

After he has gained full clarity about the good doctrine proclaimed by the sage (the Buddha), the steadfast one directs his mind to the underlying element of the factors. He recognizes, then, that the <315> (entire) tradition *(smṛtigati)* is mere conception, and in this way he quickly reaches the other shore of the ocean of virtues.

Chapter IX:
[The nature of buddhahood]

11

As long as the world exists, buddhahood is accepted as the great refuge of all beings so that they turn away from all misfortune and so that all good fortune is bestowed upon them.

12

This buddhahood, in which the seed of the obstructions of defilements and to what is to be known, which has constantly adhered (to beings) since beginningless time, has vanished as a result of extremely abundant abandonments of all kinds, consists of a transformation of the basis, which is associated with the most excellent virtues consisting of white factors. Specifically, [buddhahood] is attained on the path of knowledge, which is free from conceptions, has an extremely broad scope, and is completely pure.

13

Dwelling therein, the Perfected One surveys the world as if he were standing on a high mountain. He feels compassion for people, who take pleasure in peace (i.e., *nirvāṇa*), how much more so for other people, who take pleasure in becoming *[saṃsāra]*.

[. . .]

15

Just as it is thought about space that it is constantly all-pervasive, so it is thought about (buddhahood) that it is constantly all-pervasive. And just as space is everywhere present in the crowds of visible forms *(rūpa)*, so [buddhahood] is everywhere present in the crowds of beings. <316>

16

Just as the image of the moon cannot be seen if the vessel of water is broken, so the image of the Buddha cannot be seen in corrupt beings.

17

Just as fire flares up in one place, but goes out in another, so should it be understood about the Buddhas, that now they can be seen and now they can not be seen.

18

Just as sound emanates from (celestial) musical instruments without their being struck, so the doctrine emanates from the Buddha without any effort on his part.

19

And just as a precious gem displays its luster without exerting itself, so the Buddhas display their activities without any effort on their part.

20

Just as, uninterruptedly, in space the activities of people can be seen, so uninterruptedly, in the uncontaminated element the activities of the Victorious Ones (the Buddhas) [can be seen].

21

And just as, in space a disappearing and arising of the activities (of people) constantly takes place, so, in the uncontaminated element an arising and ceasing of the activities of the Buddhas takes place.

[. . .]

26

In the unstained element of the Buddhas, there is no unity and no multiplicity, because of bodilessness, <317> like space, and in connection with an earlier body.

[. . .]

29

Just as innumerable rays, united in the disc of the sun, constantly bring forth one and the same effect and illuminate the world,

30

so, in the unstained element, an innumerable number of Buddhas is assumed who, united in their activities, bring forth one and the same effect and call forth the light of knowledge.

31

Just as with the radiating of one single sunbeam, all of the sunbeams radiate, so is the radiating of the knowledge of the Buddhas to be understood.

32

Just as, in the activity of the sunbeam, there is no selfishness, so, in the activity of the Buddhas' knowledge, there is no selfishness.

33

Just as the world is illuminated by the sunbeams whose glow the sun emits all at once, so all that is knowable is illuminated all at once by the knowledge of the Buddhas.

34

And just as it is thought that sunbeams are hindered by clouds, etc., so the wickedness of beings constitutes a hindrance to [illumination by] the knowledge of the Buddhas. <318>

[. . .]

37

Suchness, which is no different in all (beings), if it has become pure, represents buddhahood. Therefore, all embodied (beings) carry the germ of it within them *(tadgarbha = tathāgatagarbha).*

[. . .]

51

Here (the Buddha) shows the wheel of the doctrine in many hundreds of ways, there the disappearance of birth, there manifold courses through births, here perfect enlightenment, there *nirvāṇa;* and that again and again. In doing so, he does not move from his place and yet he accomplishes everything.

52

In doing so, the Buddhas [do not] think: "This one is ripe for me. This one I must ripen. This one will now be ripened." Without an act of will *(saṃskāra = abhisaṃskāra),* everywhere in all parts of the world, people reach ripening through the three gates (of the three vehicles), by virtue of the white factors (i.e., the virtues of the Buddha).

53

Just as, through the emission of its extensive bright rays, the sun is active without effort in the ripening of seeds everywhere in all parts of the world, so, through the emission of the rays of the doctrine, the sun of the (Buddhas') doctrine that preaches peace (i.e., *nirvāṇa*) is active in the ripening of beings everywhere in all parts of the world.

54

Just as from one light an extremely great, boundless, and immeasurable abundance of light emanates without <319> it thereby exhausting itself, so, from a Buddha, an extremely great, boundless, and immeasurable abundance of ripening emanates without him thereby exhausting himself.

55

And just as the great ocean does not become saturated by the waters and is not increased by the influx of the extensive clear waters, so the element of the Buddhas is not saturated and is not increased by the constantly arriving influx of purity. This is the greatest marvel.

[. . .]

82

As long as they have not sunk underground, rivers that each have a distinct bed and distinct water, that each carry only a little water and accomplish their effect separately, are of use to only a few beings that live in the water.

83

If, however, they have reached the ocean and all now have one bed and one great body of water, and together accomplish one effect, then they are constantly of great use to the great mass of beings that live in the water.

84

Likewise, as long as they have not reached buddhahood, the sages, who have each their own distinct abode and distinct opinion, who possess little insight, and who each pursue separately their own activity, are constantly of use to only a limited number of beings.

85

If, however, they have reached buddhahood and all have the same abode, possess the same great insight, <320> and together perform the same activity, then they are constantly of use to a great crowd of beings.

CFC.4. *Introduction to samples from the Madhyāntavibhāga*

The second translated sample presents the philosophically most important parts of the first chapter of the *Madhyāntavibhāga*. This chapter contains Maitreyanātha's discussion of the Madhyamaka doctrine. He proceeds in this by shaping his doctrine in the form of the middle way, as he understands it, and thereby trying to correct and to complement the Madhyamaka doctrine. Accordingly, he also chooses a new name for his doctrine and does not speak of the *middle way*, but calls it the *doctrine of the middle and the extremes*. Essential in this is that in which he believes to have found the middle way between the extremes and his incorporation of the concept of emptiness *(śūnyatā)*.

In the first two verses Maitreyanātha's view of the middle way is already presented. Nāgārjuna had seen the middle way in the fact that both extremes, existence and non-existence, do not apply to the phenomenal world because both are, in and of themselves, not possible (*cf.* e.g., the translation of the fifteenth chapter of the *Madhyamakakārikā, above* S. 180ff.). In addition to this, however, in Nāgārjuna we already find the tendency to establish the denial of the two extremes by stating that neither of them applies exclusively since, in a certain sense, the other is also valid (*cf.* e.g., *Ratnāvalī* I, vv. 42 ff., *above* S. 212).

The Yogācāra school decided in favor of this view. Thus in the above translated section of the *Bodhisattvabhūmi* (S. 283f.), we have found the middle way explained in such a way that one cannot speak of an existence of the phenomenal world because it is mere conception and therefore unreal, but that one can just as little speak of a non-existence since the ultimate state of being, which is the basis [of the phenomenal world], is real.

And the same view holds for Maitreyanātha, except that in his case [this view] appears in a somewhat more complicated form since he does not—as does the *Bodhisattvabhūmi*—have only the phenomenal world and the ultimate state of being in view, but also takes into account the three characteristics that the *Saṃdhinirmocanasūtra* had taught [S. 280ff., 284ff.]. <321> Of these three characteristics, the imagined characteristic is pure conception; the dependent and perfect characteristic are the ultimate state of being in its polluted and its purified forms. Accordingly, the doctrine of the middle way takes the following shape for Maitreyanatha: He sees the imagined characteristic in the duality of subject and object, which conception displays to us. The dependent characteristic is, for him, the false conception, which is indeed afflicted with the deception of duality. The perfect characteristic, finally, is the ultimate state of being, insofar as it is free from this deception. Maitreyanātha thus speaks of non-existence or emptiness, but he later equates this (vv. 13–14) explicitly with the ultimate state of being, i.e., with the element of the factors. Of these then, the duality of subject and object does not exist, since it is mere conception. On the other hand, the non-existence [of this duality], i.e., the highest reality, and the false conception that is based on this, do exist. With respect to the phenomenal world, therefore, one should not speak of existence since duality does not exist, and one should not speak of non-existence since emptiness and the false conception do exist. And this is the true middle way.

Next (vv. 3–4) Maitreyanātha elucidates the central concept of the false conception *(abhūtaparikalpa)*, and starting from this concept he explains the entire phenomenal world; following which (v. 5), he briefly presents the relationship to the doctrine of the three characteristics. The false conception consists in the fact that cognition arises by displaying the appearance of object and subject. But a real object does not exist. And, without an object, no subject can exist either. This is the same inference that recurs in the description of the liberating cognition, and that we have thus already encountered above [S. 301]. It follows from this, however, that all cognition is merely a conception of something unreal. This unreality is then also concisely defined in terms of the middle way. The conceived does not exist in the way it appears, because in reality it does not exist. But it is also not completely non-existent, because it exists as a conception. However—just as Nāgārjuna teaches [S. 174f.]—bondage and liberation, and hence <322> the entire course of the world, are based on this deception of the conception, since liberation consists only in the extinction of this deception. This false conception is, in terms of the doctrine of the three characteristics, the dependent characteristic; its object, that is, the duality of subject and object, is the imagined characteristic; and the non-existence of this duality, as it ensues from liberation, is the perfect characteristic.

The next two verses (vv. 6–7) elaborate in greater detail on the briefly mentioned establishment of the unreality of conception. From the insight that only the cognition, which has the [appearing] form of the objects, is perceived, there arises the knowledge that no object-referents are perceived. But from the fact that no object-referents are apprehended, there arises the further consequence that also no cognition can be perceived, since without object-referents there is no cognition. The seeming perception is thus in reality a non-perception. But because both exist—the non-perception in accordance with the actual facts, and the perception, since, indeed, the unreal conceptual image is perceived—perception and non-perception are the same. And with that, the relative view in terms of the middle way is once again woven in.

A few remarks on the psychological foundation of the false conception follow in the next two verses (vv. 8–9). Corresponding to the general Buddhist view, this psychological foundation consists of the mind or cognition and the mental factors belonging to it, both of which are classified in terms of the three world spheres. Of these, the mind recognizes the given object in general, whereas the mental factors grasp its distinctive features. The interpretation of the second verse is difficult since Maitreyanātha hints at his views rather than expressing them and later interpreters have read Asaṅga's psychology into his words. A number of things point to the fact that Maitreyanātha distinguishes two forms of cognition, of which the first merely conveys the appearance of the object, whereas the second allows for the awareness of [the object's] perception. The first would thus correspond to the object part, the second to the subject part of the false conception. <323>

In the original, two verses then follow that enumerate the forms of pollution that condition entanglement in the cycle of existences, using the superficial systematic often found in Maitreyanātha. With this, the first half of the chapter is finished.

The second half, which now follows, deals with emptiness *(śūnyatā)* or the ultimate state of being. After a brief account of the outline of this section, Maitreyanātha first (v. 13) gives a definition of emptiness. Here he repeats the definition of the perfect characteristic given at the beginning of the chapter [v. 1], which, as we know, corresponds to the ultimate state of being, and he simply formulates it somewhat more pointedly in terms of the middle way. According to [this definition], emptiness is the non-existence of duality and the existence of this non-existence, i.e., it has a positive character. It is not a mere absence but an essence characterized by the absence of duality. As a result, in terms of a relative way of looking at things, it can be designated neither as existent nor as non-existent, and with this the middle way is once again preserved. Important, but not further elaborated upon, is the definition contained in the last part of this verse. It refers to the relationship of the ultimate state of being to the phenomenal world, in other words, of the nature of the factors *(dharmatā)* to the factors *(dharma)*. According to Maitreyanātha, this relationship is such that the two are neither distinct nor one.

The next two verses (vv. 14–15) enumerate the different names by which emptiness is also designated, and explains them. It is called *suchness (tathatā)*, because it never changes. It is called *pinnacle of the real (bhūtakoṭi)*, because it is free from any error. It is called the *signless (ānimitta)*, because it is without any sign. It is called the *highest truth (paramārthatā)*, because it is the object of the knowledge of the Noble Ones. And it is called *element of the factors (dharmadhātu)*, because the qualities *(dharma)* of the Noble Ones are based on it.

Subsequently, Maitreyanātha discusses emptiness from the point of view of bondage and liberation (v. 16), that is, in exactly the same way as otherwise in his works, where he uses the designation *element of the factors.* <324> [Emptiness] is, accordingly, either stained or unstained. It is *stained* if it is polluted through connection with the defilements. It is *unstained* if it is purified through the removal of the defilements. This pollution and purification, however, does not affect the nature [of emptiness] and does not cause any change in it since it is pure by nature, and all stains are only adventitious, as is the case with water, gold, or space (*cf. above Mahāyānasūtrālaṃkāra* XI, v. 13). The verses that now follow in the original (vv. 17–20) are an insertion, in which Maitreyanātha enumerates the sixteen types of emptiness that are taught in the *Prajñāpāramitā*. Then he continues (vv. 21–22): The polluted form of emptiness must exist, because otherwise there would be no entanglement in the cycle of existences. The purified form must exist, because otherwise no liberation would be possible. Relatively seen, [emptiness] is thus neither polluted nor unpolluted, neither pure nor impure. So here as well the principle of the middle way holds.

CFC.5. *From the "Elucidation of the Middle and of the Extremes" (Madhyāntavibhāga)*

Chapter I

1

False conception exists. There is no duality therein. There is, however, emptiness therein. And in the latter, there is also that (false conception).

2

Hence, everything is taught neither as empty nor as not-empty, due to the existence [of the false conception], to the non-existence [of duality], and to the existence [of that non-existence]. And this is the middle way.

3

Cognition arises in that it reflects object-referents, beings, the self, and perception. It has no object-referent, however, and because this [object-referent] is absent, [cognition] itself is non-existent. <325>

4

Hence, the character [of the four appearances of cognition] as false conception is established because it is not so, but is also not completely not. It is maintained that liberation (occurs) due to its vanishing.

5

The imagined, dependent, and perfect characteristic have been taught on the basis of the object-referent, the false conception, and the non-existence of duality.

6

Based on perception, non-perception arises. Based on non-perception, non-perception arises.

7

Hence, it is established that the nature of perception is non-perception. Because of that, it should be known that non-perception and perception are the same.

8

The false conception is the mind and the mental factors that belong to the three realms. In this, cognition is the seeing of the object-referent. The mental factors are directed toward its distinctive features.

9

[There are two forms of cognition:]

One is the cognition that takes note [of an object] *(pratyayavijñāna)*, [i.e., the object part,] the other is the cognition that experiences *(aupabhogika)*, [i.e., the subject part]. In this, the mental factors promote *(preraka)* determination *(pariccheda)* and experience *(upabhoga)*.

[. . .] <326>

13

The non-existence of duality and the existence of [this] non-existence is the characteristic of that which is empty. (It is thus) neither existence nor non-existence, characterized neither by distinctness nor by unity.

14

Suchness, the *pinnacle of the real,* the *signless,* the *highest truth,* and the *element of the factors,* these are, in brief, the synonyms of *emptiness.*

15

The meaning of these synonyms results respectively from the fact [that emptiness] is not different, is without error, is the suppression of (signs), is the sphere of the Noble Ones, and is the cause of the qualities of the Noble Ones.

16

[Emptiness] is polluted and pure, or stained and unstained. It is assumed that its purity is similar to the purity of the element of water, of gold, and of space.

[. . .]

21

If this [emptiness] were not polluted, all beings would be liberated. If this [emptiness] were not pure, every effort would be fruitless.

22

It is (therefore) neither polluted nor unpolluted, neither pure nor impure.

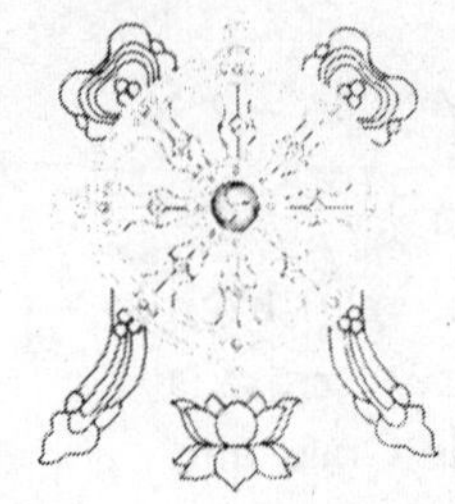

CFD. *Asaṅga (ca. 315–390 c.e.)*

The most important personality of the Yogācāra school is Asaṅga, the great student of Maitreyanātha. Asaṅga <327> was born toward the beginning of the fourth century c.e. as the son of a distinguished brahmin in Puruṣapura ([modern] Peshāwar). Initially, he belonged to the Śrāvakayāna school of the Mahīśāsaka, but turned later toward the Mahāyāna. The influence of his teacher Maitreyanātha was decisive for him. Maitreyanātha imparted his works to Asaṅga, who partly commented on them himself and partly passed them on to his brother Vasubandhu so that he could write the commentaries to them. The later legend then made out of this—once the personality of Maitreyanātha was forgotten—that Asaṅga received these works from the future Buddha Maitreya in Tuṣita heaven. Important to the development of the school was, further, that Asaṅga succeeded in winning over to his doctrine his younger brother Vasubandhu, whose activity in the service of his new convictions then became extremely extensive and successful. According to a later tradition, Asaṅga died at the age of seventy-five years.

In spite of his being a student of Maitreyanātha and in spite of the latter's strong influence on him, Asaṅga did produce significant achievements of his own: to be precise, two things in particular. Through his adoption and incorporation of the Śrāvakayāna scholasticism, he developed the Yogācāra system in such a way that it could place itself in every respect on equal terms with the great Śrāvakayāna schools of that time. Further, he surehandedly incorporated the mass of the old scholasticism of liberation into his system, which Maitreyanātha had not succeeded in doing. In this way, he established a unified edifice of doctrines that has, in its essential aspects, remained enduringly valid.

CFD.1. *The works of Asaṅga*

Of Asaṅga's numerous treatises the following are particularly important:

- The *Abhidharmasamuccaya (Compendium of Scholasticism),* in which, in reliance on the Abhidharma of the Mahīśāsaka, he gave the Yogācāra school its fundamental scholasticism.
- The *Hien yang cheng kiao louen* (*Proclamation of the Noble Doctrine;* as a makeshift, since the original title is not known, most often called *Āryadeśanāvikhyāpana* or, briefly, *Vikhyāpana*), which has been preserved only in Chinese, a systematic <328> summary of the doctrines of the gigantic *Yogācārabhūmiśāstra* (*see above* S. 265f.).
- The *Mahāyānasaṃgraha (Summary of the Mahāyāna),* the philosophically most significant work, in which he gives a systematic presentation of the fundamental doctrines of his system.

CFD.2. *The philosophical system of Asaṅga*

CFD.2.1. *Adoption of old concepts and development of new psychological concepts*

Most characteristic of Asaṅga's system is, as already mentioned, the adoption of the concepts of Śrāvakayāna scholasticism. This is especially evident in the psychology. Maitreyanātha's pure cognition, from which mistaken conceptions originate [S. 298f.], is replaced in Asaṅga by the complex of the factors of the psyche as taught by the Śrāvakayāna school, that is, the mind, i.e., the six kinds of cognition already found in the canon, and the mental factors associated with it. To this is added thinking *(manas),* as the bearer of self-consciousness, and, what is especially important, the fundamental cognition *(ālayavijñāna).*

The latter has the following origin. Since, according to general Buddhist doctrine, the factors of the psyche have only a moment's duration and immediately after their arising pass away again, the question soon arose as to how, in cases where an interruption of consciousness takes place, the stream of cognition can continue again later. For this reason, several schools of the Śrāvakayāna, among them the Mahīśāsaka, had assumed a form of cognition that underlies the conscious forms of cognition and remains uninterrupted for the entire cycle of existences or, at least, from birth until death.

In Asaṅga, the place of this cognition is now occupied by the fundamental cognition. And indeed, this assumption was all the more necessary for him, since the Yogācāra school recognized nothing outside of cognition that could have served [the conscious form of cognition] as its bearer or could have called it forth. Asaṅga thus connects with this yet another doctrine, which perhaps also had a predecessor in the Mahīśāsaka school, namely, the doctrine of the seeds *(bīja)* or of the permeation *(vāsanā)* of the fundamental cognition. According to this doctrine, every process of cognition leaves behind an imprint in the fundamental cognition. It permeates it, as it were, like an odor does a piece of cloth, and these imprints—without the stimulus of an external object—are capable of later bringing about a <329> cognition of the same kind, so that, in a beginningless uninterrupted succession of cognition and imprints, the appearance of the phenomenal world arises without any real entities existing outside of cognition. Asaṅga also explains the operation of deeds *(karma)* through similar imprints.

FD.2.2. *The appearance of the phenomenal world: the doctrine of the three characteristics*

Out of these factors of the psyche, the appearance of the phenomenal world is constituted in the following way: The concept of the *false conception,* so fundamental for Maitreyanātha, is insignificant for Asaṅga, and is only very superficially incorporated into his doctrine. In contrast to Maitreyanātha, on the other hand, the doctrine of the three characteristics provides him with the firm foundational framework.

FD.2.2.1. *The dependent characteristic*

Of these three characteristics, the dependent characteristic, being fundamental, is central. It consists of the different types of cognizance *(vijñapti)* that emerge from the fundamental cognition; and to be exact, Asaṅga recognizes eleven such types:

1–3. cognizance of the body, of the embodied, and of the one who enjoys, [i.e., the six sense-organs];
4. cognizance of that which is enjoyed by the preceding [cognizances], [i.e., the six objects];
5. cognizance of the enjoyer, [i.e., the six cognitions];
6. cognizance of time;
7. cognizance of number;
8. cognizance of place;
9. cognizance of manners of expression [*vyavahāra;* S. 341];
10. cognizance of difference between oneself and others;
11. cognizance of the good and bad destinies, of passing away and arising.

These eleven types of cognizance encompass all the forms in which the phenomenal world presents itself; and in that they emerge in this form from the fundamental cognition, the image of the phenomenal world arises.

The distinction of object and subject, so strongly emphasized by Maitreyanātha [S. 299f.], is accomplished by Asaṅga in the following way. He does not speak of the apprehended and the apprehending *(grāhyagrāhaka)*, but rather, with respect to cognition, distinguishes between an image part *(nimittabhāga)* and a seeing part *(darśanabhāga)*, which correspond to the object and subject. Both, the image part and the seeing part, are included in the types of cognizance enumerated above, specifically, as follows: According to old Buddhist doctrine, three factors must be present in every process of cognizance: the object, the sense-organ, and the corresponding cognition, and thus the canon taught a group of <330> eighteen so-called *elements (dhātu)* that encompasses the six sense-organs with the corresponding six objects and six types of cognition. But for Asaṅga, who does not recognize an external world, all of these eighteen elements are just types of cognizance and are, as such, contained in the above enumerated eleven types. More precisely, they constitute their actual core, whereas all others are only variations *(prabheda)* of them. Here, the cognizance of the body, of the embodied, and of the one who enjoys encompass the six sense-organs; the cognizance of that which is enjoyed, the six objects; and the cognizance of the enjoyer, the six types of cognition.

Hence—for Asaṅga—for every process of cognizance, three types of cognizance always arise at the same time, the first of which displays the image of the sense-organ, the second, the image of the object, and the third, the image of the corresponding cognition. In this, the cognizance that displays the image of the sense-organ forms the foundation, as it were; the cognizance that displays the image of the object represents the image part and hence the object of the process of cognizance; and the cognizance that displays the image of the corresponding cognition represents the seeing part and hence the subject.

So much for the dependent characteristic.

FD.2.2.2. *The imagined and the perfect characteristic*

Of the imagined and of the perfect characteristic, Asaṅga, like Maitreyanātha [S. 300, 305, 312], can only say that the imagined characteristic consists of object-referents that, without really existing, are reflected in the cognizance; the perfect characteristic, on the other hand, consists in the complete absence of these object-referents.

What is important and new is only his view of conception, since for him not every cognition is conception, but only mental cognition *(manovijñāna)*. Here he again follows a widespread view of the Śrāvakayāna schools that, indeed, every cognition is accompanied by conception[1] *(vikalpa)* but that the actual conceiving character belongs to mental cognition alone. With respect to mental cognition, again, as everywhere, three types of cognizance appear connected with one another. The cognizance of thinking *(manovijñapti)* forms the foundation here. The cognizance of mental cognition itself *(manovijñānavijñapti)* constitutes the seeing part. The image part, finally, consists of all six external <331> elements or spheres, from the cognizance of visual form *(rūpavijñapti)* up to the cognizance of the factors *(dharmavijñapti)*. These types of cognizance together make up conception and it is on them that the imagined characteristic is based.

---

[1] [See Frauwallner's footnote (S. 237) on *conception according to its intrinsic nature (svabhāvavikalpa)* and also Vasubandhu's discussion of the three types of conception in his *Abhidharmakośabhāṣya*, i. 33 a–b. On the other hand, see S. 268, where Frauwallner briefly speaks of the days of the early Yogācāra where one was not yet able to distinguish between perception and conceptual thinking as two distinct forms of cognition. In this context see also Vasubandhu's view, S. 355.]

CFD.2.3. *The doctrine of liberation*

The peculiarity of Asaṅga's view finds especially clear expression in the doctrine of liberation. Admittedly, the situation is more difficult, since the endeavor to incorporate the entirety of the traditional material into his system and to treat it as a whole, has resulted here in old and new ideas mixing freely with each other. In this, a number of things have remained uneven and there are also some contradictions. But if we pick out the sections in which Asaṅga expresses his own thoughts, then the objections vanish and everything merges easily and consistently with the views rendered thus far to form a unified picture.

In Asaṅga the essential aspects of the path of liberation are in accord with Maitreyanātha [S. 300f.]. He begins [S. 342] with the preparation, which consists primarily of the accumulation of merit and knowledge. Especially important therein is the hearing and correct view of the Mahāyāna doctrine. The decisive step, however, is nonconceptual knowledge *(nirvikalpakajñāna).* This knowledge first recognizes the unreality of the object-referents of cognizance, becomes conscious that without object-referents mere cognition also becomes invalid, and finally, directly beholds the ultimate state of being. Nonconceptual knowledge is followed by the subsequent knowledge *(pṛṣṭhalabdhajñāna)* that maintains the acquired insight even in the ordinary state of consciousness. The first acquisition of nonconceptual knowledge represents the path of vision *(darśanamārga).* On this path, the removal of the obstructions begins, and with this, the transformation of the basis *(āśrayaparāvṛtti)* is initiated. The continuation of this process occurs on the path of contemplation *(bhāvanāmārga),* which extends over a long period of time. The path of completion *(niṣṭhāmārga),* which brings the transformation of the basis <332> to completion after the last obstructions have been destroyed in the diamond-like concentration *(vajropamasamādhi),* finally leads to the goal and with this liberation is achieved.

Typical here is the way Asaṅga, in contrast to Maitreyanātha [S. 300f.], explains these processes psychologically. Whereas, for Maitreyanātha, they take place within the ultimate state of being, which is indeed the stainless mind [S. 298], for Asaṅga, their bearer is the mental complex, as taught by him. The process is then as follows [S. 348ff.]. First, through the hearing and correct view of the Mahāyāna doctrine, a permeation *(vāsanā)* arises that is an outflow of the ultimate state of being. This permeation does not belong to the fundamental cognition, since the latter is polluted, while [the permeation] itself is uncontaminated *(anāsrava)* and supramundane *(lokottara).* It does, however, lean on the fundamental cognition. From this permeation, nonconceptual knowledge emerges that is likewise supramundane, and it is also joined by all of the uncontaminated factors that the Bodhisattva acquires in the course of his striving. In this way, in addition to the polluted fundamental cognition and everything belonging to it, a second, purer component develops in the dependent characteristic. The further development in the course of the path of liberation now proceeds in such a way that the polluted part becomes increasingly weaker, whereas this permeation, and with it the entire pure part, gains more and more strength. This is the above-mentioned *transformation of the basis.* It ends finally in such a way that the fundamental cognition and with it the entire polluted part completely vanish and only the pure part remains [see S. 346f.].[1] And with this, liberation is attained.

---

[1] [See also in regard to this Frauwallner's discussion in his *Amalavijñāna and Ālayavijñāna*, S. 156–59.]

CFD.2.4. *Asaṅga's buddhology*

Asaṅga's buddhology also corresponds to this view of the process of liberation. Accordingly, the body of the doctrine *(dharmakāya)* of the Buddha consists of the pure factors, which remain after the transformation of the basis, together with the qualities characteristic of the Buddha, which he gains with the attainment of enlightenment [see S. 347].[1] Thus, here as well it is not the [inherent] ultimate state of being on which Asaṅga bases his thinking, but the [acquired pure part of the] complex of the mental factors. At the same time, this corresponds to the old Śrāvakayāna view that had seen the body of the doctrine in [acquisition of] the pure factors, the possession of which makes the Buddha a Buddha. Seen in detail, the ten perfections <333> of power *(vaśitā)* play a kind of central role. They are joined by the remaining pure factors. The latter are extremely numerous as here too Asaṅga integrates all that the old tradition had to offer. Likewise, he elaborates in detail on the doctrine of the three bodies of the Buddha. But all this has little philosophical significance and can—like the scholastic embellishment of the path of liberation—be left aside.

CFD.3. *Introduction to the translated sections of the Mahāyānasaṃgraha*

In the case of Asaṅga, longer continuous sections from his treatises are not suitable as translated samples, since his writing is long-winded and complicated, and he constantly weaves in material from the old scholasticism of liberation, which offers nothing to the philosophically interested reader. Thus I present a selection of single sections in which are expressed those of his views that have been portrayed above. In this,

---

[1] [See also Frauwallner's comment about difference in opinion regarding the *dharmakāya*, in his *Amalavijñāna and Ālayavijñāna*, S. 159.]

I do not consider the doctrine of the fundamental cognition and of the permeations, since it shows up again in the works of Vasubandhu, which will be rendered later [S. 352ff.].

After what has been said, the translated sections will be in general easily understandable so that a few comments will suffice:

The parts of chapter II translated here deal with the doctrine of the three characteristics and especially the way the phenomenal world assembles itself from the eleven types of cognizance. In this regard, the distinguishing of the three types of permeation in § 2 should be highlighted as characteristic for Asaṅga. Of these, [1] the *permeation of speech* belongs to the bulk of the cognizances, which as we have seen are—according to the old Yogācāra doctrine—necessarily connected with "words" (*see above* S. 268f.). [2] The *permeation of the belief in a self* appears separately, as befits the significance attributed to the self-conception and since it is linked with its own form of cognition, i.e., the so-called *defiled mind (kliṣṭaṃ manaḥ).* [3] The *permeation of the members of existence,* finally, corresponds to the form of knowledge in which the maturation of deeds in particular finds its expression. § 13 teaches an image part and a seeing part of the fundamental cognition, based on the consideration that, as cognition, it must also possess these two parts. <334>

The sections rendered from chapter III deal with the path of liberation, although with the focus on nonconceptual knowledge. § 1 begins with a precise definition of the permeation through hearing the Mahāyāna doctrine and of the corresponding cognizance from a psychological point of view. According to this definition, this cognizance is mental speech and, as a cognition, consists of an image part and a seeing part. More precisely, the image part consists of word and object-referent, hence here, of the Mahāyāna texts and their content.

§§ 7–9, which describe by what means and how the nonconceptual knowledge actually comes about, provide a good example of the way in which Asaṅga weaves together the varied traditional material and joins it with his own ideas to form a whole. In the essential aspects, he follows the doctrine of Maitreyanātha (*cf. above* S. 300f.). In order to establish the unreality of the object-referents of cognizance, he uses the old Yogācāra doctrine of mental speech and of the necessary connection of the object-referents with words. With this he connects the doctrine of the four examinations and of the four comprehensions in accordance with truth, taken from the scholasticism of liberation, and he adds his own reasons as well (§ 8 beginning = chapter II, § 11). Finally, one should note how he tries to harmonize the course of the processes with the doctrine of the three characteristics.

Chapter VIII deals exclusively with nonconceptual knowledge. The attempt in § 7 to establish the inexpressibility of the true nature of things is noteworthy. Here again Asaṅga bases himself on the old Yogācāra doctrine of the dependence of the conceived object-referents on the connection of phonemes in words. The true nature of things, however, cannot be tied to words because they do not coincide with each other, since, for example, several words can be used for one and the same thing and thus [the nature of this one thing] is inexpressible through words.

There is nothing in particular to note about chapters IX and X, which deal with the transformation of the basis and with the body of the doctrine of the Buddha. One should just bear in mind, that in the buddhology, the old doctrine of the ultimate state of being resounds again and again.

I have also tacked on a few additional paragraphs from chapter I, which <335> elucidate more precisely the doctrine of the transformation of the basis. The supramundane mind is, in this regard, nonconceptual knowledge. As for the comparison to milk and water, finally, it is to be noted that milk and water are seen as a typical image of a harmonious combination and that, according to Indian belief, the flamingo has the ability to separate the milk from this mixture while drinking.[1]

---

[1] [In the introduction (*prastāvanā*, § 2–3) to the *Mahāyānasaṃgraha*, Asaṅga briefly outlines its ten chapters:

I: the basis of the knowable *(jñeyāśraya)*, i.e., the foundational consciousness *(ālayavijñāna)*;

II: the characteristic of this knowable *(jñeyalakṣaṇa)*, i.e., the three natures *(svabhāva)*;

III: entry into this characteristic of the knowable *(jñeyalakṣaṇapraveśa)*, i.e., mere cognizance *(vijñaptimātratā)*;

IV: cause and effect of this entry *(praveśahetuphala)*, i.e., the six perfections *(pāramitā)*;

V: various contemplations of this cause and effect *(hetuphalabhāvanāprabheda)*, i.e., the ten stages of the Bodhisattva *(bodhisattvabhūmi)*;

VI: training in the highest morality *(adhiśīlaṃ śikṣā)*, i.e., the discipline *(saṃvara)* of the Bodhisattvas, that is contained in these various contemplations;

VII: training in the highest mind *(adhicittaṃ śiksā)*, i.e., the concentrations *(samādhi)* called *hero's walk*, etc., that is contained in these various contemplations;

VIII: training in the highest insight *(adhiprajñaṃ śikṣā)*, i.e., nonconceptual knowledge *(nirvikalpakajñāna)*, that is contained in these various contemplations;

IX: abandonment, fruit (of these three trainings) *(phalaprahāṇa)*, i.e., the non-abiding *nirvāṇa (apratiṣṭitanirvāṇa)*;

X: the knowledge of the fruit (of these three trainings) *(phalajñāna)*, i.e., the threefold body of the Buddha *(buddhakāya)*: the essence/nature body *(svabhāvikakāya)*, the enjoyment body *(saṃbhogakāya)*, and the emanation body *(nirmāṇakāya)*.]

CFD.4. *From the "Summary of the Mahāyāna" (Mahāyānasaṃgraha)*

Chapter II

[The characteristic of the knowable (jñeyalakṣaṇa)]

§ 1

How should the characteristic of the knowable be seen?

It is, in summary, threefold: 1. the dependent characteristic, 2. the imagined characteristic, and 3. the perfect characteristic.

§ 2

In this regard, what is the *dependent characteristic?* The cognizance that has the fundamental cognition as its seed and that belongs to the false conception *(abhūtaparikalpa)*. What is this [cognizance]?

1–3. Cognizance of the body, of the embodied, and of the one who enjoys, [i.e., the six sense-organs];
4. cognizance of that which is enjoyed by the preceding [cognizances], [i.e., the six objects];
5. cognizance of the enjoyer, [i.e., the six cognitions];
6. cognizance of time;
7. cognizance of number;
8. cognizance of place;
9. cognizance of manners of expression;
10. cognizance of difference between oneself and others;
11. cognizance of the good and bad destinies, of passing away and arising.

In this regard, cognizance of the body, of the embodied, and of the one who enjoys, the cognizance of that which is enjoyed by the preceding [cognizances], <336> the cognizance of the enjoyer, the cognizance of time, the cognizance of number, the cognizance of place, the cognizance of manners of expression are arisen from the seed of the permeation of speech *(abhilāpavāsanā)*.

Cognizance of the difference between oneself and others is arisen from the seed of the permeation of the belief in a self *(ātmadṛṣṭivāsanā).*

Cognizance of the good and bad destinies, of passing away and arising, is arisen from the seed of the permeation of the members of existence *(bhavāṅgavāsanā).*

All the realms [of the world], courses *(gataya),* wombs *(yonaya),*[1] and pollutions, which are contained in these types of cognizance, are denoted as false conception of the dependent characteristic. (On the other hand), these types of cognizance (themselves)—insofar as, being mere cognizance, they belong to the false conception and are the basis of the non-existent, erroneously appearing things—are the dependent characteristic.

§ 3

In this regard [i.e., § 1], what is the *imagined characteristic?* The appearance of this mere cognizance as an object-referent, even though no object-referent exists.

§ 4

In this regard [i.e., § 1], what is the *perfect characteristic?* The complete non-existence of the mark of an object-referent in the dependent characteristic. <337>

§ 5

In this regard [i.e., § 2], by the cognizance of the body, of the embodied, and of the one who enjoys are to be understood the six inner elements, [i.e.,] of the eye, etc.

By the cognizance of that which is enjoyed by the preceding [cognizances] is to be understood the six outer elements, [i.e.,] of visible form, etc.

By the cognizance of the enjoyer is to be understood the six elements, [i.e.,] of visual cognition, etc.

---

1 As types of existence, a Buddhist distinguishes five courses, i.e., existence as a god, a human, a ghost, an animal, or a hell being; and four wombs, corresponding to birth from an egg, from the embryonic membrane, from sweat, or through miraculous sudden appearance.

The other types of cognizances are to be regarded as variations of these types of cognizance.

§ 6

(Opponent:) What example do you have for the assertion that these types of cognizance are mere cognizance, because no object-referent exists?

(Answer:) A dream, etc., can be regarded as an example. In a dream, e.g., even though no object-referent is present and only cognition exists, the image of various object-referents appears: of a visible form, a sound, an odor, a taste, a tangible, a house, a forest, a land, a mountain, etc., and yet, at the same time, no object-referent exists. Based on this example, it can be recognized that, in all instances, only cognizance exists. The term "etc." *(above)* is to be understood such that a magical illusion, a mirage, and an optical illusion can also be regarded as examples.

(Opponent:) If, as in a dream, etc., also in the waking state in all instances only cognizance exists, why then does here, as in the case of a dream, not also the insight arise that it is nothing but cognizance?

(Answer:) It does arise for those who are awakened through the knowledge of the truth. Just as this insight does not arise in a dream, but does rather in the waking state, so <338> it does not occur in those who are not awakened through the knowledge of the truth, but rather so in those who are awakened through the knowledge of the truth.

[. . .]

§ 10

(Question:) Why do the cognizance of the body, of the embodied, and of the one who enjoys, the cognizance of that which is enjoyed by the preceding [cognizances], and the cognizance of the enjoyer arise in unison and simultaneously in every body [= existence]?

(Answer:) So that birth and the experience (of the deeds) can be completely accomplished.

(Question:) Why do the various types, [i.e.,] the cognizance of time, etc. [6–11], arise?

(Answer:) [6] Because the chain of the cycle of births that has existed since beginningless time knows no interruption. [7] Because the sphere of living beings is immeasurable. [8] Because the sphere of the surrounding world *(bhājanaloka)* is immeasurable. [9] Because the expressions that communicate the mutual activities are immeasurable. [10] Because the varieties of the grasped experience are immeasurable. [11] Because the varieties of the experience of the desired and undesired maturation of the fruit of deeds are immeasurable, and because the varieties of birth, old age and death that one suffers are immeasurable.

§ 11

(Question:) How can it be established that these [latter six] types of cognizance are mere cognizance?

(Answer:) In brief, in three ways:

1. because only they exist, since there is no object-referent,
2. because a duality is given, since they are endowed with an image *(nimitta)* [part] and a seeing *(darśana)* [part], and
3. because a multitude arises at the same time, since they arise in various forms.

These types of cognizance are in fact all, since there is no object-referent, <339> just this, (i.e., cognizance). The cognizance of the eye, etc., is endowed with image and seeing, since visible form, etc., are its image and the cognition of these is its seeing, . . . etc., up to . . . since the tactile cognition is its seeing. The cognizance of thinking has—from the cognizance of the eye up to the cognizance of factors—everything as image and the cognizance of mental cognition as seeing, because the mental cognition is conception and arises in the form of all types of cognizance.

About this, a verse states:

> Just this, the duality and the multitude, do the yogis wish to understand. For one who has entered into the mere mind, is freed from these.

[. . .]

§ 13

If the cognizance of the fundamental cognition is understood as cognizance of an object-referent, then all other types of cognizance form the cognizance of its image, [while] the cognizance of mental cognition along with its basis should be regarded as its seeing [part]. Since the types of cognizance that form the image are the occasion for the arising of the seeing, they function as the basis when this [seeing] arises in the form of the object-referent. In this way, it is certain that only cognizance exists.

[. . .]

§ 15

(Question:) If the dependent nature is the mere cognizance, which forms the basis for the appearance of object-referents, why then is it dependent and why is it called *dependent?*

(Answer:) Because it arises from the seed of its own permeation, thus it is dependent on conditions. And because once <340> it has arisen it is itself unable to exist for longer than a moment, thus it is called *dependent.*

(Question:) If the imagined nature is the appearance that is based on [the dependent nature] of the object-referents, which do not exist as object-referents, then why is it imagined, and why is it called *imagined?*

(Answer:) Because it is the occasion for the arising of the errors that consist of the conceptual imaginations of the mental cognition with their innumerable forms of appearing, thus it is imagined. And because it relies only on conceptual imagination, since an intrinsic characteristic [of the imagined nature] does not exist, thus it is called *imagined.*

(Question:) If the perfect nature is characterized by the total non-existence of the (imagined nature) [in the dependent nature], why then is it perfect, and why is it called *perfect?*

(Answer:) Because it does not change, thus it is perfect. And because it is the object-support of purity [i.e., of a purified mind] and represents the culmination of all good factors, thus it is called *perfect,* in the sense of culmination.

§ 16

(Question:) If conceptual imagination exists, then the imagined and an imagined nature also exist. What, then, is the *conceptual imagination,* what is *that which is imagined,* and what is the *imagined nature?*

(Answer:) The mental cognition is the *conceptual imagination (parikalpa)* since it is accompanied by conceptions *(vikalpa).* [Mental cognition] arises from the seed of its own permeation of speech *(abhilāpavāsanā)* and it arises from the seed of the permeation of speech of all types of cognizance. Hence it arises with the conceptions of innumerable forms of appearing, and because it conceives in that it forms in every way, it is called *conceptual imagination.*

The <341> dependent nature is *that which is imagined.*

And finally, the aspect in which the dependent nature is imagined is the *imagined nature . . .*

(Question:) How does conceptual imagination conceive? [1] What is the object-support, [2] what is the grasping of the marks, [3] what is the clinging to [the marks], [4] what is the expression of speech *[vāksamutthāna],* [5] what are the manners of expression *(vyavahāra),* and [6] what is the imputation *(samāropa)* by which [the conceptual imagination] conceives?

(Answer:) [Conceptual imagination] conceives in that it [1] finds its object-support in a name, [2] grasps the marks in the dependent nature, [3] clings to [the marks] by means of views,

[4] expresses itself in speech through reflection, [5] expresses itself through the four manners of expression: of the seen, etc., (the heard, the thought of, and the cognized), and [6] imputes existence to a non-existent object-referent.

§ 17

(Question:) Is this threefold nature of distinct or of non-distinct kind?

(Answer:) It is to be designated neither as distinct nor as non-distinct. In a certain sense, the dependent nature is dependent, in a certain sense it is imagined, and in a certain sense it is perfect.

(Question:) In what sense is the dependent nature called *dependent?*

(Answer:) Because it is dependent insofar as it arises from the dependent seed of permeation.

(Question:) In what sense is [the dependent nature] called *imagined?*

(Answer:) Because it is the occasion for the conception and is conceived through it.

(Question:) In what sense is [the dependent nature] called *perfect?*

(Answer:) Because it does not exist at all in the way as it is imagined. <342>

[. . .]

Chapter III

[Entry into the characteristic of the knowable (jñeyalakṣaṇapraveśa)]

§ 1

With this [i.e., chapter II], the *characteristic of the knowable [jñeyalakṣaṇa]* has been discussed. How, then, is the *entry into the characteristic of the knowable* to be seen? It consists of mental speech [i.e., mental cognition] the foundation of which is permeation through extensive hearing [of the doctrine of the

Great Way], does not form part of the fundamental cognition[1] but like the fundamental cognition is a seed; it [i.e., mental speech] belongs to right attention, displays upon its arising the form of doctrinal texts and their content, corresponding to the apprehended thing, and is "connected" with vision *[sadarśana]*.

§ 2

Who is it who enters into the characteristic of the knowable? A Bodhisattva, whose mind stream is permeated through extensive hearing of the doctrine of the Great Way, who has won the favor of innumerable embodiments of the Buddha, and who has fostered the roots of good through extraordinary devotion and has in this way accumulated a rich store of merit and knowledge.

§ 3

Where does he enter? With the aid of this mental speech that is "connected" with vision, that displays the image of doctrinal texts and their content, and that arises from the doctrine of the Great Way, he enters [1] into the stage of the engagement of devotion, [2] into the path of vision, [3] into the path of contemplation, and [4] into the path of completion, [1] because, he devotes himself to the instruction that all factors are mere cognizance, [2] because he recognizes this [instruction] in accordance with truth, [3] because he practices the antidote to all obstructions, and [4] because he is free from obstructions. <343>

[. . .]

§ 7

By what means and how does he enter?

He enters 1. due to mental speech that arises from the permeation through hearing, that belongs to right attention, that displays the image of doctrinal texts and their content, and

---

[1] [Because this kind of mental speech ensues from the very pure element of the factors *(dharmadhātu)* and counteracts the fundamental cognition. *See* Lamotte, S. 65ff., 153.]

that is "connected" with vision; 2. due to the four examinations *(paryeṣaṇā)*, that is, the examination of the name, of the object-referent, of the designation of the nature, and of the designation of the particularities; and 3. due to the four comprehensions in accordance with truth *(yathābhūtaparijñāna)*, that is, the comprehension in accordance with truth of the name, of the thing, of the designation of the nature, and of the designation of the particularities, since all of these cannot be perceived.

That is to say, in that the Bodhisattva makes an effort to enter into mere cognizance, he recognizes in mental speech, which appears in the form of phonemes and object-referents, that the names consisting of phonemes are mere mental speech. He recognizes that the object-referents based on the phonemes are likewise mere mental speech. And he recognizes that the nature and the particularities of the names and the object-referents are mere designations, ... In this way, on the basis of the four examinations and the four comprehensions in accordance with truth within mental speech, which displays the image of phonemes and object-referents, he enters into mere cognizance.

§ 8

How does this entry into mere cognizance take place and what does it resemble to? He enters [1] into mere (cognizance), [2] into the duality endowed with image and seeing, and [3] into the multiformity, [1] because the six object-referents: name, object-referent, designation of the nature, designation of the particularities, the nature, and the particularities, <344> are not object-referents, [2] because they present themselves as the apprehended and apprehending things, and [3] because they arise in that they simultaneously display the image of multiform object-referents.

He enters as in the case of a rope that in the dark appears as a snake. In the case of the rope, the snake is a deception because it does not exist. Those who have recognized the object-referent thus discard the apprehension of the snake that does not exist and remain with the apprehension of the rope. But the latter also is a deception if one traces it back to its subtle appearing form, since it has color, odor, taste, and the tangible as its mark. With regard to mental speech then, which displays the six appearing forms of phoneme and object-referent, as with the apprehension of the snake, the reality of the six appearing forms is dismissed. And just as, based on the apprehension of color, etc., the apprehension of the rope is also dismissed, so, based on the apprehension of the perfect nature, the apprehension of mere cognizance is also made to disappear.

§ 9

In that the Bodhisattva thus enters into the mental speech characterized by the appearing object, he enters into the imagined nature. And in that he enters into mere cognizance, he enters into the dependent nature. But how does he enter into the perfect nature?

He enters in that he eliminates the comprehension of mere cognizance. Once the Bodhisattva has caused the comprehension of an [existing] object-referent to disappear, then the mental speech originating from the permeation of the doctrinal texts that have been heard, has no possibility of arising in the form of all the object-referents. <345> Consequently, it also does not arise in the form of mere cognizance. If then with regard to all object-referents, he remains in the mere nonconceptual name and remains in such a way that he directly perceives the element of the factors, then, due to the sameness of the perceived and the perceiver, there arises within this Bodhisattva the nonconceptual knowledge of sameness. In this way, the Bodhisattva enters into the perfect nature.

[. . .]

Chapter VIII

[Training in highest insight (adhiprajñaṃ śikṣā)]

§ 1

With this [i.e., chapter VII], the excellence of the highest mind *[adhicittaṃ]* has been discussed. How, then, is the excellence of the highest insight to be seen?

Nonconceptual knowledge is to be seen as the excellence of the highest insight.

[. . .]

§ 3

The bearer of the nonconceptual knowledge of the Bodhisattvas is [1] not mind and [2] yet mind, because [the bearer] [1] recognizes no object-referent and [2] yet has emerged from it (i.e., from mind).

§ 4

The basis of the nonconceptual knowledge of the Bodhisattvas is [1] the permeation through hearing connected with speech [about the Great Way] and [2] the right attention.

§ 5

The object-support of the nonconceptual knowledge of the Bodhisattvas is the inexpressible nature of things and the suchness constituted by selflessness *(nairātmya)*. <346>

§ 6

The appearing aspect of the nonconceptual knowledge of the Bodhisattvas is the signlessness of the knowable, which serves as object-support.

§ 7

The conceived is the nature resulting from the connection [of the phonemes], and nothing else. The object-referent that results from the connection of the phonemes with one another, is the (object-referent) resulting from the connection.

If then a designation does not exist, knowledge is not engaged in the designated.

A designation does not exist (in the factors), however, because an opposition exists [between designation and designated entity]. Thus, everything is inexpressible.

[. . .]

§ 13

The final stage of the nonconceptual knowledge of the Bodhisattvas consists of the attainment of the pure three bodies [of a Buddha] and in the attainment of the perfected powers.

[. . .]

Chapter IX

[Abandonment, fruit of the three trainings (phalaprahāṇa)]

§ 1

With this [i.e., chapter VIII], the excellence of the highest insight has been discussed. How, then, is the excellence of abandonment to be seen?

The abandonment of the Bodhisattvas consists of the non-abiding *nirvāṇa (apratiṣṭhitanirvāṇa).*[1] Its mark is the transformation of the basis, which consists of the fact that while pollution has been abandoned, one still remains, without giving up the cycle of existences.

Here,

- the cycle of existences *[saṃsāra]* is the dependent <347> nature insofar as [the dependent nature] constitutes the polluted part;
- the *nirvāṇa* is [the dependent nature] insofar as [the dependent nature] constitutes the pure part;
- the basis is this dependent nature insofar as [the dependent nature] encompasses both parts;
- the transformation consists in the fact that this dependent nature, when its counteragent [i.e., nonconceptual

[1] The *nirvāṇa* that does not exclude further activity in the cycle of existences for the benefit of beings.

knowledge] arises, abandons its polluted part and becomes its pure part.

[. . .]

Chapter X

[The knowledge of the fruit (phalajñāna)]

§ 3

What is the characteristic of the body of the doctrine *(dharmakāya)* of the Buddhas? One should know that, briefly summarized, its characteristic is fivefold:

1. Its characteristic is the transformation of the basis, because it has cast off the polluted-part-forming dependent characteristic that contains all of the obstructions, and has become the pure-part-forming dependent characteristic that has gained mastery over all factors through becoming free from all obstructions.

2. Its characteristic is that its nature consists of white factors, because it has obtained the ten perfected powers *(vaśitā)* through the completion of the six perfections *(pāramitā)* . . .

3. Its characteristic is non-duality (i.e., being free from the duality of existence and non-existence, of the conditioned and the unconditioned, and of multiplicity and unity) . . .

4. Its characteristic is eternality, because it is characterized by pure suchness, because it is the effect of a previous vow, and because its activity is never completed.

5. Its characteristic is inconceivability through thinking, because pure suchness must be experienced by oneself *(pratyātmavedya)*, because it is unequalled in the world, and because it does not fall into the realm of logical thinking. <348>

§ 4

How, further, is this body of the doctrine first obtained through contact? By the nonconceptual [knowledge] and the knowledge subsequent to this, which are directed at the summarized doctrine of the Great Way [i.e., suchness *(tathatā)*]; by the fivefold energetic contemplation;[1] by the energetic accumulation of the stores (of knowledge and merit) on all of the stages *(bhūmi);* and by the diamond-like concentration *(vajropama-samādhi),* which serves to destroy the subtle, difficult to destroy obstructions. Immediately following that concentration, one is freed of all obstructions and thus obtains thereby the transformation of the basis.

[. . .]

§ 8

(Question:) Is the body of the doctrine of the exalted Buddhas distinct or is it not distinct?

(Answer:) Since basis, goal, and activity are not distinct, [the body of the doctrine] is not distinct. But since innumerable bodies do reach perfect enlightenment, it is distinct. . . .

Chapter I

[The basis of the knowable (jñeyāśraya)]

§ 45

(Opponent:) If the maturation-cognition (i.e., the fundamental cognition as the result of the maturation of deeds), which contains all the seeds, is the cause of pollution, how can it then be the seed of its counteragent, that is, of the supramundane mind *(lokottara citta)?* The supramundane mind is, namely, something unusual *[anucita]*. Hence a permeation by it does not [yet] exist. But if no permeation exists, then it must be stated from which seed [the supramundane mind] arises.

(Answer:) <349> It arises from the seed of the permeation through hearing, which is an outflow of the completely pure element of the factors.

---

[1] [Contemplation that all factors are (1) without arising *(anutpāda);* (2) without cessation *(anirodha);* (3) calm from the very beginning *(ādiśānti);* (4) *nirvāṇa* by nature *(prakṛtiparinirvṛti);* (5) essencelessness *(niḥsvabhāva).*]

§ 46

(Opponent:) Does this permeation through hearing belong to the fundamental cognition by nature or not? If it belongs to the fundamental cognition by nature, how can it then be the seed of the counteragent of this [fundamental cognition]? If, on the other hand, it does not belong to it by nature, what should then be regarded as the bearer of this seed of the permeation through hearing?

(Answer:) Until the enlightenment of the Buddhas, to whatever bearer it may adhere, the permeation through hearing adheres to the maturation-cognition insofar as it arises simultaneously together with it, just as milk and water. It does not, however, belong to the fundamental cognition, since it is the seed of the counteragent of this [fundamental cognition].

§ 47

Based on a weak permeation, a moderate permeation arises; based upon a moderate permeation, a strong permeation arises, since hearing, reflecting, and cultivating entail a strengthening.

§ 48

In this, the seed of the permeation through hearing, whether weak, mediate, or strong, should be regarded as the seed of the body of the doctrine. Since it is the counteragent of the fundamental cognition, it does not belong to the fundamental cognition by nature. And since, even though it is mundane, it is an outflow of the supramundane, completely pure element of the factors, it constitutes the seed of <350> the supramundane mind. Even if this supramundane mind has not yet arisen, it is the counteragent to the outbreak of the defilements, the counteragent to the bad course (in the cycle of existences), and the counteragent that makes all bad activity disappear. It fosters the connection with the Buddhas and Bodhisattvas. Even though it is mundane, it belongs to the body of the doctrine of the prospective Bodhisattvas and it belongs to the body of liberation of the disciples and solitary Buddhas. Thus it does not belong to the fundamental cognition; instead it belongs to the body of the doctrine and to the body of liberation. As it then develops as weak, moderate, and strong in turn, to the same extent the maturation-cognition diminishes and the basis is transformed. Once the basis is completely transformed, then the maturation-cognition, which contains all the seeds, has become seedless and is completely eliminated.

§ 49

(Opponent:) If the fundamental cognition and that which is not fundamental cognition [i.e., the permeation through hearing] coexist like milk and water, how can the one [i.e., the fundamental cognition] completely disappear, [whereas the (permeation through hearing), which is not fundamental cognition, completely develops]?

(Answer:) Just as the milk is extracted from water by a drinking flamingo . . .

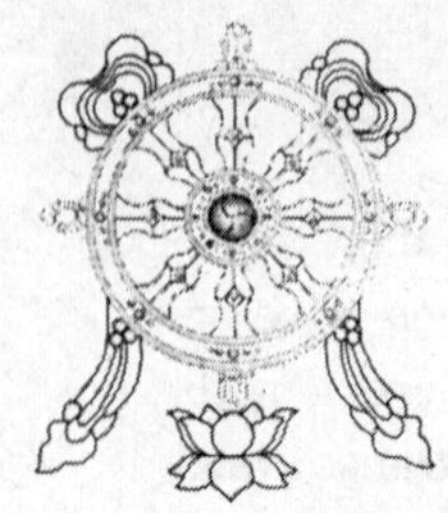

CFE. *Vasubandhu*[1]

Next to Asaṅga, the most famous personage of the Yogācāra school is his younger brother Vasubandhu [the Elder, ca. 320–80 c.e.]. He originally belonged to the Śrāvakayāna school of the Sarvāstivādins and had already made a name for himself through the composition of numerous treatises when he was won over to the Mahāyāna by Asaṅga. He then with great enthusiasm puts his talents to work in the <351> service of his new faith, for which he wrote so many works that he received the name "master of a thousand doctrinal treatises." According to legend, he is said to have died before Asaṅga.

CFE.1. *The works*

Vasubandhu's writings include numerous commentaries on the works of Maitreyanātha and Asaṅga, but his fame is based first and foremost on his commentaries on some of the most important Mahāyāna sutras. In addition, two smaller works

---

[1] [With the original section title "Vasubandhu der Ältere (ca. 320–80 c.e.)," Frauwallner follows the traditional account that reckons with one Vasubandhu as the author of all works attributed to this name. In the introduction to the two works selected here, he presents these works, however, as being authored by Vasubandhu the Younger in accordance with his theory of two Vasubandhus. *Cf.* his book *On the Date of the Buddhist Master of the Law Vasubandhu* of 1951, the note to the revised edition of the present book, S. 425, and for a recent survey of the issue of two Vasubandhus *cf.* Florin Deleanu: *The Chapter on the Mundane Path* (Laukikamārga) *in the* Śrāvakabhūmi. *A Trilingual Edition,* 2 Vols. Tokyo: The International Institute for Buddhist Studies 2006: 186–94 (with notes 206, 207 in particular).]

are preserved under the name Vasubandhu, both of which go by the title *Vijñaptimātratāsiddhi (Proof that [Everything] is Mere Cognizance),* one of which is in twenty verses *(Viṃśatikā),* the other in thirty *(Triṃśikā).* The external tradition does not permit a decision as to whether these two works come from Vasubandhu, the brother of Asaṅga, or from Vasubandhu the Younger [ca. 400–80 c.e.], the author of the *Abhidharmakośa.* In my opinion, Vasubandhu the Younger is their author, yet this difficult question cannot be discussed further here. Of these two works, the first, in twenty verses, also includes an auto-commentary by Vasubandhu himself. Its content is the proof of the unreality of the external world. The second work, in thirty verses, consists only of the verse-text. It is considered to be the last work of Vasubandhu, who is thought to have died before it was possible for him to write the intended commentary. It contains a scholasticism of the Yogācāra doctrine in a most concise form. These two works are considered to be the best summaries of the most important philosophical tenets of the school. As such, they have always enjoyed great esteem, and numerous commentaries on them have been written. Corresponding to their importance, I render them in full in what follows. I preface them with just a brief synopsis of the most important views they contain.

CFE.2. *Synopsis of the doctrines of the "Twenty Verses" and "Thirty Verses"*

In general, the following features are characteristic of these works. The philosophical interest is decidedly predominant. The old scholasticism of liberation has completely disappeared. Further, a greater deviation from Asaṅga [S. 354f.] and a reliance on the views of Maitreyanātha [S. 356] are noticeable. In the psychology, first created by Asaṅga [S. 328f.], we do find agreement in the essential points. All the <352> greater, on the other hand, are the deviations with respect to the doctrine of the phenomenal world [S. 329ff.]. To this are added unique new thoughts that pointed the way for later development, while quite often closer contact with Sautrāntika views is apparent. In terms of the shaping [of the material], finally, a precision and a taut conciseness are reached that the Śrāvakayāna scholasticism knew only in its greatest heyday.

CFE.2.1. *The mental complex as three transformations of cognition*

The details of the doctrine contained in both of these works amounts to the following. The mental complex, on which the entire phenomenal world rests, consists of three appearing forms or, as Vasubandhu expresses it, transformations *(pariṇāma)* of cognition. These are the [i] fundamental cognition, [ii] thinking, and [iii] cognizance of objects. Vasubandhu discusses each of these systematically; specifically, he deals with their nature, their support, and their object, the mental factors that accompany them, their moral character, and, finally, the exact time, and duration of their arising.

[i] The fundamental cognition *(ālayavijñāna),* as foundation of the entire mental complex and the essential bearer of the mundane personality, is, in its constitution, conditioned by the deeds that have brought about the existence in question and that in this way determine the manner of being of this existence. It is thus maturation *(vipāka)* or retribution. Its essential task is to function as the bearer of all of the seeds of the diverse permeations, in other words those imprints from which the diverse forms of cognition emerge. It is in this regard, however, a true cognition and has as such its object, namely the entire surrounding world *(bhājanaloka)* in addition to one's own body. Yet, this object is not brought into consciousness through the fundamental cognition. Vasubandhu thus advocates—as by the way Asaṅga already did before him—the bold thought that the entire phenomenal world is already the creation of

the subconsciousness and that, through the remaining processes of cognition, only secondarily parts of it are raised into consciousness. Further, as cognition, the fundamental cognition is also accompanied by mental factors *(caitta)*, but, since it remains non-conscious, only by those that accompany every cognition and are called *all-pervasive (sarvatraga)*. <353> In addition, being itself the result of previous deeds and non-conscious, it is morally undetermined. Thus it is not afflicted with defilements and is neither good nor bad. As for its occurrence, finally, it exists from beginningless time as the essential bearer of mundane existence in the uninterrupted stream of cognizance, [and will continue to do] so long as the cycle of existences endures. Only in the state of sainthood, when the transformation of the basis *(āśrayaparāvṛtti)* has taken place, is it extinguished.

[ii] Thinking *(manas)* is by nature mentation or imagining *(mananā)*. For it is the bearer of the fateful mistaken conception of a self, for which—in accordance with its importance—a continuously active form of cognition of its own is assumed. It is supported by the fundamental cognition from which it originates, and, at the same, has it as its object. The fundamental cognition is therefore the foundation of this conception of a self. Thinking is accompanied by the five all-pervasive mental factors, but especially by four defilements related to the mistaken conception of the self and that lend it its unique, disastrous character. Morally, it is undetermined since the good and bad mental factors that entail good or bad retribution are absent from it, but it is defiled. It exists throughout the entire cycle of existences and is extinguished once and for all only—as is the fundamental cognition—through the transformation of the basis in the state of sainthood. It can, however, be temporarily interrupted even earlier, specifically, in the state of the absorption of suppression *(nirodhasamāpatti)* and in the supramundane nonconceptual knowledge *(nirvikalpakajñāna)*.

[iii] Cognizance of the objects *(viṣayavijñapti)*, finally, encompasses all the remaining processes of cognizance, in other words, the six types of cognition that, in accordance with the old doctrine, are named after the six sense-organs. Its support is to be seen in the seed of the permeation, from which it has emerged. The different object-referents, which seem to belong to the external world and are reflected in it, are its object. It can be accompanied by any of the mental factors known to the scholasticism of the Yogācāra (*cf. above* S. 113ff. the rendering of Vasubandhu's *Pañcaskandhaka*): <354> the all-pervasive ones; those bound to specific objects; the good ones; the defilements; the secondary defilements; and the unbound mental factors. In [this cognizance], the volitional processes take place that constitute the deeds and determine the further course of the cycle of existences. It is thus good as well as bad, but can also be undetermined. Finally, with regard to the occurrence of the different types of cognizance of the objects, the different types of sensory cognizance arise each time that the conditions for their arising are present, that is, at times singly, at times concurrently. Mental cognition is always present except in the state of unconsciousness, thus while being anaesthetized, in the case of fainting, in the absorption of non-ideation *(asaṃjñisamāpatti)*, in the absorption of suppression *(nirodhasamāpatti)*, and finally, in the state of non-ideation *(āsaṃjñika)* that Buddhism ascribes to a certain realm of gods.

CFE.2.2. *The mental complex and the seeds of permeation*

The mental complex on which the entire phenomenal world rests is composed of these three transformations of cognition. The seeds of permeation stored in the fundamental cognition are crucial to its activity. Vasubandhu does not divide [these seeds of permeation] into three groups in the manner of Asaṅga (*see above* S. 333), but gives instead a simpler, better fitting division into two groups. Specifically, he distinguishes between the *permeation of the twofold apprehension (grāhadvayavāsanā)* and the *permeation of the deeds (karmavāsanā)*. The *permeation of the twofold apprehension* is brought about through the separate processes of cognizance, which seem to recognize an apprehended and an apprehending, and it is itself, in turn, able to bring forth similar cognitions. The *permeation of deeds* is, as its name says, conditioned by deeds, and determines the general development of the mental complex, and with this, the destiny in the cycle of existences. Above all else, it is also the principal cause—when a fundamental cognition that has, in a specific form, been the bearer of a specific existence comes to an end—for a new fundamental cognition of a different kind to arise as the bearer of a new existence.

CFE.2.3. *The mental complex in relation to the phenomenal world, highest reality, and other beings*

According to Vasubandhu, with this activity of the mental complex, the appearance of the phenomenal world comes about as follows. <355> By nature, every cognition is a conception *(vikalpa)* that conceives something unreal. This "unreal" is the duality of the apprehended and the apprehending *(grāhyagrāhaka)*. In this, the apprehended and the apprehending are not, as Asaṅga assumed, embodied by two distinct cognizances to which, as bearer, corresponding to the sense-organ, a third is added [S. 329f.]. Instead, everything is united in one cognition. In other words, this cognition itself displays the image of an object that is held to exist externally. With this, the apprehended and the apprehending is established. Further, with regard to the sense-organ, which, according to the old canonical doctrine, must be given along with an object and cognition so that a process of cognition can come about, Vasubandhu takes it to be the seed of permeation from which the corresponding cognition originates. Since every cognition is, in this way, in itself a conception, the special role that Asaṅga ascribes [S. 330] to the mental cognition is abandoned. For Vasubandhu, the latter is rather of the same type as the sensory cognition that it follows. It displays the same image as this [sensory cognition], and is thus by nature a recollection. It is differentiated from [sensory cognition] only through the fact that it consciously apprehends the corresponding object-referent.

Also important is Vasubandhu's insight that every cognition, as soon as it itself becomes an object, appears in conceived form. What is then cognized is thus not its true nature, but rather a conception like any other. With this, the relationship to the highest reality is clarified. The doctrine that everything is mere cognizance thus does not mean that the sole real entity is cognizance as it appears to us [in conceived form]. It is, rather, the true nature of [cognizance] that remains forever inaccessible to our mundane cognizance. And precisely this is the highest reality.

In addition, it is noteworthy that Vasubandhu raises the question of the multiplicity of living beings, that is, the multiplicity of cognizing subjects and their relationship to one another. In his view, the relation of different living beings to one another rests upon the fact that the distinct streams of cognition, all of which are real, are able to causally influence one another in their course. <356>

CFE.2.4. *The doctrine of liberation*

With respect to the doctrine of liberation, Vasubandhu starts, according to old custom, from the twofold bondage, which consists of the false belief in a self and in factors, while he attempts in a new and unique way to define the nature of this belief as the attribution of an extraneous essence *(upacāra)*. As for the process of liberation itself, he is concerned only with the fundamental philosophical idea, which he takes over essentially just as Maitreyanātha created it and Asaṅga retained it (*see above* S 300f. and 331f.). In the establishment of the unreality

the hell beings, there arise from the elements certain formations, which show a certain color, shape, stature, and strength, and which receive the name *guardians of hell*, etc. And they change in such a way that they seem to perform various movements, like swinging their arms, etc., to bring about fear, or that one sees mountains, in the shape of rams, come and go, and that the thorns in the iron Śālmalī forest seem to turn up and down. They are, however, in no way non-existent.

(Vasubandhu's answer [to the Sarvāstivādins]:)

v. 6

> If you accept that, through the deeds of the (hell beings), elements arise there and change in such a way, then why do you not accept the same for cognition?

Why do you not accept that their cognition changes in this way through their deeds? Why do you conceive of elements?

v. 7

> You conceive of the permeation of the deeds in one place and the fruit in another. For what reason do you not accept (the fruit) there where the permeation (resides)?

You conceive that—through the deeds of the hell beings—elements in (hell) arise and change in such a way. But the permeation of these deeds adheres to the stream of cognizance and nowhere else, so why then do you not accept that there where the permeation resides, its fruit also appears, i.e., a corresponding change of the cognition? For what reason do you conceive of the fruit there where the permeation is not? <371>

Chapter II

(Opponent:) The reason is sacred tradition. If only the cognition that displays the image of the visible form, etc., existed and not the object-referent of visible form, etc., then the Exalted One would not have taught the existence of the sphere of visible form, etc.

(Answer:) That is no reason, since:

v. 8

> The existence of the sphere of visible form, etc., was taught with a specific intention, that is, out of consideration for the people to be cultivated by it, just like (the existence) of the spontaneously appearing beings.

Just as the Exalted One taught with a specific intention that spontaneously appearing beings exist—specifically in view of the fact that the mind stream will not be interrupted in the future, in accordance with the saying: "A living being and a self do not exist; what we see are only causally conditioned factors"—likewise, the Exalted One has taught the existence of the sphere of visible form, etc., namely out of consideration for the people to be cultivated by this doctrine. It is thus a matter of a statement with a specific intention. What then is this intention?

v. 9

> Its own seed, from which a cognizance emerges, and the image that it (thereby) displays, these two the sage has designated as its double sphere.

What does this mean? Cognizance, which displays the image of visible form, arises from its seed as soon as the latter has reached a specific state of transformation *(pariṇāmaviśeṣa)*.[1] <372> This seed, then, and the image that [the cognizance] (thereby) displays, the Exalted One has designated these two as the sphere of the eye and of visible form, respectively, belonging to this cognizance. The same applies for all types of cognizance up to the cognizance of the tangible. In other words, a cognizance that displays the image of the tangible arises from its seed as soon as the latter has reached a specific state of transformation. This seed, then, and the image that [the cognizance] (thereby) displays, the Exalted One has designated these two as the sphere of the body and of the tangible, respectively, belonging to this cognizance. This then is the intention in question here.

What is the advantage of expounding the doctrine on the basis of this intention in this way?

v. 10

> In this way one attains the understanding of the essencelessness of the personality.

If the doctrine is expounded in this way, one in fact attains the understanding of the essencelessness of the personality. If one recognizes that the six types of cognition each arise from two (spheres), but that a uniform seer, hearer, etc., up to thinker does not exist, then those who should be cultivated by the doctrine of the essencelessness of the personality, attain the understanding of the essencelessness of the personality.

---

[1] The seed or impression in the subconsciousness, from which every cognition arises, matures gradually through continuous transformation until it, finally, has gained the capacity to bring forth the respective cognition in the next moment.

v. 10

If, on the other hand, the doctrine is expounded in the other way, then one attains the understanding of the essencelessness of the factors. <373>

"In the other way" means, if it is taught that (everything) is mere cognizance. How does one then come to the understanding of the essencelessness of the factors? By recognizing that everything that we see is mere cognizance, which arises in that it displays the image of the factors, visible form, etc., but that, on the other hand, a factor characterized as visible form, etc., does not exist.

(Objection:) If a factor does not exist at all, then mere cognizance also does not exist. How can you then assert it?

(Answer:) One does not attain the understanding of the essencelessness of the factors in that one thinks that a factor does not exist at all, but rather only

v. 10

according to the conceived nature.

The essencelessness of the factors exists according to the conceived nature, i.e., according to the nature that fools conceive as the apprehended and the apprehending, etc., but not according to the inexpressible nature that is the object of the Buddhas. Likewise, it is according to the nature conceived by another cognizance that one attains the understanding of the essencelessness of mere cognizance; and in that one asserts (in this sense) that (everything) is mere cognizance, one comes to the understanding of the essencelessness of all factors, not in that one completely denies the existence [of cognizance]. For otherwise, one cognizance would have another cognizance as its object-referent and it would therefore not be proven that (everything) is mere cognizance, because the cognizances would have an object-referent.

Chapter III

(Opponent:) But how can it be known that the Exalted One taught the existence of the spheres of visible form, etc., <374> with this intention, yet that these (spheres) that are individually the object of the cognizance of visible form, etc., do not (in reality) exist?

(Answer:) Because

v. 11

> [the sphere of visible form, etc.,] is an object neither as a unit, nor as a multitude of atoms, nor as the latter in a state of agglomeration *[saṃhata]*, since the individual atom is not proven.

What does this mean? The sphere of visible form, etc., which is individually the object of the cognizance of visible form, etc., is either a unit—like the whole that the Vaiśeṣika conceive—or a multitude of atoms, or these same atoms in a state of agglomeration.

Firstly, a unit cannot be an object because a whole that is different from the parts can nowhere be grasped.

Just as little can a multitude, because the atoms cannot be grasped individually.

And just as little can the (atoms) in a state of agglomeration be an object, because the atom as an individual thing is not proven.

How is it not proven? Because

v. 12

> in the case of a simultaneous connection with a group of six, a six-partedness of the atom (results).

In the case of a simultaneous connection from (all) six sides with six atoms, a six-partedness of the atoms results, because in the position of one (atom) no other can be.

v. 12

> If, on the other hand, all six are located in the same position, then the conglomeration *[piṇḍa]* would only be the size of one atom.

If the position of one atom were, at the same time, the (position) of all six, then all would be located in the same position and the whole conglomeration would thus be only <375> the size of one single atom, because one atom would not extend beyond the other. Consequently, no conglomeration would be visible.

(Opponent:) The individual atoms do not combine with one another because they are partless. Thus, this mistake need not result. When aggregated, they do, however, combine with one another; so say the Vaibhāṣikas of Kaśmīr.

(Answer:) But the amassment of atoms is nothing other than they themselves.

v. 13

> If the atom thus does not combine, then what is combined in the amassment *[saṅghāta]?* But then it is also not due to partlessness that the combination *[saṃyoga]* of the atoms does not come about.

If therefore amassment also do not combine with each other, then you cannot say that the combination of the atoms does not come about due to partlessness, since, in the case of amassment, which does have parts, you also do not admit a combination. Thus the atom as an individual thing is not proven.

Whether, furthermore, a combination of atoms is assumed or not:

v. 14

> That which is divided into spatial parts, can not possibly be a unit.

The eastern spatial part of the atom is namely different . . . etc., up to . . . the downward situated spatial part is different. How then, if a division according to spatial parts exists, can the atom, which indeed consists of these (parts), form a unit?

v. 14

Or how could there be shadow and obstruction?

If, in the case of the individual atom, there were no division according to spatial parts, how then at sunrise <376> does a shadow appear on one side and light on the other side? For there is after all no other part that the light is not able to reach.

And how does the obstruction of one atom by another take place if a division according to spatial parts is not assumed. For the atom then has no other part where, if one [atom] were to move there, it would encounter the resistance of another. But if it does not encounter resistance, then—as we already have said—all (atoms) would occupy the same position and every accumulation would therefore be the size of just one atom.

(Opponent:) Why do you not assume that shadow and obstruction belong to the conglomeration and not to the atom?

(Answer:) Do you perhaps assume that the conglomeration to which they supposedly belong is something other than the atoms? No. Thus it is said:

v. 14

If the conglomeration is nothing other, then [the atoms] do not belong to it.

If you assume that the conglomeration is nothing other than the atoms, then it is proved that they do not belong to it.

(Opponent:) The question as to whether atom or accumulation, considers only the difference in shape. But what is the point of this reflection, as long as the characteristic of visible form, etc., is not refuted?

(Answer:) What is the characteristic then?

(Opponent:) The being-the-object for the eye, etc., and the blueness, etc.

(Answer:) But this is exactly what our reflection is dealing with. It is investigating, namely, whether just this blue, yellow, etc., that is regarded as the object of the eye, etc., is a unitary thing or a multitude.

(Opponent:) And what follows from that?

(Answer:) The faults in the case of the multitude have already been discussed. <377>

v. 15

> In the case of the unit, a gradual movement, a simultaneous apprehension and non-apprehension, the existence of several separate (things), and the non-perception of the subtle would not take place.

If it is assumed that the object of the eye, blue, yellow, etc., insofar as it is not broken up *[avicchinnaṃ nānekaṃ]*, represents one individual thing, then there would be no gradual movement on earth, i.e., no walking, because everything would be traversed in a single step.

There would be no simultaneous apprehension of the front part and non-apprehension of the back part. For an apprehension and non-apprehension of the same (thing) at the same time is not possible.

Further, in one (thing), several separate (things), such as elephants, horses, etc., could not be found. For where the one is, the other would also have to be. How then can one see the two as separate? And how, on the other hand, can that which is both connected and unconnected with both of them be a unit, since after all in the gap (between the two), something is apprehended that is free from them.

Finally, if a difference of things is assumed solely due to the difference in characteristic and for no other reason, then there would be no non-perception of the subtle water beings, since they have the same constitution as the coarse ones. Therefore, a division according to atoms must certainly be assumed, and this [division] is not established as a unit. If it is not established, however, then it is also not established that visible form, etc., is the object of the eye, etc., and with that it is established that (everything) is mere cognizance. <378>

Chapter IV

(Opponent:) Existence or non-existence is determined based on the means of valid cognition. But of all means of valid cognition, sensory perception is the most important. Hence, if no object-referent exists, how does this cognizance come about: "I have perceived this through the senses"?

(Answer:)

v. 16

> The cognizance of sensory perception *(pratyakṣa-buddhi)* comes about as in sleep.

Even without an object-referent, as has already been shown previously [i.e., in verse 3].

v. 16

> Further, the object-referent is not seen at the time that [the cognizance of sensory perception] appears. So how can it be regarded as being perceived through the senses?

At the time that the cognizance of sensory perception: "This I have perceived through the senses," occurs, the object-referent is not seen because this ascertainment is brought about by mental cognition and the visual cognition is, in the meantime, past. How then can the (corresponding object-referent) be regarded as being perceived through the senses, especially by a follower of the doctrine of the momentariness of all entities, for whom, at this time, the corresponding visible form or the corresponding taste, etc., is past?

(Opponent:) Something that was not perceived before is not recollected by the mental cognition. Thus there must definitely be a perception of the object-referent and that is vision. For this reason, the visible form, etc., that represents the object [of vision] is regarded as being perceived through the senses.

(Answer:) It is not established that a perceived object-referent is recollected, for: <379>

v. 17

> We have discussed [v. 9] how a cognizance that displays its image (arises).

We have discussed how, even without an object-referent, a cognizance that displays its image—a visual cognition, etc.—arises.

v. 17

> From this (originates) recollection.

From this cognizance, a mental cognizance—which is connected with recollection, displays the same image, and conceives the visible form, etc.—originates. Thus the perception of the object-referent is not established through the arising of the recollection.

(Opponent:) If, just as in sleep, cognizance in the waking state likewise did not have a real object-referent as object, then people would likewise recognize its non-existence on their own. But this is not the case. Thus it is not correct that every perception of an object-referent, just as in sleep, does not have an object-referent.

(Answer:) This is not conclusive, since:

v. 17

> As long as one has not awakened, one does not recognize the non-existence of the objects seen in sleep.

Likewise, people who are sunk in the sleep of the permeations arisen from the habit of false conceptions, and who see, as in sleep, an unreal object-referent, are not able—as long as they have not awakened—to recognize the non-existence of [an object-referent] in accordance with truth. However, as soon as they have awakened through the acquisition of the counter-agent to [this vision of an unreal object-referent]—that is, the supramundane, nonconceptual knowledge—they recognize the non-existence of the object in accordance with truth through realizing <380> the pure mundane knowledge that follows. Hence, the situation is the same.

(Opponent:) If, with respect to beings, the cognizance that displays the image of the object-referent arises based on a specific transformation of their stream of cognizance, and not based on a specific object-referent, then how is it possible that the connection with bad and good friends and the hearing of good and bad teachings determine the cognizance of beings, if in fact this connection and this doctrine do not exist?

(Answer:)

v. 18

> The mutual determination of cognizance takes place through mutual influence.

The respective mutual determination of cognizance takes place in all beings due to the fact that their cognizances influence one another. Thus through a specific cognizance in one stream of cognizance, a specific cognizance in another stream of cognizance arises, and not through a specific object-referent.

(Opponent:) If, just as in a dream, the cognizance in the waking state has no object-referent, then why does good and bad conduct in the sleeping and not sleeping person not, in the future, result in the same desired or undesired fruit?

(Answer:) Because

v. 18

> the mind in sleep is obstructed by dullness, hence the fruit is not the same.

This is the cause of it, and not the existence of an object-referent.

(Opponent:) If all of this is mere cognizance and no one has a body or a voice, then how does <381> the death of sheep, etc., which are slaughtered by shepherds, take place? Or if their death is not caused by the shepherds, then why are they affected by the sin of the destruction of life?

(Answer:)

v. 19

> Death is a change based on a specific cognizance of another, just as through the power of thought of a Piśāca, etc., (a change such as) loss of memory, etc., (takes place) in others.

Just as through the power of thought of a Piśāca, etc., changes occur in others, such as loss of memory, the seeing of dreams, or possession by ghosts and demons, or (just as such changes) occur through the power of thought of persons endowed with miraculous powers, such as the seeing of dreams by

Sāraṇa under the influence of the noble Mahākātyāyana, or the defeat of Vemacitra through the embitterment of the thoughts of the forest-dwelling seers, in the same way, through the influence of a specific cognizance of a particular person, a change occurs in others, which counteracts the life organ, and it is through this that the interruption of the homogeneous stream of cognizance takes place, which we call *death.* So is this to be understood.

v. 20

> How, otherwise, could the emptiness of the Daṇḍaka forest have occurred through the anger of the seers.

If, however, you do not accept that the death of beings takes place under the influence of a specific cognizance of another, (then we refer to the fact that) the <382> Exalted One—in order to prove the great sinfulness of the act of violence through thoughts—asked the householder Upāli: "Did you hear, householder, how the Daṇḍaka forests, the Mātaṅga forests, and the Kaliṅga forests became empty and cleansed?" and that Upāli answered: "I have heard, Gautama, [that it occurred] through the embitterment of the thoughts of the seers."

v. 20

> How else would the great sinfulness of the act of violence through thoughts be proven thereby?

If one assumes that the beings living there were eradicated by superhuman beings who were friendly toward the (seers), and that they were not killed through the embitterment of the thoughts of the seers, how is it in this case proven that the act of violence through thought is far more sinful than the act of violence through body and speech? Through the death of so many beings as a result of the mere embitterment of their thinking, on the other hand, it is proven.

(Opponent:) If this is all mere cognizance, do the knowers of another mind then know the other mind or do they not know it? What follows from that? If they do not know it, how are they then knowers of another mind? If, on the other hand, they do know it, (then how do you assert that only cognition without an object-referent exists?)

(Answer:)

v. 21

> The knowledge of the knowers of another mind does not correspond to reality. How so? As with the knowledge of one's own mind.

How does this too not correspond to reality?

v. 21

> Because [the knowledge of one's own mind] does not know (one's mind), in the manner in which it is the domain of the Buddha. <383>

Because [the knowledge of one's own mind] does not know [this mind], in the manner in which it is in its inexpressible nature the domain of the Buddha. Both [knowledges, i.e., of another mind and of one's own mind], therefore, do not correspond to reality because they have not given up the conception of an apprehended and an apprehending, since they display false appearing images.

Regarding this (doctrine) of the mere existence of cognizance, which, with its innumerable particular statements, is unfathomably profound,

v. 22

I have composed this "Proof that (Everything) is Mere Cognizance" according to my abilities. [Mere cognizance] cannot, however, be completely grasped by thoughts.

In any form, it cannot be grasped by people like me by means of thoughts, because it is not the object of logical thinking. Whose domain is it then, in its entirety?

v. 22

It is the domain of the Buddha.

In any form, it is indeed the domain of the exalted Buddhas, since their knowledge, which encompasses everything knowable in every shape, knows no bounds.

:FE.5. *Introduction to the Triṃśikā Vijñaptimātratāsiddhi*

The *Triṃśikā Vijñaptimātratāsiddhi,* the translation of which I now present, consists of only thirty verses since Vasubandhu did not leave behind a commentary to it. Nevertheless, a more thorough explanation is unnecessary, since nearly everything needed for its understanding can be drawn from the brief introductory overview of Vasubandhu's views.

Vasubandhu begins [v. 1] with a brief reference to the two-fold cause of entanglement in the cycle of existences: the belief in a self and the belief in factors. The only thing new here is that he determines the nature of this error more precisely as an attribution *(upacāra),* i.e., through it a nature is <384> attributed to a thing that in reality does not befit it. In the present case, the attributed nature is the self and the factors. It is attributed to the different appearing forms of cognition.

Vasubandhu then describes these three appearing forms of cognition one after the other.

[1] In the description of the fundamental cognition, (vv. 2–5) the expression *site* indicates the environment *(bhājanaloka)*. By *appropriation*, the body and sense-organs are to be understood, since these appear to be incorporated into and, in a way, appropriated by the personality-stream. Equanimity as a sensation is neither pleasure nor suffering and befits the fundamental cognition, since this remains unconscious.

[2] The description of thinking (vv. 5–8) includes, besides the other determinations, an additional brief comment on the domain to which the defilements that accompany thinking belong. This question was discussed a great deal by Buddhist scholasticism with regard to all of the factors, but is without philosophical interest. Nonconceptual knowledge is designated as the supramundane path (v. 7), because this [knowledge] constitutes the supramundane part of the path of liberation.

[3] In the description of the cognizance of objects (vv. 8–16), the four unbound mental factors are enumerated as two pairs (v. 14) and are designated as twofold, i.e., they can be defiled and undefiled.

After a few verses about the character of cognition as being conception and on the operation of permeation, a brief account of the doctrine of the threefold nature of things and their threefold essencelessness (vv. 20–25) is given. Here Vasubandhu follows the old doctrine as it was presented in the *Saṃdhinirmocanasūtra* (*see above* S. 279ff.), without adding anything essentially new. With respect to the doctrine of the threefold nature, the only items of note are the comment (v. 22) that the perfect nature is neither distinct nor non-distinct from the dependent nature—which is reminiscent of how Maitreyanātha defined the relationship between the nature of the factors *(dharmatā)* and the factors (*cf. above* S. 323)—and the further comment that the dependent nature cannot be correctly understood if one has not first recognized the perfect nature. As for the threefold essencelessness, the imagined <385> nature is natureless because no intrinsic characteristic befits it; the dependent nature, because it does not exist in itself but is dependent on other things. Finally, the essencelessness of the perfect nature rests on the fact that it is the highest reality and that the latter consists of the essencelessness of the factors (*cf. above* S. 283f.).

The doctrine of liberation (vv. 26–30) follows in conclusion. The false conceptions of the belief in an 'I' and in factors and the permeations caused thereby—on which the entanglement in the cycle of existences rests—disappear only through the direct clear comprehension of mere cognizance by virtue of non-conceptual knowledge. To this end, all conceptions of objects must be removed. It is thus also not sufficient to think, in the ordinary forms of our cognition, that everything is mere cognizance because, with this, an object still remains. Only if every object, and with the object also the cognition, has disappeared, does one become directly aware of mere cognizance in its true inexpressible form. This is the supramundane nonconceptual knowledge—a non-perception, according to ordinary cognition—in which the factors of the psyche have also disappeared. This leads to the transformation of the basis and the disappearance of the twofold bondage by the belief in an 'I' and in the factors, which Vasubandhu—with an old expression already used by Maitreyanātha—designates here as *badness (dauṣṭhulya)*. With this, liberation and the entrance into the ultimate state of being occurs, which for the ordinary disciple is the body of liberation *(vimuktikāya)*; for the Buddha, the body of the doctrine *(dharmakāya)*.

CFE.6. *"Proof that (Everything) is Mere Cognizance, in Thirty Verses" (Triṃśikā Vijñaptimātratāsiddhi)*

1

The attribution of an 'I' and of factors, which takes place in a variety of ways, concerns the transformation of cognition. And this transformation is threefold: <386>

2

[it is] called [1] *maturation,* [2] *thinking,* and [3] *cognizance of objects.*

Of these, maturation is the so-called *fundamental cognition.* The latter contains all of the seeds

3

and recognizes, in an unconscious form, the appropriation [i.e., the seeds and the body endowed with the five sense-organs] and the site [i.e., the environment]. It is constantly associated with contact, attention, sensation, ideation, and will.

4

Sensation therein is equanimity. – Further, it is uncontaminated and indeterminate. Likewise contact, etc. It propagates itself in an uninterrupted flow, like a river.

5

Its disappearance occurs in the state of sainthood.

Based on it and taking it as its object-support, the cognition called *thinking* develops, which has the act of mentation as its nature,

6

is constantly accompanied by the four defilements—which are contaminated and indeterminate, are designated as belief in a self, delusion about an 'I', pride in the 'I', and love for the 'I',

7

and belong to the (domain) in which one is born—and by the other (mental factors), contact, etc. [Thinking] does not exist in a saint, in the absorption of suppression, and on the supramundane path.

8

This is the second transformation.

The third is the perception of the sixfold object. This is good, bad, and neither of the two. <387>

9

[Perception] is accompanied by the all-pervasive mental factors, by those bound to specific objects, by good [mental factors], by defilements, and by secondary defilements, and has three sensations.

10

The first are contact, etc. Those bound to specific objects are inclination, conviction, and recollection, along with concentration and insight. Faith, modesty, shame,

11

the triad of absence of greed, etc., diligence, harmoniousness, equanimity along with heedfulness, and non-violence, are the good [mental factors]. The defilements are passion, hate, delusion,

12

pride, (false) view, and doubt. And again, anger and grudge, hypocrisy, spitefulness, envy, and further, miserliness, along with deceitfulness,

13

dissimulation, wantonness, malevolence, unrestraint, shamelessness, rigidity, agitation, lack of faith, and further, laziness, negligence, forgetfulness,

14

distractedness, and thoughtlessness; remorse and languidness, contemplation and reflection. These are the secondary defilements and the (last) two pairs are each twofold, [i.e., good and bad].

15

Depending on the presence of the conditions, five types of cognition arise—at the same time or not—from the root-cognition, just like the waves on the water. <388>

16

The mental cognition always arises, except in the state of non-ideation, the two absorptions, languidness (= anaesthetization) and that fainting in which the mind is suspended.

17

This [threefold] transformation of cognition is conception. That which is conceived by it, that does not exist. Thus, all of this is mere cognizance.

18

Cognition, in fact, contains all of the seeds. Through mutual influence, the transformation develops now this way, now that way, so that now this, now that conception arises.

19

When the previous maturation is exhausted, the permeation of the deeds, along with the permeation of the twofold apprehension [i.e., the object-aspect and the subject-aspect], brings forth the (fundamental cognition) as a new maturation.

20

All things that are conceived through any kind of conception form the imagined nature. The latter does not exist.

21

The dependent nature, on the other hand, is the conception arisen from conditions. The perfect (nature) is [the dependent nature's] constant freedom from the former [i.e., the imagined nature].

22

Thus, [the perfect nature] is to be designated neither as distinct nor as non-distinct from the dependent nature, like impermanence, etc. As long as the former is not seen, the latter is not seen. <389>

23

With a view toward the threefold essencelessness of this threefold nature, the essencelessness of all factors has been taught.

24

The first [nature] is essenceless according to its characteristic. The second, because it has no independent existence. A further essencelessness results from the fact

25

that it (= the third, i.e., the perfect nature) is the highest reality *(paramārtha)* of the factors. This [reality] is also suchness, because it is such at all times. And it is, in addition, mere cognizance.

26

For as long as cognition does not abide in mere cognizance, so long does the burden *(anuśaya)* of duality [in apprehension] not disappear.

27

Also through the perception that (all) of this is mere cognizance, one does not abide in mere (cognizance) since one holds something before oneself.

28

If, on the other hand, knowledge does not perceive an object-support, then it stands firm in mere cognition, since, due to the absence of that which is apprehended, it also does not apprehend thc (cognition).

29

This is that non-perception in which the mind has disappeared *(acitta)*, it is the supramundane knowledge, <390> the transformation of the basis through the removal of the twofold badness *(dauṣṭhulya)*.

30

It is the uncontaminated element, the unthinkable, salutary, imperishable, blissful [element]. This is the body of liberation. This is the so-called (body of) the doctrine of the great sage.

With Vasubandhu, the Yogācāra school reached its apex. We do not have space here to pursue its further development in detail. It continued to flourish for a long time and in particular the sixth century is rich in renowned representatives of the school and significant works.

Further, of special importance is that the logico-epistemological school of Buddhism, which constitutes one of the high points of the entire Indian philosophy, arose from a combination of Yogācāra- and Sautrāntika-thoughts. Its classics are Dignāga (sixth century) and Dharmakīrti[1] (seventh century). This school produced a rich literature and maintained a leading position up to the beginning of the second millennium. We must leave all of this aside here, but using just a brief example, we will offer a taste of how Vasubandhu's epistemology was further developed after his time.

---

[1] [See: Erich Frauwallner: "Die Reihenfolge und Entstehung der Werke Dharmakīrti's." In *Kleine Schriften:* pp. 677–89.]

Dignāga (ca. 480–540 c.e.)[1]

Dignāga came from South India, from the region of Kāñcī, and initially belonged to the sect of the Vātsīputrīyas. Later, he turned toward the north and converted to the Yogācāra school. He spent some time in Nālandā, the center of Buddhist learning. The rest of his life, he spent in Orissa. Dignāga was an extremely prolific author. He wrote, among others, a concise commentary on the *Abhidharmakośa* <391> of Vasubandhu the Younger and a brief summary of the doctrine of the *Prajñāpāramitā.* Most significant, however, were his logical writings, through which he became the founder of the logico-epistemological school of Buddhism. After he had written numerous smaller treatises, he finally summarized his doctrines in the extensive *Pramāṇasamuccaya (Compendium of the Means of Valid Cognition),* which became the fundamental work of the new school. His logical doctrines cannot be touched upon here. In the epistemological field, his distinction between perception and conception is particularly important; also the doctrine of the different parts of cognition, which is the subject of the following translated sample.

As we have seen (*above* S. 329f.), Asaṅga had in fact distinguished within cognition an image part and a seeing part, which were allotted to two distinct knowledges. Vasubandhu had abandoned this idea [S. 355]. In Sautrāntika style, he taught only that cognition reflects the object, without

---

[1] [See: Erich Frauwallner: "Dignāga, sein Werk und seine Entwicklung." In *Kleine Schriften:* pp. 759–841.]

explicitly distinguishing between two parts of cognition. Nevertheless, in Vasubandhu also the thought appears that cognition itself becomes the object of another cognition. Following upon this, Dignāga distinguishes between two appearing forms of cognition. The appearing form of the object, which reflects itself in cognition, and cognition's own appearing form. Over and above that, however, he also acknowledges a third appearing form: the awareness. Even early on in the schools of the Śrāvakayāna, the question of how one becomes aware of a cognition had been raised. Different doctrines had been put forward, and, among others, the Mahāsāṃghika had held the view that cognition becomes aware of itself, in the way that a lamp illuminates not only objects, but also itself. Dignāga adopted this view and taught the self-awareness *(svasaṃvitti)* of cognition as its third appearing form. Hence, in his view, three appearing forms are combined in a cognition: the appearing form of the recognized object, the cognition's own appearing form, and, thirdly, the awareness. <392>

The following section from the *Pramāṇasamuccaya* then contains Dignāga's arguments for this doctrine. Here he starts from the case that—among the cognitions that succeed one another uninterruptedly in the stream of cognition and of which each has only the duration of a moment—upon one cognition that recognizes an object a second cognition follows that has this cognition itself as an object. Now, if the cognition of the object, as he says, displays only the appearing form of the object, then the cognition that recognizes [this cognition] itself can, likewise, display only this appearing form. Hence [this second cognition] would also just be a cognition of the object and no different from the first. Were, on the other hand, the first cognition to bear only its own appearing form, then the following cognitions also would not display the object's form and could therefore not recognize it as a cognition of the corresponding object. Thus, the first cognition must contain both appearing forms, that of the object and its own. The same thing also follows from the fact that one later recollects the perception of an object. For this is only possible if one can recollect both the object as well as its perception, which again presupposes both appearing forms of the corresponding knowledge.

The self-awareness of cognition can also be inferred from recollection, since just as one can only recollect an object if one has perceived it, so one can also only recollect a cognition if one has perceived it, i.e., if one has become aware of it. This becoming aware, however, can only proceed through the corresponding cognition itself. For if one has become aware of it through another cognition, then for this other cognition the same would have to apply, and hence a *regressus in infinitum* would result. In addition, one could never move on to the cognition of another object, since one cognition always recognizes only the previous one, in an infinite series. Thus the assumption that each cognition becomes aware of itself is established as absolutely necessary. <393>

From the "Compendium of the Means of Valid Cognition" (Pramāṇasamuccaya)

Chapter I

(Opponent:) How can it be recognized that cognition has two forms? (Answer:)

v. 11ab

> From the distinctness of the cognition of the object and of the cognition of this (cognition), the twofoldness of cognition results.

The cognition of an object, a visible form, etc., displays the object's image and its own. The cognition of the cognition of this object, on the other hand, displays the image of this cognition resembling the object and its own image. Otherwise, if the cognition of the object were to display only the form of the object or its own form, then the cognition of the cognition of the object would be no different, and each following cognition would not display the image of the object of the preceding cognition, because it would not have this as its object. Therefore, the twofoldness of cognition is established.

v. 11c

> And from the recollection afterwards,

"the twofoldness results," is to be added. Also because with respect to the cognition, as well as with respect to the object, a recollection of the perception arises afterwards, the twofoldness of cognition is established.

Also the self-awareness.

Why? <394>

v. 11d

> Since in the case of something not perceived, this [recollection] does not occur.

Without perception, the recollection of the seeing of an object does not occur, just like the recollection of a visible form, etc.

(Opponent:) Just like visible form, etc., the cognition is also perceived through another cognition.

(Answer:) That is not correct, since:

v. 12ab1

> In the case of perception through a separate cognition,
> an infinite series would result.

If the cognition is perceived through another cognition. How?

v. 12b2

> Since in the case of this cognition as well, recollection occurs.

Since if the cognition is perceived through another cognition, then, later, a recollection of the latter must also be observed. And if this [cognition] is thus also perceived through another cognition, [then] an infinite series would result. In addition,

v. 12cd

> under these circumstances, no moving on to another object would take place. The latter is, however, observed.

Thus, a self-awareness of cognition must certainly be assumed.

CFG. *Sthiramati and Dharmapāla (middle of sixth century c.e.)*

To conclude, I present another translated sample from Vasubandhu's school. As we already have stated, the Yogācāra school enjoyed a great flowering most particularly in the sixth century. Numerous significant representatives <395> created an abundance of works. Commentaries were written on the works of Asaṅga and Maitreyanātha. But in particular Vasubandhu's *Viṃśatikā* and *Triṃśikā Vijñāptimātratāsiddhi* constituted the starting point for numerous explanatory writings in which Vasubandhu's system was further elaborated and augmented.

The center of this lively literary activity was the famous Buddhist university of Nālandā, in Northern India, the homeland of Buddhism. Dharmapāla, the son of a minister from Kāñcī in South India, stands out as a representative of the Nālandā school. He spent his youth in the South, but later made his way to Nālandā, where he brilliantly advocated the Yogācāra doctrine in teaching and in writing. He died very early, however, at the age of thirty-two.

Alongside the Nālandā school stands the school of Valabhī in Kāthiāvār. It was founded by Guṇamati, a Southern Indian, who in the first half of the sixth century moved from Nālandā to Valabhī. Its most renowned representative is Sthiramati—a student of Guṇamati—who in his time was considered the most significant representative of the Yogācāra school, next to Dharmapāla.

Our principal source for this time and, in particular, for the two schools of Nālandā and Valabhī, is the famous Chinese pilgrim Hiuan-tsang (602 to 664 c.e.), since of the once so rich literature only a few works have been preserved. After his return from India, Hiuan-tsang wrote an extensive commentary on Vasubandhu's *Triṃśikā,* using the commentaries of ten Indian authors. In it he generally follows the doctrine of Dharmapāla, but besides that he also considers again and again the different deviating views; in particular, he also mentions Sthiramati's opinion quite regularly. The following translated sample then is taken from this work. It should be noted in this regard, however, that that which Hiuan-tsang cites as Sthiramati's opinion often does not agree with what we find expressed in Sthiramati's own works. Hiuan-tsang thus seems to base himself less on Shiramati's own works than on what he has learned in India as the doctrine of the latter's school. It would therefore be wise for us to see in the doctrines that he attributes to Dharmapāla <396> and Sthiramati, not so much the personal views of these men as the doctrines of their schools.

Similar to the translated sample from Dignāga, the following sample deals with the doctrine of the parts of cognition. According to the reports of Hiuan-tsang, the most diverse views on this subject prevailed.

Some held to Vasubandhu's view [S. 355], according to which the image of the object appears in cognition, without [any] parts having been explicitly distinguished.

For the most part though—following Dignāga's method—three parts were assumed. This was also Sthiramati's view.

Dharmapāla, finally, added yet a fourth part.

But the contrast between Sthiramati and Dharmapāla in this field rests less on the number of the assumed parts than on the following: [1] According to Sthiramati, only the awareness part is real; the image and seeing parts are mere cognizance. [2] According to Dharmapāla, all of the parts are real.

This difference of opinion has its deeper reasons:

Sthiramati, namely, follows the view of Maitreyanātha [S. 299f.] and Vasubandhu [S. 355], according to which every cognition is conception. Consequently, the image part and seeing part of every cognition belong to the imagined nature *(parikalpita svabhāva)* and are not real. Only the awareness part falls in the domain of the dependent nature *(paratantra svabhāva)* and is real.

Dharmapāla, on the other hand, takes up Asaṅga's idea [S. 330] that conception befits only thinking, and elaborates further on this, perhaps following Dignāga. For Dharmapāla, therefore, the imagined nature includes only the characteristic that is attributed to the objects of the other forms of cognition by the mental cognition *(manovijñāna)* and by thinking *(manas)*. The image part and seeing part of all of these forms of knowledge belong to the dependent nature and are real.

Hence, for Sthiramati the entire phenomenal world is mere conception. For Dharmapāla, reality befits [the phenomenal world]; it is just, according to his doctrine, not a matter of an external world, but instead merely a matter of appearing forms of cognition.

This difference of opinion also has its effect with respect to the doctrine of liberation, where the connection to Maitreyanātha [S. 300f.] and Asaṅga [S. 331f.] is once again apparent:[1]

For <397> Sthiramati, in the case of liberation—in connection with the transformation of the basis *(āśrayaparāvṛtti)*—all cognition disappears since [cognition] is mere conception, and only suchness remains.

According to Dharmapāla, all forms of cognition undergo a transformation, but they continue to exist even in the liberated one.

---

[1] [See in this context also Erich Frauwallner's *Amalavijñāna and Ālaya-vijñāna*, S. 154–59.]

The first section of the translated sample comes from the commentary to the third verse of the *Triṃśikā* and deals with the words "(the fundamental cognition) recognizes, in an unconscious form, the appropriation [i.e., the seeds and the body endowed with the five sense-organs] and the site [i.e., the environment]." – First a brief explanation of the individual words is given. Then Hiuan-tsang moves on to the question of the appearing form *(ākāra)* of cognition and, in doing so, discusses the doctrine of its parts. For this he uses material of the most diverse origins, which he attempts as much as possible to unify in that he starts from the simplest view and advances to the most difficult and tries in conclusion to show that all of these views have the same meaning.

Without speaking of any parts, § 1 describes according to Vasubandhu's own doctrine, how the image of the object, which provides the object of the process of cognizance, appears in cognition. The last sentence, which designates this process of cognizance as the seeing part, is Hiuan-tsang's addition.

In § 2, two parts of cognition are distinguished, the apprehended *(ālambya)* and the apprehending *(ālambaka)*, and their existence is established. The establishment of the existence of the image of the apprehended is the same as that which was already current in the Śrāvakayāna school of the Sautrāntikas. Without this image, in other words, no reason would exist for the corresponding cognizance to recognize exactly this object and no other. The characteristic of the apprehender must be given in order for cognition to take place at all.

Next [§ 3], follow two scholastic discussions:

The first deals with the question of what the object-support *(ālambana)*, the appearing form *(ākāra)*, and the substance *(dravya)* of cognition are, thus, its object, its activity, and its actual nature.

The second deals with the question of how mind and mental factors relate to each other with respect to their support, their object-support, their <398> appearing form, and their substance.

In both cases, Hiuan-tsang starts from the Śrāvakayāna view of the reality of the external world, since in both we are dealing with discussions that date from even the Śrāvakayāna scholasticism. Now according to [Śrāvakayāna scholasticism], for each cognition, the outer object is to be regarded as the object-support, the image part as the appearing form, and the seeing part as the nature. The support of a cognition and of the mental factors belonging to it are one and the same, namely, the sense-organ. Likewise, the object-support, namely, the outer object; and the appearing form, namely, the image of the object in cognition. On the other hand, while cognition and the mental factors, themselves, are indeed the same in terms of number—since they all show up individually—in terms of their character, cognition, sensation, etc., are of course different.

All of this shifts as soon as one denies the existence of external objects, and at the same time it becomes necessary to assume an additional third part of cognition, namely, the awareness part. For in this case, the image part is to be regarded as the object-support for each cognition; the seeing part as the appearing form; and the awareness part as the nature. The support, namely, the sense-organ, is the same for the mind and the mental factors. Likewise, the object-support, i.e., in this case the image of the object in the cognition. On the other hand, the appearing form, namely, the activity of cognition, of sensation, etc., is different, and, likewise, the character of cognition, of sensation, etc., itself. The proof of the existence of the awareness part, which is briefly outlined at this opportunity, is the same as in Dignāga, i.e., that without it no recollection of mental processes would be possible.

Since Dignāga was the one who decisively shaped the doctrine of the three parts of cognition, Hiuan-tsang also offers, as a kind of supplement, the form in which the doctrine of the object-support, appearing form, and substance of cognition appears in Dignāga. For in the circles of logicians and epistemologists to which Dignāga belonged, the question was formulated differently:

Firstly, one did not speak of cognition in general, but <399> of the means of valid cognition, since one tried to determine these first and foremost. And one inquired about the object of the means of valid cognition *(prameya)*, about these means themselves *(pramāṇa)*, and about their result *(pramāṇaphala)*. According to the verse cited from Dignāga (*Pramāṇasamuccaya* I, v. 10), these three are then apportioned to the three parts of cognition in the following way: The image part is the object, the seeing part the means of valid cognition, and the awareness part is the result.

§ 4 offers Dharmapāla's view. He teaches a fourth part of cognition, that is, the awareness of the awareness. The reasons that lead him to this are: that the awareness part, as with every part of cognition, would have to be recognized by another part; in addition, [the awareness part] as awareness is sensory perception *[pratyakṣa]*, hence a means of valid cognition, and like any such, must have a result. This leads to the assumption of a fourth part of cognition that recognizes the awareness part. [The fourth part of cognition] itself is in turn recognized by the awareness part, and so the circle is closed and an infinite series—as Dignāga had feared it (*cf.* S. 393)—is avoided. The fourth part, by the way, recognizes only the third part and not the second part, because this latter part is already recognized by the third and thus there remains nothing more to recognize. Besides this, it should also be noted that, with respect to sensory cognition, the second part is sensory perception, hence a means of valid cognition. With respect to mental cognition, [the second part] can, as inference, likewise be a means of valid cognition. As recollection, on the other hand, it is not. Everything else is easily understandable.

The last paragraph [§ 5] tries, finally, to show how the different views of the number of the parts of cognition can be harmonized with each other:

The last two parts can be regarded as a unit, since they are both awareness. In this way, only three parts remain.

One can, however, also view the last three parts as a unit, since they can all, as apprehending, be classed as the seeing part. This results in only two parts.

And, finally, all of the parts can be regarded as a unit, since their nature as cognizance *[vijñapti]* is the same. <400>

CFG.1. *From Hiuan-tsang's "Proof that (Everything) is Mere Cognizance" (Tch'eng wei che louen)*

What is the appearing form and the object-support of this cognition [i.e., the fundamental cognition]? The answer reads:

v. 3

> It recognizes, in an unconscious form, the appropriation and the site.

Cognizance *(vijñapti)* is its appearing form, because cognition has its appearing form in cognizance.

"Site" means location, i.e., the environment, because it is the location of all beings.

"Appropriation" is twofold: [1] the seeds and [2] the body endowed with the sense-organs.

By "seeds," the permeation by mark, name, and conception is to be understood.

By "body endowed with the organs," the material organs and the bearer of the sense-organs is to be understood.

These two are appropriated by cognition, i.e., integrated into its nature, because they share its fate.

Appropriations and site are the object-support (of cognition).

§ 1

At the time that, through the power of the causes and conditions, the fundamental cognition arises according to its nature, there occurs its inner transformation into the seeds and the body endowed with the sense-organs, [and] its outer transformation into the environment. [The fundamental cognition] has its object-support in this transformation, because with [the transformation's] help its appearing form (= the cognizance) comes into existence. Here *cognizance* is to be understood as the cognitive activity—of the maturation-cognition—that is directed to its object-support. This activity of cognizance belongs to the seeing part. <401>

§ 2

At the time that it arises according to its nature, every defiled cognition displays the image of the characteristic of the apprehended *(ālambya)* and of the apprehending *(ālambaka)*. The same is true of the (mental) factors connected with it. The image of the characteristic of the apprehended is called the *image part*. The image of the characteristic of the apprehending is called the *seeing part*.

For if the mind and the mental factors did not display the characteristic of the apprehended, then either they could not apprehend the object that is their object-support, or they would each have to apprehend all of the (objects), since their own object would [then] become the same as the other [objects] and the other [objects] would become the same as their own.

And if the mind and the mental factors did not display the characteristic of the apprehending, then they could not apprehend, like the ether, etc., or the ether, etc., would likewise apprehend.

Thus mind and mental factors must necessarily possess this double characteristic. And accordingly it says in the sutra:

> Everything is mere perception, perceived objects do not exist. The perceiving and the perceived part appear separately on their own.

§ 3

Those who assume that there are objects as object-support outside of cognition, say that the external object is the object-support (of cognition), the image part the appearing form, and the seeing part the substance, because [the seeing part] is the characteristic of the nature of the mind and of the mental factors. Here the mind and the mental factors have the same support, the same object-support, and the same appearing form, namely, the same appearing image. The <402> substance, although the same in terms of number, differs in terms of characteristic, since the characteristic of cognition, of sensation, of becoming aware, etc., differs.

Those, on the other hand, who admit that outside of cognition there are no objects as object-support, say that the image part is the object-support (of cognition), the seeing part the appearing form, and the nature—which forms the foundation of the image [part] and the seeing part—the substance. This [nature] is the awareness part. If this [part] did not exist, one could not recollect the mind and the mental factors, just as objects not previously seen can of course not be recollected. Here the mind and the mental factors have the same support, namely, the same sense-organ, the same object-support, that is, the same appearing image. The appearing form differs, because the activity of cognition, of sensation, etc., differs. Likewise, the substance, although the same in terms of number, differs in terms of characteristic, since the nature of cognition, of sensation, etc., is a different one.

Thus the mind and mental factors, if correctly examined, each have three parts at the time of their arising, since [1] the object of the means of valid cognition, [2] the means of valid cognition, and [3] the result of the means of valid cognition are to be distinguished, and because the image part and the seeing part must necessarily have one nature as foundation. Accordingly, it is stated in a verse of the *Compendium of the Means of Valid Cognition* (*Pramāṇasamuccaya;* chap. I, v. 10):

> The appearing image, which displays itself, is the object of the means of valid cognition. The means of valid cognition and its results are to be found in the appearing forms of the apprehender, and in awareness. These three are therefore nothing separate from each other. <403>

§ 4

But if the mind and mental factors are considered in detail, then they must have four parts, three parts as above and, as the fourth, the awareness-awareness part. For who would, if the latter would not exist, bring the third part to awareness? For since it is a part of the mind, it must, like all others, be brought to awareness. Further, the awareness part would have to have no result, whereas all means of valid cognition necessarily have a result. Also, the seeing part cannot be the result of the third, since the seeing part sometimes does not belong to the means of valid cognition. Consequently, the seeing part cannot bring the third to awareness, because the nature of awareness is necessarily sensory perception.

Of these four parts, the first two are outer, the last two inner (parts).

The first is only an object-support.

The last three are both simultaneously (the apprehended and the apprehending):

In this, the second part apprehends only the first. It is a means of valid cognition, or else, it is not. It can be perception, or also inference.

The third part apprehends the second and the fourth.

The awareness-awareness part apprehends merely the third, but not the second, because [the awareness-awareness part] has nothing more to do.

The third and the fourth parts both are sensory perception.

The mind and the mental factors are composed of four parts. They are at once the apprehended and the apprehending. Therefore, the flaw of an infinite series does not apply. And they are neither one nor separate. Thus, it is valid that everything is mere cognizance. Consequently, it is stated in a verse of a sutra:

> The mind of beings is of two types. All parts, inner and outer, are entangled in the apprehended and <404> the apprehending. Seeing has manifold variations.

This verse means: The mind of beings is composed of two types of parts. All of these, be they inner or outer, are entangled in the apprehended and the apprehending. Seeing has many manifold variations: means of valid cognition, non-means of valid cognition, sensory perception, or inference. In this, seeing is namely the seeing part.

§ 5

These four parts can also be summarized as three, since the fourth is contained in the awareness part.

They also can be summarized as two, since the last three are all contained in the seeing part, as they are, by nature, the apprehending. Indeed the expression "seeing" means the apprehending.

Finally, they can also be summarized as one, because their nature is not different. Accordingly, it is stated in a verse of the *Laṅkāvatāra:*

> While it is attached to its own mind, the mind develops in that it displays an outer object. But that which is seen does not exist. Therefore, it is stated that there is merely mind.

Likewise, it is stated in numerous passages that there is only the mind. For with the expression "only mind," the mental factors are included.

Thus the appearing form of cognition is cognizance. And cognizance is the seeing part of cognition.

> I follow with a few more sentences from the commentary to verse 20 that illuminate the difference in view with respect to the reality of the parts of cognition. Of the views presented, the first belongs to the school of Sthiramati, the second to the school of Dharmapāla. It is noteworthy here that in Sthiramati the adduced references to scripture lead back to Maitreyanātha (*Madhyāntavibhāga* I, *see above* S. 324f.), <405> and in Dharmapāla to Asaṅga (*Mahāyānasaṃgraha* II, § 11 and § 2, *see above* S. 338f. and 335).

What is the characteristic of the imagined nature, and how does it differ from the dependent nature? Some hold that—due to beginningless false permeation—the mind and mental factors that belong to the three spheres, although by nature a unity, appear as a duality when they arise as duality, namely, as a seeing part and an image part, i.e., as the apprehended and the apprehending. As an assumption, these two parts exist, but not as established. [In the *Madhyāntavibhāga*] this characteristic is called *imagined*. However, the nature on which these two (parts) rest, actually arises based on conditions. This nature is thus in no way non-existent and is called *dependent*.

Others hold that the two parts into which every mind and its mental factors transform themselves through the power of permeation arise from causes and are thus likewise dependent.

Based on these [causes], conception erroneously assumes a real existence and non-existence; unity and difference; both at once and neither of the two; etc. These twofold opposites are called *imagined*. Scripture states, in fact, that the mere means of valid cognition, the mere duality, and the mere multitude are designated as *dependent*. Also the treatise says that . . . the eleven types of cognizance belong to the dependent (nature).

In conclusion, I render one paragraph from the very end of the treatise, which shows how the doctrine of the unreality of the phenomenal world presents itself according to the views of the two schools [of Sthiramati and Dharmapāla].

First [§ 1], the doctrine of Sthiramati is formulated. According to this, only cognition itself exists. The entire phenomenal world is mere appearance.

Then [§ 2] follows <406> Dharmapāla's view. According to him, cognition develops into the phenomenal world. This world is therefore real, only it is not external, but rather within cognition.

Then [§ 3], an opponent brings forth the objection that in this case it would not be justifiable to state that merely cognizance exists, since the objects are also real.

This objection is first countered from Dharmapāla's point of view, and then the author concludes by once again returning to Sthiramati's view, which offers no point of attack for such an objection.

1

The image part, etc., which develops based on cognition, does not belong, as does the nature of cognition, to the dependent (characteristic) and is not real. For otherwise, it would not be proven that everything is mere cognizance, since it would be assumed that both cognition and the inner objects are real.

2

Or, the image part and the seeing part of cognition are arisen from causes. They are thus both dependent, and unreal or real like the cognition itself. The expression "mere (cognizance)" only refutes outer objects, but does not deny the inner objects. Otherwise, suchness would also have to be unreal, (since it is not cognition).

3

(Opponent:) If therefore, as well as cognition, the inner objects are also not unreal, why then do you only state that merely cognizance exists, and not the objects too?

(Answer:) Cognition is only inside, but the objects are, at the same time, also outside. Because one could possibly fall victim to the mistake that they are outside, it has just been taught that merely <407> cognizance exists. Or, because fools mistakenly believe in objects, then through this bring about defilements and deeds, sink into the cycle of existences, and do not attempt to get out through contemplation of the mind, for this reason, out of compassion for them, it has been proclaimed that merely cognizance exists, so that they find liberation from the cycle of existences through contemplation of the mind—but not by assuming that the inner objects, just like the outer, do not exist at all. Or, the image part, etc., is by nature cognition. Only through the power of permeation does the image of several parts arise. The true nature of cognition is, however, suchness. Thus, separate from the nature of cognition, there are no factors of their own. Here the mental factors are [thus] also indicated by the expression "cognition," because the mind is necessarily associated with the mental factors. <408>

Sources and Literature & Supplementary Remarks

SOURCES AND LITERATURE

(S = source material, E = editions, T = translations)

GENERAL

H. Oldenberg. *Buddha, sein Leben, seine Lehre, seine Gemeinde,* Stuttgart und Berlin 1923.

H. v. Glasenapp. *Der Buddhismus in Indien und im fernen Osten,* Berlin-Zürich 1936.

L. de La Vallée Poussin. Bouddhisme. *Opinions sur l'histoire de la dogmatique,* Paris 1925.

———. *Le dogme et la philosophie du Bouddhisme,* Paris 1930.

E. Conze. *Buddhism its Essence and Development,* Oxford 1951.

Regamey. *Buddhistische Philosophie* (Bibliographische Einführungen in das Studium der Philosophie, No. 20/21), Bern 1950.

A. THE TEACHING OF THE BUDDHA

Canonical texts *(Tripiṭaka):*

S: The canon of the Ceylonese branch of the school of the Sthavira (Pāli canon) [Pali Canon: Online Database: *http://www.bodhgayanews.net/pali.htm*], and also numerous fragments of the canons of other schools, are preserved in the original; in addition, the most important texts exist in Chinese translations, which go back to different schools; in the Tibetan *bka' 'gyur* (Kanjur), only a few texts of the old canon were included.

E: The authoritative edition of the Pāli canon was undertaken by the
<409> Pali Text Society, London 1882ff.; more recently, a new edition with translation is being published in Paris. The best edition of the Chinese translations is found in the Taishō edition of the Chinese Tripiṭaka, ed. by J. Takakusu and K. Watanabe, Tokyo 1924–29. [Chinese Buddhist Electronic Text Association (CBETA): *http://www.cbeta.org/index.htm*]. For the Tibetan translations one is generally dependent

on the Tibetan blockprints.[1] [ACIP: *http://www.asianclassics.org/research_site/index.html*].

T: The most important texts are translated in the *Sacred Books of the Buddhists* and in the *Translation Series of the Pali Text Society*, London; besides this, numerous partial translations exist in diverse languages. The rendered sections are taken from the following texts:

- The sermon of Benares = *Mahāvagga* I, 6, 17–29
  [*http://www.bodhgayanews.net/tipitaka.php?record=10*];
- The Buddhist path of liberation = *Majjhimanikāya* 51 (Vol. I, pp. 345ff.)
  [*http://www.bodhgayanews.net/tipitaka.php?record=3345*];
- *Ānanda* = *Saṃyuttanikāya* XLIV, 10 (Vol. IV, pp. 400f.)
  [*http://www.bodhgayanews.net/tipitaka.php?record=5099*];
- *The Discourse of Vatsagotra and the Fire* = *Majjhimanikāya* 72 (Vol. I, pp. 483ff.)
  [*http://www.bodhgayanews.net/tipitaka.php?record=3466*];
- *The Account of Enlightenment* = *Mahāvagga* I, 1, 1–3
  [*http://www.bodhgayanews.net/tipitaka.php?record=1*];
- *The Great Discourse of the Foundations of Origination* = *Dīghanikāya* XV, 1–9
  [*http://www.bodhgayanews.net/tipitaka.php?record=2430*]
  Dīghanikāya XV, 19–22
  [*http://www.bodhgayanews.net/tipitaka.php?record=2435*];
- *The Discourse of the Bearer of the Burden* is translated according to the Chinese of Tsa a-han (T. 99, k. 3, p. 19a15–b1)
  [*http://www.cbeta.org/result/normal/T02/0099_003.htm*].

Pratītyasamutpādasūtra:

S: Sanskrit original
[*http://www.uwest.edu/sanskritcanon/dp/index.php?q=node/35&textID=409d327524b16c86df*]

---

[1] In the following, I cite the Pāli texts according to the Pali Text Society, the Chinese translations according to the Taishō edition of the Tripiṭaka, the Tibetan translations according to the Complete Catalogue of the Tibetan Buddhist Canons, ed. by H. Ui and others, Sendai 1934.

Chin. translation, T. 124

[*http://www.cbeta.org/result/normal/T02/0124_001.htm*];

Tib. translation, Nr. 211.

My translation follows the inscriptively preserved Sanskrit text, *see* N. P. Chakravarti, "Two Brick Inscriptions from Nālandā" (*Epigraphia Indica*, XXI/1931–1932, pp. 193–99).

Pratītyasamutpādavyākhyā:

S: Fragments of the Sanskrit original; Tib. translation, Nr. 3995.

E: G. Tucci. *A Fragment from the Pratītyasamutpāda of Vasubandhu* (Journal of the <410> Royal Asiatic Society, 1930, pp. 611–23). – The translation corresponds to Tucci, pp. 616–19.

Śālistambasūtra:

S: Sanskrit original

[*http://www.uwest.edu/sanskritcanon/dp/index.php?q=node/35&textID=a2d3127542217a7eb6*];

five Chin. translations, T. 708–712

[*http://www.cbeta.org/result/normal/T16/0708_001.htm*; *...T16/0709_001.htm*; *...T16/0710_001.htm*; *...T16/0711_001.htm*; *...T16/0712_001.htm*];

Tib. translation, Nr. 210.

E: In L. de La Vallée Poussin. *Théorie des douze causes*, Gand 1913, pp. 68ff. (Contains the Tibetan text and a reconstruction of the Sanskrit original on the basis of the numerous fragments). The newly found Sanskrit original was not available to me.

B. THE SCHOLASTICISM (ABHIDHARMA) OF THE WAY OF HEARERS (ŚRĀVAKAYĀNA)

Milindapañhā:

S: Pāli Text

[*http://www.bodhgayanews.net/tipitaka.php?record=14822*; next sections begin: *...14836*; *...14843*; *...14846*; *...14847*];

Chin. translation, T. 1670 a and b

[*http://www.cbeta.org/result/normal/T32/1670a001.htm*; *http://www.cbeta.org/result/normal/T32/1670b001.htm*].

E: *The Milindapañho, being Dialogues between King Milinda and the Buddhist Sage Nāgasena,* ed. by V. Trenckner, London 1928.

T: T. W. Rhys Davids. *The Questions of King Milinda* (Sacred Books of the East, vol. 35–36), Oxford 1890 and 1894.

F. O. Schrader. *Die Fragen des Königs Menandros,* Berlin 1907.

L. Finot. *Les questions de Milinda* (Collection des Classiques de l'Orient, vol. 8), Paris 1923.

P. Demiéville. *Les versions chinoises du Milindapañha* (Bulletin de l'École Française d'Extrême-Orient, tome 24/1925, pp. 1–258).

Vasubandhu the Younger:

Abhidharmakośa:

S: Sanskrit original;

two Chin. translations, T. 1558–1560

[Hsüan-tsang:

http://www.cbeta.org/result/normal/T29/1558_001.htm;

Paramārtha:

http://www.cbeta.org/result/normal/T29/1559_001.htm;

Kārikās (Hsüan-tsang):

http://www.cbeta.org/result/normal/T29/1560_001.htm];

Tib. translation, No. 4089–4090

[Kārikās:

http://www.asianclassics.org/research_site/webdata/monastic/open/html/TD4089N.html;

Bhāṣya Part 1:

http://www.asianclassics.org/research_site/webdata/monastic/open/html/TD4090I1.html;

Bhāṣya Part 2:

http://www.asianclassics.org/research_site/webdata/monastic/open/html/TD4090I2.html].

Of the newly found Sanskrit original, so far only the verse text has been published by V. V. Gokhale, *The Text of the Abhidharmakośakārikā of Vasubandhu* (Journal of the Bombay Branch of the Royal Asiatic Society, New Series, Vol. 22/1946, pp. 73–102).

T: L. de La Vallée Poussin. *L'Abhidharmakośa de Vasubandhu; traduit et annoté,* 6 vols., Paris-Louvain 1923–1931 (according to the Chinese translation of Hiuan-tsang). – The translated parts correspond to the following sections: <411>

- A soul does not exist = T. 1558, k. 9, pp. 47b24–48c8 (in La Vallée Poussin III, pp. 56–65)
  [*http://www.cbeta.org/result/normal/T29/1558_009.htm*];
- From "Refutation of the Person" (in La Vallée Poussin IX, pp. 230ff., 238ff., 256f.) =
  T. 1558, k. 29, pp. 152b24–153b2; 153b12–c12
  [*http://www.cbeta.org/result/normal/T29/1558_029.htm*];
  T. 1558, k. 30, p. 155a23–b9
  [*http://www.cbeta.org/result/normal/T29/1558_030.htm*];
- A substance does not exist = T. 1558, k. 12, p. 66c15–23 (in La Vallée Poussin III, pp. 213f.)
  [*http://www.cbeta.org/result/normal/T29/1558_012.htm*];
- The momentariness of things = T. 1558, k. 13, pp. 67c11–68b1 (in La Vallée Poussin IV, pp. 4–8)
  [*http://www.cbeta.org/result/normal/T29/1558_013.htm*];
- The seemingly and the truly real = T. 1558, k. 22, p. 116b10–29 (in La Vallée Poussin VI, pp. 139ff.)
  [*http://www.cbeta.org/result/normal/T29/1558_022.htm*];
- The nature of acquisition = translated according to the incomplete edition of the Tibetan text in the Bibliotheca Buddhica XX, pp. 158,15–161,20 (in La Vallée Poussin II, pp. 181ff.);
- Suppression through knowledge = Bibl. Buddh. XX, pp. 9,8–10,11 (in La Vallée Poussin I, pp. 8f.);
- Nirvāṇa as non-existence = T. 1558, k. 6, pp. 34a12–35a3 (in La Vallée Poussin II, pp. 278–86)
  [*http://www.cbeta.org/result/normal/T29/1558_006.htm*].

Pañcaskandhaka:

S: Chin. translation, T. 1612
[*http://www.cbeta.org/result/normal/T31/1612_001.htm*];
Tib. translation, No. 4059.
My translation follows the Chinese version.

Harivarman,

Tattvasiddhi:

S: Chin. translation, T. 1646
[*http://www.cbeta.org/result/normal/T32/1646_001.htm*].
The rendered section (k. 16, pp. 368c13–369a27) was also translated by L. de La Vallée Poussin in *Mélanges chinois et bouddhiques*, V/1936–1937, pp. 208–10.

C. THE SCHOOLS OF THE GREAT WAY (MAHĀYĀNA)

The oldest literary documentation of the Great Way

Aṣṭasāhasrikā Prajñāpāramitā:

S: Sanskrit original
[*http://www.uwest.edu/sanskritcanon/dp/index.php?q=node/35&textID=ff1588e3e4301c794e*];
six Chin. translations, the oldest from the years 172 and 179 c.e.,
T. 220, k. 538–555
[*http://www.cbeta.org/result/normal/T07/0220_538.htm*
up to:
http://www.cbeta.org/result/normal/T07/0220_555.htm] and
T. 224–228
[*http://www.cbeta.org/result/normal/T08/0224_001.htm*
up to:
http://www.cbeta.org/result/normal/T08/0228_001.htm];
Tib. translation, Nr. 12
[*http://www.asianclassics.org/research_site/webdata/monastic/open/html/KD0012I.html*].

E: Rájendralála Mitra. *Ashṭasáhasriká; a Collection of Discourses on the Metaphysics of the Maháyána School of the Buddhists* (Bibliotheca Indica 110), Calcutta 1888; reprinted, with some <412> improvements, in *Abhisamayālaṃkārāloka of Haribhadra*, ed. by Unrai Wogihara, Tokyo 1932–1935.

T: M. Walleser. *Prajñā Pāramitā, die Vollkommenheit der Erkenntnis* (Quellen der Religionsgeschichte, Bd. 6, Gruppe 8), Göttingen 1914 (partial translation).
The following sections were translated according to the edition of Rājendralāla Mitra (all of which are also included in the Chin. translation from 179 c.e., although with deviations in wording):
chap. 1, pp. 3,12–6,10 (T. 224, k. 1, pp. 425c4–426a4
[*http://www.cbeta.org/result/normal/T08/0224_001.htm*]);
chap. 2, pp. 45,1–47,20 (T. 224, k. 1, p. 430b23–c22
[same URL as before]);
chap. 22, pp. 399,12–400,17 (T. 224, k. 7, p. 462a23–b14
[*http://www.cbeta.org/result/normal/T08/0224_007.htm*]);
chap. 1, pp. 20,13–21,12 (T. 224, k. 1, p. 427c2–13
[same URL as before]);
chap. 8, pp. 190,8–192,20 (T. 224, k. 3, p. 442b26–c20
[*http://www.cbeta.org/result/normal/T08/0224_003.htm*]).

Ratnakūṭa (Kāśyapaparivarta):

S: Sanskrit original, in an incomplete Central Asian manuscript
[*http://folk.uio.no/braarvig/getskt_kpv.php* (Sanskrit; Chinese; Tibetan);
http://www.uwest.edu/sanskritcanon/dp/index.php?q=node/35&textID=0d5b0251cf911162ac];
four Chin. translations, the oldest from the years 178–84 c.e.,
T. 310, No. 43, k. 112
[*http://www.cbeta.org/result/normal/T11/0310_112.htm*], and
T. 350–352
[*http://www.cbeta.org/result/normal/T12/0350_001.htm*
up to:
http://www.cbeta.org/result/normal/T12/0352_001.htm];
Tib. translation No. 87.

E: A. von Staël-Holstein. *The Kāçyapaparivarta; a Mahāyānasūtra of the Ratnakūṭa Class; edited in the original Sanskrit, in Tibetan and in Chinese*, Shanghai 1926.

The Madhyamaka school

Nāgārjuna:

Madhyamakakārikā:

S: Sanskrit original
[*http://www.uwest.edu/sanskritcanon/dp/index.php?q=node/35&textID=4673a1cbc57363b8294*];

Chin. translation (with the commentary by Ts'ing mou), T. 1564
[*http://www.cbeta.org/result/normal/T30/1564_001.htm*];

Tib. translation, Nr. 3824
[*http://www.asianclassics.org/research_site/webdata/monastic/open/html/TD3824N.html*].

E. L. de La Vallée Poussin. *Mūlamadhyamakakārikās de Nāgārjuna avec la Prasannapadā Commentaire de Candrakīrti* (Bibliotheca Buddhica IV), St.-Petersbourg 1913.

T: M. Walleser. *Die buddhistische Philosophie in ihrer geschichtlichen Entwicklung. – 2. Teil: Die Mittlere Lehre (Mādhyamakaśāstra) des Nāgārjuna,* rendered according to the Tibetan version, Heidelberg 1911. – 3. *Teil: Die mittlere Lehre des Nāgārjuna,* rendered according to the Chinese version, Heidelberg 1912. *See also under* Candrakīrti.

Vigrahavyāvartanī:

S: Sanskrit original
[*http://folk.uio.no/braarvig/getskt_vgv.php* (Sanskrit, Chinese, Tibetan, English; entire text);
http://www.uwest.edu/sanskritcanon/dp/index.php?q=node/35&textID=1eed29b9ed10fcdd4 (*kārikās* only)];

Chin. <413> translation, T. 1631
[*http://www.cbeta.org/result/normal/T32/1631_001.htm*];

Tib. translation,
No. 3828
[*http://www.asianclassics.org/research_site/webdata/monastic/open/html/TD3828M.html*] and
No. 3832
[*http://www.asianclassics.org/research_site/webdata/monastic/open/html/TD3832M.html*].

E: K. P. Jayaswal and Rāhula Sāṅkṛityāyana. *Vigrahavyāvarttanī by Āchārya Nāgārjuna; with the Author's own Commentary* (Appendix to the Journal of the Bihar and Orissa Research Society, Vol. XXIII, Part III), Patna 1937.

T: Susumu Yamaguchi. *Traité de Nāgārjuna pour écarter les vaines discussions; traduit et annoté* (Journal Asiatique, tome 215/1929, pp. 1–86).

G. Tucci. *Vigrahavyāvartanī by Nāgārjuna; Translation from the Chinese and Tibetan Text* (In *Pre-Diṅnāga Buddhist Texts on Logic from Chinese Sources*, Gaekwad's Oriental Series, No. XLIX), Baroda 1929.

Johnston, E.H. and A. Kunst. *Vigrahavyāvartanī*, as reproduced with tr. in K. Bhaṭṭacharya: *The Dialectical Method of Nāgārjuna*, Motilal Banarsidass, Delhi 1978

Ratnāvalī:

S: Fragments of the Sanskrit original [*http://www.uwest.edu/sanskritcanon/dp/index.php?q=node/35&textID=2660279af4e11b01b*];

Chin. translation, T. 1656 [*http://www.cbeta.org/result/normal/T32/1656_001.htm*];

Tib. translation, Nr. 4158 [spring yig, gc 107a1–126a4: *http://www.asianclassics.org/research_sie/webdata/monastic/open/html/TD10171/TD10171-9.html*].

E: G. Tucci. *The Ratnāvalī of Nāgārjuna* (Journal of the Royal Asiatic Society, 1934, pp. 307–25, and 1936, pp. 237–52) (k. 1, 2 [beginning] and 4; Sanskrit text with English translation).

Āryadeva:

Catuḥśataka:

S: Fragments of the Sanskrit original [*http://www.uwest.edu/sanskritcanon/dp/index.php?q=node/35&textID=ef30048c74d5c1f7e*];

partial Chinese translation, T. 1570 [*http://www.cbeta.org/result/normal/T30/1570_001.htm*];

Tib. translation, No. 3846

[*http://www.asianclassics.org/research_site/webdata/monastic/open/html/TD3846M.html*].

E: Haraprasād Shāstri. *Catuḥśatikā by Ārya Deva* (Memoires of the Asiatic Society of Bengal, Vol. III/1914, No. 8, pp. 449–514).

Vidhushekhara Bhattacharya. *The Catuḥśataka of Āryadeva; Sanskrit and Tibetan Texts, with copious extracts from the commentary of Candrakirtti, reconstructed and edited,* Part II (Visva-Bharati Series, No. 2), Calcutta 1931.

T: G. Tucci. *Studi Mahāyānici I; La versione cinese del Catuḥçataka di Āryadeva confrontata col testo sanscrito e la traduzione tibetana* (Rivista degli Studi Orientali, X/1923–1925, pp. 521–90).

Buddhapālita:

Mūlamadhyamakavṛtti:

S: Tib. translation, No. 3842

[*http://www.asianclassics.org/research_site/webdata/monastic/open/html/TD3842M.html*].

E: M. Walleser. *Mūlamadhyamakavṛtti; tibetische Übersetzung* (Bibliotheca Buddhica XVI), S.-Petersburg 1913–14 (incomplete).

Bhāvaviveka:

Prajñāpradīpa:

S: Chin. translation <414> T. 1566

[*http://www.cbeta.org/result/normal/T30/1566_001.htm*];

Tib. translation, No. 3853

[*http://www.asianclassics.org/research_site/webdata/monastic/open/html/TD3853M.html*].

E: M. Walleser. *Prajñā-Pradīpaḥ; a Commentary on the Madhyamaka* Sūtra (Bibliotheca Indica 226), Calcutta 1914 (incomplete).

Tchang tchen (Hastaratna ?):

S: Chin. translation, T. 1578

[*http://www.cbeta.org/result/normal/T30/1578_001.htm*].

T: L. de la Vallée Poussin. *Madhyamaka. – II. L'auteur du Joyau dans la main. – III. Le Joyau dans la main* (Mélanges chinois et bouddhiques, II/1932–1933, pp. 60–138).

Candrakīrti:

Prasannapadā:

S: Sanskrit original;

Tib. translation, No. 3860

[*http://www.asianclassics.org/research_site/webdata/monastic/open/html/TD3860M.html*].

E: *See* Nāgārjuna.

T: Th. Stcherbatsky. *The Conception of Buddhist Nirvāṇa,* Leningrad 1927 (contains a translation of the first and twenty-fifth chapters).

St. Schayer. *Ausgewählte Kapitel aus der Prasannapadā* (V, XII bis XVI), *Einleitung, Übersetzung und Anmerkungen* (Polska Akademja Umiejetności, Prace komisji orientalistyczny No. 14), Krakow 1931.

[———. German translation of chapter X of the Prasannapadā in Rocznik Orientalistyczny 7, 1929–1930, pp. 26–52.]

Madhyamakāvatāra:

S: Tib. translation, No. 3861–62

[*dbu ma la 'jug pa:*

http://www.asianclassics.org/research_site/webdata/monastic/open/html/TD3861N.html;

dbu ma la 'jug pa'i bshad pa zhes bya:

http://www.asianclassics.org/research_site/webdata/monastic/open/html/TD3862M.html].

E: L. de la Vallée Poussin. *Madhyamakāvatāra par Candrakīrti; traduction tibétaine* (Bibliotheca Buddhica IX), St. Pétersbourg 1912.

T: L. de la Vallée Poussin. *Madhyamakāvatāra; introduction au traité du milieu de l'Ācārya Candrakīrti, avec le commentaire de l'auteur, traduit d'après la version tibétaine* (Muséon VIII/1907, pp. 249–317; XI/1910, pp. 271–358; XII/1911, pp. 235–328) (incomplete).

The school of Sāramati

Sāramati:

Ratnagotravibhāga:

S: Sanskrit original

[*http://www.uwest.edu/sanskritcanon/dp/index.php?q=node/35&textID=d8ee716b28e3399ee16*];

Chin. translation, T. 1611

[*http://www.cbeta.org/result/normal/T31/1611_001.htm*];

Tib. translation, No. 4024

[*http://www.asianclassics.org/research_site/webdata/monastic/open/html/TD4024N.html*].

E: E. H. Johnston. *The Ratnagotravibhāga Mahāyānottaratantraśāstra* (The Journal of the Bihar Research Society, Vol. XXXVI, Part I), Patna 1950.

T: E. Obermiller. *The Sublime Science of the Great Vehicle to Salvation, being a Manual of Buddhist Monism. The Work* <415> *of Ārya Maitreya with a Commentary by Āryāsaṅga, translated from the Tibetan with* introduction and notes (Acta Orientalia, IX/1931, pp. 81–306).

The Yogācāra school

Bodhisattvabhūmi:

S: Sanskrit original

[*http://www.uwest.edu/sanskritcanon/dp/index.php?q=node/35&textID=2c8271d89f1460a1d9a*];

three Chin. translations,

T. 1579, k. 35–50

[*http://www.cbeta.org/result/normal/T30/1579_035.htm*
up to:
http://www.cbeta.org/result/normal/T30/1579_050.htm],

T. 1581

[*http://www.cbeta.org/result/normal/T30/1581_001.htm*]

T. 1582

[*http://www.cbeta.org/result/normal/T30/1582_001.htm*];

Tib. translation, No. 4037
[*http://www.asianclassics.org/research_site/webdata/monastic/open/html/TD4037M.html*].

E: Unrai Wogihara. *Bodhisattvabhūmi; a statement of the whole course of the Bodhisattva (being fifteenth section of Yogācārabhūmi),* Tokyo 1930–1936. – pp. 37,1 and 43,24–48,6 were translated.

Saṃdhinirmocanasūtra:

S: five Chin. translations, T. 675–679
[*http://www.cbeta.org/result/normal/T16/0675_001.htm*
up to:
http://www.cbeta.org/result/normal/T16/0679_001.htm];
Tib. translation, No. 106
[*http://www.asianclassics.org/research_site/webdata/monastic/open/html/KD0106M.html*].

E: É. Lamotte. *Saṃdhinirmocanasūtra. L'explication des mystères. Texte tibétain; édité et traduit* (Univ. de Louvain, recueil de travaux publiés par les membres des Conférences d'Histoire et de Philologie, 2e série, 34e fasc.), Louvain-Paris 1935. – My translation follows the Tibetan.

Maitreyanātha:

Mahāyānasūtrālaṃkāra:

S: Sanskrit original
[*http://www.uwest.edu/sanskritcanon/dp/index.php?q=node/35&textID=f005e1a32cc417568fb* (*kārikās* only)];
Chin. translation, T. 1604
[*http://www.cbeta.org/result/normal/T31/1604_001.htm*];
Tib. translation, No. 4020 [sems tsam, phi 1a1-39a4:
http://www.asianclassics.org/research_site/webdata/monastic/open/html/TD10122.html].

E: Sylvain Lévi. *Asaṅga, Mahāyāna-Sūtrālaṃkāra; exposé de la doctrine du Grand Véhicule selon le système Yogācāra; édité et traduit* (Bibliothèque de l'École des Hautes Études, sciences historiques et philologiques, fasc. 159 & 190), Paris 1907–1911.

Madhyāntavibhāga:

S: Sanskrit original

[*http://www.uwest.edu/sanskritcanon/dp/index.php?q=node/35&textID=9687e18555923109*];

two Chin. translations, T. 1599–1600

[*http://www.cbeta.org/result/normal/T31/1599_001.htm*;

http://www.cbeta.org/result/normal/T31/1600_001.htm];

Tib. translation, No. 4021 [sems tsaṁ, phi 40b1–45a6:

http://www.asianclassics.org/research_site/webdata/monastic/open/html/TD10122/TD10122-3.html].

E: Susumu Yamaguchi. *Pien tchong pien louen,* Nagoya 1934 (contains the Tibetan and the Chinese translations with the commentary by Vasubandhu). Fragments of the unpublished Sanskrit original in: Susumu Yamaguchi. *Sthiramati, Madhyāntavibhāgaṭīkā; exposition systematique du Yogācāravijñaptivāda,* <416> Nagoya 1934, and: Vidhushekhara Bhattacharya and G. Tucci. *Madhyāntavibhāgasūtrabhāṣyaṭīkā of Sthiramati,* Part I (Calcutta Oriental Series, No. 24), London 1932.

T: Th. Stcherbatsky. *Madhyāntavibhaṅga. Discourse on Discrimination between Middle and Extremes, ascribed to Maitreya and commented by Vasubandhu and Sthiramati. Translated from the Sanskrit* (Bibliotheca Buddhica XXX), Leningrad 1936 (was not available to me).

Asaṅga:

Mahāyānasaṃgraha:

S: four Chin. translations,

T. 1592–1594

[Buddhaśānta:

http://www.cbeta.org/result/normal/T31/1592_001.htm;

Paramārtha:

http://www.cbeta.org/result/normal/T31/1593_001.htm;

Hiuan-tsang:

http://www.cbeta.org/result/normal/T31/1594_001.htm]

T. 1596

[Dharmagupta:

http://www.cbeta.org/result/normal/T31/1596_001.htm];

Tib. translation, No. 4048 [sems tsam, ri 1a1–43a7:
http://www.asianclassics.org/research_site/webdata/monastic/open/html/TD10133.html].

E: É. Lamotte. *La Somme du Grand Véhicule d'Asaṅga (Mahāyāna-saṃgraha)*, Tome I, Versions tibétaine et chinoise (Hiuan-tsang), Tome II, traduction et commentaire (Bibliothèque du Muséon 7), Louvain 1938.

Vasubandhu

Viṃśatikā:

S: Sanskrit original
[*http://www.uwest.edu/sanskritcanon/dp/index.php?q=node/35&textID=6906a9ddb861e622e*];

three Chin. translations, T. 1588–1590
[*http://www.cbeta.org/result/normal/T31/1588_001.htm*
up to:
http://www.cbeta.org/result/normal/T31/1590_001.htm];

Tib. translation,
No. 4056 [sems tsam, shi 3a4–4a2:
http://www.asianclassics.org/research_site/webdata/monastic/open/html/TD10135.html]
up to:
No. 4057 [sems tsam, shi 4a3–10a2:
http://www.asianclassics.org/research_site/webdata/monastic/open/html/TD10135.html].

E: Sylvain Lévi. *Vijñaptimātratāsiddhi; deux traités de Vasubandhu, Viṃśatikā et Triṃśikā* (Bibliothèque de l'École des Hautes Études, fasc. 245), Paris 1925.

L. de la Vallée Poussin. *Vasubandhu, Viṃśatikākārikāprakaraṇa; traité des vingt ślokas avec le commentaire de l'auteur* (Muséon XIII/1912, pp. 53–90) (Tibetan text with translation).

T: Sylvain Lévi. *Matériaux pour l'étude du système Vijñaptimātra* (Bibliothèque de I'École des Hautes Études, fasc. 260), Paris 1932 (contains a translation of the *Viṃśatikā* and *Triṃśikā*).

Junyu Kitayama. *Metaphysik des Buddhismus* (Veröffentlichungen des Orientalischen Seminars der Universität Tübingen, 7. Heft), Stuttgart 1934 (contains, pp. 234–68, a translation of the *Viṃśatikā*).

Triṃśikā:

S: Sanskrit original
[*http://www.uwest.edu/sanskritcanon/dp/index.php?q=node/35&textID=3ea808e159e43f226*];
two Chin. translations, T. 1586–1587
[*http://www.cbeta.org/result/normal/T31/1586_001.htm; http://www.cbeta.org/result/normal/T31/1587_001.htm*];
Tib. translation, No. 4055 [sems tsam, shi 1a1–3a3: *http://www.asianclassics.org/research_site/webdata/monastic/open/html/TD10135.html*].

E: *See Viṃśatikā.*

T: *See Viṃśatikā.*
H. Jakobi. *Triṃśikāvijñapti des Vasubandhu mit Bhāṣya des Ācārya Sthiramati* <417> (Beiträge zur indischen Sprachwissenschaft und Religionsgeschichte, 7. Heft), Stuttgart 1932.

Dignāga:

Pramāṇasamuccaya:

S: Tib. translation, No. 4203–4204
[*http://www.asianclassics.org/research_site/webdata/monastic/open/html/TD4203M.html; http://www.asianclassics.org/research_site/webdata/monastic/open/html/TD4204M.html*].

E: H.-R. Rangaswamy Iyengar. *Diṅnāga's Pramana Samuccaya* (Chapter 1), with Vṛitti, Ṭika and Notes edited and restored into Sanskrit, Mysore 1930 (completely unusable).

Hiuan-tsang:

Tch'eng wei che louen:

S: Chin. original, T. 1585
[*http://www.cbeta.org/result/normal/T31/1585_001.htm*].

T: L. de la Vallée Poussin. *Vijñaptimātratāsiddhi, la Siddhi de Hiuan-tsang,* traduite et annotée (Buddhica, Premiere Série: Mémoires – Tome I & V), Paris 1928–1929. <418>

ADDITIONAL HELPFUL URLs

Source materials

- Access to Insight:
  http://www.accesstoinsight.org/index.html.
- Digital Library & Museum of Buddhist Studies:
  http://buddhism.lib.ntu.edu.tw/BDLM/en/index.htm
- Digital Sanskrit Buddhist Canon:
  http://www.uwest.edu/sanskritcanon/dp/index.php?q=node/33
- GRETIL – Göttingen Register of Electronic Texts in Indian Languages:
  http://www.sub.uni-goettingen.de/ebene_1/fiindolo/gretil. htm#Tipit
- The Online Tibetan to English Dictionary and Translation Tool:
  http://www.thdl.org/tibetan/servlet/org.thdl.tib.scanner.OnLineScannerFilter?thdlBanner=on
- The Pali Text Society's Pali-English dictionary:
  http://dsal.uchicago.edu/dictionaries/pali/index.html
- Peking Tripitaka Online Search: The ShinBuddhist Comprehensive Research Institute: Otani University:
  http://web.otani.ac.jp/cri/twrp/tibdate/Peking_online_search.html
- Sanskrit, Tamil and Pahlavi Dictionaries:
  http://webapps.uni-koeln.de/tamil/
- Thesaurus Literaturae Buddlucae:
  http://folk.uio.no/braarvig/tlb.html

Supplementary Remarks

More than fifteen years have passed since the present book was written. During this time numerous specialized works have appeared, so that it seems advisable to point out at least the most important thereof.

First, the large text editions should be mentioned:

In the years 1956–1961, a complete edition of the Pāli canon was published in Nālandā, in the *Nālandā-Devanāgarī-Pāli-Series* under the supervision of Bhikkhu J. Kashyap. The previous editions served as the basis, first and foremost the Burmese Chaṭṭhasaṅgāyana edition. A corresponding edition of the Pāli commentaries is planned. – Further, a new edition of the Taishō edition of the Chinese Tripiṭaka is currently in publication. – The edition of the *Tibetan Tripitaka* published in 1957 by the Tibetan Tripitaka Research Institute in Tokyo, under the supervision of Daisetz T. Suzuki, is particularly valuable and welcome. It contains a reduced photographic reproduction of the Peking blockprint of 1737 c.e., taken from the copy at the Otani University in Kyoto. A detailed catalogue and index to the latter was published in 1962. With this the Tibetan canon is no longer available only in rare original block prints. – The series of *Buddhist Sanskrit Texts,* published in Darbhanga by the Mithila Institute of Post-Graduate Studies and Research in Sanskrit Learning, is also very commendable. It contains, among others, works that had been out of print for centuries and that <419> are now once again available. Finally, particular importance is also to be attributed to the *Tibetan Sanskrit Works Series,* published by the Kashi Prasad Jayaswal Research Institute, in Patna. In it Buddhist works appear, the manuscripts of which were obtained or photographed in Tibet by Rāhula Sānkrityāyana, and which were thus saved for research. Unfortunately, their publication is proceeding only very slowly.

GENERAL

With respect to presentations of a general nature, I would like to note the following: a thirteenth edition of Oldenberg's book was published in 1959, with an afterword by H. v. Glasenapp that contains supplements and additions, as well as an appraisal of Oldenberg's achievements. E. Conze's book, *Buddhism, its Essence and Development,* is also available in a German translation under the title *Der Buddhismus, Wesen und Entwicklung,* Stuttgart 1953 (Urban-Bücher 5). In the meantime, another work of a general nature by E. Conze has also been published: *Buddhist Thought in India,* London 1962. Further, a good general presentation is offered by A. Bareau, *Der indische Buddhismus,* Stuttgart 1964 (in *Religionen der Menschheit,* Bd. 13: Die Religionen Indiens III). Although it deals only briefly with Buddhist doctrine within the larger framework, I would also like to mention the extensive work of Ét. Lamotte, *Histoire du Bouddhisme Indien, des origins à l'ère Śaka,* Louvain 1958 (Bibliothèque du Muséon, vol. 43).

THE TEACHING OF THE BUDDHA

For the canonical texts translated in this section, I would like to limit myself to referring to the <420> above mentioned collective editions of the canons. – An edition of the *Śālistambasūtra,* by N. Aiyaswami Sastri, Adyar, was published in 1950 (*The Adyar Library Series,* No. 76). However, it contains only a retranslation from the Tibetan.

THE SCHOLASTICISM (ABHIDHARMA) OF THE ŚRĀVAKAYĀNA

André Bareau has published a series of works—which should be considered as fundamental—on the doctrines of the different schools of the Śrāvakayāna. In particular, *Les sects bouddhiques du Petit Véhicule,* Saigon 1955 (Publications de l'École Française d'Extrême-Orient, vol. 38) should be mentioned.

As far as the Abhidharma works of the older period are concerned, the manuscript findings in Tibet did not produce anything worth mentioning. The editions that have appeared lately in India are retranslations from the Chinese and are not very reliable. In addition, as I have previously mentioned in this book, in terms of content and form, these works are extremely unyielding and scarcely of any interest to wider circles. As to what they do offer that is of philosophical importance, I refer the reader to my presentation in the third volume of my *History of Indian Philosophy,* which I hope to finish before too long, and until then, to my "Abhidharma-Studien" (*Wiener Zeitschrift für die Kunde Süd- und Ostasiens,* Bd. 7/1963 and 8/1964).[1]

The Sanskrit text of Vasubandhu's *Abhidharmakośa* was finally published just recently; *Abhidharm-Koshabhāṣya of Vasubandhu,* ed. by P. Pradhan, Patna 1967 (Tibetan Sanskrit Works Series, Vol. 8). Also of importance is that among the manuscripts in Tibet, parts of a work from the school of Saṃghabhadra—who in contrast to Vasubandhu's tendency toward the Sautrāntika holds the <421> orthodox doctrine of the Sarvāstivādins—were also found; this work was published by Padmanabh S. Jaini, *Abhidharmadīpa with Vibhāṣāprabhāvṛtti; critically edited with notes and introduction,* Patna 1959 (Tibetan Sanskrit Works Series, Vol. 4).

---

[1] [Frauwallner's third volume was never written. For an edition of some remaining essays and a survey of the complete plan of Fr.'s "History" *cf. Erich Frauwallner's Posthumous Essays.* Translated from the German by Jayandra Soni, Aditya Prakashan, New Delhi 1994. – Frauwallner's "Abhidharma-Studien" were continued until 1973 and subsequently collected and published in English: *Studies in the Abhidharma Literature and the Origins of Buddhist Philosophical Systems.* Translated by Sophie Francis Kidd. SUNY Press, Albany 1995.]

THE SCHOOLS OF THE MAHĀYĀNA

The oldest literary documentation of the Mahāyāna

As for the *Prajñāpāramitā* literature, one must point out the works of E. Conze in particular. Among others, we have also from him a translation of the *Aṣṭasāhasrikā Prajñāpāramitā,* which was published in Calcutta 1958 as Nr. 284 of the *Bibliotheca Indica.* A collection of his most important essays was recently published under the title *Thirty Years of Buddhist Studies: Selected Essays by E. Conze,* Oxford 1967. A new edition of the text of the *Aṣṭasāhasrikā Prajñāpāramitā,* as well as the commentary by Haribhadra, was brought out by P. L. Vaidya as nr. 4 of the *Buddhist Sanskrit Texts,* Darbhanga 1960.

The Madhyamaka school

A new edition of Nāgārjuna's *Madhyamakakārikā,* together with the commentary by Candrakīrti, was published by P. L. Vaidya as nr. 10 of the *Buddhist Sanskrit Texts,* Darbhanga 1960. It also includes in the appendix, the *Vigrahavyāvartanī* as well as the *Ratnāvalī.* Moreover, after the first edition of the *Vigrahavya-avartanī* by K. P. Jayaswal and R. Sāṅkrityāyana, a far better critical edition by E. H. Johnston and A. Kunst was published (in: *Mélanges chinois et bouddhiques,* vol. 9/1951, pp. 99–152). Further, wc must mention R. Gnoli, *Nāgārjuna, Madhyamaka-kārikā, Vigrahavyāvartanī, Catuḥstava, introduzione, traduzione e note,* Torino 1961.

The first chapter of Buddhapālita's *Vṛttiḥ* <422> was dealt with in the meantime by I. Datar in a separate study ("A study of the first chapter of Buddhapālita's Mūlamadhyamakavṛtti," *Journal of the Bombay Branch of the Asiatic Society,* Vol. 26/1951, pp. 129–39). The first chapter of Bhāvaviveka's *Prajñāpradīpa* was translated by Y. Kajiyama (*Wiener Zeitschrift für die Kunde Süd- und Ostasiens,* Bd. 7/1963, pp. 37–62 and Bd. 8/1964, pp. 100–30).

From Candrakīrti's *Prasannapadā*—only individual chapters of which had earlier been translated, specifically, in addition to the works by Th. Stcherbatsky [chapters 1 and 25] and St. Schayer [chapters 5, 10, 12–16] already noted, the seventeenth chapter by Ét. Lamotte (in *Mélanges chinois et bouddhiques*, vol. 4/1936, pp. 265–88)—we now also have translations of the other chapters. Specifically, of chapters 18–22 by J. W. de Jong (*Cinq chapitres de la Prasannapadā*. Buddhica, documents et travaux, 1re série, t. 9, Paris 1950); of chapters 2–4, 6–9, 11, 23–24, and 26–27 by J. May (*Candrakīrti, Prasannapadā Madhyamakavṛtti; douze chapitres traduits du sanskrit et du tibétain; accompagnés d'une introduction, de notes et d'une édition de la version tibétaine*, Collection Jean Przyluski, t. 2, Paris 1959).

The school of Sāramati

With respect to the *Ratnagotravibhāga*, an extensive study by J. Takasaki has been published, which is of the utmost importance for the assessment of the text: *A Study on the Ratnagotravibhāga (Uttaratantra), being a Treatise on the Tathāgatagarbha Theory of the Mahāyāna Buddhism*, Roma 1966 (Serie Orientale Roma 33). – A detailed presentation on the Tathāgatagarbha- and Gotra-theory, which is so important for this school, will soon appear in a book by D. Seyfort Ruegg. <423>

The Yogācāra school

A new edition of the *Bodhisattvabhūmi* by N. Dutt (Tibetan Sanskrit Works Series, Vol. 7) appeared in Patna 1966. In addition, large parts of the other sections of the *Yogācārabhūmi* have been found among the Buddhist Sanskrit manuscripts photographed by Rāhula Sānkrityāyana in Tibet. Of these, so far *The Yogācārabhūmi of Ācārya Asaṅga*, ed. by Vidhushekhara Bhattacharya, Part I, Calcutta 1957, has been published. This contains the first five sections of the work. The thirteenth section, the *Śrāvakabhūmi,* was taken on for publication by A. Wayman. So far only the *Analysis of the Śrāvakabhūmi Manuscript* by A. Wayman, Berkeley and Los Angeles 1961 (University of California Publications in Classical Philology, vol. 17), and the text of the short sections 8, 9, and 14, which happened to be included in the manuscript of the *Śrāvakabhūmi,* under the title "The Sacittikā and Acittikā Bhūmi and the Pratyekabuddhabhūmi (Sanskrit texts)" by A. Wayman (*Journal of Indian and Buddhist Studies,* Vol. 8/1960, pp. 375–79) have appeared. Contrary to A. Wayman's opinion, I am holding to my own view that the *Yogācārabhūmi* is a gradually developed work of the school, and refer for this to L. Schmithausen's *Zur Literaturgeschichte der älteren Yogācāra-Schule* (Zeitschrift der Deutschen Morgenländischen Gesellschaft. Supplementa I: Vorträge des XVII. Deutschen Orientalistentages in Würzburg, Wiesbaden 1969, pp. 811–23).

Likewise, I am holding to the view that in Maitreyanātha we must see a historical personality to whom a number of works are to be ascribed, which are connected by the same characteristic views and therefore allow the conclusion of identical authorship. With respect to these works, important new publications should be mentioned. The text of the *Abhisamayālaṃkāra,* <424> with the Tibetan translation, was already published in 1929 by Th. Stcherbatsky and E. Obermiller as nr. 23 of the *Bibliotheca Buddhica.* An edition with the commentary by Haribhadra was brought out by G. Tucci (Gaekwad's Oriental Series, Vol. 62, Baroda 1932) and by U. Wogihara (Tokyo 1932–1935). In addition, E. Obermiller had given a presentation of the doctrine in *Acta Orientalia,* Vol. 11/1932–1933. In the meantime, a translation of the text by E. Conze has appeared: *Abhisamayaalaṃkāra, Introduction and translation from the original text,* Roma 1954 (Serie Orientale Roma 6). C. Pensa published an older commentary than Haribhadra's with *L'Abhisamayālaṃkāravṛtti di Ārya-Vimuktisena, primo abhisamaya,* Roma 1967 (Serie

Orientale Roma 37). Haribhadra's own commentary has been reprinted in the edition of the *Aṣṭasāhasrikā Prajñāpāramitā* by P. L. Vaidya (Buddhist Sanskrit Texts, No. 4, Darbhanga 1960).

An edition of the Sanskrit text of the *Madhyāntavibhāga* together with the commentary by Vasubandhu appeared in G. M. Nagao *Madhyāntavibhāga-bhāṣya: a Buddhist philosophical treatise edited for the first time from a Sanskrit manuscript,* Tokyo 1964. J. Nozawa published the Tibetan translation, together with a fragment of the Sanskrit text, of another work by Maitreyanātha—the *Dharmadharmatāvibhaṅga,* along with the corresponding commentary by Vasubandhu—under the title "The Dharmadharmatāvibhaṅga and the Dharmadharmatāvibhaṅga-vṛtti" in the felicitation volume for S. Yamaguchi (*Studies in Indology and Buddhology,* Kyoto 1955).

Of Asaṅga's works mentioned in this book, the *Abhidharma Samuccaya of Asanga,* ed. by Pralhad Pradhan, <425> Santiniketan 1950 (Visva-Bharati Studies 12) has been published in the meantime. This edition is based on an incomplete manuscript of the Sanskrit text. That which is missing in the manuscript has been retranslated from the Chinese and Tibetan, although not always satisfactorily. Sthiramati's commentary, which was also found in its Sanskrit original by Rāhula Sānkrityāyana, served as valuable aid in this. This commentary itself has, however, not been published so far.

With respect to Vasubandhu's *Viṃśatikā Vijñaptimātratāsiddhi* and *Triṃśikā Vijñaptimātratāsiddhi,* further examinations seem to confirm my assignment of these to the younger Vasubandhu; *cf.* L. Schmithausen, "Sautrāntika-Voraussetzungen in Viṃśatikā und Triṃśikā" (*Wiener Zeitschrift für die Kunde Süd- und Ostasiens,* Bd. 11/1967, pp. 109–36). In any case, the *Abhidharmakośa, Karmasiddhi, Viṃśatikā* and *Triṃśikā* clearly belong to one and the same sequence of development.

Of Dignāga's principal work, the *Pramāṇasamuccaya*, the first part has, in the meantime, appeared under the title *Dignāga, On Perception, being the Pratyakṣapariccheda of Dignāga's Pramāṇasamuccaya; from the Sanskrit fragments and the Tibetan versions*. Translated and annotated by Masaki Hattori, Cambridge, Massachusetts 1968 (Harvard Oriental Series, Vol. 47). Dignāga's smaller works are printed at the end of my essay "Dignāga, sein Werk und seine Entwicklung" (*Wiener Zeitschrift für die Kunde Süd- und Ostasiens*, Bd. 3/1959, pp. 83–164). <426>

Appendices

APPENDIX I: AMALAVIJÑĀNA AND ĀLAYAVIJÑĀNA. A CONTRIBUTION TO THE EPISTEMOLOGY OF BUDDHISM.[1]

[A. Introduction

AA. The dispute as to whether *amalavijñāna* or *ālayavijñāna* is the foundation of cognition and of the entire phenomenal world

AB. The purpose of the essay

B. The investigation

BA. The facts about the dispute in China

BB. The facts about the dispute in India

BBA. The doctrine of the world soul, *brahman* or *ātman*, as the standard or model for later Indian philosophy

BBB. The bearer of cognition and the relationship of highest reality to phenomenal world in the Sāṃkhya system

BBC. The bearer of cognition and the relationship of highest reality to phenomenal world in Buddhism

BBC.1. Sarvāstivāda, Madhyamaka, Yogācāra

BBC.2. The development of the doctrines of the Yogācāra: Sāramati, Maitreyanātha and Asaṅga

BBC.3. The Mahāsāṃghikas' doctrine of pure cognition

BBC.4. Sāramati's system

BBC.5. Maitreyanātha's system

BBC.6. Asaṅga's system

C. The result of the investigation]

---

[1] First published in: *Alt- und Neu-Indische Studien* 7, Hamburg 1951, pp. 148–59; also published in *Kleine Schriften*, Wiesbaden 192, pp. 637–48.

A. INTRODUCTION

AA. *The dispute as to whether amalavijñāna or ālayavijñāna is the foundation of cognition and of the entire phenomenal world*

In his brilliant article on the authenticity of the *Mahāyāna-śraddhotpādaśāstra*,[1] P. Demiéville has pointed out an interesting dispute that occupied the Buddhist schools of China in a lively way in the sixth and seventh centuries c.e. At issue was the question of whether stainless cognition *(amalavijñāna)* or fundamental cognition *(ālayavijñāna)* is to be seen as the foundation of cognition and the entire phenomenal world.

Demiéville has outlined the essential aspects of the different opinions of the schools and the course of the discussion with wonderful clarity. In one thing he was mistaken, however, since he concludes his description with the words (p. 46):

> La querelle était vraiment bien vaine, car en fait, qu'on classe le *vijñāna* pur comme une section de l'*ālaya* ou qu'on en fasse un neuvième *vijñāna* sous le nom d'*amala*, cela importe assez peu au fond de la doctrine. Mais les Chinois se sont toujours montrés friands de classifications verbales, et il n'y a pas lieu de s'étonner qu'ils aient pu tant discuter sur une question en somme si superficielle.

> The dispute was truly quite in vain, since whether in fact one classifies pure cognition *(vijñāna)* as part of the *ālaya* or makes of it a ninth cognition *(vijñāna)* under the name of *amala*, makes very little difference to the heart of the doctrine. But the Chinese have

---

[1] P. Demiéville, *Sur l'authenticité du Ta tch'eng k'i sin louen*, Bulletin de la Maison Franco-Japonaise, série française, tome II, No. 2/1929.

persistently shown themselves to be fond of verbal classifications, so it is no surprise that they were able to create so much discussion about a question that is in fact so superficial.

AB. *The purpose of the essay*

In this entire discussion he has thus seen nothing but a subordinate dispute among the schools. This, however, is not right. In reality, this is one of the most fundamental and most difficult questions in the whole of Buddhist and of Indian epistemology. To demonstrate this and to place the problem in its proper context within the historical development [of Indian philosophy] is the purpose of the following essay.

3. THE INVESTIGATION

3A. *The facts about the dispute in China*

The facts, as Demiéville has demonstrated them, are the following:[1]

In the year 508 c.e., two Buddhist missionaries, Bodhiruci and Ratnamati, came from India to China. Both belonged to the idealistic Yogācāra school and both relied first and foremost on Vasubandhu the Elder's[2] commentaries on various Mahāyāna sutras. It was Vasubandhu's *Daśabhūmikaśāstra* in particular that both of them considered to be the fundamental text and that they both translated into Chinese. Nonetheless, their followers formed two separate schools of thought. The crux of the dispute that lead to this split can be clearly recognized in

---

[1] pp. 30ff.

[2] [For a recent survey of the issue of two Vasubandhus *cf.* Florin Deleanu: *The Chapter on the Mundane Path* (Laukikamārga) *in the* Śrāvakabhūmi. *A Trilingual Edition,* 2 Vols. Tokyo: The International Institute for Buddhist Studies 2006: 186–94 (with notes 206, 207 in particular).]

the surviving reports. It had to do with the foundation of all cognition. According to Bodhiruci, the foundation of all cognition is the *ālayavijñāna* (fundamental cognition), according to Ratnamati, it is the *tathatā* (suchness). Ratnamati's view was later supported by the great Indian missionary Paramārtha, who came to China in 546 c.e. He too belonged to the <149> Yogācāra school, though for him the fundamental text was Asaṅga's *Mahāyānasaṃgraha*. Paramārtha taught that the foundation of all cognition is not the *ālayavijñāna,* but rather a further cognition, the *amalavijñāna* (stainless cognition). The dispute soon subsided, however. The final word rested, in the seventh century, on the authority of Hiuan-tsang, who, in contrast to Paramārtha, sided with the *ālayavijñāna.*

In order to understand this entire discussion, we must first grasp two things:

Firstly, as can clearly be drawn from traditional reports,[1] the issue at hand is a dispute about the interpretation of the ancient texts. Both camps, Bodhiruci just like Ratnamati and Paramārtha just like Hiuan-tsang, base themselves on the same texts, from which they extrapolate their own view. Thus while the starting points of their different views were present in the ancient texts, the elaboration of the problem and the differing of the schools based thereon are more recent.

Secondly, it is important that tradition traces the origin of the dispute back to India.[2] This of course suggests itself, since the leading personalities of the aforementioned schools were either themselves Indian or, as in the case of Hiuan-tsang, directly dependent on the Indian tradition. So, the doctrine of *amalavijñāna* is traced back to the school of Sthiramati, and the doctrine of *ālayavijñāna* to Dharmapāla. The picture we have of the Yogācāra school in India during the sixth century is indeed

[1] Demiéville, pp. 38ff.

[2] Demiéville, p. 43.

dominated by the comprehensive activity of commentators concerned with the works of Asaṅga and Vasubandhu, in particular Vasubandhu's *Triṃśikā Vijñaptimātratāsiddhi.* The center of this [activity] was the great Buddhist university at Nālandā. At the beginning of the sixth century, however, a respected teacher from Nālandā, Guṇamati, had moved to Valabhī in Kāṭhiāvār and there founded his own school, which reached the height of its success under his pupil Sthiramati. At the same time, Nālandā came into full flower under the great teacher Dharmapāla. In connection with this we hear often of an opposition between the two schools, specifically that Shiramati followed the old masters *(pūrvācarya),* while Dharmapāla advocated a more progressive direction. The different views about the *amalavijñāna* and the *ālayavijñāna* thus also hark back to the opposition between these two schools. The doctrine of the *amalavijñāna* comes from the school of Valabhī. And in fact, its principal representative, Paramārtha, lived in neighboring Mālava. The doctrine of the *ālayavijñāna,* on the other hand, originates in Nālandā. And it is well known that Hiuan-tsang found his ultimate authority in Dharmapāla.

3. *The facts about the dispute in India*

With this we come to the question of what lead to this difference of opinion in India and what underlies it. But in order to answer this question, we have to go a ways further back.

3A. *The doctrine of the world soul, brahman or ātman, as the standard or model for later Indian philosophy*

The most important, though not the only stream of development of the older Indian philosophy originated in the *Upaniṣads*. It was here that the doctrine of the world soul, the *brahman* or *ātman,* was created, which then remained largely authoritative and exemplary. <150> Even in the most ancient times, we can already see the tendency to place the *brahman* far above everything worldly; to proclaim it to be inconceivable and free from all worldly definitions. In the end only three definitions remained in the most important doctrine; specifically that handed down under Yājñavalkya's name, which the later Vedānta brought together in the term *saccidānanda:* it [i.e., *brahman*] is being, it is consciousness, and it is bliss. The same tendency, however, also continued in the schools that arose later from the same stream of development, in particular in the relevant doctrines of the Epic, in Buddhism, and in Sāṃkhya. Here as well one sought to elevate the highest reality beyond everything worldly, indeed, even more emphatically. [Thus:]

[1] Its definition as bliss, particularly characteristic of Yājñavalkya's doctrine, was generally dropped.

[2] Yet also in its definition as being, one often saw a worldly concept that does not apply to the highest reality. Thus as early as in the doctrines of the Epic we find the highest reality described as neither being nor non-being.[1] And this occurs most pointedly in the Madhyamaka school of Buddhism.

[3] But the greatest difficulties were presented by its third definition as consciousness. To simply let this go was not an easy decision to make since to see in the soul the bearer of cognition too readily suggested itself. To retain it, on the other hand, entailed very undesirable consequences. Special importance was attributed to the eternal untouchedness and immutability of the highest reality, since that is all that places it beyond the becoming and ceasing and the pain thereof, which belongs intrinsically to the earthly world. But from this it follows that the highest reality can also not be active, since any activity means a change and thus a ceasing and arising. This [argument] was particularly used against the proponents of the belief in a highest

---

[1] *Mahābhārata* XII, 201, v. 27.

creator-god. The same also applies, however, to cognition. This is also a process and as such, a change. And thus one arrived at the conclusion that cognition cannot belong to the highest reality. One could not, on the other hand, simply deny cognition to the highest reality, since in that case, one had to ask oneself: what kind of connection, if any at all, would there be between the highest reality and the earthly world? Who then experiences existence and entanglement and release?

The bearer of cognition and the relationship of highest reality to phenomenal world in the Sāṃkhya system

The Sāṃkhya system tried to resolve these difficulties as follows. It was held that cognition and mental processes in general do not belong to the soul *(puruṣa)*, which here corresponds to the *ātman* or the highest reality, but rather to the mental organism. They are qualities of the mental organ, the *buddhi*. This latter, however, is not itself capable of cognition, since consciousness itself merely adheres to the soul. Thus one thought to preserve the soul's character as the bearer of cognition, and on the other hand, to relieve it of all events and the changes related to them. Its opponents inexorably pointed out, however, that any occurrence of awareness, as it must be ascribed to the soul as the highest subject, by necessity has the soul's changeability and thus its impermanence as a consequence. To this context <151> belongs the oft-quoted verse, which I presume is derived from Vasubandhu's *Paramārthasaptatikā:*[1]

> *varṣātapābhyāṃ kiṃ vyomnaś carmaṇy asti tayoḥ phalam /*
> *carmopamaś cet so 'nityaḥ khatulyaś ced asatphalaḥ //*

---

[1] Yaśomitra, *Sphuṭārthā*, p. 699, 25; *Yuktidīpikā* (Calcutta S. S.), p. 105, 4; *Nyāyavārttika* (Kashi S. S.), p. 355, 4, etc.

> How can rain and sunshine affect space! Yet they affect the skin.
> Now if (the soul) is akin to skin, then it is impermanent. Yet if it is akin to space, then it is impervious to being affected.

Finally, after several vain attempts,[1] the following theory was arrived at. It was held that the *buddhi* resembles a two-sided mirror. On one side, the perceived objects are reflected, on the other side, the consciousness of the soul, which thus passes over to the *buddhi,* so to speak, and enables it to cognize the objects. Thus it was thought possible to attribute all events in the process of cognition exclusively to the *buddhi* and yet at the same time to hold on to the soul as the principle of cognition. In doing so, this co-operation of soul and *buddhi* was carefully formulated in the following way:[2]

> *apariṇāminī hi bhoktṛśaktir apratisaṃkramā ca pariṇāminy arthe pratisaṃkrānteva tadvṛttim anupatati, tasyāś ca prāptacaitanyopagraharūpāyā buddhivṛtter anukāramātratayā buddhivṛttyaviśiṣṭā hi jñānavṛttir ity ākhyāyate.*

> Although the soul's capability to cognize is unchanging and cannot pass over to any (other entity), it nevertheless passes over to the changeable *buddhi,* so to speak, and follows its activity. And only because it follows the activity of the *buddhi,* which has thus adopted the form of consciousness, it is said that the activity of the soul is not different from the activity of the *buddhi.*

---

[1] *Cf.* here the presentation in the first volume of my *History of Indian Philosophy*.

[2] Vyāsa, *Yogabhāṣya* (Ānandāśrama S. S.), pp. 89, 2 and 197, 4.

But this theory was too forced for it to succeed in broader circles. Indeed, it was unanimously rejected by all the schools other than the Sāṃkhya.

3BC. *The bearer of cognition and the relationship of highest reality to phenomenal world in Buddhism*

3BC.1. *Sarvāstivāda, Madhyamaka, Yogācāra*

Buddhism followed very different paths to the resolution of the question of the relationship of the highest reality to the phenomenal world and the question of the bearer of cognition. Here, from the beginning, all mental processes were attributed exclusively to the mental factors, without recourse to a soul or an ultimate state of being. In this way the difficulties discussed above were avoided. A soul had thus also become superfluous, however, and the fully developed scholasticism (Abhidharma), of the Sarvāstivāda in particular, also did not shy away from completely denying a soul.

But for the schools that did not go so far, the original problem continued to exist to its full extent, and this was particularly true for the schools of the Mahāyāna. The latter had emerged from the circles of mystics who could not be talked out of their belief in the ultimate state of being, which they had experienced in the state of meditation. This, however, left them still faced with the same old difficulties.

It is true that the most extreme school, the Madhyamaka, was little affected by all of this—although it was they in particular who emphasized the inconceivability of the highest reality the most pointedly and thus took the contrast to the phenomenal world <152> to its extreme—but this was only so because they did not ask the decisive questions.

For the Yogācāra school, on the other hand, the difficulties were all the greater, and all the more so since they viewed the phenomenal world as conception. For them, therefore, the question of the bearer of cognition must by necessity have been of central importance. And with this we are already approaching the circles from which our investigation began.

BBC.2. *The development of the doctrines of the Yogācāra: Sāramati, Maitreyanātha and Asaṅga*

In discussing the doctrines of the Yogācāras, we will follow the course of development that proceeded essentially in the following way.

The Yogācāra school was originally, as even the name suggests, a school that concerned itself above all else with questions relating to liberation and that had developed an extensive scholasticism on this subject. As with most of the Mahāyāna schools, [the early Yogācāra school] was closely connected with the circles of the Mahāsaṃghikas, but did not possess a philosophical system of its own. While it did also address metaphysical questions, this did not go beyond a few isolated attempts and there was no actual system to speak of.

The creation of such a system was the achievement of Maitreyanātha who melded the existing attempts with the doctrine of an ultimate state of being and with the buddhology of Sāramati's school to form a unit, and thus strove at the same time for a synthesis with the tenets of the Mādhyamikas.

What was still missing though, was a fully developed scholasticism of the type the Śrāvakayāna schools had developed, a scholasticism that systematically arranged all factors, and especially those of the phenomenal world, and discussed them in philosophically clearly defined terms. [The Yogācāra] school first achieved this thanks to Asaṅga. Asaṅga, who came from the Śrāvakayāna school of the Mahīśāsakas, developed and expanded the Yogācāras' Abhidharma based on the doctrines of his former school. He built a monumental system of doctrines atop the foundation laid by Maitreyanātha, while also making use of the old scholasticism of liberation. In all its essential features this system of doctrines has continued to be authoritative for this school.

BC.3. *The Mahāsāṃghikas' doctrine of pure cognition*

For the issues that concern us here, we must now first draw upon a theorem of the Mahāsāṃghikas—the influence of which can still be detected in various places in the Mahāyāna treatises[1]—specifically, their doctrine of pure cognition. As early as the Pāli canon, we occasionally find the sentence:

> *pabhassaraṃ idaṃ bhikkhave cittaṃ taṃ ca kho āgantukehi upakkilesehi upakkiliṭṭhaṃ.*[2]
>
> This mind, o monks, is brightly luminous. It is polluted through adventitious pollutions.

Here then, a form of mind is spoken of, which is by nature pure and to which all contaminations attach themselves in only an adventitious manner, without affecting it in its essence. The Mahāsāṃghika school adopted this view and developed it into a firm theorem that is rendered in the following way in Vasumitra's well-known treatise on the Buddhist schools and their tenets (T 2031, p. 15c27; theorem 42 [35][3]):

> The nature of the mind is pure in its original state *(prakṛtiviśuddha).* However, when it is polluted by adventitious *(āgantuka)* pollutions *(upakleśa),* it is called *impure.* <153>

---

[1] Compare La Vallée Poussin's references and citations in *Abhidharmakośa* VI, p. 299, footnote 1 and *Vijñaptimātratāsiddhi,* pp. 109f.

[2] *Anguttaranikāya* I, 10ff.

[3] The Chinese texts are cited according to the Taishō edition of the Tripiṭaka.

What is not certain is what place this pure mind occupied within the Mahāsāṃghikas' system. According to the Tibetan tradition,[1] it was counted as one of the nine unconditioned factors *(asaṃskṛtā dharmāḥ)*. What is certain, on the other hand, is that it served as the foundation of all mental processes[2] and that a lasting essence was attributed to it.[3]

Sāramati's system

The same views of the pure mind were taken over by Sāramati and were transferred to the ultimate state of being. For Sāramati, the ultimate state of being holds the central position in his doctrine, while everything else becomes less important. More specifically, his version of the ultimate state of being has features quite similar to the *ātman* of the *Upaniṣads*. It is true that its inconceivability and ineffability are occasionally emphasized, but he does not avoid any statement at all—as is consistently done in the Madhyamaka system. A description such as the following is quite reminiscent of the tone of the *Upaniṣads* (*Uttaratantra*,[4] T 1611, p. 835a18–25; Ob. I, vv. 77–79; [J. vv. 80–82]):

---

[1] *Cf.* M. Walleser, *Die Sekten des alten Buddhismus*, Heidelberg 1927, p. 27.

[2] *Cf.* the doctrine of the *mūlavijñāna* (root cognition), La Vallée Poussin, *Vijñaptimātratāsiddhi*, pp. 178f.; E. Lamotte, "Karmasiddhiprakaraṇa," *Mélanges chinois et bouddhiques* IV/1936, p. 250; E. Lamotte, *La Somme du Grand Véhicule*, Tome II, Louvain 1938, p. 27 and 7*.

[3] This we can see from the polemic in the *Mahāvibhāṣāśāstra* and in Saṅghabhadra's *Nyāyānusāra*; *cf.* La Vallée Poussin, *Abhidharmakośa* VI, p. 299, footnote 1.

[4] Translated from the Tibetan by E. Obermiller, *The Sublime Science of the Great Vehicle to Salvation, being a Manual of Buddhist Monism, the Work of Ārya Maitreya with a Commentary by Āryāsaṅga*, in Acta Orientalia IX/1931, pp. 81–306. The [Tibetan] text is not appended, the translation therefore not verifiable. Since, as far as I know, the fragments of the original Sanskrit texts are not yet published and I do not at the moment have access

It is not born and it does not die, it does not sicken and it does not age, because it is eternal, lasting, pure, and immutable.

Because it is eternal, it is not born, since it is without even a mental *(manomaya)* body.

Because it is lasting, it does not die, since it is also without imperceptible transformation.

Because it is pure, it does not sicken, since it is not permeated by defilements *(kleśa)*.

And because it is immutable, it does not age, since it is also not adhered to by uncontaminated formations *(anāsrava saṃskāra)*.

Beyond this, quite specific qualities are actually attributed to the ultimate state of being, such as, for example, the four qualities

---

to a Tanjur, I quote according to Ratnamati's Chinese translation, but add the verse numbers according to Obermiller.

Supplementary note by Erich Frauwallner:

Since the composition of this essay, the Sanskrit original of the *Uttaratantra (Ratnagotravibhāga)* by E. H. Johnston (J) has been published in the *Journal of the Bihar Research Society* XXXVI/1950. The passages from the Chinese translation reproduced above deviate from the original Sanskrit in some details. In terms of the ideas put forward, nothing has changed. Since the division of the verses in Obermiller is often flawed, his numbering of the verses differs from that of the Sanskrit text. The above-mentioned verses correspond in the following way: v. 30 = 30; v. 34 = 35; v. 46 = 47; v. 48 = 49; vv. 51f. and 61f. = 52f. and 62f.; vv. 58ff. = 59ff.; vv. 77–79 = 80–82.

[J. vv. 80–82:

na jāyate na mriyate bādhyate no na jīryate /
sa nityatvād dhruvatvāc ca śivatvāc chāśvatatvataḥ //80//
na jāyate sa nityatvād ātmabhāvair mano-mayaiḥ /
acintya-pariṇāmena dhruvatvān mriyate na saḥ //81//
vāsanā-vyādhibhiḥ sūkṣmair bādhyate na śivatvataḥ /
anāsravābhisaṃskāraiḥ śāśvatatvān na jīryate //82//]

of purity, self, bliss, and eternity.[1] This ultimate state of being is the *dharmakāya* of the Buddha and is inherent as an element *(dhātu)* or germ *(gotra)* in all sentient beings.

This same ultimate state of being now also shows the characteristic features of the *viśuddha citta* [pure mind]. It is consciousness in its intrinsic nature[2] and it is designated as *vimala citta*[3] [stainless mind] or *viśuddha citta*.[4] Above all, it is pure in its original state.[5] All of the contaminations that the entanglement in cyclic existence entails <154> are merely adventitious. More precisely, in ordinary people [the ultimate state of being] is completely contaminated, in Bodhisattvas partially contaminated and partially pure, and in Buddhas completely pure.[6] This is elaborated upon through numerous analogies, among which the image of space is the most popular. Of these many examples, one will suffice (T 1611, p. 814a18–21 = 832c4–7 [*cf.* T 1626, p. 893b1f.] and 814b7–10 = 832c22–25; Ob. I, vv. 51f. and 61f.; [J. vv. 52f. and 62f.]):

> Just as space pervades everything and, because of its subtlety, is not soiled by dust, similarly Buddha-nature pervades all sentient beings and is not soiled by defilements *(kleśa)*.[7]

---

[1] T 1611, p. 814a8f. = 829b9f.; Ob. I, v. 34; [J. v. 35].

[2] Ob. p. 187, A 6 *sems kyi rang bzhin don dam pa'i bden pa = cittasvabhāva paramārthasatyam;* T 1611, p. 814a29 = 832c15 *tseu sing ts'ing tsing sin.*

[3] For example T 1611, p. 814a17 = 832b8; Ob. I, v. 48; [J. v. 49].

[4] For example T 1611, p. 814b2ff. = 832c17ff.; Ob. I, vv. 58ff.; [J. vv. 59ff].

[5] *tseu sing chang pou jan,* T 1611, p. 814a6 = 828b21; Ob. I, v. 30; [J. v. 30]; *cf.* T 1626 *(Dharmadhātuviśeṣatā-śāstram),* p. 892b27.

[6] T 1611, p. 814a14f. = 832a11f.; Ob. I, v. 46; *cf.* T 1626, p. 893a5f.

[J. v. 47:

aśuddho 'śuddha-śuddho 'tha suviśuddho yathā-kramam /
sattva-dhātur iti prokto bodhisattvas tathāgataḥ //47//]

[7] [J. v. 52:

Just as the entire world arises and ceases supported by space, similarly all vital energies arise and cease supported by this uncontaminated element *(anāsrava dhātu).*[1]

[. . .]

The pure mind, like space, is without cause, without condition, and without the totality (of causes and conditions) *(sāmagrī),* it knows no arising, abiding, and ceasing.[2]

Just like space, the pure mind is constantly bright and unchanging. Due to false conception, it becomes polluted by the adventitious stains of defilements.[3]

Maitreyanātha's system

These views of Sāramati's constitute one of the most important components out of which Maitreyanātha constructed his system. In [Maitreyanātha] as well, the ultimate state of being, which he most often calls the *element of the factors (dharmadhātu)* or also *suchness (tathatā),* occupies the center of the system. It is true

---

yathā sarva-gataṃ saukṣmyād ākāśaṃ nopalipyate /
sarvatrāvasthitaḥ sattve tathāyaṃ nopalipyate //52//]

1 [J. v. 53:

yathā sarvatra lokānām ākāśa udaya-vyayaḥ /
tathaivāsaṃskṛte dhātav indriyāṇāṃ vyayodayaḥ //53//]

2 [J. v. 62:

na hetuḥ pratyayo nāpi na sāmagrī na codayaḥ /
na vayayo na sthitaś citta-prakṛter vyoma-dhātuvat //62//]

3 [J. v. 63:

cittasya yāsau prakṛtiḥ prabhāsvarā
na jātu sā dyaur iva yāti vikriyām /
āgantukai rāgamalādibhis tv asāv upaiti
saṃkleśam abhūtakalpajaiḥ //63//]

that here, due to the strong Madhyamaka influence, it is treated more abstractly, but the essential features are the same.[1] It is all-pervasive like space, undivided and unvarying. As an element *(dhātu)* or seed *(bīja)*, it is inherent in all sentient beings,[2] and in its pure form, it constitutes the nature of the Buddha.[3] First and foremost, however, it again bears the characteristic features of the *viśuddha citta* [pure mind]. It is mental, pure by nature, and only adventitiously polluted. This is shown very clearly, for example, by the following verses from the fifth chapter of the *Madhyāntavibhāga*.[4] Maitreyanātha enumerates here the various kinds of errorlessness *(aviparyāsa)* and in doing so says (vv. 19b–23a):

> */ chos kyi dbyings ni ma gtogs par // 'di ltar chos yod ma yin te //* 19b
> */ de'i phyir spyi'i mtshan nyid der // de ni phyin ci ma log pa'o /* 20a

---

[1] *Cf.* to this in particular the ninth chapter of the *Mahāyānasūtrālaṃkāra*, ed. Sylvain Lévi, Paris 1907–1911.

[2] For example, IX, v. 15.

[3] For example IX, v. 59.

[4] Ed. Susumu Yamaguchi, Nagoya 1935 (Tibetan and Chinese text); the Sanskrit original has to my knowledge not yet been published. [*Cf.* now: Gadjin M. Nagao: *Madhyāntavibhāga-Bhāṣya: Buddhist Philosophical Treatise Edited for the First Time from a Sanskrit Manuscript.* Suzuki Research Foundation: Tokyo 1964:

> *dharmadhātuvinirmukto yasmād dharmo na vidyate //* 19b
> *sāmānyalakṣaṇaṃ tasmāt sa ca tatrāviparyayaḥ /* 20a
> *viparyastamanaskārāvihāniparihāṇitaḥ //* 20b
> *tadaśuddhir viśuddhiś ca sa ca tatrāviparyayaḥ /* 21a
> *dharmadhātor viśuddhatvāt prakṛtyā vyomavat punaḥ //* 21b
> *dvayasyāgantukatvaṃ hi sa ca tatrāviparyayaḥ /* 22a
> *saṃkleśaś ca viśuddhiś ca dharmapudgalayor na hi //* 22b
> *asattvāt trāsatāmānau nātaḥ so 'trāviparyayaḥ //* 23a

Verses 5.19b–23a are numbered 19–22 in Nagao's edition.]

Since there is no factor that would be separated from the element of the factors *(dharmadhātuvinirmukto yasmād dharmo na vidyate)*, therefore that is errorlessness with respect to the common characteristic.

/ *phyin ci log gi yid la byed // ma spangs pa dang spangs pa las* // 20b
/ *de ni ma dag rnam dag ste // de yang de la ma log pa'o* / 21a

The impurity and purity of the (element of the factors) through the not-vanishing or vanishing of erroneous thinking *(viparyastamanaskāra)*, that is errorlessness with respect to them, [i.e., impurity and purity].

/ *chos kyi dbyings ni rang bzhin gyis // rnam par dag phyir nam mkha bzhin* // 21b
/ *gnyis ni glo bur gyung ba ste // de yang de la ma log pa'o* / 22a

That these two (impurity and purity) are adventitious, since the element of the factors is pure by nature, like space *(dhurmadhātor viśuddhatvāt prakṛtyā vyomavat)*; that is errorlessness in regard to it, [i.e., their being adventitious].

/ *chos rnams dang ni gang zag gi // kun nas nyon mongs rnam dag med* // 22b
/ *med phyir de bas skrag dang dngang // med de de 'dir ma log pa'o* / 23a. <155>

For pollution and purification do not apply to the factors and the person *(pudgala)*, since these do not exist. Therefore neither fear nor pride is appropriate here. That is errorlessness with respect to it, [i.e., absence of fear and pride].

Maitreyanāthā is, furthermore, also acquainted with the three-fold division of sentient beings, according to whether they are impure, impure and pure, or completely pure.[1] And he elucidates the pollution and purification of the ultimate state of being, in a way very similar to Sāramati's, namely through analogies. In particular, he compares them to the purely adventitious cloudiness, to which water, gold, or space are subject, and following which the original purity reasserts itself.[2]

From all of this we can see that Maitreyanātha teaches an ultimate state of being that, similar to the *ātman* of the *Upaniṣads*, is inherent in all living beings, and also that thus, for him, this ultimate state of being is the bearer of existence and of cognition. With this though, we come to the question of where Maitreyanātha stands regarding the problems discussed above and how he resolves the difficulty of attributing the processes of cognition to the ultimate state of being.

Regarding this, it must be said that this difficulty does not, in fact, exist for him. Like Sāramati's, his doctrine has undergone its own development from its own presuppositions and hence has not inherited these problems. We have seen that Sāramati unhesitatingly attributed positive qualities to the ultimate state of being, and so, like Maitreyanātha, he does not find anything objectionable in thinking the ultimate state of being capable of action. Indeed, for the buddhology of both of them it is even required, since for them—since the ultimate state of being also constitutes the essence of the Buddha—the entire activity of the Buddha must by necessity also emanate from [the ultimate state of being]. Maitreyanātha most clearly explains this in the ninth chapter of his *Mahāyānasūtrālaṃkāra,* in which for example, he compares the activity of the Buddha, which occurs without

---

[1] *Madhyāntavibhāga* IV, vv. 15b–16a.

[2] *Cf. Madhyāntavibhāga* I, v. 16, *Mahāyānasūtrālaṃkāra* XI, v. 13, and the final remarks of the *Dharmadharmatāvibhāga*.

striving *(ābhoga)*, to the shining of a jewel or to the sound of celestial instruments that resound without being struck (v. 18f.); or in which he presents the example of the sun, which without effort, without selfishness, and without moving, illuminates everything (vv. 29ff. and 51ff.).

This leaves only the question then, of how Maitreyanātha conceives of the interplay between the ultimate state of being and the factors of the psyche with respect to cognition, and how he envisions the details of the mental processes at all.

Here, however, we encounter a gap in his system. Over all, it is one of the most characteristic features of the earliest Mahāyāna that it is without a philosophically clearly defined terminology and a systematics comparable to the Śrāvakayāna Abhidharma. The one-sided interest in the scholasticism of liberation and in the metaphysical questions related to the ultimate state of being prevented their development. The old canonical terms <156> were generally considered to be sufficient, and when necessary, particular ideas were borrowed from the Śrāvakayāna scholasticism. Such is also the case with Maitreyanātha. In vain we search in him for a fully developed psychology, comparable for example, to that of the Sarvāstivāda. While it is true that he is the first to attempt to change this, particularly in the first chapter of his *Madhyāntavibhāga,* he does not progress beyond mere beginnings. A systematics is still missing. The terms and expressions are idiosyncratic and strange. And it is typical that, for example, the name *ālayavijñāna,* the most characteristic term of the later Yogācāra school, does not appear [in Maitreyanātha's writings]. The credit for having brought about a fundamental change in all of this goes to his great disciple Asaṅga, to whom we must now turn our attention.

BBC.6. *Asaṅga's system*

As already mentioned, Asaṅga systematically introduced the philosophical conceptions of the Śrāvakayāna into the Yogācāra system and adapted them to its needs. In his work, therefore, we also find a fully developed psychology:[1] the long familiar six kinds of cognition, to which is added the *manas* [thinking] as the bearer of the I-awareness, and finally the *ālayavijñāna* [fundamental cognition], which forms the foundation of the whole of the mental processes and of which—incidentally—prototypes could already be found in the Śrāvakayāna. Similar to the Śrāvakayāna schools, he also provides a detailed list of all of the factors of the psyche that are associated with cognition *(caitta).* He bases his psychology on these factors and with them he explains all of the mental processes. In this, surprisingly, we can then see the strongest contrast to Maitreyanātha, since for Asaṅga, as for the schools of the Śrāvakayāna, not only are the aforementioned factors of the psyche independently acting factors, but all of the processes of entanglement in cyclic existence and of liberation also take place within them. Next to them, the ultimate state of being—positioned centrally in Maitreyanātha—recedes completely into the background; but as surprising as this may appear on first sight, it is in fact quite natural.

In its scholasticism the Śrāvakayāna had created a highly developed philosophical system with very specific ways of thinking. Given this superior system, it is little wonder that in attempting to make it one's own, anyone approaching it without a firm philosophical foundation of their own would be compelled to follow its lead, and forced to think in these ways. Otherwise, one would have first had to develop one's own new manner of thinking, and this was not in Asaṅga's interest,

---

[1] A systematic synopsis of this is found at the beginning of the *Abhidharmasamuccaya* (T 1605) as well as that of the *Vikhyāpana* (T 1602).

who after all had his origins in the Śrāvakayāna. However, this Śrāvakayāna scholasticism understood mental processes only as the play of independently acting mental factors. There was no place in this system for an ultimate state of being in Sāramati's sense. And it is typical that the ultimate state of being, where it was incorporated into a Śrāvakayāna-style list of factors, is in no way an entity of a completely different type relative to the other [conditioned and unconditioned] factors, but rather—as a factor just like any other—it was listed among the unconditioned factors *(asaṃskṛta dharma)*.[1] <157>

Hence, in Asaṅga, the process of liberation—wherein the uniqueness of his view shows itself especially clearly—proceeds in the following way. Similarly to the Śrāvakayāna scholasticism,[2] he begins by distinguishing between polluted *(sāṃkleśika)* and pure *(vaiyavadānika)* factors. The fundamental cognition, the *ālayavijñāna*, along with all of the polluted factors that attach themselves to it, constitutes the foundation of cyclic existence. The preparation for liberation occurs in that—through hearing the Mahāyāna teachings and through their correct comprehension—pure factors are called forth that, along with their seeds, attach themselves to the mental complex of the *ālayavijñāna*. These pure factors are strengthened and increased in the course of the continued path of liberation. Finally, liberation

---

1 *Cf.* the suchness *(tathatā)* of the good, bad, and indeterminate factors in the list of the unconditioned factors of the Mahīśāsaka (in Vasumitra, T 2031, p. 17a8f.), and subsequently in Asaṅga's *Abhidharmasamuccaya* (T 1605, p. 666a21ff.) and *Vikhyāpana* (T 1602, p. 484b29ff.); see also Vasubandhu's *Mahāyānaśatadharmaśāstra* (T 1614, p. 855c19) and *Pañcaskandhaka* (T 1612, p. 850a19ff.); regarding the development of the term [i.e., *asaṃskṛta*] in the Yogācāra school, *cf.* further *Vijñaptimātratāsiddhi*, T 1585, p. 6b15ff. (La Vallée Poussin, pp. 72ff.).

2 *Cf.* the fundamental division between *sāsrava* (impure; contaminated) and *anāsravā* (pure; uncontaminated) *dharmas*, with which Vasubandhu opens his *Abhidharmakośa*.

occurs by means of the liberating nonconceptual knowledge *(nirvikalpaka jñāna)*, which reaches its peak at the end of the path of liberation. This [knowledge] namely brings forth a transformation *(parāvṛtti)* of the mental complex through which the polluted factors vanish and the pure factors alone remain. With this, liberation is attained. The complex of pure factors that alone now continues to exist is the *dharmakāya* of the Buddha. To express this in Asaṅga's own words (*Mahāyānasaṃgraha* IX, 1):[1]

> a. *de la 'khor ba ni gzhan gyi dbang gi ngo bo nyid de kun nas nyon mongs pa'i char gtogs pa'o //*
>
> The cycle of existences is the dependent nature *(paratantra svabhāva)*[2] insofar as [the dependent nature] constitutes the polluted part.
>
> b. *mya ngan las 'das pa ni de nyid rnam par byang ba'i char gtogs pa'o //*
>
> The *nirvāṇa* is [the dependent nature] insofar as [the dependent nature] constitutes the pure part.
>
> c. *gnas ni de nyid gnyi ga'i char gtogs pa ste / gzhan gyi dbang gi ngo bo nyid do //*
>
> This dependent nature, which encompasses both parts, is called the *basis (āśraya).*

---

[1] I quote according to the paragraph divisions in the edition of E. Lamotte, *La Somme du Grand Véhicule* (Bibliothèque du Muséon 7), Louvain, 1938.

[2] This is how the Yogācāra school refers to the entire complex of the factor of the psyche, on which the deception of the phenomenal world is based.

d. *gzhan gyur pa ni gang gzhan gyi dbang gi ngo bo nyid de nyid kyi gnyen po skyes na gang kun nas nyon mongs pa'i cha ldog cing rnam par byang ba'i char gyur pa'o //*

The transformation of the basis consists in the fact that this dependent nature, when its counteragent *(pratipakṣa)* arises, abandons its polluted part and becomes its pure part.

Of the *dharmakāya* he says further (X, 3):

gnas gyur pa'i mtshan nyid ni sgrib pa thams cad pa kun nas nyon mongs pa'i char gtogs pa'i gzhan gyi dbang gi ngo bo nyid rnam par log na sgrib pa thams cad las rnam par grol zhing chos thams cad la dbang sgyur ba nye bar gnas pa rnam par byang ba'i char gtogs pa'i gzhan gyi dbang gi ngo bo nyid gyur pa'i phyir ro //

Its characteristic is the transformation of the basis, because it has cast off the dependent nature that forms the polluted part and contains all obstructions (*āvaraṇa*), and it has become the dependent nature that forms the pure part <158> and has gained mastery over all factors through becoming free from all obstructions.

C. THE RESULT OF THE INVESTIGATION[1]

We thus come to the conclusion that on the question of the bearer of all mental processes a sharp difference of opinion exists between the two leaders of the Yogācāra school. Whereas Maitreyanātha locates it in the element of the factors *(dharmadhātu)*, that is to say, in the ultimate state of being, Asaṅga sees it in the complex of the factors of the psyche that group themselves around the *ālayavijñāna*.

Asaṅga did not completely supplant Maitreyanātha's doctrine, however, since the treatises of both were handed down alongside each other as the fundamental texts of the [Yogācāra]

---

[1] Editorial addition: The result of this investigation may be summarized by the following chart:

	Maitreyanātha		**Asaṅga**	
	unique:	*dharmadhātu*	unique:	*ālayavijñāna*
CHINA	**Ratnamati**		**Bodhiruci**	
	508 arrives in China		508 arrives in China	
	unique:	*tathatā*	unique:	*ālayavijñāna*
	both follow:			
	the commentaries of Vasubandhu [the Elder], in particular the *Daśabhūmikaśāstra*			
	Paramārtha		**Hiuan-tsang**	
	546 arrives in China		602–664	
	unique:	*amalavijñāna*	unique:	*ālayavijñāna*
	follows:	*Mahāyānasaṃgraha*		
INDIA	**school in Valabhī**		**school in Nālandā**	
	Guṇamati			
	≈ first half of the 6th cent.			
	Sthiramati		Dharmapāla	
	≈ middle of 6th cent.		≈ middle of 6th cent.; ca. 510–70	
	unique:	*amalavijñāna*	unique:	*ālayavijñāna*

school. It is thus only natural that this difference of opinion exerted its influence on the later school. Hence there arouse within the school various movements that decided in favor of one view or the other, and that then sought, in accordance with Indian custom, to interpret the entire tradition from their own point of view. And a last reverberation of this difference of opinion within the school is what we encounter in the Chinese reports discussed at the beginning of this [essay]. Ratnamati does advocate Maitreyanātha's line of thought, and Bodhiruci that of Asaṅga. Paramārtha attempts to reinterpret Asaṅga's principal work from Maitreyanātha's point of view, whereas Hiuan-tsang turns back again to Asaṅga's original view.[1]

How this dispute among the schools otherwise unfolded, especially in India itself, must be shown by further research, provided that it manages to piece together a realistic depiction of the history of the Yogācāra school from the rubble that confronts us. Nevertheless, a few things can already be said here.

The Chinese tradition connects the dispute with the difference of opinion between the schools of Nālandā and Valabhī, and this may be correct. However, whether Dharmapāla and Sthiramati were the principal representatives of the two views remains open to question. Their names have likely been invoked because they were well known as the most significant representatives of the two schools,[2] but by no means can they be the originators

---

[1] In his *Vijñaptimātratāsiddhi*, Hiuan-tsang mentions both views, i.e., the one that suchness *(tathatā)* is the basis of the transformation of the mental complex and that the *ālayavijñāna* completely vanishes [in this process], and the other that the *ālayavijñāna* is the basis and that cognition continues to exist and only undergoes a change in its character (*cf.* T 1585, k. 9, p. 51a3ff. and k. 10, p. 55a10ff.; in La Vallée Poussin pp. 610f. and 665). He himself leans toward the second view.

[2] Hiuan-tsang especially, when he refers to the doctrines of Sthiramati and Dharmapāla, seems to have their own treatises less in mind than the doctrines of their schools, as he had become acquainted with them in India.

of the difference of opinion on this issue, since when Bodhiruci and Ratnamati came to China [in 508], Dharmapāla had not yet been born and Sthiramati was no more than a boy. In addition, the most extensive treatise of Sthiramati's that has been found and published thus far,[1] the *Madhyāntavibhāgaṭīkā*, does not express any explicit support of Maitreyanātha's view by Sthiramati. Signs of the dispute can, however, also be detected here. Sthiramati was in fact not the first commentator on the *Madhyāntavibhāga* but had several predecessors, of which we can name at least one: Candrapāla. Thus, when it comes to important questions, [Sthiramati] <159> again and again presents several attempts at an explanation, and thereby the old difference of opinion between the doctrines of Maitreyanātha and Asaṅga becomes apparent. To give but one example: In the course of explaining the fourth chapter, Sthiramati comes to speak of the *dharmakāya* and says in this context:[2]

> *sarvāvaraṇaprahāṇat tatpratipakṣānāsravadharmabīja-pracayāc cāśrayaparāvṛttyātmakaḥ sarvadharmavaśa-vartī anālaya iti buddhānām dharmakāyaḥ . . . anye tu niḥśeṣāgantuka-malāpagamāt suviśuddho dharma-dhātur eva dharmatākāyo dharmakāya iti varṇayanti.*

> The *dharmakāya* of the Buddhas consists of the transformation of the basis, in that all obstructions are removed and the seeds of the uncontaminated factors that form their counteragent are accumulated; it has power over all factors and is without the fundamental cognition.[3] . . .

---

[1] Unfortunately, the Tibetan translations of these treatises are not available to me [at the moment].

[2] Sthiramati, *Madhyāntavibhāgaṭīkā, exposition systématique du Yogācāra-vijñaptivāda*, éd. par Susumu Yamaguchi, Nagoya 1934, p. 191, 4ff.

[3] Since this [fundamental cognition] vanishes with the polluted factors.

> Others, on the other hand, say that the element of the factors, completely purified through the removal of all adventitious stains, is called the *dharmakāya*, since the nature of the factors *(dharmatā)*, in this case, is the body *(kāya)*.[1]

The first opinion corresponds to Asaṅga's view, the second to Maitreyanātha's.

With this, the questions raised at the beginning [of this essay] have found their answer and our investigation comes to an end. We have succeeded in tracing the dispute between the different representatives of the Yogācāra school, as documented in Chinese [sources], back to its origins. In doing so it has become evident that underlying it is one of the most interesting and controversial problems of the more ancient Indian Philosophy. And I hope that at the same time, new light has also been shed on the history of the Yogācāra school; a school of such great importance, yet one whose understanding is still obstructed by great difficulties.

---

[1] This is an attempt to explain the expression *dharmakāya*. According to this explanation, it derives from *dharmatākāya*, by dropping the suffix *tā*.

APPENDIX II: BIBLIOGRAPHY OF ERICH FRAUWALLNER[1]

Abbreviations:

JAOS	Journal of the American Oriental Society
WZKM	Wiener Zeitschrift für die Kunde des Morgenlands
WZKS	Wiener Zeitschrift für die Kunde Südasiens
ZDMG	Zeitschrift der deutschen morgenländischen Gesellschaft
ZII	Zeitschrift für Indologie und Iranistik

1921

- De synonymorum, quibus animi motus significantur, usu tragico. Dissertation, Wien (unpublished).

1925

- Untersuchungen zum Mokṣadharma. Die nicht-sāṃkhyistischen Texte. JAOS 45, pp. 51–67.
- Untersuchungen zum Mokṣadharma. Die sāṃkhyistischen Texte. WZKM 32, pp. 179–206.

1926

- Untersuchungen zum Mokṣadharma. Das Verhältnis zum Buddhismus. WZKM 33, pp. 57–68.
- Untersuchungen zu den älteren Upaniṣaden. ZII 4, pp. 1–45.

1927

- Zur Elementenlehre des Sāṃkhya. WZKM 34, pp. 1–5.

1929

- Bemerkungen zu den Fragmenten Dignāgas. WZKM 36, pp. 136–39.

---

[1] [This bibliography is based on the one by Franco-Preisendanz—in the new reprint of Frauwallner's *Die Philosophie des Buddhismus* (Akademie Verlag, Berlin)—that excludes book reviews, for an alphabetical list of which see: WZKS 1978.]

1930

- Dignāgas Ālambanaparīkṣā. Text, Übersetzung und Erläuterungen. WZKM 37, pp. 174–94.
- Beiträge zur Apohalehre. – I. Dharmakīrti. WZKM 37, pp. 259–83.

1932

- Jñānaśrī. WZKM 38, pp. 229–34.
- Beiträge zur Apohalehre. – I. Dharmakīrti. Übersetzung. WZKM 39, pp. 247–85.

1933

- Beiträge zur Apohalehre. – I. Dharmakīrti. Übersetzung. (Fortsetzung). WZKM 40, pp. 51–94.
- Zu den Fragmenten buddhistischer Logiker im Nyāyavārttikam. WZKM 40, pp. 281–304.
- Dignāga und Anderes. Festschrift für Moriz Winternitz. Leipzig, pp. 237–42.

1934

- Dharmakīrtis Sambandhaparīkṣā. Text und Übersetzung. WZKM 41, pp. 261–300.

1935

- Beiträge zur Apohalehre. – I. Dharmakīrti. Zusammenfassung. WZKM 42, pp. 93–102.
- Dharmottaras Kṣaṇabhaṅgasiddhiḥ. Text und Übersetzung. WZKM 42, pp. 217–58.

1936

- Beiträge zur Geschichte des Nyāya. – I. Jayanta und seine Quellen. WZKM 43, pp. 263–78.

1937

- Zu den Fragmenten buddhistischer Autoren in Haribhadras Anekāntajayapatākā. WZKM 44, pp. 65–74.
- Beiträge zur Apohalehre. – II. Dharmottara. WZKM 44, pp. 233–87.

1938

- Bhāvanā und Vidhiḥ bei Maṇḍanamiśra. – I. Bhāvanā. WZKM 45, pp. 212–52.
- Der arische Anteil an der indischen Philosophie. (Kurzfassung) ZDMG 92/Heft 2/3, pp. *9*–*10*.

1939

- Der arische Anteil an der indischen Philosophie. WZKM 46, pp. 267–91.

1942

- Die Bedeutung der indischen Philosophie. (Kurzfassung) ZDMG 96/Heft 3, pp. *40–42*.

1944

- Die Bedeutung der indischen Philosophie. Der Orient in deutscher Forschung, Vorträge der Berliner Orientalistentagung, hrsg. H. H. Schaeder, Leipzig, pp. 158–69.

1951

- On the Date of the Buddhist Master of the Law Vasubandhu. Serie Orientale Roma Vol. III, Roma.
- Amalavijñānam und Ālayavijñānam. Beiträge zur indischen Philologie und Altertumskunde, Walther Schubring zum 70. Geburtstag dargebracht, (Alt- und Neu-Indische Studien 7), Hamburg, pp. 148–59.

1952

- Die buddhistischen Konzile. ZDMG 102, pp. 240–61.
- Die ceylonesischen Chroniken und die erste buddhistische Mission nach Hinterindien. Actes du IVe Congrès International des Sciences Anthropologiques et Ethnologiques, Vienne 1952, Tome 2, pp. 192–97.

1953

- Geschichte der indischen Philosophie. 1. Band. Die Philosophie des Veda und des Epos, der Buddha und der Jina, das Sāṃkhya und das klassische Yoga-System. Salzburg. (Second newly composed edition by Andreas Pholus, Aachen 2003).

1954

- Die Reihenfolge und Entstehung der Werke Dharmakīrti's. Asiatica, Festschrift Friedrich Weller zum 65. Geburtstag, Leipzig, pp. 142–54.

1955

- Der Stand der Erforschung der indischen Philosophie. ZDMG 105 (1955): Bericht über die Mitglieder-Versammlung der D. M. Gesellschaft am 31. Juli 1955 in Hamburg, pp. 55–56.
- Candramati und sein Daśapadārthaśāstram. Studia Indologica, Festschrift für Willibald Kirfel, (Bonner Orientalistische Studien, 3), Bonn, pp. 65–85.
- Die Anthropologie des Buddhismus. Anthropologie Religieuse, Supplements to Numen, Vol. 2, Leiden, pp. 120–32.

1956

- Die Anfänge der indischen Logik (Auszug aus dem Vortrag). Anzeiger der phil.-hist. Klasse der Österr. Akad. d. Wiss., Jg. 1956, Nr. 6, pp. 97–98.
- Geschichte der indischen Philosophie. 2. Band. Die naturphilosophischen Schulen und das Vaiśeṣika-System, das System der Jaina, der Materialismus. Salzburg. (Second newly composed edition by Andreas Pohlus, Aachen 2003).
- The Earliest Vinaya and the Beginnings of Buddhist Literature. Serie Orientale Roma VIII, Roma.
- Die Philosophie des Buddhismus. Philosophische Studientexte. Texte der indischen Philosophie. Bd. 2, Berlin. (2. unveränd. Auflage, Berlin 1958; 3. durchges. Auflage, Berlin 1969; 4. gegenüber der 3. durchges. unveränd. Auflage, Berlin 1994).

1957

- The historical data we possess on the Person and the Doctrine of the Buddha. East and West 7, pp. 309–12.
- Zu den buddhistischen Texten in der Zeit Khri-Sroṅ-Lde-Btsan's. WZKS 1, pp. 95–103.
- Vasubandhu's Vādavidhiḥ. WZKS 1, pp. 104–46.
- The Editions of Mallavādī's Dvādaśāranayacakram. WZKS 1, pp. 147–51.

1958

- Zur Erkenntnislehre des klassischen Sāṃkhya-Systems. WZKS 2, pp. 84–139.

1959

- Dignāga, sein Werk und seine Entwicklung. WZKS 3, pp. 83–164.
- Indische Philosophie. Die Philosophie im XX. Jahrhundert, Stuttgart, pp. 49–67.

1960

- Das Eindringen der Sprachtheorie in die indischen philosophischen Systeme. Indologen-Tagung 1959. Verhandlungen der Indologischen Arbeitstagung in Essen-Bredeney, Villa Hügel, 13.–15. Juli 1959. Göttingen, pp. 239–43.
- Sprachtheorie und Philosophie im Mahābhāṣyam des Patañjali. WZKS 4, pp. 92–118.
- Devendrabuddhi. WZKS 4, pp. 119–23.

1961

- Mīmāṃsāsūtram I, 1, 6–23. WZKS 5, pp. 113–24.
- Landmarks in the History of Indian Logic. WZKS 5, pp. 125–48.
- Geschichte und Aufgaben der Wiener Indologie. Anzeiger der phil.-hist. Klasse der Österr. Akad. d. Wiss., Jg. 1961, Nr. 10, Wien, pp. 77–95.
- Dignāga, die Entwicklung eines indischen Philosophen. Wissenschaftliche Zeitschrift der Martin-Luther-Universität Halle-Wittenberg, Jahrgang 10 (1961), pp. 1410–12.

1962

- Aus der Philosophie der śivaitischen Systeme. Deutsche Akad. d. Wiss. zu Berlin, Vorträge und Schriften, Heft 78, Berlin.
- Kumārila's Bṛhaṭṭīkā. WZKS 6, pp. 78–90.

1963

- Abhidharma-Studien. – I. Pañcaskandhakam und Pañcavastukam. WZKS 7, pp. 20–36.

1964

- Abhidharma-Studien. – II. Die kanonischen Abhidharma-Werke. WZKS 8, pp. 59–99.
- Mahatma Gandhi. Die geistig-politischen Profile der Gegenwart in Asien. Eine Auswahl von Vorträgen der Seminare der Österreichischen Unesco-Kommission, Wien, pp. 21–31.

1965

- Prabhākara Upādhyāya. WZKS 9, pp. 198–226.

1966

- Raghunātha Śiromaṇi. WZKS 10, pp. 86–207.

1967

- Raghunātha Śiromaṇi (1. Fortsetzung). WZKS 11, pp. 140–208

1968

- Materialien zur ältesten Erkenntnislehre der Karmamīmāṃsā. Österr. Ak. d. Wiss., phil.-hist. Kl., Sitzungsber., 259. Band, 2. Abh., Wien. (Veröffentl. d. Komm. f. Sprachen u. Kulturen Süd- und Ostasiens, Heft 6).

1970

- Die Lehre von der zusätzlichen Bestimmung (upādhiḥ) in Gaṅgeśa's Tattvacintāmaniḥ. Österr. Ak. d. Wiss., phil.-hist. Kl., Sitzungsber., 266. Band, 2. Abh., Wien. (Veröffentl. d. Komm. f. Sprachen und Kulturen Süd- und Ostasiens, Heft 9).
- Raghunātha Śiromaṇi (2. Fortsetzung). WZKS 14, pp. 161–208.
- Der ursprüngliche Anfang der Vaiśeṣika-Sūtren. Seminar on Aspects of Religion in South Asia. School of Oriental and African Studies, London (hectographic reproduction).
- Preface to a reprint of H. Jacobi, Das Rāmāyaṇa. Darmstadt, pp. V–VIII.

1971

- Die Entstehung der Buddhistischen Systeme. Nachrichten der Akademie der Wiss. in Göttingen, I. Phil.-hist. Klasse. Jg. 1971 Nr. 6, pp. 115–27 [3]–[15].
- Abhidharma-Studien. – III. Der Abhisamayavādaḥ. – IV. Der Abhidharma der anderen Schulen. WZKS 15, pp. 69–121.

1972

- Abhidharma-Studien. – IV. Der Abhidharma der anderen Schulen (Fortsetzung). WZKS 16, pp. 95–152.
- Zum Vṛttikāragranthaḥ. WZKS 16, pp. 165–67.

1973

- Abhidharma-Studien. – V. Der Sarvāstivādaḥ. Eine entwicklungsgeschichtliche Studie. WZKS 17, pp. 97–121.
- History of Indian Philosophy. Vols. I and II. Tr. V.M. Bedekar. Delhi. (Reprints 1984, 1993, 1997, 1999).

1982

- Kleine Schriften. Ed. Gerhard Oberhammer and Ernst Steinkellner. Glasenapp-Stiftung Vol. 22. Wiesbaden.

1984

- Nachgelassene Werke. Vol. I: Aufsätze, Beiträge, Skizzen. Ed. Ernst Steinkellner. Österr. Akad. d. Wiss., phil.-hist. Klasse, Sitzungsberichte Band 438 = Veröffentlichungen der Kommission für Sprachen und Kulturen Südasiens Heft 19. Wien.
- Historia filozofii indyjskiej. Tom I–II. Tr. Przełożył Leon Żylicz. Warszawa.

1992

- Nachgelassene Werke. Vol. II: Philosophische Texte des Hinduismus. Ed. Gerhard Oberhammer and Chlodwig H. Werba. Österr. Akad. d. Wiss., phil.-hist. Klasse, Sitzungsberichte Band 588 = Veröffentlichungen der Kommission für Sprachen und Kulturen Südasiens Heft 26. Wien.

1994

- Erich Frauwallner's Posthumous Essays. Transl. Jayendra Soni. Delhi. (Transl. of Nachgelassene Werke I, 1984).

1995

- Studies in Abhidharma Literature and the Origins of Buddhist Philosophical Systems. Tr. Sophie Francis Kidd under the supervision of Ernst Steinkellner. SUNY Series in Indian Thought: Texts and Studies. New York.

2003

- New edition of Geschichte der indischen Philosophie by Andreas Pohlus. Geisteskultur Indiens. Klassiker der Indologie 4.1–2. Aachen.

APPENDIX III:
SELECTED EDITIONS (E), TRANSLATIONS (T), RESOURCES (R), AND LITERATURE AFTER THE THIRD EDITION (1969)

With specific regard to the sources adduced and English translations and interpretations.

GENERAL:

Bechert, Heinz and others. 2000. *Der Buddhismus I. Der indische Buddhismus und seine Verzweigungen,* (Die Religionen der Menschheit 24,1). Stuttgart-Berlin-Köln: Verlag W. Kohlhammer.

R: *Encyclopedia of Indian Philosophies. Vol. I. Bibliography.* Compiled by Karl H. Potter. 1970. Delhi: Motilal Banarsidass. (*http://faculty.washington.edu/kpotter/*)

R: *Encyclopedia of Indian Philosophies. Vol. VII. Abhidharma Buddhism to 150 A.D.* Ed. Karl H. Potter and others. 1996. Delhi: Motilal Banarsidass.

R: *Encyclopedia of Indian Philosophies. Vol. VIII. Buddhist Philosophy from 100 to 350 A.D.* Ed. Karl H. Potter and others. 1999. Delhi: Motilal Banarsidass.

R: *Encyclopedia of Indian Philosophies. Vol. IX. Buddhist Philosophy from 350 to 600 A.D.* Ed. Karl H. Potter and others. 2003. Delhi: Motilal Banarsidass.

Frauwallner, Erich. 1982. Kleine Schriften. Herausgegeben von Gerhard Oberhammer und Ernst Steinkellner. Wiesbaden: Franz Steiner Verlag GmbH.

Gethin, Rupert. 1998. *The Foundations of Buddhism.* Oxford: Oxford University Press.

Harvey, Peter. 1990. *An Introduction to Buddhism. Teachings, History* and Practices. Cambridge: Cambridge University Press.

Herman, A. L. 1983. *An Introduction to Buddhist Thought. A Philosophic History of Indian Buddhism.* Lanham: University Press of America.

Kajiyama, Yuichi. 1989. *Studies in Buddhist Philosophy (Selected Papers)*. Edited by Katsumi Mimaki et al. Kyoto: Rinsen Book.

Kalupahana, David J. 1976. *Buddhist Philosophy. A Historical Analysis.* Honolulu: The University Press of Hawaii.

Keown, Damien. 1996. *Buddhism. A Very Short Introduction*. Oxford: Oxford University Press.

La rivelazione del Buddha. Vol. I: I testi antichi, a cura e con un saggio introduttivo di Raniero Gnoli. Traduzioni e commento di Claudio Cicuzza, Raniero Gnoli e Francesco Sferra. 2001. (I Meridiani. Classici dello Spirito). Milano: Arnoldo Mondadori Editore.

La rivelazione del Buddha. Vol. II: Il Grande veicolo, a cura e con un saggio introduttivo di Raniero Gnoli. Introduzione ai testi tradotti di Claudio Cicuzza e Francesco Sferra con contributi di Mauro Maggi e Cristina Pecchia. 2004. (I Meridiani. Classici dello Spirito). Milano: Arnoldo Mondadori Editore.

Lamotte, Étienne. 1988. *History of Indian Buddhism from the Origins to the Śaka Era,* translated from the French by Sara Webb-Boin under the supervision of Jean Dantinne. (Publications de l'Institut Orientalist de Louvain 36). Louvain-La-Neuve.

R: Nakamura, Hajime. 2007 (1980[1]). *Indian Buddhism. A Survey with Bibliographical Notes,* Delhi: Motilal Banarsidass.

Schmithausen, Lambert. 1973. "Spirituelle Praxis und philosophische Theorie im Buddhismus." In *Zeitschrift für Missionswissenschaft* und Religionswissenschaft 57: pp. 161–86.

———. 1978. "Zur Struktur der erlösenden Erfahrung im indischen Buddhismus." In *Transzendenzerfahrung, Vollzugshorizont des Heils.* Edited by Gerhard Oberhammer. Wien: De Nobili Research Library; pp. 97–119.

Siderits, Mark. 2007. *Buddhism as Philosophy. An Introduction.* Aldershot, Hampshire: Ashgate Publishing Ltd.

Takasaki, Jikido. 1987. *An Introduction to Buddhism.* Translated by Rolf W. Giebel. Tokyo: Tōhō Gakkai.

Vetter, Tilmann. 1988. *The Ideas and Meditative Practices of Early* Buddhism. Leiden: E. J. Brill.

Warder, A. K. 1996 (1970[1]). (Revised Edition). *Indian Buddhism*. Delhi: Motilal Banarsidass.

Williams, Paul with Anthony Tribe. 2000. *Buddhist Thought. A Complete Introduction to the Indian Tradition*. London: Routledge.

The World of Buddhism. Buddhist Monks and Nuns in Society and Culture. Heinz Bechert and Richard Gombrich (eds). 1984. London: Thames and Hudson.

A. THE TEACHING OF THE BUDDHA

Canonical texts (Tripiṭaka):

Saṃyuttanikāya:

T: *The Connected Discourses of the Buddha. A Translation of the Saṃyutta Nikāya*. Translated by Bhikkhu Bodhi. 2000. Boston: Wisdom Publications.

Majjhimanikāya:

T: *The Middle Length Discourses of the Buddha. A New Translation of the Majjhima Nikāya*. Original translation by Bhikkhu Ñāṇamoli. 1995. Translation edited and revised by Bhikkhu Bodhi. Boston: Wisdom Publications.

Dīghanikāya:

T: *Dīgha Nikāya. Thus have I heard: The Long Discourses of the Buddha*. Translated from the Pali by Maurice Walshe. 1995[2] (1987[1]). Boston: Wisdom Publications.

Non-canonical texts:

Pratītyasamutpādavyākhyā:

E: Muroji, Yoshihito. 1991. "Vedanā- und Tṛṣṇāvibhaṅga in der *Pratītyasamutpādavyākhyā*. Tibetischer Text mit Entsprechungen im Sanskrit." In Mikkyō Bunka 173, 98–74.

———. 1993. *Vasubandhu's Interpretation des* Pratītyasamutpāda. *Eine kritische Bearbeitung der* Pratītyasamutpādavyākhyā (Saṃskāra- *und* Vijñānavibhaṅga), (Alt- und Neu-Indische Studien 43). Stuttgart: Franz Steiner Verlag.

Śālistambhasūtra:

E: Schoening, Jeffrey D. 1995. *The Śālistambha Sūtra and its Indian Commentaries.* Vol. I: Translation with Annotation; Vol. II: Tibetan Editions, (Wiener Studien zur Tibetologie und Buddhismuskunde 35,1,2). Wien: Arbeitskreis für tibetische und buddhistische Studien Universität Wien.

E&T: Reat, N. Ross. 1993. *The Śālistambasūtra: Tibetan Original, Sanskrit Reconstruction, English Translation, Critical Notes (including Pāli parallels, Chinese version and ancient Tibetan fragments).* Delhi: Motilal Banarsidass.

T: Cooper, J. M. 1992. "The Śālistambhasūtra." In *Buddhist Studies Review* 8,1–2; pp. 21–57.

B. THE SCHOLASTICISM (ABHIDHARMA) OF THE WAY OF THE HEARERS (ŚRĀVAKAYĀNA)

General:

T: Broeck, José van den. 1977. *La saveur de l'immortel (A-p'i-t'an Kan Lu Wei Lun).* La version chinoise de l'*Amṛtarasa* de Ghosaka. Publications de l'Institut Orientaliste de Louvain, 15. Louvain-la-neuve: Institut Orientaliste. – Chinese Text URL (T 1553):

http://www.cbeta.org/result/normal/T28/1553_001.htm

Cox, Collett. 1995. *Disputed Dharmas: Early Buddhist Theories on Existence.* (Studia Philologica Buddhica: Monograph Series XI). Tokyo: The International Institute for Buddhist Studies. – Chinese Text URL (T 1562):

http://www.cbeta.org/result/normal/T29/1562_012.htm

Dhammajoti, Kuala Lumpur. 1998. *Entrance into the Supreme Doctrine (Skandhila's Abhidharmāvatāra).* Colombo, Postgraduate Institute of Pali and Buddhist Studies. – Chinese Text URL (T 1554):

http://www.cbeta.org/result/normal/T28/1554_001.htm

———. 2007a. *Sarvāstivāda Abhidharma.* Third Edition. Centre of Buddhist Studies. The University of Hong Kong.

———. 2007b. *Abhidharma Doctrines and Controversies on Perception.* Third Revised Edition. Centre of Buddhist Studies. The University of Hong Kong.

T: Dessein, Bart. 1999. *Saṃyuktābhidharmahṛdaya. Heart of Scholasticism with Miscellaneous Additions.* Delhi: Motilal Banarsidass. – Chinese Text URL (T 1552):

http://www.cbeta.org/result/normal/T28/1552_001.htm

Frauwallner, Erich. 1995. *Studies in Abhidharma Literature and the Origins of Buddhist Philosophical Systems.* Translated from the German by Sophie Francis Kidd under the supervision of Ernst Steinkellner. (SUNY Series in Indian Thought: Text and Studies). Albany: State University of New York Press.

Griffith, Paul. 1986. *On Being Mindless: Buddhist Meditation and the Mind-Body Problem.* La Salle, Ill.: Open Court.

Jaini, Padmanabh S. 1977. *Abhidharmadīpa with Vibhāṣāprabhāvṛtti.* Critically edited with notes and introduction (pp. 1–144). Patna: Kashi Prasad Jayaswal Research Institute.

———. 2001. *Collected Papers on Buddhist Studies.* Delhi: Motilal Banarsidass. – Sanskrit root text:

http://www.uwest.edu/sanskritcanon/dp/index.php?q=node/35&textID=ff0da13b8c3349909ad

JIABS. 2003. *The Sautrāntikas.* Journal of the International Association of Buddhist Studies. Volume 26, Number 2: General Introduction, by Robert Kritzer, 201–24; On the School Affiliation of Aśvaghoṣa: 'Sautrāntika' or 'Yogācāra'? by Nobuyoshi Yamabe, 225–54; Bhadanta Rāma: A Sautrāntika before Vasubandhu, by Takumi Fukuda, 255–86; Sautrāntika and the Hṛdaya Treatises, by Bart Dessein, 287–321; Sautrāntika, by Yoshifumi Honjo, 321–30; Sautrāntika in the Abhidharmakośabhāṣya, by Robert Kritzer, 331–84.

Rospatt, Alexander von. 1995. *The Buddhist Doctrine of Momentariness. A Survey of the Origins and Early Phase of this Doctrine up to Vasubandhu.* (Alt- und Neu-Indische Studien 47). Stuttgart: Franz Steiner Verlag.

Sadakata, Akira. 1999. *Buddhist Cosmology. Philosophy and Origins.* Tokyo: Kosei Publishing.

Schmithausen, Lambert. 1967. "Sautrāntika-Voraussetzungen in Viṃśatikā und Triṃśikā." *Wiener Zeitschrift für die Kunde Süd- und* Ostasiens 11: pp. 109–36.

Willemen, Charles and Bart Dessein, Collett Cox. 1998. *Sarvāstivāda* Buddhist Scholasticism. Leiden: E. J. Brill.

T: Willemen, Charles. 2006. *The Essence of Scholasticism. Abhidharmahṛdaya. T 1550. Revised edition with a completely new introduction.* Delhi: Motilal Banarsidass. – Chinese Text URL (T 1550): *http://www.cbeta.org/result/normal/T28/1550_001.htm*

Specific texts and authors:

Milindapañhā:

T: *Milinda's Questions, Vol. I.* Translated from the Pali by I. B. Horner. 1969[2] (1963[1]). (Sacred Books of the Buddhists vol. XXII). London: Luzac & Company Ltd.

T: *Milinda's Questions, Vol. II.* Translated from the Pali by I. B. Horner. 1969[2] (1964[1]). (Sacred Books of the Buddhists vol. XXIII). London: Luzac & Company Ltd.

T: *Milindapañha. Ein historisches Gipfeltreffen im religiösen Weltgespräch.* Aus dem Pāli von Nyanatiloka. Herausgegeben und bearbeitet von Nyayaponika. 1998. O. W. Barth Verlag.

T: *Entretiens de Milinda et Nāgasena.* Traduit par Édith Nolot. 1995. Paris: Gallimard.

Vasubandhu,

Abhidharmakośa:

E: *Abhidharm-koshabhāṣya of Vasubandhu.* Edited by P. Pradhan. 1967. Patna: K. P. Jayaswal Research Institute. (Revised Second Edition with Introduction and Indices, Etc., by Aruna Haldar 1975).

E: *Abhidharmakośabhāṣya of Vasubandhu, Chapter I: Dhātunirdeśa.* Edited by Yasunori Ejima. 1989. (Bibliotheca Indologica et Buddhologica 1). Tokyo: Sankibo Press.

E: *Abhidharmakośabhāṣya of Vasubandhu, Chapter IX: Ātmavāda-pratiṣedha.* (Bibliotheca Indologica et Buddhologica 11). Edited by Jong Cheol Lee. 2005. Tokyo: Sankibo Press.

T: *Abhidharmakośabhāṣyam [translated into French] by Louis de La Vallée Poussin.* English translation by Leo M. Pruden. 1988–1990. Vols. 1–4. Berkeley: Asian Humanities Press.

T: *Indian Buddhist Theories of Persons: Vasubandhu's "Refutation of the Theory of a Self."* Translated by James Duerlinger. 2003. London: Routledge Curzon (Chapter 9).

T: Hall, Bruce Cameron. 1983. *Vasubandhu on 'Aggregates, Spheres, and Components': Being Chapter One of the 'Abhidharmakośa'.* Ph.D. diss., Harvard University.

R: *Index to the Abhidharmkośabhāsya (P. Pradhan Edition).* – 1973. Part 1: Sanskrit–Tibetan–Chinese. – 1977. Part 2: Chinese–Sanskrit. – 1978. Part 3: Tibetan–Sanskrit. Tokyo: Daizo Shuppan.

Pañcaskandhaka:

E: *Vasubandhu's Pañcaskandhaka.* Critically edited by Li Xuezhu and Ernst Steinkellner, with a contribution by Toru Tomabechi. 2008. (Sanskrit Texts from the Tibetan Autonomous Region 4). Beijing-Vienna: China Tibetology Publishing House – Austrian Academy of Sciences Press.

T: *Seven works of Vasubandhu: the Buddhist psychological doctor.* Translated and edited by Stefan Anacker. 1984. Delhi: Motilal Banarsidass; pp. 49–82.

T: *Le traité des cinq agrégats (Pañcaskandhaprakaraṇa de Vasubandhu).* Traduit et annoté par Jean Dantinne. 1980. Bruxelles: Institut Belge des Hautes Études Bouddhiques.

T: *The Inner Science of Buddhist Practice. Vasubandhu's Summary of the Five Heaps with Commentary by Sthiramati.* 2009. Ithaca: Snow Lion Publications.

C. THE SCHOOLS OF THE GREAT WAY (MAHĀYĀNA)

General:

Brunnhölzl, Karl. 2003. *The Center of the Sunlit Sky: Madhyamaka in the Kagyü Tradition*. Ithaca: Snow Lion Publications.

Buescher, Hartmut. 2008. *The Inception of Yogācāra-Vijñānavāda*. Beiträge zur Kultur- und Geistesgeschichte Asiens 62. Wien: Verlag der Österreichischen Akademie der Wissenschaften.

Harris, Ian Charles. 1991. *The Continuity of Madhyamaka and Yogācāra* in Indian Mahāyāna Buddhism. Leiden: E.J. Brill.

Kritzer, Robert. 1999. *Rebirth and Causation in the Yogācāra Abhidharma*. Wiener Studien zur Tibetologie und Buddhismuskunde, Heft 44. Wien: Arbeitskreis für Tibetische und Buddhistische Studien Universität Wien.

T: Mathes, Klaus-Dieter. 1996. *Unterscheidung der Gegebenheiten von ihrem wahren Wesen (Dharmadharmatāvibhāga). Eine Lehrschrift der Yogācāra-Schule in tibetischer Überlieferung*. Swisttal-Odendorf: Indica et Tibetica Verlag. – Tibetan text of Vasubandhu's Dharmadharmatāvibhāgavṛtti:

http://www.asianclassics.org/research_site/webdata/monastic/open/html/TD4028I.html

Nagao, Gadjin M. 1991. *Mādhyamika and Yogācāra. A Study of Mahāyāna Philosophies. Collected Papers of G. M. Nagao*, Edited, Collated, and Translated by L. S. Kawamura in Collaboration with G. M. Nagao. Albany: State University of New York Press.

R: Powers, John. 1991. *The Yogācāra School of Buddhism: A Bibliography*. Metuchen, N. J.: Scarecrow Press.

T: *Abhidharmasamuccaya*. The Compendium of the Higher Teaching (Philosophy) by Asaṅga. Originally translated into French and annotated by Walpola Rahula. 1971. English version from the French by Sara Boin-Webb. 2001. Fremont: Asian Humanities Press. – Sanskrit text:

http://www.uwest.edu/sanskritcanon/dp/index.php?q=node/35&textID=644091f3a5b359f4dfd

Ruegg, David Seyfort. 1969. *La Théorie du Tathāgatagarbha et du Gotra. Études sur la Sotériologie et la Gnoséologie du Bouddhisme.* Paris: École Française d'Extrême-Orient.

———. 1981. *The Literature of the Madhyamaka School of Philosophy in India.* (A History of Indian Literature VII,1). Wiesbaden: Otto Harrassowitz.

Schmithausen, Lambert. 2007 (1987[1]). *Ālayavijñāna. On the Origin and the Early Development of a Central Concept of Yogācāra Philosophy. Part I: Text; Part II: Notes, Bibliography and Indices.* Tokyo: The International Institute for Buddhist Studies.

Tachikawa, Musashi. 1997. *An Introduction to the Philosophy of Nāgārjuna.* Translated by Rolf W. Giebel, Delhi: Motilal Banarsidass.

T: Tola, Fernando and Carmen Dragonetti. 2004. *Being as Consciousness: Yogācāra Philosophy of Buddhism.* Delhi, Motilal Banarsidass. – Sanskrit text URLs:

Ālambanaparīkṣā:

http://www.uwest.edu/sanskritcanon/dp/index.php?q=node/35&textID=ac7935c4b5d4306c4

Ālambanaparīkṣāvṛttiḥ:

http://www.uwest.edu/sanskritcanon/dp/index.php?q=node/35&textID=423ef50ce1b5ac8ff

Trisvabhāvakārika:

http://www.uwest.edu/sanskritcanon/dp/index.php?q=node/35&textID=7b25c8832fd7727e1

Viṃśatikākārikā:

http://www.uwest.edu/sanskritcanon/dp/index.php?q=node/35&textID=6906a9ddb861e622e

Waldron, William S. 1994–1995. "How Innovative is the *Ālayavijñāna?*" In *Journal of Indian Philosophy.* – Part I: 22 (1994): pp. 199–258; Part II: 23 (1995): pp. 9–51.

———. 2003. *The Buddhist Unconscious. The Ālaya-vijñāna in the Context of Indian Buddhist Thought.* London: RoutledgeCurzon.

Williams, Paul. 1989. *Mahāyāna Buddhism. The Doctrinal Foundations.* London: Routledge.

1. The Madhyamaka school

Aṣṭasāhasrikā Prajñāpāramitā:

Schmithausen, Lambert. 1977. "Textgeschichtliche Beobachtungen zum 1. Kapitel der Aṣṭasāhasrikā Prajñāpāramitā." In *Prajñāpāramitā and Related Systems (Studies in honor of Edward Conze).* Ed. by Lewis Lancaster. (Berkeley Buddhist Series 1); pp. 35–80.

Ratnakūṭa (Kāśyapaparivarta):

T: *A Treasury of Māhāyāna sūtras: Selections from the Mahāratnakūta sūtra.* Translated from the Chinese by the Buddhist Association of the United States (ed. by Garma C. C. Chang). 1983. University Park: Pennsylvania State University Press.

Nāgārjuna,

Madhyamakakārikā:

E: *Mūlamadhyamakakārikāḥ.* Edited by J. W. de Jong. 1977. Madras: Adyar Library and Research Centre.

E&T: Kalupahana, David K. 1986. *Nāgārjuna. The Philosophy of the Middle Way, Mūlamadhyamakakārikā.* Albany: State University of New York Press.

T: *The Fundamental Wisdom of the Middle Way, Nāgārjuna's Mūlamadhyamakakārikā.* Translation and Commentary by Jay Garfield. 1995. Oxford: Oxford University Press.

Vigrahavyāvartanī:

E&T: Bhattacharya, Kamaleshwar. 1971. "The dialectical method of Nāgārjuna, translation of the 'Vigrahavyāvartanī' from the original Sanskrit with introduction and notes." In *JIP* 1, pp. 217–61. (Reprinted in Delhi 1978: *The dialectical method of Nāgārjuna: Vigrahavyāvartanī.* Translated from the original Sanskrit with introduction and notes by Kamaleswar Bhattacharya, text critically edited by E.H. Johnston and Arnold Kunst. 1986². Delhi: Motilal Banarsidass).

E&T: Edited in Sanskrit and Tibetan in Christian Lindtner. In *Nagarjuniana: Studies in the Writings and Philosophy of Nāgārjuna*. By Christian Lindtner. 1982. (Indiske Studier 4). Copenhagen: Akademisk Forlag; pp. 70–86.

E: Yonezawa, Yoshiyasu. 2008. "Vigrahavyāvartanī. Sanskrit Transliteration and Tibetan Translation." In *Journal of Naritasan Institute for Buddhist Studies* 31, pp. 209–33.

Ratnāvalī:

E: *Nāgārjuna's Ratnāvalī, Vol. I, the Basic Texts (Sanskrit, Tibetan, Chinese)*. By Michael Hahn. 1982. (Indica et Tibetica 1). Bonn: Indica et Tibetica Verlag.

T: *The Precious Garland and The Song of the Four Mindfulnesses*. Translated and edited by Jeffrey Hopkins and Lati Rimpoche with Anne Klein. 1975. London: George Allen and Unwin Ltd.

Āryadeva, *Catuḥśataka:*

E&T: *Āryadeva's Catuḥśataka. On the Bodhisattva's Cultivation of Merit and Knowledge*. By Karen Lang.1986. (Indiske Studier 7). Copenhagen: Akademisk Forlag.

E&T: Tillemans, Tom J. F. 1990. *Materials for the study of Āryadeva, Dharmapāla and Candrakīrti: the Catuḥśataka of Āryadeva, chapters XII and XIII, with the commentaries of Dharmapāla and Candrakīrti: introduction, translation, Sanskrit, Tibetan and Chinese texts, notes*. (Wiener Studien zur Tibetologie und Buddhismuskunde Heft 24). Wien: Arbeitskreis für Tibetische und Buddhistische Studien Universität Wien (2 vols) (Chapters 12–13).

T: *Āryadeva's Four Hundred Stanzas on the Middle Way. With Commentary by Gyel-tsap*. Translated by Ruth Sonam Rinchen with additional Commentary by Geshe Sonam Rinchen. Ithaca, N. Y.: Snow Lion Publication.

Buddhapālita, *Mūlamadhyamakavṛtti:*

T: Feher, Judit. 1984. "Buddhapālita's Mūlamadhyamakavṛtti: Arrival and Spread of *Prāsaṅgika-Madhyamika* Literature in Tibet." In: Ligeti, Louis (ed.), *Tibetan and Buddhist Studies Commemorating the 200th Anniversary of the Birth of Alexander Csoma de Körös,* Vol. 1. (Bibliotheca Orientalis Hungarica 29,1). Budapest: Akadémiai Kiadó; pp. 211–40 (Chapter One).

E&T: Lindtner, Christian. 1981. "Buddhapālita on Emptiness." In *Indo-Iranian Journal* 23; pp.187–217 (Chapter Eighteen).

Bhāvaviveka, *Prajñāpradīpa:*

E: Lindtner, Christian. 1984. "Bhavya's Controversy with Yogācāra in the Appendix to *Prajñāpradīpa,* Chapter XXV." In: Ligeti, Louis (ed.), *Tibetan and Buddhist Studies Commemorating the 200th Anniversary of the Birth of Alexander Csoma de Körös,* Vol. 1. (Bibliotheca Orientalis Hungarica 29,1). Budapest: Akadémiai Kiadó; pp. 77–97.

T: Kajiyama, Yuichi. 1963–1964. "Bhāvaviveka's Prajñāpradīpaḥ (1. Kapitel)." *Wiener Zeitschrift für die Kunde Süd- und Ostasiens,* Bd. 7, 8. (Reprinted in *Studies in Buddhist Philosophy,* Kyoto; pp. 417–74). (Chapter 1, translated into German).

T: Ames, William L. 1993–1995, 1999–2000. "Bhāvaviveka's Prajñāpradīpa, A translation of Chapter One: 'Examination of causal conditions' *(pratyaya).*" In *Journal of Indian Philosophy,* 21, 1993, pp. 209–60; 22, 1994, pp. 93–116. (Chapter Two. In *Journal of Indian Philosophy,* 23, 1995, pp. 295–365; Chapters Three, Four, Five. In *Buddhist Literature* 1, 1999, pp. 1–119. Chapters Six, Seven. In *Buddhist Literature* 2, 2000, pp. 1–91).

T: Eckel, M. David. "Bhāvaviveka's Critique of Yogācāra Philosophy in Chapter XXV of the *Prajñāpradīpa.*" In: Lindtner, Christian (ed.), *Miscellanea Buddhica.* (Indiske Studier 5). Copenhagen: Akademisk Forlag 1985; pp. 25–75.

Candrakīrti,

Prasannapadā:

E&T: MacDonald, Anne. 2003. *The Prasannapadā's Chapter One: Editions and Translations.* PhD dissertation, University of Vienna (publication forthcoming).

E&T: Timme Kragh, Ulrich. 2006. *Early Buddhist Theories of Action and Result. A Study of Karmaphalasambandha. Candrakīrti's Prasannapadā, Verses 17.1–20.* (Wiener Studien zur Tibetologie und Buddhismuskunde 64). Wien: Arbeitskreis für Tibetische und Buddhistische Studien Universität Wien.

T: Ruegg, David Seyfort. 2002. *Two Prolegomena to Madhyamaka Philosophy. Candrakīrti's* Prasannapadā Madhyamakavṛttiḥ *on* Madhyamakakārikā *I.1 and Tsoṅ kha pa Blo bzaṅ grags pa/rGyal tshab dar ma rin chen's dKa' gnad/gnas brgyad hyi zin bris. Annotated Translations.* (Studies in Indian and Tibetan Madhyamaka Thought Part 2). (Wiener Studien zur Tibetologie und Buddhismuskunde 54). Wien: Arbeitskreis für Tibetische und Buddhistische Studien Universität Wien; pp. 1–135.

Madhyamakāvatāra:

E Sanskrit text of chapters one to five:
http://www.uwest.edu/sanskritcanon/dp/index.php?q=node/35&textID=dd79e10fef63096b02d

T: *Madhyamakāvatāraḥ und Madhyamakāvatārabhāṣyam (Kapitel VI, Vers 166–226).* Übersetzt und kommentiert von Helmut Tauscher. 1981. (Wiener Studien zur Tibetologie und Buddhismuskunde 5). Wien: Arbeitskreis für Tibetische und Buddhistische Studien Universität Wien.

T: *The Moon of Wisdom: Chapter Six of Chandrakirti's* Entering the Middle Way. *With commentary from the Eighth Karmapa Mikyö Dorje's* Chariot of the Dagpo Kagyü Siddhas. Translated under the guidance of Khenpo Tsültrim Gyamtso Rimpoche by Ari Goldfield, Jules Levinson, Jim Scott & Birgit Scott. 2005. Ithaca: Snow Lion Publications.

T: *Introduction to the Middle Way. Chandrakirti's Madhyamaka-avatara; with commentary by Jamgön Mipham.* Translated by the Padmakara Translation Group. 2002. Boston: Shambhala Publications.

2. The school of Sāramati

Sāramati, *Ratnagotravibhāga:*

E: *Cf.* Schmithausen, Lambert. 1971. "Philologische Bemerkungen zum Ratnagotravibhāga." *Wiener Zeitschrift für die Kunde* Südasiens 15; pp. 123–77.

T: Mathes, Klaus-Dieter. 2008. *A Direct Path to the Buddha Within. Gö Lotsāwa's Mahāmudrā Interpretation of the Ratnagotra-*vibhāga. Somerville: Wisdom Publications.

T: *Buddha Nature. The Mahayana Uttaratantra Shastra by Arya Maitreya; written down by Arya Asanga; commentary by Jamgön Kongtrül Lodrö Thayé "The Unassailable Lion's Roar."* Explanations by Khenpo Tsultrim Gyamtso Rimpoche. Translated by Rosemarie Fuchs. 2000. Ithaca: Snow Lion Publications.

3. The school of the Yogācāra

Bodhisattvabhūmi:

T: Tatz, Mark. 1986. *Asanga's Chapter on Ethics with the Commentary of Tsong-kha-pa, The Basic Path to Awakening, The Complete Bodhisattva.* Lewiston, N.Y: The Edwin Mellen Press (Part I, Chapter 10).

T: Deleanu, Florin. 1986. *The Chapter on the Mundane Path* (Laukikamārga) *in the* Śrāvakabhūmi. *A Trilingual Edition (Sanskrit, Tibetan, Chinese), Annoted Translation and Intoductory Study.* 2 Vols. Studia Philologica Buddhica, Monograph Series XX. Tokyo: The International Institute for Buddhist Studies.

Saṃdhinirmocanasūtra:

T: *Wisdom of Buddha: the Saṃdhinirmocana Sūtra*. Translated by John Powers. 1994. (Tibetan Translation Series 16). Berkeley: Dharma Publishing.

Maitreyanātha,
Mahāyānasūtrālaṃkāra:

E: *Mahāyāna-sūtrālaṅkāra of Asaṅga*. Edited by S. Bagchi. 1970. (Buddhist Sanskrit Texts 13) Darbhanga: The Mithila Institute of Post-Graduate Studies and Research in Sanskrit Learning.

T: *The Universal Vehicle Discourse Literature (Mahāyāna-sūtrālaṃkāra) by Maitreyanātha/Āryāsaṅga, together with its Commentary (Bhāṣya) by Vasubandhu*. Translated from Sanskrit, Tibetan, and Chinese by L. Jamspal, R. Clark, J. Wilson, L. Zwilling, M. Sweet, R. Thurman. 2004. (Tanjur Translation Initiative Treasury of the Buddhist Science series). New York: American Institute of Buddhist Studies at Columbia University.

Madhyāntavibhāga:

T: *Seven Works of Vasubandhu: The Buddhist Psychological Doctor*. Translated and edited by Stefan Anacker. 1984. Delhi: Motilal Banarsidass; pp. 191–286.

T: Kochumutton, Thomas A. 1982. *A Buddhist Doctrine of Experience. (A New Translation and Interpretation of the Works of Vasubandhu the Yogācarin)*. Delhi: Motilal Banarsidass Publishers; pp. 27–89; 235–246.

Asaṅga, *Mahāyānasaṃgraha:*

E&T: *The Realm of Awakening. A Translation and Study of the Tenth Chapter of Asaṅga's Mahāyānasaṅgraha*. Introduction by John P. Keenan. Translation and Notes by Paul J. Griffiths, Noriaki Hakamaya, John P. Keenan, and Paul L. Swanson (with the assistance of Alex Naughton, John Newman, and Heng-ching Shih). Texts by Paul J. Griffiths and Noriaki Hakamaya. 1989. New York: Oxford University Press.

T: Chapter Eight translated, with Gadjin Nagao's commentary, by Leslie Kawamura, "Nirvikalpaka-jñāna: awareness freed from discrimination." In *From Benares to Beijing: Essays on Buddhism and Chinese Religion* (ed. Koichi Shinohara and Gregory Schopen). 1991. Oakville, Ontario, pp. 41–68.

T: *The Summary of the Great Vehicle by Bodhisattva Asaṅga.* Translated from the Chinese of Paramārtha (Taishō, vol. 31, no. 1593) by John P. Keenan. 1992. Berkeley: Numata Center for Buddhist Translation and Research 1992.

Vasubandhu,

Viṃśatikā:

T: *Seven Works of Vasubandhu: The Buddhist Psychological Doctor.* Translated and edited by Stefan Anacker. 1984. Delhi: Motilal Banarsidass; pp. 157–79.

T: Kochumutton, Thomas A. 1982. *A Buddhist Doctrine of Experience. (A New Translation and Interpretation of the Works of Vasubandhu the Yogācarin).* Delhi: Motilal Banarsidass; pp. 165–96; 260–75.

T: Tola, Fernando and Carmen Dragonetti. 2004. *Being as Consciousness: Yogācāra Philosophy of Buddhism.* Delhi, Motilal Banarsidass; pp. 53–186.

Triṃśikā:

E: Buescher, Hartmut. 2007. *Sthiramati's Triṃśikāvijñaptibhāṣya. Critical Editions of the Sanskrit Text and its Tibetan Translation.* Wien: Verlag der Österreichischen Akademie der Wissenschaften.

T: *Seven Works of Vasubandhu: The Buddhist Psychological Doctor.* Translated and edited by Stefan Anacker. 1984. Delhi: Motilal Banarsidass; pp. 181–90.

T: Kochumutton, Thomas A. 1982. *A Buddhist Doctrine of Experience. (A New Translation and Interpretation of the Works of Vasubandhu the Yogācarin).* Delhi: Motilal Banarsidass; pp. 127–163; 254–259.

Dignāga, *Pramāṇasamuccaya:*

E: Steinkellner, Ernst. 2005. *Dignāga's Pramāṇasamuccaya, Chapter 1. A hypothetical reconstruction of the Sanskrit text with the help of the two Tibetan translations on the basis of the hitherto known Sanskrit fragments.*

http://ikga.oeaw.ac.at/Mat/dignaga_PS_1.pdf

INDICES

INDICES

A. *General index of terms*[1]

A

[1] The technical terms marked by an asterix are based on the source materials and added by the translator. The page numbers listed refer to samples of these terms that do not cover all the occurrences of the terms in the book.

C

E

F

G

J

K

L

N

P

Q

R

T

Sanskrit terms[1]

[1] To ease the search for the general reader, ordered according to the Roman alphabet.

c. *Names of texts*[1]

[1] To ease the search for the general reader, ordered according to the Roman alphabet.

Index of names

About the Author

Prof. Erich Frauwallner, born December 28, 1898, took part in WWI from 1916 to 1918, and after the war studied Classical Philology at Vienna University for which his doctoral thesis was approved in 1921. In 1922 he took the state examination and began teaching Classical Greek and Latin in Vienna. He had no academic mentor in Indology and Indian philosophy; instead he used his methodological competence as a Classicist to guide himself. In 1925 he published his first indological paper. In 1928 he received permission to teach Indology at Vienna University. After Austria's annexation by Nazi Germany, Frauwallner was appointed extraordinary professor of Indology and Iranian Studies in August 1939. Drafted again in April 1943, he served close to Vienna to the end of the WWII. In June 1945, he was dismissed from the University for his party membership, and in 1948 sent into early retirement. In 1952 Frauwallner received the permission to teach again and in 1955 was appointed extraordinary professor and became full member of the Austrian Academy of Sciences. Appointed full professor in 1960 at the newly opened Institute of Indology, he retired in 1963.

Frauwallner founded, in 1957, the *Wiener Zeitschrift für die Kunde Süd- und Ostasiens.* He was widely acknowledged throughout the international scholarly community for his numerous path-breaking studies and the *History of Indian Philosophy* (1953, 1956), an exposition of Indian thought that in its methodology and presentation can be considered as the basis of all further research. Frauwallner was also a fascinating and motivating teacher and drew a number of gifted students to Vienna during his last years at Vienna University. He was honored in 1972 by the honorary membership of the Deutsche Morgenländische Gesellschaft and in 1973 became corresponding member of the Academy of Sciences at Göttingen. Frauwallner died on July 5, 1974.

Lodrö Sangpo (Jürgen Balzer) — the translator — is a Gelong in the Karma Kagyü Order. Born in Stuttgart, Germany, in 1952, he studied Educational Science and became an elementary school teacher. A student of the late Ven. Trungpa Rinpoche, he received his first ordination in the Karma Kagyü Sangha in 1984, in France, and then moved to Gampo Abbey, Canada. In 1987, he received the Bhikshu ordination in the USA and afterwards completed the traditional three-year retreat and a four-year study retreat. He served for a few years as Acting Director of Gampo Abbey and was one of the co-founders of the Nitartha Institute for Higher Buddhist Studies. Now he is a senior teacher at the Vidyadhara Institute, the monastic college of Gampo Abbey. His focus of study is on the systematic traditions of Buddhist Abhidharma. He has prepared a new annotated English translation of Louis de La Vallée Poussin's French translation of Vasubandhu's *Abhidharmakośabhāṣya*, soon to be published.

Ernst Steinkellner — the supervisor of the translation — obtained his Ph.D. in Indology under Erich Frauwallner in 1963. He received permission to teach at Vienna University in 1967. In 1971 he was appointed guest lecturer and in 1972 associate professor at the University of Pennsylvania (USA). In 1973 he was called to Vienna University where he founded the Department for Tibetology and Buddhist Studies, which he headed until 2000. In 1977 he founded the *Wiener Studien zur Tibetologie und Buddhismuskunde.* From 1998 to 2006 he served as director of the Institute for the Cultural and Intellectual History of Asia of the Austrian Academy of Sciences. In 2008 he received the Ludwig Wittgenstein Prize of the Austrian research community.

Thanks to an agreement between the Austrian Academy of Sciences and the Chinese Tibetology Research Center in Beijing, Ernst Steinkellner gained access to the treasure of the Sanskrit manuscripts in Tibet. The study of these manuscripts ushers in a new era in the research on Indian Buddhism.